MOR
The Ul

"There is, by definition, no subject of greater existential importance than death, and in his extraordinary fifty-year career as a courageous psychiatrist and consciousness researcher, Stanislav Grof has penetrated as deeply as anyone into this mystery of mysteries. THE ULTIMATE JOURNEY *is an astonishingly comprehensive summation of psychological understanding, scientific observation, and spiritual wisdom concerning dying and death, and their profound interconnection with birth and rebirth. For individuals given to thoughtful reflection about the meaning of life, as well as for humanity as a whole at this critical threshold in its collective journey, this book is an essential work for our time."*

—Richard Tarnas, professor of philosophy and psychology, California Institute of Integral Studies, author of *The Passion of the Western Mind* and *Cosmos and Psyche*

"Stanislav Grof, world-renowned pioneering psychiatrist and researcher of the potentials of psychedelic psychotherapy, who has made extraordinarily significant contributions to our understanding of the birth experience and how it relates to the transpersonal dimensions of human existence, in this book turns his attention to the other end of the life cycle. Summarizing his own earlier work in using psychedelics to help prepare one for dying, as well as the research of many other scientists in thanatology and Near-Death Experience (NDE), and reviewing the literature of the world's great mystical traditions, this work demonstrates that the experiences of people in special states of consciousness lead to a vastly different and more expansive perspective on the meaning of death. Such death-and-rebirth experiences can also connect us to the deeper transpersonal dimensions of life, and lead to a much more accepting and peaceful spiritual attitude toward death than that afforded by either materialist science or conventional religious systems. We can be grateful to Dr. Grof and MAPS for making this tremendously important work available."

—Ralph Metzner, Ph.D., psychologist, coauthor of *The Psychedelic Experience*, author of *The Well of Remembrance* and *The Unfolding Self*

"A comprehensive and penetrating study of death and life from the master himself. This wonderful work combines impeccable scholarship, wide-ranging cross-cultural studies, and moving encounters with death and transcendence to renew our communion with the cycle of life. A treasure trove of insights. No one but Stanislav Grof could have written this book."

—Christopher Bache, Ph.D., author of *Dark Night, Early Dawn*

"Based on a half century of research, Stanislav Grof provides a brilliant and exciting survey of ancient and contemporary evidence for other dimensions of reality and afterlife survival of consciousness. A book of fundamental importance."

—Michael Harner, Ph.D., anthropologist, founder of The Foundation for Shamanic Studies, and author of *The Way of the Shaman*

THE ULTIMATE JOURNEY

The Ultimate Journey:

Consciousness and the Mystery of Death

The Ultimate Journey

THE ULTIMATE JOURNEY:
Consciousness and the Mystery of Death

Stanislav Grof, M.D.

MAPS

THE MULTIDISCIPLINARY ASSOCIATION FOR PSYCHEDELIC STUDIES

100% of the profits from the sale of this book will be devoted to psychedelic psychotherapy research.

THE ULTIMATE JOURNEY:
CONSCIOUSNESS AND THE MYSTERY OF DEATH
ISBN 0-9660019-9-0 (paperback)

MAPS, 309 Cedar Street, #2323, Santa Cruz, CA 95060
Voice: (831) 429-MDMA (6362) • Fax: (831) 429-6370
e-mail: askmaps@maps.org
www.maps.org

Editor: Elizabeth Gibson
Project Managers: Valerie Mojeiko, Randolph Hencken, M.A. and Brandy Doyle
Cover & book design: Mark Plummer
Cover image of Eagle Nebula © T.A. Rector & B.A. Wolpa, NOAO, AURA
Text set in Figural Book for the Macintosh

Printed in the United States of America by McNaughton & Gunn, Saline, MI

CONTENTS

An Interview with Peter Gasser, M.D. – MAPS-sponsored LSD/End-of-Life Researcher

By David Jay Brown

IN 2008, SWISS PSYCHIATRIST PETER GASSER, M.D., became the first medical researcher in over three decades to obtain government approval to do therapeutic research with LSD. This was the first government-approved LSD study since Stanislav Grof was forced to shut down his research in 1972. Gasser's LSD/end-of-life anxiety study is being sponsored by the Multidisciplinary Association for Psychedelic Studies (MAPS, see page 353.)

David: Can you talk a little about how you started doing LSD research, and what it feels like to be the first researcher to receive government approval to do human studies with LSD in thirty-five years?

Peter: In January, 2006 — around the time that we held the symposium for Albert Hofmann's 100th birthday celebration — MAPS Executive Director Rick Doblin, Ph.D. and I were walking through the snowy Swiss mountains. While we were walking, Rick said that he thought that it would be great to do research with LSD again, as MAPS had just successfully launched studies with MDMA. After speaking with Rick, I began the process of gaining approval and meeting all the requirements. Getting a license to work with LSD felt like a great honor. It also filled me with a sense of hope, because it meant the end of a thirty-five year Ice Age, where all therapeutic research with LSD was totally blocked.

David: What have you learned from Stanislav Grof's work that helps you conduct your own research?

Peter: When some friends of mine discovered that I would be working with people who were seriously ill, or possibly dying, they gave me a warning. They told me that they thought the work would be too heavy of an emotional burden for me. However, one friend also recommended that I read Stan Grof's book "The Ultimate Journey," which I wasn't familiar with at the time. Grof's book taught me to have an open, natural, and interested attitude toward the patients in this study. At that time I had no special training in psycho-oncology [the psychological aspects of cancer], although I had some experience over the years working with people suffering from life-threatening diseases.

From Grof's book "The Ultimate Journey," I learned that the issues that people faced in his studies were basically the same issues of our common human condition, only in a different intensity and priority. Grof's book is a rich treasure chest, filled with cultural, historical, philosophical, and religious links that help us to understand the individual psychological process. Like Carl Gustav Jung, Grof is an author with an extremely broad background of knowledge about the history of mankind — in all its shapes. He is capable of linking the individual process with the collective process — which may be a great comfort and relief, especially for dying people.

David: What kind of process and struggles did you have to go through to get your LSD study approved?

Peter: During the approval process for the study, there were two critical questions that needed to be addressed. The first one was: Is it possible to convince the Ethics Committee that the potential risk of LSD-assisted psychotherapy is not higher than in other drug research studies, and that the potential benefits that could be gained from this study make it worth doing? As you can imagine, the answer to these questions can't be obtained with any kind of mathematical precision, and rather depends upon the attitudes and prejudices of the members of the committee. Ethical decisions are always decisions of personal judgment, even if they rely on a clear and rational decision process. Fortunately, the Ethics Committee was able to discuss the question of LSD-assisted therapy in an open manner, and after much discussion, finally, it was decided that yes, such work could be done.

The second question was: Will the authorities at the Ministry of Health be influenced by political processes that might inhibit an approval of our study? It was satisfying to learn that their work was based on legal, ethical, and scientific requirements. I am convinced that Kairos — the Greek God of the opportune moment — was lending a hand, as something that brings together and orchestrates so many factors, and results in a success like this, must have played a role. It was greatly satisfying for everyone involved in this study that Albert Hofmann was still alive when the research began. He witnessed that steps were being taken to help develop LSD into what it only sometimes was — a medicine.

David: Can you share an anecdote or two from your studies, and talk a little about how your subjects are responding to the LSD-assisted psychotherapy?

Peter: Since we have a placebo-controlled design — and because of the obvious inherent difficulties involved with giving inactive placebos to subjects in psychedelic drug studies — the placebo patients also receive a very low dose of the active drug, which is 20 micrograms of LSD. Albert Hofmann said that he was convinced that even a low dose of 20 micrograms was enough to create a psychic effect in people — and he was right! One patient (who received a placebo) reported that he had a very realistic impression that the floor of the room we were in opened up and the devil appeared. Although this scene was quite short, it was very realistic.

Of course, the 200 microgram dose that the experimental subjects receive is much more powerful and longer lasting. I was very touched when one subject, a 57-year-old man suffering from metastatic gastric cancer, reported his LSD session. It was his first session in the study, as well as the first experience with hallucinogens in his life. He went out of his body, and he had the experience of flying like a bird, which was very fulfilling for him. Then he flew up higher and higher, until he met his dead father. The patient had a difficult relationship with his father, who would withdraw from confrontational family situations, leaving the patient alone with his overwhelming mother.

Although his father had died a long time ago, the patient was full of criticism and reproach toward him. However, his encounter on LSD was very different. He felt free. It was just two men meeting at the same level, without any father/son dynamics. The patient loved feeling the closeness, and there was no longer any feeling of building up an inner wall when he thought of him. Later the subject said that he thought that in his process of dying it was very important for him to meet with his father at his place, where the dead people are, and to feel their presence in the vicinity without any fear or negative feelings.

David: Have you seen anything in your sessions that influenced your understanding of, or perspective on, death?

Peter: For me, one of the most satisfying aspects of my work in this study comes from my encounter with the patients. People who are going to die automatically put more emphasis on the "here and now." They search and long for intensity and open awareness right now — not in some distant future which might not exist. This is what makes working with these people so rich.

David: What sort of promise do you see for the future of LSD research?

Peter: With this pilot study that we're now doing, my vision is to show that LSD-assisted psychotherapy is safe and effective — so that we can plan further studies based on that result. This would not be something new for insiders, but it would be new to much of the world — because it would be based on research that meets the medical requirements of contemporary drug research. I absolutely believe that LSD has broad potential for healing and relief.

The Dancer. An anthropomorphic figure, possibly a dancing shaman, from the Gabillou cave.

FOREWORD

IF THERE WERE A LIST OF THE MOST influential people in the 20th century (and now a bit beyond), Stanislav Grof would be among them. The importance of altered states of consciousness is now coming to be increasingly recognized, and no one has worked this domain as productively as the author of this book.

Grof's work began in Czechoslovakia, where for four years he worked in an interdisciplinary complex of research institutes in Prague and for another seven in the newly founded Psychiatric Research Institute. On coming to the United States in 1967 he continued his investigations at the Research Unit of Spring Grove State Hospital in Baltimore, MD, and in the Maryland Psychiatric Research Center. Two covering facts about his work are worth noting before proceeding. First, in the use of psychedelics for therapeutic and personality assessment, his experience is by far the vastest that anyone has amassed, covering as it does over 3,000 sessions in which he spent a minimum of five hours with the subject. In addition, his studies cover another 800 cases his colleagues at Baltimore and Prague conducted. Second, in spanning the Atlantic, his work covers the two dominant approaches to psychedelic therapy that have been developed: psycholytic therapy (used at Prague and in Europe generally) which involves numerous administrations of low to medium doses of LSD or its variants over a long therapeutic program, and psychedelic therapy (conducted in America) which involves one or a few high doses in a short period of treatment.

The relevant point of this tremendous database for this, Grof's latest book, is that it is the experience of dying and being reborn—the "ultimate journey" that awaits us all—that effects the cure. That sentence is worth the reader's pausing for a moment to ponder, for its implication is enormous. If, even intellectually—cognitively, cerebrally—we were convinced that death is indeed followed by rebirth, this might go a long way toward curing nothing less than our lives. For fear is life's disease. We have it from Carl Jung that he had never had a patient over forty years of age whose problems did not root from his fear of approaching death.

The great virtue of this book is that, using what was said in the preceding paragraph as its centerpiece, it encircles that centerpiece from all the relevant angles: historical, theoretical, therapeutic, scientific, and philosophical. I don't need to enlarge on this point, for a glance at the book's table of contents will make it immediately clear. Being a philosopher myself, I particularly like Grof's chapter on "Dimensions of Consciousness: New Cartography of the Human Psyche," but I have said enough. The best thing I can now do for this signally important book is to stop standing between the reader and Stanislav Grof himself.

Huston Smith
Berkeley, California

ACKNOWLEDGMENTS

THE IDEAS AND CONCEPTS discussed in this book are based on observations and experiences from more than half a century of my research on non-ordinary states of consciousness, which has been not only an exciting scientific exploration of the human psyche, but also a fascinating journey of self-discovery and personal transformation. Over the years I have received invaluable support, encouragement, and inspiration from many people who have played an important role in my life and shared with me their knowledge and wisdom—some of them as teachers, others as close friends and fellow seekers, and many of them in all these roles.

I would like to express my deep appreciation for the pioneers who conducted the ground-breaking research of death and dying and opened the field of thanatology: Elisabeth Kübler-Ross for her research on the dying process and psychological work with dying patients, Karlis Osis for his deathbed observations of physicians and nurses, Russell Noyes, Raymond Moody, Kenneth Ring, Michael Sabom, Bruce Greyson, and others for their paradigm-breaking research on near-death experiences, and Carl Simonton and Stephanie Matthews-Simonton for their exploration of psychological factors in the etiology and therapy of cancer.

My special appreciation goes to the people who played a pivotal role in the development of psychedelic therapy with cancer patients—Eric Kast, Valentina Pavlovna Wasson, Sidney Cohen, and particularly Aldous and Laura Huxley. In her book, *This Timeless Moment,* Laura offers an extraordinary account of her life with Aldous, including his ideas regarding work with dying people, and particularly the moving experience of his own death transformed by LSD, which she administered to him at his request. I feel deeply grateful to Laura for her permission to include selected passages from this important document as the Appendix to this book.

This book could not have been written without the experiences and observations from the period of my life when I was Clinical and Research Fellow and later Chief of Psychiatric Research at the Maryland Psychiatric Research Center in Catonsville,

Maryland, where I was privileged to participate in the Spring Grove Experiment, the last surviving official U.S. research program of psychedelic therapy. Over the years we conducted several large controlled studies with groups of neurotic patients, alcoholics, and narcotic drug addicts. We also administered psychedelics to mental health professionals for training purposes and conducted a program of psychedelic therapy for cancer patients, which is described at some length in this book.

I initially arrived in the United States for a one-year stay, which became permanent exile after the Soviet invasion of Czechoslovakia. The Spring Grove staff members welcomed me with much love into their research team and opened their homes to me. I spent seven years in Baltimore in this personally nourishing and professionally stimulating environment of like-minded friends. This period represents an unforgettable time of my life and a source of many wonderful memories. The research we did together at the Maryland Psychiatric Research Center using psychedelic therapy with terminal cancer patients is one of the most important sources of information for this book. I feel immense gratitude to this extraordinary group of people.

Sanford Unger was the main architect and conceptual thinker of the Spring Grove research project and of its various controlled studies. In the early years of my stay in Baltimore, Sandy, his wife Eve, and their two little daughters became my second family. Walter Pahnke's enthusiasm, energy, and dedication were essential for launching the programs of LSD and DPT psychotherapy with cancer patients. His background in medicine, psychology, and religion, combined with his unique personality, qualified him as the ideal person to head the research of psychedelic therapy with the dying. Walter himself died a tragic death in July 1971, before he could see the completion of his projects. William Richards played an important role in the LSD and DPT studies both as research theorist and as therapist.

In various stages of research, other staff members of the Maryland Psychiatric Research Center participated in the Spring Grove research as psychedelic therapists. Grateful acknowledgment is made to Thomas Cimonetti, Robert Leihy, the late Franco Di Leo, John Lobell, John Rhead, Robert Soskin, Sidney Wolf, and Richard Yensen. Mark Schiffman and Lockwood Rush operated the media department at the center. As a result of their commitment and enthusiasm, much of the case material described in this book was preserved in the form of videotape records. Helen Bonny contributed to the psychedelic studies in a unique combination of roles as musical advisor, co-therapist, and research assistant.

I would like to express my appreciation to Nancy Jewell, Karen Leihy, and the late Ilse Richards for their sensitive and dedicated participation in the cancer project as nurses and co-therapists. All three showed extraordinary interest, enthusiasm, and initiative in their work and accepted with great understanding all the extra duties imposed on them by the unusual nature of psychedelic therapy with cancer patients. I would also like to acknowledge the role my ex-wife Joan Halifax played in the cancer study in the course of her one-year stay in Baltimore. During that time, she worked with me as co-therapist in the sessions of cancer patients, including some whose case histories are included in this book, and co-authored with me an earlier book on death and dying. She also introduced me to many of her anthropologist friends, and these connections helped me put my research findings into a larger cross-cultural perspective.

Special appreciation is due to Albert A. Kurland, Director of the Maryland Psychiatric Research Center and Assistant Commissioner for Research of the Maryland State Department of Mental Hygiene. Although his responsible position and complex administrative duties made it impossible for him to participate in actual clinical work on the project, his role as coordinator, organizer, and advisor was crucial. Charles Savage, Associate Director of the Maryland Psychiatric Research Center, deserves respectful acknowledgment for the invaluable support and encouragement he granted to the projects over the years.

The experimental program of psychedelic therapy with cancer patients could not have been carried out without the unique understanding and cooperation of Louis E. Goodman, attending surgeon and head of the Oncology Clinic at Sinai Hospital. Also, the members of the medical staff of this hospital deserve appreciation for their interest, help, and willingness to provide their resources for this unexplored and highly sensitive area. My special thanks go to the agencies that provided the necessary funding for the Spring Grove research endeavors, namely the Department of Mental Hygiene of the State of Maryland and the National Institutes of Health. Especially significant was the financial support of the Mary Reynolds Babcock Foundation, which allowed these activities to be expanded in depth at a most critical time. I also wish to acknowledge the administrative and financial help of the Friends of Psychiatric Research, Inc., in Baltimore.

This book extends far beyond clinical work with psychedelics into other disciplines—anthropology, comparative religion, philosophy, and mythology. I feel very grateful to my friends and colleagues who introduced me to these fields and offered me important and valuable information. I am deeply indebted to Native American, Mexican, and South American shamans, who shared with me the world view and the practice of this ancient healing art. Here I reserve a special place in my heart for Don José Matsuwa, a centenarian Huichol shaman from Central Mexico, who for many years was an important teacher and special friend of my wife Christina and myself.

Angeles Arrien, an anthropologist trained in the Basque mystical tradition, has been a true friend and a living example of how to integrate the feminine and masculine aspects of one's psyche and how to walk the mystical path with practical feet. Michael and Sandra Harner, who also belong to our most intimate circle of friends, have given me much support, encouragement, and opportunity to share unconventional observations and adventures. Michael, who combines the role of a respectable academician and a person who received shamanic initiation during his fieldwork in the Amazon, provides an important model and example for my own life.

In July 1973, I had the unique opportunity to participate in a symposium entitled "Ritual: Reconciliation in Change," conceived and coordinated by Margaret Mead and Mary Catherine Bateson, Margaret's daughter by Gregory Bateson. During long and stimulating discussions with thirteen other participants, which took place for nine days at Burg Wartenstein in Austria, I learned some invaluable lessons concerning rites of passage and their importance for human society. This meeting planted in my mind many seeds that over the years developed into the form expressed in this book.

Gregory Bateson, with whom I had the privilege to spend hundreds of hours of intense personal and intellectual interaction during the two and a half years before his death, when we both were scholars-in-residence at the Esalen Institute in Big Sur, California, was an important teacher and a special friend. Gregory's incisive critique of mechanistic thinking in science and his creative synthesis of cybernetics, information and systems theory, psychiatry, and anthropology have had a profound influence on my own development.

Joseph Campbell, seminal thinker, master teacher, and a dear friend, played a very important role in my personal, as well as professional life. He radically changed my understanding of mythology and showed me its paramount importance for psychiatry, psychology, and for a deeper understanding of human life and death. Over the years, his truly encyclopedic knowledge of world mythology helped me understand many experiences that my clients had in various non-ordinary states of consciousness.

Rick Tarnas, psychologist, philosopher, scholar of history, and brilliant astrologer, has been a close friend of mine for more than three decades. Our numerous private discussions and classes and seminars we have taught over the years on non-ordinary states, archetypal psychology, and astrology have been for me a continuing adventure of intellectual discovery and rich source of inspiration.

Frances Vaughan and Roger Walsh, pioneers of transpersonal psychology, who both have made major contributions to the field, belong to a small circle of friends that has been regularly meeting in the Bay Area. These meetings have given me the opportunity to discuss many of the ideas described in this book and receive invaluable insights. Ram Dass, an archetypal spiritual seeker, who has regularly participated in these meetings, has shared with us his intimate experiences concerning the promises and pitfalls of the spiritual path. His wisdom and ability to turn all aspects of his life into spiritual learning and teaching have inspired us all.

Swami Paramahamsa Muktananda, head of the Siddha Yoga lineage, granted me and my wife Christina inestimable help on our spiritual journey. Frequent close contact with this extraordinary human being, extended over many years, gave us the unique opportunity to observe and experience the powerful influence of a vital spiritual tradition on human lives. The conference of the International Transpersonal Association (ITA) in February 1982 in Bombay, which Christina and I organized in cooperation with Muktananda's Ganeshpuri ashram, was an unforgettable experience.

Jack Kornfield, transpersonal psychologist and Vipassana Buddhist teacher, has during the last thirty years played a unique role in our life as an extraordinary spiritual teacher, dear friend, coworker, and fellow seeker. A rare example of a prominent representative of the spiritual field who "walks his talk," Jack teaches as much by his being as by his brilliant lectures spiced with exquisite humor. We have been truly blessed by having Jack and his family in our life.

Huston Smith, world renowned religious scholar, philosopher, and author, has been my dear friend and important teacher since the time of our first meeting in the late 1960s when he participated in our Spring Grove psychedelic research program in Baltimore. His books, lectures, and movies have comprised for me a treasure trove of information about the great religions of the world and about the mystical world view. I am particularly grateful that he found time in his busy schedule to write the foreword to this book.

Additional spiritual teachers who have profoundly influenced my life, my work, and my spiritual journey were Tibetan Buddhists Lama Govinda, Chögyam Trungpa, and Sogyal Rinpoche, and Benedictine monk Brother David Steindl-Rast. Christina and I also enjoyed for many years close friendship with Ajit Mookerjee, renowned Tantric scholar and author of many books on Tantric science, art, and ritual. During his visits at Esalen and as our guide during a pilgrimage through sacred places in India, he shared with us much of his profound knowledge of this extraordinary spiritual system.

Special thanks go to Tav and Cary Sparks, our close friends and co-workers for more than two decades. They both have played a pivotal role in our Holotropic Breathwork training and in workshops and conferences in many different parts of the world—Tav as my travel companion, co-leader, and in recent years Head of the training and Cary as the Administrative Director of the training and soul of all the projects. I am deeply grateful to Michael Marcus, Janet Zand, John Buchanan, Bokara Legendre,

Bob Schwartz, and Betsy Gordon, who over the years have granted generous support to my work.

My list of acknowledgements would not be complete without expressing my profound gratitude to Christina, my wife, lover, best friend, coworker, and fellow spiritual seeker, for everything she has contributed to my life and to our joint projects. Among others, she founded the Spiritual Emergence network (SEN) and has co-developed with me the Holotropic Breathwork, a powerful form of therapy and self-exploration that will be often mentioned in this book. She has also made a unique contribution to the understanding of the relationship between addiction, attachment, and the spiritual quest. My appreciation comes with a profound apology for all the times when my work on this book encroached on our private life.

Those whose contribution to this volume was absolutely essential and to whom I am deeply indebted and immensely grateful cannot be mentioned by name. I am referring here to many hundreds of psychiatric patients, who during their psychedelic sessions explored with enormous courage deep recesses of their psyches and shared with me their insights and discoveries. The same applies to many thousands of participants in our Holotropic Breathwork workshops and training. My special thanks go to all our Spring Grove cancer patients, for whom symbolic experiential encounters with death in their sessions represented an immediate preparation for their ultimate journey. Without the gracious cooperation of these brave individuals and their families, this book could not have been written.

Finally I would like to express my thanks to several people who played a critical role in the publication of this book. Over the years, Rick Doblin, President of the Multidisciplinary Association for Psychedelic Studies (MAPS) and the publisher of this book, has shown extraordinary effort to correct the misconceptions about psychedelic substances engendered by unsupervised use, sensation-hunting journalists, and poorly informed legislators and to achieve legalization of responsible use of these extraordinary tools. Rick's invitation provided the necessary stimulus for me to write this comprehensive treatise on the psychological, philosophical, and spiritual aspects of death. For the final form of this book, I am very grateful to Elizabeth Gibson, who edited the manuscript, for the deep knowledge of the subject, meticulous attention to detail, and loving dedication with which she carried out this task; to Mark Plummer, for his beautiful design for the book's cover and his artistic and technical help with the rich illustrations that accompany the text; and to Brandy Doyle for her careful final supervision of all the different aspects of the publication process. I also wish to thank Yahia Kabil for his generous help with the sections on Islam. I appreciate the many careful corrections made by Renn Butler to the original manuscript.

INTRODUCTION

Modern psychology has discovered how powerful the birth trauma is to the individual's life. What about the "death trauma"? If one believes in the continuity of life, should one not give it equal consideration?
– Laura Huxley, author of *This Timeless Moment*

DYING AND DEATH are the most universal and personally relevant experiences for every single individual. In the course of life, we all lose relatives, friends, teachers, and acquaintances and eventually face our own biological demise. Yet it is quite extraordinary that until the late 1960s, the Western industrial civilization showed an almost complete lack of interest in the subject of death and dying. This attitude has been displayed not only by the general public, but also by scientists and professionals for whom this subject should be of great interest—medical doctors, psychiatrists, psychologists, anthropologists, philosophers, and theologians. The only plausible explanation for this situation is massive denial of death and psychological repression of everything related to it.

Death and Dying in Preindustrial Societies

This disinterest is even more striking when we compare it to the attitude toward mortality found in preindustrial societies, where the approach to death and dying was diametrically different. Death dominated and captivated the imagination of people in ancient high cultures and provided inspiration for much of their art and architecture.

In Egypt, preoccupation with the Afterlife found its expression in monumental pyramids, large necropolises, magnificent tombs, and in countless paintings and sculptures. In pre-Hispanic Mesoamerica of the Mayans and the Aztecs, pyramids, temples, and even ballcourts were sites of elaborate rituals revolving around death. The mausoleum in Halicarnassus in Asia Minor, the tomb of Mausolus of Caria (a provincial governor of the Persian Empire) was built for him by his wife Artemisia and was considered one of the seven wonders of the ancient world.

Another great example of the ancient funeral monuments is the tomb of the Chinese Emperor Qin near Xian in the Shaanxi province, where more than 7,000 sculptures of larger-than-life-size terra-cotta warriors and horses were also buried to protect him in the Afterlife. According to archaeological research, even the legendary Minoan palace in Crete was not a royal residence, but a gigantic necropolis (Wunderlich 1972). The great Moghul dynasty in India left us beautiful tombs and mausoleums, such as the tomb of Akbar the Great and the legendary Taj Mahal, built by Shah Jahan for his beloved wife Noor Mahal. These are just a few examples of how powerfully the theme of death influenced ancient civilizations.

Death has been equally important for preindustrial native societies throughout history. Much of the aboriginal art of various parts of the world depicts the world of spirits, the posthumous journey of the soul, and particularly the all-important realm of the ancestors, beings who have been both venerated and feared. The common denominator of many funeral rites of native people is their steadfast belief in the Afterlife and their ambivalent attitude toward the deceased. Many aspects of these rites reflect an effort to facilitate and hasten the transition of the deceased to the spirit world. However, a countervailing theme can be observed with almost the same frequency—an effort to establish ceremonial relationship between the quick and the dead to obtain safety and protection. Specific features of many funeral rituals can be interpreted in terms of helping the dead in their posthumous journey, as well as preventing them from returning.

Death as Transition to Other Realities

The difference between the attitude toward death in the industrial civilization and in the preindustrial societies can best be illustrated by comparing the situation of the individuals dying in these two different contexts. The cosmologies, philosophies, and mythologies of the ancient cultures and native groups, as well as their spiritual and ritual lives, reflect a clear message that death is not the absolute and irrevocable end of everything. Consciousness, life, or existence in some form continues after the biological demise. A special variation of this belief is the widespread concept of reincarnation. In addition to the element of disembodied existence following individual death, reincarnation also involves return to material existence in a new body. In Hinduism, Buddhism, and Jainism this belief is connected with the law of karma, according to which the quality of individual incarnations is specifically determined by the person's merits and debits from preceding lifetimes.

Eschatological mythologies generally agree that the soul of the deceased undergoes a complex series of adventures in consciousness. The posthumous journey of the soul is sometimes described as travel through fantastic landscapes that bear some similarity to those on earth, other times as encounters with various archetypal beings, or as passage through a sequence of non-ordinary states of consciousness. In some cultures the soul reaches a temporary realm in the Beyond, such as the Christian Purgatory or the Lokas of Tibetan Buddhism, in others an eternal abode—Heaven, Hell, Paradise, or the sun realm. Such cultures accept without question the existence of other, normally invisible spiritual domains, such as astral realms and the world of the ancestors.

Preindustrial societies thus seemed to agree that death was not the ultimate defeat and end of everything, but an important transition. The experiences associated with death were seen as visits to important dimensions of reality that deserved to be experienced, studied, and carefully mapped. The dying were familiar with the eschatological cartographies of their cultures, whether these were shamanic maps of the funeral landscapes or sophisticated descriptions of the Eastern spiritual systems, such as those found in the *Bardo Thödol*, the Tibetan Book of the Dead. This important text of Tibetan Buddhism deserves special notice, since it represents an interesting counterpoint to Western civilization's exclusive pragmatic emphasis on productive life and denial of death. The Tibetan Book of the Dead describes the time of death as a unique opportunity for spiritual liberation from the cycles of death and rebirth and a period that determines our next incarnation, if we do not achieve liberation. In this context, the intermediate states between lives (bardos) can be seen as more important than incarnate existence, and consequently it is essential to prepare for them by systematic practice during one's lifetime.

Another characteristic aspect of ancient and preindustrial cultures that colors the experience of dying is their acceptance of death as an integral part of life. Throughout life, people living in these cultures spend time around dying people: handling corpses, observing cremation, and living with the remnants of their relatives. For a Westerner, a visit to a place like the holy Hindu city Varanasi (Benares), where this attitude is expressed in its extreme form, can be a profoundly shattering experience. In addition, dying people in preindustrial cultures typically die in the context of an extended family, clan, or tribe. Thus at this critical time of passage they can receive meaningful emotional support from people whom they intimately know. Powerful rituals are conducted at the time of death to help individuals face the ultimate transition, or even provide specific guidance for dying, such as the approach described in the *Bardo Thödol.*

Holotropic States of Consciousness in Death and Dying

The practice of various forms of experiential training for dying was an extremely important factor influencing the attitude toward death and the experience of dying in preindustrial societies. The common denominator of such practices was that they involved non-ordinary states of consciousness, or a special important subgroup of these states, for which I have coined the term "holotropic" (Grof 1992). This composite word literally means "oriented toward wholeness" or "moving in the direction of wholeness" (from the Greek *holos* = whole and *trepein* = moving toward or in the direction of something). These states, induced by psychedelic substances and by an entire spectrum of non-drug techniques, or occurring spontaneously, have great healing and transformative potential and represent an important source of information about consciousness, the human psyche, and nature of reality. The significance which the ancient and aboriginal cultures attributed to holotropic states is reflected in the amount of time and energy dedicated to the development of these "technologies of the sacred."

Among the experiences occurring in holotropic states are profound sequences of psychospiritual death and rebirth and feelings of cosmic unity, which have the potential to radically transform the attitude toward death and the process of dying itself. Ancient and preindustrial societies provided many socially sanctioned contexts to experience such states. The oldest of such institutions is *shamanism*, an ancient spiritual system and healing art intimately connected with holotropic states of consciousness and with death and dying. The career of many shamans begins with the "shamanic illness," a spontaneous initiatory crisis involving a visionary journey into the Underworld, experience of psychological death and rebirth, and ascent into supernal realms. The knowledge of the realm of death acquired during this transformation makes it possible for the shaman to move freely back and forth between the two worlds and use these journeys for healing purposes and for obtaining knowledge. He or she can also mediate such journeys for others.

Anthropologists have described another context that makes it possible to practice dying—*rites of passage*. These are elaborate rituals conducted by various aboriginal cultures at the time of important biological and social transitions, including birth, circumcision, puberty, marriage, menopause, and dying. These rites employ various effective mind-altering technologies. Closer examination of the states induced by them and of the external symbolism surrounding them reveals that they revolve around the triad birth-sex-death and the experience of psychospiritual rebirth. People living in these cultures have during their lifetime numerous opportunities to experience and transcend death. At the time of their biological demise, they are thus entering a familiar territory.

Closely related to the rites of passage were the *ancient mysteries of death and rebirth*, complex sacred and secret procedures that also involved powerful mind-altering techniques. They existed in many different parts of the world, but were particularly prevalent in the Mediterranean area. These initiatory events were based on mythological stories of deities symbolizing death and rebirth—Babylonian Inanna and Dumuzi, Egyptian Isis and Osiris, and the Greek Dionysus, Attis, Adonis, and others. The most famous of them were the Eleusinian Mysteries, based on the myth of Persephone's abduction into the Underworld by Hades and her periodic return to the world. These mysteries were conducted at Eleusis, a small town near Athens, every five years without interruption for a period of almost 2,000 years. The experiences of death and rebirth in these mysteries had the reputation of freeing the initiates from the fear of death and radically transforming their way of life.

Of particular interest for transpersonally-oriented researchers are various *mystical traditions and the great spiritual philosophies of the East*. Here belong the various systems of yoga, various schools of Buddhism from Theravada and Tibetan Vajrayana to Zen, Taoism, Sufism, Christian mysticism, Kabbalah, and many others. These systems developed effective forms of prayers, meditations, movement meditations, breathing exercises, and other powerful techniques for inducing holotropic states with profoundly spiritual components. Like the experiences of the shamans, initiates in the rites of passage, and neophytes in ancient mysteries, these procedures offered the possibility of confronting one's mortality and impermanence, transcending the fear of death, and radically transforming one's being in the world.

The description of the resources available to dying people in preindustrial cultures would not be complete without mentioning *the books of the dead*, such as the Tibetan *Bardo Thödol*, the Egyptian *Pert Em Hru*, the Aztec *Codex Borgia*, the Mayan *Ceramic Codex*, and the European *Ars moriendi*. These texts described in detail the experiences that one can encounter after biological death and during the posthumous journey of the soul. As discussed in Chapter 6, the same texts serve another important function: they can also be used during one's lifetime as manuals for spiritual practice and guides for self-exploration involving holotropic states of consciousness.

As we have seen, an individual dying in one of the ancient or native cultures had experienced an intensive training for death in a variety of rituals involving holotropic states of consciousness and was equipped with a spiritual and philosophical belief system that transcended death. He or she died in the nourishing context of the extended family and fellow tribesmen and women, often with expert ritual guidance through the stages of dying. In some cultures, the basis for such guidance was provided by cartographies transmitted by oral tradition or special texts describing the experiential territories which the dying had to traverse.

Approach to Death and Dying in Industrial Societies

The situation of an average person dying in one of the industrial societies is radically different. Such an individual typically has a pragmatic and atheistic world view or is at least very profoundly influenced by the exposure to it. According to Western science and its monistic materialistic philosophy, the history of the universe is essentially the history of developing matter. Life, consciousness, and intelligence are more or less accidental and insignificant by-products of this development and appeared on the scene after many billions of years of evolution of passive and inert matter in a trivially small part of an immense universe. There is no place for spirituality of any kind in a world where reality is defined solely as material, tangible, and measurable.

Role of Religion

Although religious activities are generally permitted and even formally encouraged, from a strictly scientific point of view, any involvement in spirituality is considered an irrational activity indicating emotional and intellectual immaturity: lack of education, primitive superstition, and regression to magical and infantile thinking. Direct experiences of spiritual realities are seen as manifestations of a serious mental disease, as psychotic distortions of reality caused by a pathological process afflicting the brain. Religion, bereft of its experiential component, has largely lost the connection to its deep spiritual source and consequently is increasingly empty and meaningless—no longer a positive and useful force in our life. In this form, it cannot compete with the persuasiveness of materialistic science backed up by its technological triumphs. In the absence of experientially-based, viable spirituality, well-educated people are likely to be atheistic and those less intellectually savvy tend to succumb to delusional forms of fundamentalism.

View of Consciousness

According to Western neuroscience, consciousness is an epiphenomenon of matter, a product of the physiological processes in the brain, and thus critically dependent on the body. The death of the body, more specifically the brain, is seen as the absolute end of any form of conscious activity. Belief in life after death, posthumous journey of the soul, abodes of the Beyond, and reincarnation have been relegated to the realm of fairy tales and handbooks of psychiatry and are seen as products of wishful thinking of primitive or simple-minded people who are unable to accept the obvious biological imperative of death. This approach has pathologized much of the spiritual and ritual history of humanity.

Very few people, including most scientists, realize that we have absolutely no proof that consciousness is actually produced by the brain. Moreover, we do not have even a remote notion how this could possibly happen; no scientist has ever attempted to specifically address how the formidable gap between matter and consciousness could be bridged. Even so, the basic metaphysical assumption that consciousness is an epiphenomenon of matter remains one of the leading myths of Western materialistic science and profoundly influences our entire society. There also is no scientific proof for the absence of a spiritual dimension in the universal scheme of things, whereas ample evidence can be found for the existence of normally invisible numinous dimensions of reality. However, under present circumstances, the current official world view of the industrial civilization and official forms of religious worship do not offer much support for dying people.

Scientific Interest in Death and Dying

Until the 1970s, this perspective on death also effectively inhibited scientific interest in the experiences of dying patients and of individuals in near-death situations. The rare exceptions received very little attention, whether they were popular books for the general public, such as Jess E. Weisse's *The Vestibule* and Jean-Baptiste Delacour's *Glimpses of the Beyond* (Weisse 1972, Delacour 1974), or scientific treatises, such as the thorough study of deathbed observations of physicians and nurses conducted by Karlis Osis (Osis 1961). These contributions were relegated to the realm of parapsychology and dismissed as scientifically irrelevant.

This situation changed after the publication of Elisabeth Kübler-Ross' groundbreaking book *On Death and Dying* (Kübler-Ross 1969) and of Raymond Moody's international bestseller *Life After Life* (Moody 1975). Since then, Ken Ring, Michael Sabom, and other pioneers of thanatology have amassed impressive evidence about the extraordinary characteristics of near-death experiences, from accurate extrasensory perception during out-of-body experiences to the profound personality changes following them. Information from these studies has been widely publicized in best-selling books, TV talk shows, Hollywood movies and other forms of media. As a result, professionals and lay audiences are now familiar with the basic features of near-death experiences. Yet these paradigm-shattering observations, despite their potential to revolutionize our understanding of the nature of consciousness and its relationship to the brain, are still dismissed by most professionals as irrelevant hallucinations produced by biological crises of the body and the brain. Near-death experiences are also not routinely recorded and examined as important aspects of the patients' medical history, and most medical facilities offer no specific psychological services to help survivors integrate them.

Conditions of Dying and Death

People dying in Western societies often lack effective human support to ease their transition. We try to protect ourselves from the emotional discomfort associated with death by removing sick and dying people into hospitals and nursing homes. The emphasis is on life-support systems and mechanical prolongation of life, often beyond any reasonable limits, rather than supportive human milieu and quality of the remaining days. The family system has disintegrated, and children often live far from the parents and grandparents. Consequently contact with relatives during a medical crisis is often formal and minimal. In addition, mental health professionals, who have developed specific forms of psychological support and counseling for a large variety of emotional crises, still lack effective ways of helping the dying with their transition. Consequently meaningful help is not available for those facing the most profound of all imaginable crises, one that affects simultaneously the biological, emotional, interpersonal, social, philosophical, and spiritual aspects of the individual.

All this occurs in the much larger context of collective denial of impermanence and mortality that characterizes Western industrial civilization. Much of our encounter with death comes in a sanitized form, where a team of professionals mitigates its immediate impact. In its extreme expression, it includes postmortem barbers and hairdressers, tailors, make-up experts, and plastic surgeons who make all kinds of cosmetic adjustments to the corpse before it is shown to relatives and friends. The media create more distance from death by diluting it into empty statistics and reporting in a matter-of-fact way about the thousands of victims of wars, revolutions, and natural catastrophes. Movies and TV shows further trivialize death by capitalizing on violence and immunizing modern audiences against its emotional relevance with countless scenes of dying, killing, and murder in the context of entertainment. Clearly the conditions of life existing in modern developed countries do not offer much ideological or psychological support for people who are facing death.

Overview of This Book

In this book I explore the findings of consciousness research that have revolutionized theoretical understanding of dying and death and opened new ways of working with dying people. In the first part I discuss at some length the ancient and aboriginal ritual and spiritual practices that can help us understand the experience of death, develop effective ways of making dying easier, and make it a meaningful part of life. Individual chapters focus on various forms of training for dying—shamanism, rites of passage, ancient mysteries, and various mystical and Eastern spiritual systems, and the posthumous journey of the soul. After the discussion of these ritual and spiritual practices, I have dedicated a special chapter to the ancient books of the dead—the Tibetan *Bardo Thödol*, the Egyptian *Pert Em Hru*, the Aztec *Codex Borgia*, the Mayan *Ceramic Codex*, and the European *Ars moriendi*.

The second part of this book reviews the findings of modern studies that throw new light on a variety of phenomena related to death and dying. This discussion begins with the new expanded cartography of the psyche that has emerged from my 50 years of research of psychedelic therapy, Holotropic Breathwork, and spontaneous psychospiritual crises. This map is a necessary prerequisite for any serious approach to the problems discussed in this book, from various forms of ritual transformation to the question of consciousness on the threshold of death. I then address in separate chapters various areas of research relevant for the question of survival of consciousness after death—near-death experiences, karma and reincarnation, and communication with discarnate consciousness.

The final chapters of this book focus on the Spring Grove Program, a major research effort to investigate psychedelic therapy with terminal cancer patients. In these chapters I outline the history of this treatment modality, describe the therapeutic process, include several illustrative case histories, and analyze the clinical results. The closing chapter reviews the psychological understanding of death from Freud's early speculations to the transpersonal perspective that has emerged from psychedelic therapy and other areas of modern consciousness research, including the current renewal of psychedelic research. This chapter also explores the practical relevance of the material discussed in this book for individuals living in technological societies and possible sociopolitical implications of the new insights for the understanding of the current global crisis and its alleviation. The Appendix, contributed by Laura Huxley, includes excerpts regarding Aldous Huxley's conscious approach to death from her book *This Timeless Moment: A Personal View of Aldous Huxley* (L. Huxley 1968).

The Sorcerer from Les Trois Frères. A cave painting of a mysterious composite figure combines various male symbols—antlers of a stag, eyes of an owl, tail of a wild horse or wolf, human beard, and paws of a lion.

1
SHAMANISM: THE ARCHAIC TECHNIQUES OF ECSTASY

The witch doctor succeeds for the same reason
the rest of us (doctors) succeed. Each patient carries
his own doctor inside him. They come to us not knowing this truth.
We are at our best when we give the doctor who resides
within each patient a chance to go to work.
– Albert Schweitzer, German physician,
theologian, philosopher, and musician

EXPERIENTIAL TRAINING FOR DYING can be traced back tens of thousands of years, to the dawn of humanity and the practice of shamanism, an ancient art of healing and the first form of spiritual practice for which we have archaeological records. The term "shaman" is most likely derived from the Tunguso-Manchurian word *saman*, meaning literally "he or she who knows." This name reflects the deep respect for the profound knowledge of the psyche and of the nature of reality that shamans possess. In its narrower and more specialized anthropological sense, this term refers to Siberian native healers and their use of ceremonial costume, the one-sided drum, trance state, and visionary journeys. In its broader sense, it has been widely used for a variety of native healers in different parts of the world, who have also been popularly known as medicine men, witch doctors, sorcerers, or wizards.

A unique feature of shamans, when compared to other healers, is their use of holotropic states of consciousness for healing themselves and others and for a variety of other purposes. Shamans have the reputation of being able to diagnose, heal, and cause diseases, communicate with the worlds beyond, and use extrasensory perception to foretell the future. Among other feats they reportedly see things happening in remote places, locate lost people and objects, influence weather, and monitor the movement of game animals. They are viewed as guardians of the psychic and ecological equilibrium of their people, intermediaries between the seen and unseen, masters of spirits, and supernatural healers.

Shamanism is extremely ancient, probably at least thirty to forty thousand years old; its deepest roots can be traced far back to the Paleolithic era. The walls of the famous caves in Southern France and northern Spain, such as Lascaux, Font de Gaume, Les Trois Frères, La Gabillou, Altamira, and others are decorated with beautiful images of animals and mythical creatures with striking magical and ritual significance. Paintings and carvings of strange figures in many of these caves combine human and animal features and undoubtedly represent ancient shamans. Among the most famous are the "Sorcerer" from Les Trois Frères, the "Dancer" from La Gabillou, and the "Beast Master" from Lascaux. Also well known is the hunting scene on the wall in the Lascaux cave complex, which shows a wounded bison and a lying figure of a shaman with an erect penis. The origins of shamanism can be traced back to a yet older Neanderthal cult of the cave bear and its animal shrines from the interglacial period found in the grottoes in Switzerland and southern Germany.

Shamanism is not only ancient, but also universal; it can be found in North and South America, in Europe, Africa, Asia, Australia, Micronesia, and Polynesia. The fact that shamanism has pervaded so many different cultures throughout human history suggests that the holotropic states that the shamans induce engage what the anthropologists call the "primal mind"—a basic and primordial aspect of the human psyche that transcends race, sex, culture, and historical time. Shamanic techniques and procedures have survived until this very day in cultures that have escaped the deleterious influence of Western industrial civilization.

Initiatory Experiences

Shamanism is closely related to death and dying. The career of many shamans begins with a spontaneous visionary state. This initiatory crisis, or "shamanic illness," as Western anthropologists call it, usually takes the form of a profound experience of psychospiritual death and rebirth and represents extraordinary experiential training for actual death. The initiatory crisis is not always spontaneous. Practicing shamans sometimes initiate their apprentices into the shamanic profession by inducing similar experiences with the use of powerful mind-altering procedures, such as psychedelic plants or a combination of drumming, rattling, chanting, dancing, fasting, and sleep deprivation. They also use these methods in their own journeying and when they are helping others.

In their initiatory visionary states, future shamans typically experience a journey into the Underworld, the realm of the dead. Here they are attacked by vicious demons and subjected to agonizing ordeals. Flesh is scraped from their bones, their eyeballs are torn out, and blood is sucked out of their vessels. Their bodies are hacked to pieces, boiled in cauldrons, reduced to skeletons, and dismembered. After the novice shaman has been completely annihilated, the pieces of his or her body are usually distributed among the spirits of various diseases. It is understood that in the future the shaman will be able to heal diseases caused by evil spirits, who during the initiatory crisis had feasted on his or her body. Although the details of these experiences vary considerably among different tribes and individual shamans, they all share the general atmosphere of horror and inhuman suffering.

On the journey to the land of the dead, the shaman might brave icy winds, burning forests, stormy rivers, and bloody streams. The Underworld is a dangerous and terrifying place. It may be supported by human bones, carpeted with women's hair, teeming with toads and lizards, filled with dark boiling waters where countless souls wail in agony. The novice shaman might cross a dangerous black river and travel on boats with corpses or spirit canoes. The rapids are flaming whirlpools, the landscape breeds sickness and death, and the evil Mistress of the Underworld rules a village of man-eaters. Altaic shamans traverse landscapes with gloomy forests and high mountains, strewn with bones of their dead predecessors and their mounts. They then confront the Lord of the Underworld, who howls and bellows like a maddened bull, appease him through gifts and trickery, and return on a wild gander. A Yakut shaman must travel through the throat and body of a monster serpent whose bowels have sharp spikes.

After the experience of death, dismemberment, and total annihilation, the shaman experiences rebirth. He or she acquires new flesh, new blood, and new eyes and ascends to the supernal realms, most often by climbing the World Tree, which joins together the three worlds and is connected with the primeval waters of life circulating through all of nature. The shaman can also experience transformation into a bird, such as an eagle, thunderbird, hawk, or condor and fly into the solar realm or alternatively be carried there by such a bird. Additional archetypal ways of reaching the supernal realms are climbing a rainbow, a chain of arrows, a holy mountain, or a pole with nine notches. From Lapland to Patagonia, from ancient times to today, the archetypes activated during shamanic ordeals and exaltations are astonishingly similar.

In this process of descent into the Underworld, death and rebirth, and ascent to the celestial realms, future shamans realize their solar identity. They experience a deep connection with forces of nature and with animals, both in their actual physical form and in their archetypal form. In the shamanic lore, these latter forces are known as "power animals" and possess certain unique features: capability to talk, to appear in human form, and navigate in an atypical element. (For example, a land mammal or serpent power animal can fly.) Power animals are not individuals in the ordinary sense; they represent the entire genus or species, such as Coyote, Bear, or Raven. The visionary experiences of the initiatory crisis typically bring deep insights into the nature and origin of diseases and help future shamans heal themselves from various emotional, psychosomatic, and often even physical disorders, which had previously plagued their lives. For this reason, anthropologists often refer to shamans as "wounded healers."

To be recognized as a shaman requires successful completion of the initiatory crisis, integration of the achieved insights, and attainment of adequate or superior functioning in everyday reality. The experience of a dramatic holotropic state is not sufficient, in and of itself, to qualify an individual as a shaman. Native cultures are capable of distinguishing real shamans from persons who are ill or crazy. Accomplished shamans are able to enter holotropic states at will, in a controlled way, and for a specific purpose, such as healing, extrasensory perception, and exploration of alternate dimensions of reality. They can also induce such states in other members of their tribes and play the role of "psychopomps," in which they provide the necessary support and guidance for those traversing the complex territories of the Beyond.

This account of the initiation of an Avam-Samoyed shaman, recorded by A. A. Popov, illustrates the experiences that open individuals to a shamanic career:

> Stricken with smallpox, the future shaman remained unconscious for three days, so nearly dead that on the third day he was almost buried. He saw himself go down to Hell and, after many adventures, was carried to an island, in the middle of which stood a young birch tree, which reached up to Heaven. It was the Tree of the Lord of the Earth, and the Lord gave him a branch of it to make himself a drum. Next he came to a mountain; passing through an opening, he met a naked man plying the bellows at an immense fire on which was a kettle. The man caught him with a hook, cut off his head, and chopped his body to bits and put them all into the kettle. There he boiled the body for three years, and then forged him a head on an anvil. Finally he fished out the bones, which were floating in a river, put them together, and covered them with flesh. During his adventures in the Other World, the future shaman met several semi-divine personages, in human or animal form, and each of them revealed doctrines to him or taught him secrets of the healing art. When he awoke in his yurt, among his relatives, he was initiated and could begin to shamanize (Popov 1936).

A Yakut myth describes the ordeals associated with the birth of shamans:

> The Mother of Animals, a large female eagle with iron feathers, claws, and beak, hatches shamans—the great ones for three years on high branches of the tree and less eminent ones one year on lower branches of the tree. The baby is entrusted to a spirit-shamaness who has one eye, one hand, and one leg. She feeds him blood in a cradle of iron and then hands him to three black spirits who hack him to pieces and scatter the remains. The shaman will be able to heal the diseases whose evil source has been given a piece of his flesh. Great shamans experience dismemberment three times.

Although the shamanism of the Siberian and Ural-Altaic peoples has received the primary attention of anthropologists and ethnographers, similar practices and experiences, including initiatory illness, exist among peoples in Southeast Asia, Australia, Oceania, Africa, and among Indians in North and South America. According to renowned authority Mircea Eliade, shamans have contributed considerably to the knowledge of death and of the experiences associated with it ("funerary geography") (Eliade 1964). The stories of their journeys are also among the most important sources of eschatological mythology. Through repeated magical journeys of the shamans, the unknown and terrifying world of death assumed form and structure and gradually became more familiar and acceptable to their people. Little by little, the region of death became knowable, and death itself was seen primarily as a rite of passage to a spiritual mode of being.

Healing and Transformative Potential of the Shamanic Crisis

Mircea Eliade referred to shamanism as the "archaic technique of ecstasy" in the sense of its original Greek meaning—stepping out of oneself (ek-stasis). The visionary journeys of the shamans are not always blissful and joyful; they often are dark and agonizing. As we will see in Chapter 8, many experiences characterizing the shamanic initiatory crises, such as being engulfed, subjected to extreme emotional and physical suffering, being tried by fire, exposed to scatological materials, and dismembered, are known from the sessions of psychedelic subjects focusing on the process of psychospiritual death and rebirth.

Mainstream psychiatry and anthropology tend to ascribe pathological labels to the psychospiritual crises of the shamans and to the shamans themselves. The diagnoses range from schizophrenia, borderline psychosis, and epilepsy to severe hysteria and "culturally constituted defense." The shamanic crisis is distinctly different from schizophrenia. It has unusual phenomenology with great emphasis on the mystical dimension, no progressive deterioration of personality, and superior functioning in the culture. Master shamans are at home in the non-ordinary, as well as ordinary reality, and they operate successfully in both realms. Typically they participate actively in social, economic, and even political affairs—as hunters, gardeners, farmers, politicians, artists, and responsible family members. Shamans display remarkable energy and stamina, a high level of intelligence, and considerable leadership skills. They have superior grasp of complex data concerning myth and rituals but, above all, they have profound knowledge of the experiential territories of dying and death.

Modern consciousness research and psychotherapeutic work with individuals experiencing spontaneous episodes of non-ordinary states of consciousness have brought a radically new perspective to the "shamanic illness." Properly understood and supported, psychospiritual crises of various kinds can result in healing, spiritual opening, and deep positive transformation of personality. They can also provide profound insights into the nature and dimensions of the human psyche, emotional and psychosomatic disorders, and the nature of reality. Shamanic initiatory crises thus belong to a large category of experiences which can break down rigid ego structures and reconstitute them in a positive way (Dabrowski 1967, Silverman 1967 and 1970, Perry 1974 and 1976). Rather than being manifestations of mental illness, psychospiritual crises represent "spiritual emergencies" and offer the potential for healing and profound transformation (Grof and Grof 1990).

2
RITES OF PASSAGE: DEATH AND REBIRTH IN RITUAL TRANSFORMATION

Are you willing to be sponged out, erased, canceled,
Made nothing? Are you willing to be made nothing?
Dipped into oblivion?
If not, you will never really change.
– D.H. Lawrence, *Phoenix*

RITUAL EVENTS KNOWN AS RITES of passage represent another important example of socially sanctioned institutions that have provided experiential training for dying in ancient civilizations and native cultures. This term was coined by the Dutch anthropologist Arnold van Gennep, who recognized their importance and universal distribution and wrote the first scientific treatise on the subject (van Gennep 1960). Ceremonies of this kind once existed in all known native cultures and are still being performed in many preindustrial societies. Their main purpose is to redefine, transform, and consecrate individuals, groups, and even entire cultures.

Rites of passage mark critical changes in the life of an individual or a culture. Their timing frequently coincides with major physiological transitions, such as childbirth, circumcision, puberty, marriage, menopause, and dying—occasions in which the body, psyche, social status, and sacred role of the initiates are changing significantly. Similar rituals are also associated with initiation into warrior status, acceptance into secret societies, calendrical festivals of renewal, and geographical moves of human groups into new territories.

In Western industrial civilization, the time of major transition from one stage in life to another is usually fraught with a negative value judgment. This is certainly true for puberty, middle age, senescence, and, of course, dying. Even birth has taken on a negative cast in our culture, where the delivering mother is routinely relegated to the role of the patient and goes to a hospital to deliver her child. Old people are also denigrated, as well as those afflicted by diseases, particularly those who have been designated as "terminally ill." Such persons are between life and death and therefore no longer viable social entities; for this reason, the dying are often seen as social and economic burdens.

Typical Stages of Rites of Passage

Arnold van Gennep recognized that in all the cultures he had studied, rituals of this kind followed a standard pattern with three distinct stages: separation, transition, and incorporation. In the first stage, *separation*, the initiated individuals are removed from their social fabric—family, clan, and the rest of the tribe. During the ensuing period of isolation, they may be completely alone or may share this unsettling situation with their peers. Loss of the familiar ground and absence of a new one to replace it relegate them to an indeterminate state of liminality, a limbo condition described by anthropologists as being "betwixt and between." Initiates typically react to this situation with a feeling of intense grief over the loss of the old way of being and can also become afraid of uprootedness, of the unexpected, and of the unknown. In this sense their experience is very similar to a "spiritual emergency," where familiar reality is forcefully replaced by the challenges of the inner world. However, in group initiations conducted in tribal rites of passage this frightening period of separation has its positive side in that the neophytes typically develop a deep sense of bonding and community with each other.

At this point, the elders impart the culture's cosmology and mythology and prepare the initiates for the next stage of the ritual, the transition. Such thorough and thoughtful preparation is essential for the optimal outcome of the transformative process. The initiates obtain much of this information indirectly through mythological stories, songs, and dance. The elders also share their knowledge of the experiential territories the initiates are about to traverse. In this way the initiates learn that the journey that is ahead of them, as strange and ominous as it might seem, has a timeless dimension. It has been and will be traveled by many others—by sacred ancestors, as well as by past and future initiates. Knowing the universal nature of this process can be reassuring for the neophytes and help them face the difficult aspects of the transformation process.

In the second stage, which van Gennep termed *transition*, the neophytes move from predominantly intellectual learning to profound direct experiences of holotropic states of consciousness, induced by powerful mind-altering procedures, "technologies of the sacred." These methods combine in various ways drumming and other forms of percussion, music, chanting, rhythmic dancing, changes of breathing, and cultivation of special forms of awareness. Extended social and sensory isolation, such as a stay in a cave, desert, arctic ice, or in high mountains, also plays an important role in inducing holotropic states. Some of the more extreme physiological interventions include extended sleep deprivation, dehydration, fasting, using powerful laxatives and purgatives, massive bloodletting, genital mutilation, and infliction of excruciating pain. The extreme nature of many of these techniques emphasizes the value that various human groups have traditionally ascribed to holotropic states.

Among the most powerful technologies of the sacred are various psychedelic plants. Their use for ritual and spiritual purposes reaches back thousands of years. The legendary divine potion referred to as "haoma" in the ancient Persian *Zend Avesta* and as "soma" in India was used by the Indo-Iranian tribes several millennia ago and was probably the most important inspiration of the Vedic religion and philosophy. Preparations from different varieties of hemp have been smoked and ingested under various names (hashish, charas, bhang, ganja, kif, marijuana) in the Oriental countries, in Africa, and in the Caribbean area for recreation, pleasure, and during religious ceremonies. They have represented an important sacrament for such diverse groups as the Brahmans, certain Sufi orders, ancient Skythians, and the Jamaican Rastafarians.

Ceremonial use of various psychedelic materials also has a long history in Central America. Highly effective mind-altering plants were well known in several pre-Hispanic Indian cultures—among the Aztecs, Mayans, and Toltecs. Most famous of these are the Mexican cactus peyote (*Lophophora williamsii*), the sacred mushroom teonanacatl (*Psilocybe mexicana*), and ololiuqui, seeds of different varieties of the morning glory plant (*Ipomoea violacea* and *Turbina corymbosa*). These materials have been used as sacraments until this day by the Huichol, Mazatec, Chichimeca, Cora, and other Mexican Indian tribes, as well as the Native American Church.

The famous South American yajé or ayahuasca is a decoction from a jungle liana (*Banisteriopsis caapi*) combined with other plant additives. The Amazonian area and the Caribbean islands are also known for a variety of psychedelic snuffs. Aboriginal tribes in Africa ingest and inhale preparations from the bark of the iboga shrub (*Tabernanthe iboga*) and use them in small quantities as stimulants and in larger dosages in initiation rituals for men and women. The psychedelic compounds of animal origin include the secretions of the skin of certain toads (*Bufo alvarius*) and the meat of the Pacific fish *Kyphosus fuscus*. This list represents only a small fraction of psychedelic materials that have been used over many centuries in ritual and spiritual life of various countries of the world.

Various combinations of these practices induce in the initiates profound experiences resulting in healing, spiritual opening, deep personality transformation, and a higher level of integration. Such experiences typically take the form of psychospiritual death and rebirth and encounter with numinous dimensions of reality. In the context of such rituals, these experiences are then interpreted as dying to the old role and being born into the new one. For example, in the puberty rites the initiates enter the ritual as boys or girls and emerge from it as adults, with all the rights and duties that come with this status.

The third stage in van Gennep's triad is *incorporation*, in which the individual is reintegrated into his or her community in a new role, defined by the type of the ceremony: as an adult, a married person, a parent, a warrior, and so on. In a rite of passage, the individual or social group leaves behind one mode of being and, after passing through a period of liminality, moves into another, completely new existential condition. Newly initiated persons are not the same as those who entered the initiation process. Having undergone a deep psychospiritual transformation, they have a personal connection with the numinous dimensions of existence, a vastly expanded world view, a better self-image, and a different system of values. Because they have faced and survived a convincing experience of personal annihilation, they have transcended their identification with the body and ego, lost fear of death, and attained a new attitude toward life.

Okipa Rite of Passage

An example of a powerful and complex rite of passage was the Okipa festival of the Mandans, a tribe of North American Plains Indians who lived on the Missouri River. This ritual, which involved extreme physical pain and mutilation, shows how highly some cultures value transformative experiences and to what extremes they are willing to go in pursuing them. Certainly many other similar rites of passage are not nearly as radical or as elaborate as the Okipa festival. Although the core of this extraordinary ritual was initiation of young men into adulthood and into warrior status, it also included ceremonial dances for the purpose of securing successful buffalo hunts and appeasing evil spirits, and a celebration of the ending of the mythological flood.

The Okipa ritual began as a ceremonial figure representing the First Man, the Original Ancestor, painted with white clay and wearing a splendid robe, led the group of young male initiates covered with clay of different colors to the ceremonial site. After smoking his sacred medicine pipe, the "First Man" gave the initiates an encouraging talk and appointed an old medicine man to be the Master of the Ceremonies, who made sure that none of the young men escaped from the lodge, ate, drank, or slept during the four days of preparation for the ordeal. Through prayers, he also maintained connection with the Great Spirit, asking for the success of the procedure. During this preparation time, the rest of the tribe gathered outside of the lodge, where they performed several rituals and provided various forms of entertainment around the Great Canoe, a reminder of the flood. They chanted many prayers to the Great Spirit, asking for continuous supply of buffaloes and encouragement for the young initiates. Much of their energy was focused on invocations of the Evil Spirit, O-kee-hee-dee. This type of effort to come to terms with the dark aspects of existence is characteristic of the rites of passage and healing ceremonies in many cultures.

On the fourth day, a masked figure representing O-kee-hee-dee finally appeared, almost naked and painted mostly black, with some white. Adorned with a colossal wooden penis that had a black shaft and a large vermillion head, he stormed the village and ran around in a frenzy, chasing women and wreaking havoc. The general panic and chaos kept building and then reached a sudden turning point when the Master of the Ceremonies confronted the Evil Spirit and immobilized him by the charm of his sacred pipe. O-kee-hee-dee, bereft of his magic power, was tantalized, ridiculed, and humiliated, particularly by the women, and chased out of the village.

The women's triumphant return with his gigantic penis as a trophy was the signal for the beginning of the ordeal in the lodge. There the young initiates were raised above the ground by cords attached to skewers piercing their flesh. Heavy weights, such as shields, bows, quivers, and buffalo skulls, were suspended from the skewers, and the initiates were rotated around a pole until they lost consciousness. They were then lowered to the ground, and when they regained consciousness, their little fingers were chopped off and offered to the Great Spirit.

The final stage of the Okipa ceremony was the Last Race. With the weights still attached to their bodies, the young men were taken outside to the ceremonial area, where they ran in large circles, dragging the weights behind them, each striving to endure longer than his peers, without collapsing or "dying," as it was called. Even after they fainted, totally exhausted by physical exertion and excruciating pain, the initiates were dragged around until all of the weights were torn out from their flesh. Their mangled bodies lay on the ground until they regained consciousness and staggered through the crowds to their lodges, where they were welcomed by their relatives, who congratulated them on their great achievement. The immature youngsters who they had been were considered to have died in this ordeal and been reborn as adults and brave warriors.

While these practices might seem extreme from a Western point of view, ceremonies of this kind typically enhance several key attributes: emotional and physical wellbeing, one's sense of personal strength and independence, feelings of deep connection with nature and the cosmos, and a sense of social belonging and cohesion. The inner experiences and external events of the rite of passage communicate to the neophytes a profound message, the core insight of all human transformative processes, including spiritual emergencies: one can suffer through the chaos of liminality and dying, undergo an experience of total annihilation and death and emerge feeling healed, reborn, rejuvenated, and stronger than before. This awareness reduces greatly the fear of death and enhances one's ability to enjoy life. Such transformation profoundly benefits not only the individual initiates but also the entire community.

In the Okipa rite of passage a significant part of the transformative ordeal was enacted in a realistic and concrete way; however, this is not the only possibility. Various mind-altering techniques of a much gentler kind can trigger similar sequences of suffering, death, and rebirth by activating the psyche's own inner repositories, without any physical damage to the body. A purely symbolic experience of this kind can have an identical impact. In individuals undergoing spiritual emergencies, episodes of this kind often occur spontaneously. Even a cursory comparison reveals that many of the aspects of rites of passage are closely related to the phenomenology of psychedelic and holotropic experiences, which originate on the perinatal (birth-related) level of the unconscious. (The perinatal level of the unconscious is discussed in Chapter 8).

Themes of Birth, Sex, and Death in Rites of Passage

The inner experiences of initiates in these rituals involve a unique mixture of themes related to birth, sex, and death, the same triad that characterizes experiences associated with the reliving of the final stage of birth (see Chapter 8). The external symbolism used in the initiatory procedures reflects the same strange amalgam of these three important aspects of life. For example, the initiation hut might be referred to as "vagina" or "womb," and often the same term also means tomb. In some cultures, the word used for gestation applies equally to burial and to ritual initiation. Conversely, tombs are often built in the shape of wombs, and the dead are buried in fetal position. Pregnant women can be referred to as being dead and are considered reborn after they deliver their children. Among the Iatmul, a New Guinea tribe, the entrance into the initiation hut is called the clitoris gate.

Rites of passage often use symbolic allusions to biological birth to support the experience of the "second birth" and ritual transformation. Initiates are frequently stripped of all their clothes, their heads and bodies are shorn, blood of sacrificial animals is poured over their heads, and their scalps might be smeared with feces. In some instances, initiates are wrapped for several days in hides. Such practices are clearly attempting to recreate the situation of prenatal life, birth, and postnatal care. The emotional and physical suffering, painful separation, and struggle for survival involved in many rites of passage closely resemble comparable phenomena that characterize perinatal experiences, both actual in real life and symbolic in holotropic states. In perinatal sessions, experiences of psychospiritual death and rebirth are typically intermingled with reliving of biological birth and often also have a strong sexual component. In rites of passage, the encounter with death, which is an integral part of birth, can be staged in such a realistic fashion that it involves serious risk of physical trauma or even biological destruction of the initiate.

The similarity between rites of passage and the perinatal process in deep experiential work can be seen not only in relation to the specific content of the two, but also in their general pattern. Van Gennep's stage of separation closely parallels the onset of biological delivery, when the uterine contractions compress the arteries supplying oxygen and nourishment to the fetus, and the uterine cervix is still closed. This interruption of the placental circulation between the mother and the child severs the meaningful connection between them and effectively separates them from each other. Van Gennep's stage of transition then corresponds to the experience of the passage through the birth canal after the cervix opens. This death and birth struggle marks the radical transformation of the aquatic organism (the fetus) into an air-breathing organism (the newborn). Finally, van Gennep's stage of incorporation has its perinatal counterpart in the child's reunion with its mother after the experience of (re)birth.

Societal Implications

Rites of passage are cultural and spiritual events, in which initiates can experience, confront, and express powerful emotions and physical energies associated with perinatal and transpersonal matrices, which we all harbor in deep recesses of our unconscious psyche. In view of the elemental nature of the psychological forces involved, uncontrolled manifestation and acting out of these energies could be destructive for the community. In this context it is important to consider the conclusions of Arnold van Gennep, Victor Turner, Margaret Mead, Mircea Eliade and other outstanding anthropologists, namely that rites of passage are institutions of critical importance for the cohesive and harmonious functioning of the community (van Gennep 1960, Turner 1969, Mead 1973, Eliade 1958).

Thus the absence of meaningful rites of passage might contribute to the various forms of social psychopathology observed in contemporary society. Many impulses of a destructive and antisocial nature, instead of being acted out and expressed with social sanctioning in a safe and structured sacred context, leak insidiously into our everyday life and manifest in a number of individual and societal problems. Many researchers have suggested that the escalating sexual acting-out, delinquency, and abuse of alcohol and narcotics among adolescents in the industrial countries could be remedied by meaningful rites of passage for this age group (Mead 1973; Mahdi, Foster, and Little 1987; Mahdi, Christopher, and Meade, 1996).

The Beastmaster. Detail from a large wall painting in *Les Trois Frères* cave shows an anthropomorphic figure, most likely a Paleolithic shaman, surrounded by animals.

3
ANCIENT MYSTERIES OF DEATH AND REBIRTH

Nothing is higher than these mysteries. They have
sweetened our character and softened our customs;
they have made us pass from the condition of savages to true humanity.
They have not only shown us the way to live joyfully, but
they have taught us to die with hope.
-Marcus Tullius Cicero describing the Eleusinian Mysteries
(*De Legibus*)

THE MYSTERIES of death and rebirth represented another important form of experiential training for dying in the ancient world. These ritual events were based on mythological stories featuring various deities, who died and were brought back to life, or visited the Underworld, the realm of the dead, and safely returned. Understanding the dynamics of these mysteries and their relationship to the stories of death and rebirth of gods and heroes requires an entirely new interpretation of the nature and function of myths. Myths are traditionally considered to be products of human fantasy and imagination. However, the work of C. G. Jung and Joseph Campbell brought about a radically new understanding of mythology. According to these two seminal thinkers, myths are not fictitious stories about adventures of imaginary characters in nonexistent countries and thus arbitrary products of individual human fantasy. Rather, myths originate in the collective unconscious of humanity and are manifestations of the primordial organizing principles of the psyche and the cosmos, which Jung called archetypes (Jung 1976).

Archetypes and the Imaginal World

Archetypes are timeless primordial principles underlying, forming, and informing the fabric of the material world. The tendency to interpret the world in terms of archetypal principles first emerged in ancient Greece and was one of the most striking characteristics of Greek philosophy and culture. Archetypes can be seen from several different perspectives (Tarnas 2006). In Homeric epics they took the form of personified mythological figures or deities, such as Zeus, Poseidon, Hera, Aphrodite, or Ares. In the philosophy of Plato, they were described as pure metaphysical principles—transcendent Ideas, Forms, or divine *archai*—which existed independently in a realm not accessible to ordinary human senses. In modern times, C. G. Jung revived and reformulated the concept of archetypes, describing them primarily as psychological principles (Jung 1959).

For many centuries, two schools of philosophy have hotly debated the nature of Platonic Ideas. While the realists have asserted that they are ontologically real and supraordinated to the material world, nominalists have seen them as nothing more than "names," abstractions from objects, which we encounter in everyday life. Modern psychology and consciousness research have brought important supportive evidence for the position of the realists. Jungians refer to the world of the archetypal figures and realms as "imaginal" to distinguish it from imaginary products of the individual human mind. Although it can be accessed through intrapsychic self-exploration, the imaginal world has objective existence, and those who experience it can reach consensual agreement on its various aspects.

Archetypes are timeless essences, cosmic ordering principles which can also manifest as mythic personifications, or specific deities of various cultures. They express themselves through the individual psyche and its deeper processes, but they do not originate in the human mind and are not its products. They are supraordinated to the individual psyche and function as its governing principles. According to Jung's later work, archetypes are "psychoid" in nature; they operate in the twilight zone between consciousness and matter. They shape not only the processes in the human psyche, but also the events in the physical world and human history.

James Hillman offers a brilliant description of archetypes in the preface to his book *Re-Visioning Psychology*:

> All ways of speaking of archetypes are translations from one metaphor to another. Even sober operational definitions in the language of science or logic are no less metaphorical than an image which presents the archetypes as root ideas, psychic organs, figures of myth, typical styles of existence, or dominant fantasies that govern consciousness. There are many other metaphors for describing them: immaterial potential of structure, like invisible crystals in solution or forms in plants that suddenly show forth under certain conditions; patterns of instinctual behavior like those in animals that direct actions along unswerving paths; the genres

and topoi in literature; the recurring typicalities in history; the basic syndromes in psychiatry; the paradigmatic thought models in science; the worldwide figures, rituals, and relationships in anthropology (Hillman 1977).

In mythology, the basic archetypal figures, realms, and themes, in their most general and abstract form, are universally distributed: specific variations of these basic mythological motifs exist in different cultures and at various periods of history. For example, a powerful universal archetype, that of the Great Mother Goddess, takes in various cultures the forms of specific mother goddesses, such as Isis, Virgin Mary, Cybele, or Kali. Similarly, the concepts of Heaven, Paradise, and Hell can be found in many cultures of the world, but the specific form of these archetypal domains varies from one instance to another. The same is true for timeless themes, such as that of the evil stepmother, the prodigal son, or the death and rebirth of gods and heroes. The "collective unconscious," Jung's term for the place where archetypes reside, represents a shared cultural heritage of all humanity throughout the ages.

The Hero with A Thousand Faces

In 1948, after many years of systematically studying mythologies of various cultures of the world, Joseph Campbell published his ground-breaking book *The Hero with a Thousand Faces*, which in the following decades profoundly influenced research and understanding in the field (Campbell 1968). Analyzing a broad spectrum of myths from various parts of the world, Campbell realized that they all contained variations of one universal archetypal formula, which he called the monomyth. This was the story of the hero, either male or female, who leaves his or her home ground and, after fantastic adventures, returns as a deified being. Campbell found that the archetype of the hero's journey typically has three stages, similar to those described earlier as characteristic sequences in traditional rites of passage: separation, initiation, and return. The hero leaves the familiar ground or is forcefully separated from it by an external force, is transformed through a series of extraordinary ordeals and adventures, and finally is again incorporated into his or her original society in a new role.

A typical myth of the heroic journey begins when the ordinary life of the protagonist is suddenly interrupted by the intrusion of elements that are magical in nature and belong to another order of reality. Campbell refers to this invitation to adventure as a "call." If the hero responds to the call and accepts the challenge, he or she embarks on an adventure that involves visits to strange territories, encounters with fantastic animals and superhuman beings, and numerous ordeals. This adventure often culminates in an experience of death and subsequent rebirth. After the successful completion of the journey, the hero returns home and lives a full and rewarding life as a deified being—worldly leader, healer, seer, or spiritual teacher. In Campbell's own words, the basic formula for the hero's journey can be summarized as follows: "A hero ventures forth from the world of common day into a region of supernatural wonder; fabulous forces are encountered and a decisive victory is won; the hero comes back from this mysterious adventure with the power to bestow boons on his fellow man."

Campbell's inquisitive and incisive intellect went beyond simply recognizing the universality of this myth over time and space. His curiosity drove him to ask what makes this myth universal. Why does the theme of the hero's journey appeal to cultures of all times and countries, even if they differ in every other respect? Campbell's answer has the simplicity and unrelenting logic of all brilliant insights: the monomyth of the hero's journey is a blueprint for the transformative crisis, which all human beings can experience when the deep contents of the unconscious psyche emerge into consciousness. The hero's journey describes nothing less than the experiential territory that an individual must traverse during times of profound transformation.

Death and Rebirth of Gods and Heroes

The encounter with death and subsequent rebirth is a particularly powerful theme that recurs with remarkable frequency in the mythology of the hero's journey. Mythologies of all times and countries feature dramatic stories about gods, goddesses, heroes, and heroines who have died and been resurrected. Variations on this theme describe mythological characters who have descended into the realm of the dead and, having undergone unimaginable ordeals and challenges, returned to earth endowed with special powers. The central theme of the Christian religion, the death and resurrection of Jesus, is the most familiar such story, one that has profoundly influenced human history. However, this theme is not in any way unique to Christianity and plays an important role in the mythologies of many cultures and historical periods.

The oldest stories of death and rebirth are the Sumerian myth of the goddess Inanna and her descent into the Underworld and the Egyptian myth describing the death, dismemberment, and resurrection of Osiris. Among the contributions of Greek mythology are the narratives describing the abduction of the goddess Persephone into the Underworld, the dismemberment and rebirth of Dionysus, and the encounters with death experienced by Attis, Adonis, and Orpheus. The underworld adventures of the Greek heroes Hercules, Theseus, and Odysseus also belong to this category. The Mayan Hero Twins Hunahpu and Xbalanque and the Aztec Plumed Serpent Quetzalcoatl are famous Mesoamerican examples of mythological beings who experienced death and rebirth. In a less obvious symbolic form, the same motif is sometimes represented as the experience of being devoured and regorged by a terrifying monster. The examples here range from the biblical Jonah, who spent three days and nights in the belly of the "great fish," to the Greek hero Jason and Saint Margaret of Antioch, who were both swallowed by a dragon in their respective stories and later managed to escape.

Psychedelic research and work with experiential therapies have shown that the archetype of death and rebirth is closely connected with biological birth. This explains why this motif is so universal and appears so frequently in mythology. Passage through the birth canal is a life-threatening event and, as a result, death and birth are deeply linked in our unconscious. Consequently sequences of psychological death and rebirth are among the most frequent experiences observed in holotropic states induced by various means, as well as those occurring spontaneously. They play an extremely important role in the process of psychological transformation and spiritual opening.

The Mysteries of Death and Rebirth

In many parts of the world, the myths of death and rebirth provided the ideological basis for sacred mysteries, powerful ritual events in which neophytes experienced death and rebirth and profound psychospiritual transformation. Very little is known of the methods used in these mysteries to induce holotropic states, since they were either kept secret or the specific information about them was lost over time. However, these procedures were probably similar to those used in shamanic practices and rites of passage: drumming, chanting, dancing, changes in respiratory rhythm, exposure to physical stress and pain, and experiencing seeming or actual life-threatening situations. Among the most effective tools were undoubtedly mind-altering potions containing plant materials with psychoactive properties.

The powerful and often terrifying experiences induced in the initiates represented unique opportunities to contact deities and divine realms and were perceived as necessary, desirable, and ultimately healing. Moreover in some cases, voluntary exposure to these extreme states of consciousness was considered a protection against true insanity, as illustrated by the Greek myth of Dionysus, who invited the citizens of Thebes to join him in what he called the Lesser Dance. This term referred to the rapture of the Bacchanalia, orgiastic rituals which involved ingesting alcoholic beverages, wild dancing, and the unleashing of powerful emotions and instinctual drives. Dionysus promised the Thebans that the Lesser Dance would take them to places they never dreamed possible. When they refused his offer, he felt offended and forced them into the Greater Dance of Dionysus, a spell of dangerous madness, in which they mistook their prince for a wild animal and killed him. The insane queen personally impaled the severed head of her son on a spear and carried it back into the city.

As this popular myth indicates, the ancient Greeks realized that the dangerous forces harbored in the psyche must be expressed in the proper context. The powerful experiences that initiates encountered in the mysteries, particularly psychospiritual death and rebirth, had a remarkable healing and transformative potential in this regard. We can refer here to the testimony of two giants of ancient Greek philosophy, Plato and Aristotle. It is especially significant that this testimony originated in Greece, the cradle of European civilization, since Westerners tend to ignore the evidence from "primitive" and exotic cultures where shamanism or rites of passage were practiced.

In his dialogue *Phaedrus*, Plato discusses four types of madness conferred by the gods: erotic madness due to possession by Aphrodite and Eros, prophetic madness from the intervention of Apollo, artistic madness due to inspiration by one of the Muses, and ritual or telestic madness caused by Dionysus. The great philosopher vividly describes the therapeutic potential of telestic madness and uses an example from the less-known variety of the Greek mysteries, the Corybantic rites. Wild dancing to flutes and drums, culminating in an explosive emotional release, resulted in a state of profound relaxation and tranquility (Plato 1961a).

Plato's famous disciple Aristotle was the first to state explicitly that the process of fully experiencing and releasing repressed emotions, which he called catharsis (purification), represented an effective treatment of mental disorders. Aristotle said that the mysteries of death and rebirth provided a powerful context for this process; specifically that wine, aphrodisiacs, and music could be used to induce extraordinary arousal of passions leading to a healing catharsis. He supported the basic thesis of the Orphic cult (one of the most important mystical schools of the time)—that the chaos and frenzy of the mysteries were conducive to greater order.

Among the oldest mysteries of death and rebirth were the Babylonian and Assyrian rites of Ishtar and Tammuz, based on the myth of the Mother Goddess Inanna (Ishtar) and her descent into the Underworld ruled by her sister, the terrible goddess Ereshkigal. The purpose of Ishtar's visit to the realm of the dead was to obtain an elixir that would restore to life the vegetation god Tammuz, who was both her son and husband. In the ancient Egyptian temples of Isis and Osiris, initiates underwent complex ordeals under the guidance of high priests to overcome the fear of death and gain access to esoteric knowledge about the universe and human nature. During this procedure, neophytes experienced identification with the god Osiris, who according to the myth underlying these mysteries was killed and dismembered by his evil brother, Seth. Osiris was subsequently brought back to life by his two sisters, Isis and Nephtys, and became the ruler of the Underworld. In this context, the theme of death and rebirth was linked to the diurnal-nocturnal cycle and to the archetypal journey of the sun god across the sky and through the Underworld.

Mystery religions and sacred rites were abundant in ancient Greece, Asia Minor, and the neighboring countries. The Eleusinian Mysteries were based on an esoteric interpretation of the myth of the Greek fertility goddess Demeter and her daughter Persephone. Persephone was kidnapped by Hades, the god of the Underworld, but was then released by him at the intervention of Zeus, with the condition that she would return to Hades for one third of each year. This myth, usually considered an allegory about the cyclical growth of plants during the seasons of the year, became for the Eleusinian initiates a symbol for the spiritual struggles of the soul, periodically imprisoned in matter and liberated.

The Orphic cult revolved around the legend of the deified Thracian bard Orpheus, the incomparable musician and singer, who visited the Underworld in an unsuccessful effort to liberate his beloved Eurydice from the bondage of death. Orpheus himself died a tragic death when he was torn to pieces by Ciconian women for interfering in the Bacchanalia. According to the legend, his severed head, thrown into the Hebrus River, continued to sing and give forth oracles. The Dionysian rites, or Bacchanalia, were based on the mythological story of the young Dionysus, who was dismembered by the Titans and then resurrected when Pallas Athene rescued his heart. In the Dionysian rites, the initiates experienced identification with the murdered and reborn god by drinking intoxicating beverages, orgiastic dancing, running through the countryside, and eating raw animal flesh. The Samothracian mysteries of the Corybants were closely related to the Dionysian festivals. The associated ritual drama depicted the murder of Cadmillus by his three brothers.

The Mithraic cult, another major mystery religion of antiquity, was the sister religion of Christianity and its very serious competitor for a world religion. It began to spread throughout the Roman Empire in the first century A.D., reached its peak in the third century, and succumbed to Christianity at the end of the fourth century. At the cult's height, the underground Mithraic sanctuaries (*mithraea*) could be found from the shores of the Black Sea to the mountains of Scotland and to the border of the Sahara Desert (Ulansey 1989).

The famous myth of Adonis, another story about a dying god, inspired many mysteries in the ancient world. During her pregnancy, his mother Smyrna was turned into a myrrh tree by the gods. Adonis was born when a wild boar opened the tree with its tusks and freed the baby. Aphrodite was so charmed by Adonis' beauty that she handed him over to the care of Persephone, the goddess of the Underworld. When Persephone later refused to return Adonis, Zeus decided that he should spend one third of each year with Persephone and one third with Aphrodite. The remaining third was left to his discretion, but legend has it that Adonis always spent two thirds of each year with Aphrodite. Mysteries based on this myth were annually celebrated in many parts of Egypt, Phoenicia, and Byblos. The closely related Phrygian mysteries were held in the name of Attis, a deity who castrated himself, died, and was resurrected by the Great Mother Goddess Cybele. His self-mutilation and death were the result of frenzy which Agdistis, the mother of Attis, imparted on him in her jealous rage to prevent him from getting married.

The myth underlying the Nordic mysteries of Odin (Wotan) was the story of Odin's murdered and resurrected favorite son, Balder. According to the myth, Balder was young and beautiful and was the only peaceful god in Valhalla. The trickster Loki, the personification of evil, duped the blind god of fate, Hoder, to shoot Balder with a mistletoe arrow, the only weapon that could hurt him. Balder was pierced through the heart and died. Hel, the goddess of death, moved by the pleas of the heartbroken gods, promised to send Balder back to the land of the living on one condition: everything in the world, dead or alive, must weep for him. And everything did weep, except Loki, and so Balder had to remain in the Underworld. However, the myth predicted that after the final Battle of Ragnarok, when a new world was to arise from its ashes, Balder would be reborn. In the mysteries of Odin the neophyte drank sanctified mead from a bowl made of a human skull. Identified with Balder, the initiate underwent a sacred ordeal in a complex of nine underground chambers and was able to unveil the mystery of Odin, the most precious secrets of nature and the human soul.

In the Druidic mysteries of Britain the boundary between symbolic and biological death was rather blurred. After having been buried alive in a coffin, the candidate was sent to sea in an open boat as a symbolic reenactment of the death of the Sun God. In this unusual ordeal many initiates lost their lives; those who survived the demanding ritual were referred to as reborn.

The specifics of the mind-altering procedures involved in these secret rites have remained for the most part unknown. However, the sacred potion *kykeon* that played a critical role in the Eleusinian Mysteries was most likely a concoction containing alkaloids of ergot similar to LSD. It is also highly probable that psychedelic materials were involved in the bacchanalia and other types of rites. Ancient Greeks did not know how to distill alcohol and yet, according to the reports, the wines used in Dionysian rituals had to be diluted three to twenty times, and a mere three cups brought some initiates "to the brink of insanity" (Wasson, Hofmann, and Ruck 1978). Only the addition of psychedelic materials to these alcoholic beverages could account for such a profound effect on the psyche.

The cultural importance of these mysteries for the ancient world and their as yet unacknowledged role in the history of European civilization become evident when we realize that among their initiates were many famous and illustrious figures of antiquity. The list of neophytes included the mathematician Pythagoras, the philosophers

Plato, Aristotle, and Epictetus, the military leader Alkibiades, the playwright Euripides, the historian Plutarch, and the poet Pindaros. Another famous initiate, Emperor Marcus Aurelius, was fascinated by the eschatological hopes offered by these rites. Roman statesman and philosopher Marcus Tullius Cicero took part in these mysteries and wrote an exalted report about their effects and their impact on the antique civilization in his book *De Legibus* (Cicero 1977).

The Mysteries of Eleusis

The most important mysteries of antiquity were celebrated for almost two thousand years (c. 1500 B.C.–A.D. 400) in honor of the Greek fertility goddess Demeter and her daughter Persephone at Eleusis, a Greek town situated about sixteen miles west of Athens. They represent a particularly good example of these important practices both because of their cultural significance and the amount of information we have about them.

The events leading to the founding of the shrine of Eleusis are described in an epic poem from around the end of the seventh century B.C., known as *The Homeric Hymn to Demeter*:

> One day, while Persephone, daughter of Zeus and Demeter, was picking flowers in the lovely meadows, she was abducted by Hades, god of the Underworld. Her mother searched for her in vain, finally learning from Helios of the abduction of her daughter. Sorely afflicted, Demeter became alienated from Olympus, since she even came to know that Zeus had been in agreement with the kidnapping. After an unsuccessful search for Persephone, Demeter came to Eleusis dressed as a simple woman and found friendly abode in the palace of the king of Eleusis, Keleos, and his wife Metaneira. Engaged as a nurse for their son Demophon, she tried to make him immortal by immersing him in fire. When this became known, she revealed her divinity and in gratitude for the friendly hospitality, she founded a temple in Eleusis.
>
> To castigate the Olympian gods for the abduction of her daughter, Demeter caused all of the vegetation on Earth to die, threatening humankind with extinction. The gods feared the loss of the prayers and sacrifices of humanity and begged Demeter to make the Earth fruitful again. This plea was not granted until Zeus ordered his brother Hades in the Underworld to return Persephone to her mother. Mother and daughter returned to Olympus, but henceforth Persephone had to spend a third of the year with her husband in the Underworld. When she did, winter reigned on the earth. Yet every year, when Persephone returned to earth in the spring, the plant world awoke anew with flowers and bore fruits.

> Before Demeter returned to the other gods on Olympus, she instructed the kings of Eleusis, Keleos and Triptolemus, how to celebrate the rites in her temple. These were secret precepts, Mysteries, to be closely guarded. Divulging them and profaning them was punished by death. In appreciation of the propitious outcome of the drama of Eleusis, Demeter bestowed upon Triptolemus, the first initiate of Eleusis, a sprig of grain and bade him to instruct humankind in agriculture, an art which had not been known to them before (Wasson, Hofmann, and Ruck 1978).

The cult of Demeter and Persephone in Eleusis, which initially had been of only local importance, soon became an important part of Athenian citizenship and eventually developed into a pan-Hellenic institution. By the second half of the fifth century B.C., in the classical period of Greek culture, participation in the Eleusinian rituals, earlier restricted to Athenians, was open to all Greeks. In Hellenistic and imperial times, the mysteries had even greater prestige and were open to initiates from the entire Roman Empire. The extraordinary duration of the Eleusinian Mysteries, which were conducted regularly and without interruption every 5 years for a period of almost 2,000 years, is impressive testimony for the power and impact of the experiences they offered. Furthermore, the mysteries did not end simply because they ceased to attract the attention of the antique world. The ceremonial activities in Eleusis were brutally interrupted when the Christian Emperor Theodosius interdicted participation in the mysteries and all other pagan cults. Shortly afterward, in A.D. 395, the invading Goths destroyed the sanctuary.

Whatever was offered in Eleusis to the initiates had to be something really extraordinary if, for many centuries, thousands of people, including many prominent figures of antiquity, were willing to travel long distances to participate. One frequent suggestion is that some form of theatrical performance was given. However, the main hall of the Eleusinian sanctuary (telestrion) was architecturally totally unsuited for this purpose. As other ancient sites such as Epidauros show, the Greeks were able to build astonishing amphitheaters with superior acoustics. The rows of massive pillars of the Eleusinian telestrion, a large chamber occupying its center (anaktoron), and the number of participants (3,000 and possibly more), would have made it impossible for many initiates to observe the show. The many surviving account books also do not record any expenses for actors or stage props. In addition, the Greeks were very sophisticated with regard to theater and could not be easily tricked and fooled, particularly not the likes of Pindaros and Sophocles, both of whom testified to the mysteries' power and extraordinary value.

The accounts of the Eleusinian experiences contained many references to astonishing visions of supernaturally brilliant light, often described in terms of antitheses and polarities, such as darkness and light or terror and bliss. Thus Aelius Aristides, writer and orator who lived during the Roman Empire, wrote that Eleusis was "both the most awesome and the most luminous of all the divine things that exist among men." Some of the most impressive visions involved encounters with deities, particularly the goddess Persephone. Emperor Marcus Aurelius, himself an initiate, counted the mysteries among "those endowments which manifest the solicitude of the gods for humanity." Another interesting aspect of the Eleusinian experiences involved allusions to biological birth. For example, Hippolytus (c. A.D. 170-236) reports: "Under a huge fire, the hierophant shouts: The Mistress has given birth to a sacred child, Brimo to Brimos." All the above characteristics apply equally to psychedelic experiences and other types of holotropic states.

An important key to this enigma is that the hierophants administered to all participants the sacred potion, called "kykeon," before the climax of the initiation. This suggests the possibility that kykeon was a preparation with remarkable psychoactive properties. Only a psychedelic potion could predictably induce such powerful experiences in thousands of people at the same time. This notion is further supported when one considers that at one point during the Classical Age (around 415 B.C.), it was discovered that many aristocratic Athenians were conducting private mysteries in their homes. This profanation of the mysteries resulted in a crackdown and infliction of harsh penalties. While it would have been hardly possible to replicate in private homes intricate theatrical special effects, it would have been easy to carry a jar of kykeon from Eleusis to Athens.

Albert Hofmann, the father of LSD, mycologist Gordon Wasson (whose story of the discovery of Mexican magic mushrooms is described in Chapter 12), and Greek scholar Carl A. P. Ruck published after years of thorough study a treatise called *The Road to Eleusis* (Wasson, Hofmann, and Ruck 1978). They concluded that kykeon contained a psychedelic ingredient obtained from ergot, with effects similar to LSD and to the Mesoamerican sacrament ololiuqui. To give kykeon its consciousness-altering properties, the Eleusinian priests merely had to collect the ergot, which was very common in the vicinity of the temple, pulverize it, and add it to the potion. Ergot could easily have been used as a sacrament in the temple of the goddess of grain, Demeter. At one point of the Eleusinian ritual, the priests actually presented an ear of grain to the initiates, as a reference to the barleycorn planted in the earth, which dies in order to give life to a new plant. Here we find a symbol of the annual rotation of Persephone from the darkness of the Underworld to the light of Olympus, as well as a symbol of the permanence of life in the eternal cycle of death and rebirth.

Pindaros, the greatest lyric poet of ancient Greece and himself an initiate, wrote about the impact the Eleusinian initiation had on the participants:

Blessed is he who, having seen these rites,
undertakes the way beneath the Earth.
He knows the end of life, as well as
its divinely granted beginning.

Dramatic mythological sequences portraying death and rebirth and other numinous experiences are extremely frequent in experiential psychotherapy, as well as in episodes of spontaneous psychospiritual crises ("spiritual emergencies"). In holotropic states this mythological material emerges spontaneously from the depths of the psyche, without any programming and often to the surprise of everybody involved. Archetypal images and entire scenes from the mythology of various cultures often appear in the experiences of individuals who have no intellectual knowledge of the mythic figures and themes they are encountering. Such archetypes as Persephone, Dionysus, Osiris, and Wotan, as well as Jesus Christ, seem to reside in the psyche of modern Westerners and come alive in holotropic states.

4
DEATH AND REBIRTH IN THE GREAT RELIGIONS OF THE WORLD

The man who dies before he dies
does not die when he dies.
– Abraham a Sancta Clara,
17th century German Augustinian monk

TECHNOLOGIES OF THE SACRED have not been limited to shamanism, rites of passage of native cultures, and the ancient mysteries. Several great religions of the world developed more or less sophisticated psychospiritual procedures specifically designed to induce holotropic experiences. These use various combinations of fasting, sitting or moving meditation, visualizations, prayer, chanting, dancing, and breathing exercises. Under the right circumstances such approaches can induce an extraordinary array of experiences originating in the deep recesses of the human psyche, including a profound encounter with death and psychospiritual death and rebirth. They can thus provide effective experiential training for dying.

Eastern Spiritual Philosophies and Practices

Many such practices have been developed in connection with the Eastern spiritual philosophies. Different schools of yoga, which originated within the context of Hinduism, offer a broad spectrum of refined methods of meditation combining in various ways fasting, physical postures (asanas), gestures (mudras), and mental concentration. An important part of the yogic tradition is the work with breath and the use of sound in the form of sacred chants (kirtans and bhajans) and repetition of auspicious syllables, words, or phrases (mantras). In India, the understanding of the potential of breath to change consciousness and its use in spiritual practice were raised to the level of science (pranayama). Hinduism also has the concept of dvija, which means literally a person who is twice born and very likely refers to the experience of psychospiritual death and rebirth. Dvija is an individual who has realized that he or she is not a body of flesh and bones, but pure consciousness. Buddhism contributed a great variety of meditation techniques to the armamentarium of the technologies of the sacred, such as the Vipassana insight meditation of Theravada, the esoteric practices of Vajrayana, zazen and the work with koans in Soto and Rinzai Zen, the fire-breath meditation, and many others.

One of the most interesting and sophisticated technologies of the sacred is Tantra, a system that crosses the boundaries of individual religions and represents esoteric branches of Hinduism, Buddhism, and Jainism. Tantra is an elaborate system of psychospiritual practice using sacred geometrical diagrams (yantras), mandalas, mudras, mantras, asanas, and breathing exercises. The culmination of the practice of Vamamarga (left-handed Tantra) is panchamakara, a ritual which involves sacred sexual union (maithuna) performed in yogic asanas. The preparation for this union heightens the senses by using incense, flowers, music, sacred chants, and gentle touches to induce in the two partners experiential identification with archetypal beings, the deities Shiva and Shakti. The use of Ayurvedic herbal mixtures combining strong aphrodisiacs with psychedelic ingredients gives the experience of panchamakara an unparalleled power.

The fascinating aspect of the Tantric practice is that it is based on an extraordinary spiritual vision of existence and a comprehensive scientific world view that was astonishingly advanced for the time of its origin. Tantric scholars developed a profound understanding of the universe, which has been validated in many ways by modern science. The Tantric world view featured sophisticated models of space and time, the concept of the Big Bang, and such elements as a heliocentric arrangement of the planets, interplanetary attraction, spherical shape of the earth and planets, and entropy. Additional achievements of Tantra included advanced mathematics using decimal count and zero and highly refined abstract and figurative spiritual art (Mookerjee and Khanna 1977). Tantric practitioners and scholars also created detailed experiential maps of the subtle body with its many channels (nadis) and centers (chakras).

Practices in Judaism, Christianity, and Islam

Powerful methods of inducing holotropic states of consciousness have also been used in the three great religions from the Middle East—Judaism, Christianity, and Islam. Approaches designed to induce or facilitate direct spiritual experiences are characteristic for the mystical branches of these great religions and for their monastic orders. Medieval Kabbalists produced a series of techniques for reaching ecstatic states. The best known and most influential representative of ecstatic Kabbalah was Avraham Abulafia, the author of various methods for uniting with God. He specifically stated that his aim was to mediate experiences similar to or even identical with those of the ancient Jewish prophets. Other examples from the Jewish mystical history are also significant—the practices of the Askhenazic Hasidic masters, Hasidic dances, and the practice of Devequt, communion with God. To induce mystical experiences, the Essenes of the Dead Sea Scrolls, members of an apocalyptic sect of Judaism, used very effective breathing techniques and a form of baptism that brought the initiates close to death by drowning.

Technologies of the sacred pervade the history of Christianity. The experiences of the Desert Fathers, early Christian hermits practicing asceticism in the Egyptian desert, were facilitated by fasting, dehydration, extreme heat, and the partial sensory deprivation caused by the monotony of the desert. The Hesychasts were Christian monks who believed that it was possible to achieve—by an elaborate system of asceticism, detachment from earthly concerns, submission to an approved master, and unceasing prayer—the vision of mystic light, which was for them none other than the uncreated light of God. This vision could be facilitated by a specific technique, which included such elements as holding the body immovable for a long time, pressing the chin against the breast, holding the breath, and turning the eyes in. Studies have explored the parallels between Hesychasm and the Indian yogic practices, particularly kundalini yoga (Matus 1984). Also among the Christian methods of inducing mystical experiences were the exercises of St. Ignatius of Loyola, founder of the Jesuits, whose method of prayer involved visual imagination as a way to come closer to God.

Religious scholar Dan Merkur concluded on the basis of his research that the early Jews and Christians used psychedelic materials as part of their religious rites. In his book, *The Mystery of Manna: The Psychedelic Sacrament of the Bible* (Merkur 2000), he uses the example of manna, the miraculous bread that the Israelites ingested before they beheld the glory of Yahweh appearing in a cloud. Merkur suggests that this incident was in fact an initiation into a psychedelic mystery cult that induced spiritual visions through bread containing ergot—a psychoactive fungus with active ingredients related to LSD. Furthermore, this example was only one in an unbroken tradition of Western psychedelic sacraments, from Moses and manna to Jesus and the Eucharist. According to Merkur, when this practice became unacceptable to the religious orthodoxy, it was perpetuated in secret by Gnostics, Masons, and Kabbalists. John Allegro, member of an international team formed to decipher the Dead Sea Scrolls, went even farther. In his controversial book *The Sacred Mushroom and the Cross*, Allegro contended that Judaism and Christianity had their origins in fertility cults of the ancient Near East that used psychedelic mushrooms in their rituals (Allegro 1970).

Clearly the experience of psychospiritual rebirth, or second birth, has played an important role in Christianity from its early days to the present. In a very interesting passage in the third chapter of the Gospel of John, Jesus talks about the importance of being born again: "Unless one is born again, he cannot see (enter) the kingdom of Heaven." Nicodemus, who takes Jesus' statement literally, cannot understand how he, a large, grown man, could pass through his mother's pelvis and be born again. In an obvious reference to psychospiritual rebirth, Jesus explains that he is not talking about being born from flesh, but about "being born from above, from water and Spirit."

Medieval Christian monks used meditation with guided imagery to experience death and rebirth. One such exercise involved envisioning one's own death and the successive decomposition of the body. Another one was experiential identification with Jesus' suffering, death on the cross, and resurrection (*imitatio Christi*).

Sufis, the mystics of Islam, have for centuries been using spiritual music, intense breathing, and devotional chants in their sacred ceremonies (known as zikers or dzikres). The sects of whirling dervishes are known for their intoxicating, trance-inducing dance. Like the mystics of other great religions, the Sufis have been in conflict with the official religious authorities and have suffered serious persecution in many Muslim countries. Mansur al-Hallaj, the famous Sufi ecstatic and poet known as the "martyr of mystical love" was actually imprisoned and burnt alive for stating the insights he had attained in ecstatic raptures: "Ana'l Haqq—I am God, the Absolute Truth, the True Reality." Al-Suhrawardi, Muslim theologian, philosopher, and founder of the "illuminationist" school of philosophy, was charged with heresy by rivals in the Muslim clergy and was condemned to death, earning himself the name "al-Maqtul" ("the Killed'). Even Ibn al-Arabi, "The Greatest Master," author of the Meccan Revelations and probably the most influential figure in the history of Sufism, was persecuted and imprisoned.

Mystics have encountered very difficult challenges in organized religions, even though their direct experiences of numinous dimensions of reality in holotropic states of consciousness have provided inspiration for all great religious movements. Such experiences, moreover, are essential to preserving the vitality and relevance of religious creeds.

5
THE POSTHUMOUS JOURNEY OF THE SOUL

Lend, lend your wings! I mount! I fly!
O grave! where is thy victory?
O death! where is thy sting?
- Alexander Pope, *The Dying Christian to his Soul*

PREINDUSTRIAL HUMAN GROUPS believed that death does not terminate human existence entirely and that, in one way or another, life and consciousness continue after the cessation of the vital processes in the body. Consequently they provided for their members elaborate maps of the Beyond and guidelines for the posthumous journey of the soul. The specific descriptions of the Afterlife vary among cultures and ethnic groups separated historically and geographically, but the general concepts are very similar. Sometimes the image of the Afterworld is very concrete and real, not dissimilar to earthly existence. More frequently the realms of the world beyond have special characteristics distinguishing them from anything known on earth. Whether or not the residing place of the soul is a familiar environment, the soul's journey to the Afterworld is often seen as a complex process of transitions and transformations through many different levels and realms.

Abodes of the Beyond and the Archetypal World

Three abodes of the Beyond—Heaven, Paradise, and Hell— appear with extraordinary frequency in eschatological mythology and show almost universal distribution across religions, cultures, geographic areas, and historical periods. Less common is the concept of an intermediate state or place, such as Purgatory or Limbo. Heaven is generally considered to be "above," related to the human experience of the sky and including the sun, the moon, and the stars. It is a domain of bliss, joy, and light inhabited by higher spiritual beings and righteous discarnate humans. Paradise is another abode of the Beyond destined for the blessed, a place of extraordinary happiness, joy, peace, and delight. As its name indicates (in Old Persian "pairidaeza" means enclosed garden), Paradise is usually represented as a beautiful garden or park, with exotic trees bearing luscious fruit, rivers of life, and gorgeous birds and animals. Occasionally, Paradise is situated in some other form of extraordinary natural scenery, such as an island or aurora borealis. By contrast, Hell is usually the realm "below," under the surface of the earth, located in a system of subterranean caverns. It is a chthonic region of darkness and gloom associated with terror, despair, and physical suffering. Hell's inhabitants are evil demonic creatures taking delight in exposing their victims to unimaginable tortures.

The erroneous belief that these abodes of the Beyond are located in the physical universe—Heaven in the interstellar space, Paradise somewhere in a hidden area on the surface of our planet, and Hell in the interior of the earth—led to a bizarre and entirely unnecessary conflict between science and religion. Astronomers have used extremely sophisticated devices, such as the Hubble telescope, to explore and map carefully the entire "vault of Heaven." Results from these efforts, which have of course failed to show any Heaven replete with God and angels, are taken as definitive proof that such spiritual realities do not exist. Similarly, in cataloguing and mapping every acre of the planetary surface, explorers and geographers have found many areas of extraordinary natural beauty, but none of them match the descriptions of Paradise found in spiritual scriptures. Geologists have discovered that the core of our planet consists of layers of solid and molten nickel and iron, and its temperature exceeds that of the sun's surface. This earthly core is encased in layers of dense and mostly solid silicate rock—not a very plausible location for the caves of Satan.

This seeming conflict between religion and science is ludicrous and reflects a fundamental misunderstanding on both sides. As Ken Wilber has pointed out, there cannot possibly be a real conflict between genuine science and authentic religion. Any such "conflict" likely reflects a problem of "bogus science" and "bogus religion," where either side seriously misunderstands the other's position and undoubtedly represents a false version of its own discipline (Wilber 1982). Modern studies of holotropic states have shown that Heaven, Paradise, and Hell are ontologically real; they represent distinct and important states of consciousness that all human beings can under certain circumstances experience during their lifetime. Thanatology has amassed convincing evidence that such experiences especially happen in connection with dying and death.

In his ground-breaking essay, *Heaven and Hell*, Aldous Huxley suggested that concepts such as Hell and Heaven represent subjective realities experienced in very concrete and convincing ways during non-ordinary states of mind induced by psychedelic substances or various powerful non-drug techniques (Huxley 1959). Celestial, paradisean, and infernal visions are important components of the experiential spectrum of psychedelic inner journeys, near-death states, mystical experiences, as well as shamanic initiatory crises and other types of "spiritual emergencies." Psychiatrists often see such experiences in their patients but because of their inadequate model of the psyche they misinterpret them as manifestations of mental disease, caused by a pathological process of unknown etiology instead of realizing that the matrices for these experiences exist in deep recesses of the unconscious of every human being.

An astonishing aspect of holotropic experiences of various provenances that feature eschatological themes and motifs is that their content can be drawn from the mythologies of any culture of the world, including those of which the subject has no intellectual knowledge. C. G. Jung demonstrated this extraordinary fact for mythological experiences of any kind occurring in dreams and psychotic experiences of his patients. Based on this observation, Jung realized that the human psyche also contains, besides the Freudian individual unconscious, a collective unconscious, a repository of the entire cultural heritage of humanity. Knowledge of comparative mythology is thus more than a matter of personal interest or an academic exercise; it is a very important and useful tool for individuals involved in experiential therapy and self-exploration, and a necessary prerequisite for those who support and accompany them on their journey.

Case History Examples: Significance of the Collective Unconscious for Psychotherapy

Some remarkable episodes from my own clinical practice illustrate the significance of the collective unconscious for psychotherapeutic work. The first involves Otto, one of my clients when I worked in the Psychiatric Research Institute in Prague as principal investigator in a research program of psychedelic therapy.

Otto was accepted into the program because he suffered from depression and severe pathological fear of death (thanatophobia). In one of his psychedelic sessions, he experienced a powerful sequence of psychospiritual death and rebirth. As this experience was culminating, he had a vision of an ominous entrance into the Underworld guarded by a terrifying pig goddess. At this point, he suddenly felt an urgent need to draw a specific geometrical design. Usually I asked my clients to stay in a reclining position during their sessions with their eyes closed in order to keep the experiences internalized. However, Otto opened his eyes, sat up, and asked me to bring him some sheets of paper and drawing utensils.

He drew with great urgency and extraordinary speed an entire series of complex abstract patterns. Showing deep dissatisfaction and despair, he kept impulsively tearing and crumpling these intricate designs as soon as he finished them. He was very disappointed with his drawings and was getting increasingly frustrated, because he was not able to "get it right." When I asked him what he was trying to do, he was unable to explain. He said that he simply felt an irresistible compulsion to draw these geometrical patterns and was convinced that drawing the right kind of design was somehow a necessary condition for successfully completing his session.

The theme clearly had a strong emotional charge for Otto, and it seemed important to understand it. At that time, I was still strongly influenced by my Freudian training, and I tried my best to identify the unconscious motives for this strange behavior by using the method of free associations. We spent much time on this task, but without any real success. The entire sequence simply did not make any sense. Eventually the process moved to other areas, and I stopped thinking about this situation. The entire episode had remained a complete mystery for me until many years later, when I moved to the United States.

Shortly after my arrival in Baltimore, I was invited to give a lecture for a conference of the Society for Art, Religion, and Science in New York City, entitled "The Grotesque in Art." My presentation explored the problem of the Grotesque, drawing on my observations from psychedelic research, and included a slide show of my clients' paintings. Joseph Campbell was also a participant at the conference, a renowned scholar considered by many as the greatest mythologist of the twentieth century and possibly of all times. He was fascinated by my descriptions of the experiences of patients reliving their birth and by the paintings they had made. At his request, I sent him a manuscript summarizing the findings of my research in Prague. It was a thick volume, entitled *Agony and Ecstasy in Psychiatric Treatment*, a work which was never published in its original form and later became the source for five books discussing different aspects of my work.

After a few initial encounters, Joseph and I became good friends, and he came to play a very important role in my personal and professional life. My wife Christina had developed an independent friendship with him when she was his student at Sarah Lawrence College. Joseph's intellect was remarkable, and his knowledge of world mythology truly encyclopedic. He loved the material from psychedelic research, particularly my concept of the basic perinatal matrices (BPMs; see Chapter 8), which helped him understand the ubiquity and universal nature of the motif of death and rebirth in mythology. After we moved to California I saw Joseph regularly, since he was a frequent guest at Esalen Institute, where he conducted his own workshops and participated as guest faculty in the month-long seminars that Christina and I conducted there.

After a few days at Esalen, Joseph usually tired of the Institute's menu, which he called "rabbit food," and was ready for a good steak and the Glenlivet whiskey that he loved. Christina and I invited him regularly to our house for homemade dinners, catering to his culinary preferences. Over the years, we had many fascinating discussions, during which I shared with him observations of various obscure archetypal experiences of participants in our workshops that I was not able to identify and understand. In most instances, Joseph had no difficulties identifying the cultural sources of the symbolism involved.

During one of these discussions, I remembered the above episode from Otto's session and shared it with him. "How fascinating," said Joseph without any hesitation, "it was clearly the Cosmic Mother Night of Death, the Devouring Mother Goddess of the Malekulans in New Guinea." He went on to tell me that the Malekulans believed they would encounter this deity during the Journey of the Dead. She had the form of a frightening female figure with distinct pig features. According to the Malekulan tradition, she sat at the entrance into the Underworld and guarded an intricate sacred labyrinthine design.

The Malekulan boys had an elaborate system of rituals that involved breeding and sacrificing pigs. The pig that each boy bred through his childhood represented his mother. Slaying this pig in the context of the puberty ritual helped male members of the tribe overcome the dependency on their human mothers, on women in general, and eventually on the Devouring Mother Goddess. The Malekulans spent an enormous amount of time during their lifetimes practicing the art of labyrinth drawing, since its mastery was considered essential for a successful journey to the Beyond. Joseph, with his astonishing lexical knowledge of mythology, was thus able to solve this challenging puzzle which I had encountered during my research in Prague.

The remaining questions, that even Joseph was not able to answer, were: why this particular mythological motif was so intimately connected with Otto's tedious emotional symptoms, why Otto had to encounter this Malekulan deity as part of his therapy, and why this experience was so important for its successful outcome. However, in the most general sense, the task of mastering problems associated with the posthumous journey of the soul certainly made good sense for somebody whose main symptom was thanatophobia, pathological fear of death. The choice of the Malekulan symbolism in this particular case has remained a mystery.

I have described Otto's case in some detail because it illustrates several important points. In holotropic states various themes from eschatological mythology become experiential reality and are intimately connected with psychological issues of the individual and his or her emotional and psychosomatic problems. The fact that neither I nor Otto had intellectual knowledge of the Malekulan culture represents supportive evidence for Jung's idea of the collective unconscious. The rather esoteric elements of the ritual and spiritual life of this New Guinea tribe, which spontaneously emerged in Otto's session, required the extraordinary encyclopedic mind of the greatest mythologist of our time to be understood. And, finally, this episode also demonstrates the close association between eschatological mythology and the rites of passage.

I include here another brief example of a similar situation from the early years of my psychedelic research at the Psychiatric Research Institute in Prague. In this case, I was able to understand the imagery and its symbolism without Joseph's help, although not immediately. This episode is from an LSD session of Alex, who volunteered for the program of psychedelic therapy after many months of unsuccessful traditional therapy for anxiety states, including a phobia of darkness.

In the advanced stage of his therapy, one of Alex's sessions was dominated by memories of his prenatal existence—he became a fetus in his mother's belly, tasting the amniotic fluid, sensing his connection with the maternal body through the umbilical cord, and being acutely aware of the changes in his mother's emotional and physical condition. As he was experiencing a blissful state during a period when his prenatal existence was undisturbed, the embryonic scene suddenly opened into a glorious vision of the aurora borealis.

Alex was floating in its radiance as a pure spirit, without any awareness of his physical body, and was experiencing an ecstatic rapture. He was surrounded by other similar ethereal beings engaged in a joyful dynamic activity. At one point, he noticed that this activity was some strange ballgame, since a round object was being playfully passed from one of these beings to another. Eventually, he realized to his great surprise that the object that was being tossed around was the head of a walrus.

As in Otto's case, free associations did not provide any information to elucidate this strange, yet obviously emotionally very important experience. Eventually we gave up, and the process moved to some other areas. Years later I spent several hours in a bookstore in San Francisco searching randomly for any books that would fall into my area of interests. To my surprise, I came across a book of Eskimo mythology which included a passage on the ideas concerning the Afterlife. Apparently the Eskimo people believe that the highest level of Heaven is located in the aurora borealis, a glorious place, always bright, without snow or storm. Happy spirits reside there and enjoy using a walrus head to play ball. According to the Eskimo lore, the aurora is actually caused by streams of light that reflect the excitement and energy of the game. Alex's mysterious LSD experience thus represented accurate insight into the mythology of a culture of which he had no previous knowledge.

For people living now, holotropic states of consciousness mediate access to a wide range of mythological experiences from various cultures of the world. Historically this is a new phenomenon, one which deserves special notice. All ancient and native cultures used in their ritual and spiritual practices powerful consciousness-expanding procedures and means ("technologies of the sacred"), including psychedelic plants. Yet people living in those societies experienced with reasonable consistency predominantly archetypal figures and motifs specific to their respective cultures. Otherwise, characteristic and easily recognizable discrete mythologies would not exist. Although certain universal archetypes are certainly shared by many cultures, their specific expressions are culture-bound. For instance, we do not find the Dhyani Buddhas from the Tibetan Book of the Dead on the funeral ceramics of the ancient Maya or sculptures of Jesus on the cross in the ancient Hindu temples.

This new capacity of the human psyche (or property of the collective unconscious) is closely related to worldwide cultural and technological developments in recent centuries. Until the end of the fifteenth century Europeans were generally unaware of the New World and similarly, Native Americans had no knowledge of Europe and its inhabitants. Until the Chinese invasion in 1949, Tibet was relatively secluded and had little connection with the rest of the world. Only a few exceptional individuals, such as Alexandra David-Neel and Lama Govinda functioned as cultural brokers. In the first decades of the twentieth century, some areas on the planet had not yet been discovered by Westerners.

That situation has changed rapidly, as jet travel, telephone, radio, television, and most recently the Internet are transforming the planet into a "global village." For the first time in history, we have access to translations of spiritual scriptures and recordings of ritual and spiritual music of all times and countries, as well as visiting teachers of all religions. With the material surfacing from the full range of the collective unconscious in spontaneous and induced holotropic states, knowledge of world mythology, in general, and eschatological mythology, in particular, has thus become an extremely important tool for psychiatrists, psychologists, and psychotherapists. Passing knowledge of the archetypal world is also essential for everybody involved in the spiritual journey and in the adventure of self-exploration and self-discovery. With this in mind, we will now take a brief excursion into the most important themes of eschatological mythology from a cross-cultural perspective.

Heaven, Paradise and the Theme of Divine Judgment

The concept of the final home of the righteous after death—Heaven or Paradise—appears in many different variations. The ancient Hebrews envisioned Heaven as the world above (Shamayim) and saw it as the dwelling place of Yahweh. In the Jewish tradition, the Garden of Eden had different levels: a lower Garden of Eden and an upper Garden of Eden. In the lower Garden of Eden, the souls inhabited the bodies of the same form as during the deceased's lifetime, and they experienced various types of spiritual pleasures. In the upper Garden of Eden, the souls dwelled in their true essence and enjoyed various types of spiritual pleasures that were greater and more exalted than the pleasures of the lower Garden.

When a person died, the soul (nefesh) ascended to the Lower Garden of Eden. The body that it occupied was of a very refined nature—simply an energy form that did not require physical food and drink. It received its sustenance through a higher form of the sense of smell. Afterwards, the soul ascended further to the Upper Garden of Eden (Neshamah), where it was sustained by the radiance of the Divine Presence. The righteous sat with their crowns on their heads, delighting in the incandescence of the Divine Presence. They derived pleasure from seeing and had no need to eat or drink. Stories from the Jewish mystical tradition commonly feature places similar to Christian Heaven and Purgatory, wandering souls, and reincarnation.

The Christian concept of Heaven combines the Hebraic image of a region in the sky with the Greek ideas of concentric celestial spheres and of the spiritual journey. The followers of Jesus, who come to Heaven, enjoy the presence of God, angels, and saints, and contemplate His being. Christian mythology has an entire hierarchy of angels; the concentric tiers of this pantheon feature in descending order the Seraphim, Cherubim, Thrones (or Wheels), Dominations, Virtues, Powers, Principalities, Archangels, and Angels. Another abode of the blessed in the Christian tradition is Paradise or the Garden of Love; this concept derives from the myths of the Golden Age and the Garden of Eden. The symbolism involves a geographical location, elements of pristine nature, walls of gold, and roads paved with emeralds. Four rivers originate in the garden and flow in four cardinal directions. Any negative emotions and tendencies are absent; lion and lamb lie peacefully side by side. Yet another abode of the Christian blessed is the Celestial City, with spectacular architecture and streets paved with gold, silver, and precious stones.

Divine judgment, a recurrent archetypal theme in eschatological mythology, is an important component of the Christian posthumous journey. Christianity distinguishes two kinds of moral reckoning. The first occurs at the time of death of an individual person and involves weighing of souls. Less frequently, the separation of the just from the sinners occurs on a bridge or on a ladder leading to Heaven. The art depicting the judgment of the dead typically features images of devils and angels fighting for the soul and often specifically focuses on archangel Michael as the partisan for the souls of the deceased. The second type of moral reckoning, the Last Judgment, is predicted to happen at the end of time when the tombs open and all the dead will be judged again. Christian art abounds in paintings and reliefs of the Last Judgment, with Jesus Christ depicted as a stern judge surrounded by the four mystical beasts of the Apocalypse—lion, eagle, bull, and winged man. The just are seen ascending into Heaven or entering the Garden of Love, and the damned are devoured by the mouth of Hell.

The Qur'an promises the believers entrance into Heaven and relegation of the infidels to Hell. The glory of the seven heavens and Paradise is described in the *Miraj Nameh*, a mystical legend of Muhammad's miraculous nocturnal journey. Accompanied by Archangel Gabriel and riding al-Buraq, his celestial steed with a crowned human head, Muhammad visits the regions of the Beyond: seven heavens, Paradise, and the Hell realm Gehenna. Each of the heavens is associated with a precious metal or stone and harbors earlier prophets. In the Seventh Heaven, Muhammad has an encounter with Allah, during which he experiences "ecstasy approaching annihilation" and is given instructions for the prayers of his followers.

The Muslim Paradise is an oasis with beautiful gardens, luscious trees bearing exquisite fruit, exotic birds, and rivers of pure water, honey, and oil. Life in this idyllic setting reflects male Arab tastes, fantasies, and dreams. Men are clad in the richest silken robes and brocades and adorned with bracelets of gold and silver and crowns set with pearls. Lying on couches in rooms richly decorated with silken carpets and pillows, they enjoy perpetual youth, beauty, and vigor and feast on exquisite food, fruit, and wine. Enticing music and singing further enhance the extraordinary sensual pleasures which this realm has to offer. But the most extraordinary delights are provided by unlimited hosts of *houris*, ravishing black-eyed young women created of pure musk, waiting in pavilions of hollow pearls to serve the pleasures of the faithful. Having given their undivided attention to their clients and satisfied their sexual desires, the houris resume their virginal status. The pleasures of Paradise are so overwhelming that God will give to everyone the potentialities of a hundred individuals.

The theme of divine judgment is also an important aspect of Islamic religion. The ethical history of the deceased is thoroughly examined by two angels, Munker and Nakeer, who come to interrogate the dead. Those who are found righteous are refreshed by air and perfume, and a door is opened for them toward Paradise. Infidels are clad in garments from Hell and then pass through infernal doors into Hell, where they are enveloped by the heat and pestilential wind until the grave closes in on them and crushes their ribs. There they remain in agony until the day of resurrection. The Muslim tradition speaks also of the Sirat, which is a bridge over Hell, "finer than a hair and sharper than a sword," which all departed must cross. Believers are able to keep their balance and cross successfully; unbelievers slip and plunge into the infernal abyss.

The Zoroastrian concept of the abodes of the Beyond are vividly portrayed in the *Book of Arda Viraf*, which describes the hero's spiritual visions induced by wine and a "narcotic," very likely the Zoroastrian psychedelic sacrament haoma. During Viraf's visionary journey, two spiritual guides—divine messenger Srosh and the angel Adar—

take him on a visit to Heaven and Hell and explain each place to him in detail. The *Zend Avesta* teaches that after death the soul can reach Heaven by following a succession of increasingly bright lights: the Stars (good thoughts), the Moon (good words), and the Sun (good deeds). During the posthumous journey, the souls must cross a gloomy river of tears, which their relatives and friends have shed during their mourning and lamentation. If the survivors have shown excessive grief, the departed find the river of tears to be a formidable obstacle and an impasse that makes crossing impossible. The souls of just people who reach Heaven, such as good rulers and monarchs, truthful speakers, religious leaders, and "virtuous women who consider their husbands as lords," are clad in gold- and silver-embroidered garments and enjoy the presence of archangels, angels, and guardian angels.

Certain aspects of the Zoroastrian posthumous journey deserve special notice. The motif of divine judgment again plays an important role. Three days after death and the painful separation of the soul from the body, the just meet the image of their own self disguised as a ravishingly beautiful fifteen year-old girl. For the wicked ones, the self appears in the shape of a profligate naked woman, decayed, filthy, and stinking. A deity named "Just Rashnu" weighs the evil deeds of the departed against their noble deeds. The deceased then undergo a special ordeal: they must try to cross the Cinvato paratu, or "Bridge of the Separator." To the just the bridge appears wide and comfortable, and they easily pass across it to eternal bliss. For those who are found wicked, the bridge displays its other side, which is extremely narrow and resembles a razor's edge. As they attempt to cross it, their bad deeds take the form of vicious hounds howling and attacking them. The wicked lose balance and fall into the gaping maw of the demon Vizarsh and enter Hell. However, the final judgment has to wait until the apocalypse, when a final decisive battle will take place. After Ahura Mazda's victory over the army of Ahriman, Earth and Heaven will be united, and Ahura Mazda's kingdom will flourish.

The Heaven of ancient Greeks was located on the top of Mount Olympus, the abode of Twelve Olympians, principal gods of the Greek pantheon, who resided in beautiful crystal palaces. Here also was located the throne of Zeus, the principal deity. Ten gods were always considered Olympians: Zeus, Hera, Poseidon, Ares, Hermes, Hephaestus, Aphrodite, Athena, Apollo, and Artemis. Demeter, Dionysus, Hades, and Hestia were the variable gods among the twelve. On Mount Olympus, the gods feasted on nectar and ambrosia, which brought them immortality. At the same time, Greek gods were anthropomorphic and manifested human emotions and character traits, including various foibles. They had fierce conflicts and passionate love affairs with each other and mingled freely with people, engendering demigods, such as Heracles, Achilles, Theseus, and Perseus.

The paradisean realms of the classical Greeks were the Isles of the Blest and the Plain of Elysium, located over the waters of the Atlantic at the world's end. According to references found in Homer, Pindar, and Strabo, the Elysian Plain had an ideal climate with no rain, snowfall, or strong wind—only gentle breezes of Zephyrus. The air was permeated with perfumes, and nature was stunningly beautiful, with meadows of crimson roses and trees bearing golden fruit and incense. The land was so fertile that it bore honey-sweet fruit three times a year. Life was as easy as one can imagine. Inhabitants enjoyed music and poetry, played draughts, and participated in different sports of their choice, such as riding horses and wrestling.

The Orphic mystics, who taught salvation as a release from matter and earthly bondage, saw the Elysian Fields as a joyful resting place for pure spirits, at first located in an Underworld of strange brightness, and later in the upper regions of the sky. The Pythagoreans and other groups in ancient Greece believed in reincarnation and transmigration of the souls (metempsychosis). According to Plato, the dead were judged in a meadow by Aeacus, Minos, and Rhadamanthus and were consigned either to the gloomy Tartarus or to the Isles of the Blest. Subsequently they drank from the stream of Lethe, the river of oblivion, and forgot all their previous experiences.

In Nordic mythology, the heavenly realm has a strong martial emphasis and is known as Valhalla, Hall of the Slain, presided over by Odin (Wotan), the chief deity of the Norse pantheon. Odin is a god of war and death, but also of wisdom and poetry. He learned the secrets of the runes and nine powerful songs when he hung for nine days on the World Tree Iggdrasil, pierced by his own spear. Odin also gained immense wisdom when he traded one of his eyes for a drink from the Well of the Highest Wisdom, guarded by the giant Mimir. His companions are two wolves, two ravens, and his eight-footed steed Sleipnir.

Valhalla is a giant hall with 540 doors. Its rafters are spears, and the roof is made of shields. Breast plates are strewn all around. A wolf guards the western door, and an eagle hovers over it. Here Odin's messengers and spirits of war, the Valkyries ("Choosers of the Slain"), beautiful young women mounted on winged horses and armed with helmets and spears, bring half of the heroes who have died on the battle fields. Access to Valhalla is gained strictly on the basis of martial prowess. Warriors engage in splendid tournaments during the day and at night feast together on pork and mead. These heroes, the Einherjar, are prepared in Valhalla for the oncoming battle of Ragnarok, the Twilight or Doom of the Gods.

According to the ancient Vedic tradition, particularly the Rgveda, Heaven was the realm of the fathers, who went there after death to be with the gods. This realm was associated with the sky, and the dead were associated with the stars. Yama, who was the first human to die and also the ruler of the dead, reigned in the realm of light in the outer sky. The lives of all the worthy deceased were free of pain and care. They enjoyed music, sexual fulfillment, and sensual pleasures—essentially the delights of earthly life, but greatly enhanced. The welfare of those who died critically depended on their participation in rituals, offerings, and sacrifices to the gods while on earth. Agni, the god of fire, provided the purification of the deceased, a necessary prerequisite for successful posthumous journey.

Later Yama became the lord of the infernal regions. His mount was a fierce, black buffalo, a form which Yama on occasions also assumed himself. He used a rope noose to catch his victims and a mace to punish them. According to the Mahabharata, his abode called Yamalya featured a magnificent palace built by the architect Vishwakarma at the request of Brahma. Opposite its south door were four pits where the wicked were punished. Three other doors were reserved for the entrance of the good so that they did not have to see the place of punishment when they went to be judged. Brahma ordered Vishwakarma to form a vast trench and fill it with water. He then asked the fire god Agni to enter this river and make the water boil. After death each person was obliged to swim across this river, which gave harmless passage to good souls, while evil ones suffered torments and pangs. Yama functioned also as the judge of the dead and sent the wicked to suffer in the appropriate parts of Hell and the people with noble deeds to a particular part of Heaven.

Hinduism brought a different world view, reflecting the philosophical and spiritual ideas of the Upanishads. Here the emphasis was on cyclical continuity of existence—a series of lives, deaths, and rebirths, karma and reincarnation. In this context, Heaven and Hell came to be seen not as places of ultimate destiny, but as intermediate states alternating with a series of earthly existences. Traditional Hindu cosmology includes fourteen transcendental realms: half are above the earth (seven Upper Worlds or "Heavens"—Sapta Urdhvaloka); and the other half are under the earth (seven Underworlds or "Hells"—Sapta Adholoka). The nature of the passage of the soul (jiva) from one earthly existence to another through one of the Heavens or Hells is determined by karma, a cumulative record of one's thoughts, words, and actions in the entire series of existences.

Hindu mythology is extremely rich and describes many celestial and paradisean realms. The most important is Mount Meru, a golden mountain in the center of the universe, and the axis of the world. It is the abode of gods, and its foothills are the Himalayas. As the world axis, Mount Meru reaches down below the ground, into the nether regions, as far as it extends into the heavens. All the principal deities have their own celestial kingdoms on or near it, where their devotees reside with them after death, while awaiting their next reincarnation. In Vishnu's Heaven, Vaikuntha, the god and his consort Lakshmi, the goddess of good fortune, generosity, beauty, and purity, rest among white lotuses, surrounded by pools lined with gold and precious jewels and reflecting their radiance. Shiva's Heaven is on Mount Kailas, where he dwells with his consort Parvati.

Buddhism shares with Hinduism a cyclical view of history and of individual existence. The samsaric world, the world of space, time, and history is transitory and in constant flux. Buddhist mythology abounds in heavens, paradises, and hells, too numerous to describe here. The corpus of basic texts of Theravada Buddhism known as Pali canon or Tipitaka ("Three Baskets") does not offer a systematic account of the various hells and heavens. Generally, the lower six heavens and the various hells are included in kamaloka, the lower universe of sensuality, where desire is the primal motivation. The six heavens of the sensual realm of kamaloka harbor kings, gods, and bodhisattvas. The Buddhist heavens of the other two realms can be attained only by rigorous spiritual discipline and practice; the first of these, rupaloka (the world of forms), is the realm of radiant gods with subtle form and the second, arupaloka (the formless world), is the realm of beings with pure mental life. The paradises of the five Dhyani Buddhas or Tathagatas of Tibetan Buddhism deserve special notice and are discussed in Chapter 6.

Although glorious, the divine realms described by Buddhism are not free from involvement in the cycles of samsaric existence and do not represent the most desirable ultimate goal of Buddhist spiritual seekers. Rather they are intermediate states between one earthly existence and another, temporary stations for those who are not ready to give up personal desires and attachments and achieve total release from the bondage of personality—enlightenment, which transcends even the highest of the Heavens. The same is true for Hells, which represent only temporary stations in the cycle of death and rebirth. The ultimate goal of the Buddhist seeker is to reach nirvana. In the original Hinayana (Smaller Vehicle Buddhism), nirvana meant final release from the cycle of death and rebirth, extinguishing the "thirst of flesh and blood" (trsna or tanha) and moving beyond the realm of material existence. In later Buddhism (Mahayana or the Greater Vehicle Buddhism), nirvana could be achieved during material existence if one could extinguish the three "poisons" responsible for the suffering in the world—ignorance, desire, and anger.

The concept of divine realms exists also in Mesoamerican eschatological mythology. The Aztecs distinguished three different paradises where souls went after death. The first and lowest of these, Tlalocan, land of water and mist, was a place of abundance, bliss, and serenity. The happiness experienced there was of a very earthly variety. The dead sang songs, played leapfrog, and chased butterflies. The trees were laden with fruit, and the land was covered with maize, pumpkins, green peppers, tomatoes, beans, and flowers. By contrast, Tlillan-Tlapallan was the Paradise of the initiates who were followers of Quetzalcoatl, the god-king symbolizing psychospiritual death and rebirth. It was referred to as the land of the fleshless, an abode for those who had learned to live outside their physical bodies and were unattached to them. The highest Paradise was Tona-tiuh Ichan, House of the Sun, a place for those who achieved full illumination. These privileged ones were chosen as daily companions of the sun and lived a life of pure delight. The Maya recognized certain categories of the dead as being privileged—warriors who fell in battle, women who died in childbirth, priests, and persons who committed suicide by hanging. These were immortal and enjoyed eternal happiness in the Maya Paradise beneath the sacred ceiba tree, the World Tree that crossed all celestial spheres.

The image of a glorious place of the dead appears also in the lore of many native cultures. Thus, for example, the Native American tribes of the Great Plains imagine the dwelling place of the dead, Happy Hunting Grounds, as a vast rolling prairie, where the deceased dance and feast. Spirits of dead warriors ride beautiful stallions and catch thunderbolts with their bare hands. Similar realms of Indians who live east of the Mississippi and in South America have a strong agricultural emphasis and focus on cultivation of maize and agrarian festivities. In both North and South America, the trance states of shamans seem to have inspired the belief in two souls, one of which can be separated from the body during one's life. The shamans also provided information about the journey of the soul into the realm of the dead. Their tales included reports about obstacles that the soul encounters in the Beyond—wild rivers, slippery trunks joining the banks of rushing streams, walls of fire, and threatening monsters that try to drive the traveler insane.

As mentioned earlier, Eskimo people envision their dead in the radiance of aurora borealis, joyfully playing with the head of a walrus. Australian Aborigines believe that death is the final rite of passage that takes one from the profane world to the sacred universe. It is an ecstatic journey patterned after the first journey of the supernatural beings and the mythic ancestors. According to the Aborigines' mythology, man has two souls. The true essential one, the primordial and preexistent spirit, comes from Heaven and, at death, it goes back to live forever in the Eternal Dreaming (alcheringa), where it was before birth. The other soul remains on earth and enters another person. Variations on the realm of the fortunate dead can be found among African tribes, in Polynesian societies, and many human groups in other parts of the world.

Hell and Purgatory

The concept of Hell or Purgatory, a place where the departed will be exposed to inhuman tortures, is equally ubiquitous. In the Hebraic tradition the land of the dead is She'ol, a great pit or walled city under the earth, "the land of forgetfulness," "the land of silence," where discarnate human beings live in dust, darkness, and ignorance, all covered by maggots and forgotten by Yahweh. It is a land of shadows, since the "spirit" or "breath of life" (ruah) through which human beings are endowed by God with life has departed. A later Jewish form of the Afterlife abode of the damned was Gehenna, a deep valley with burning fire, where the wicked were tormented by flames. Originally, Gehenna was a valley west and south of Jerusalem, where from the 10th to the 7th century B.C. Israelites burned children as sacrifices to the Ammonite god Moloch. The imagery of the burning of humans supplied the concept of "hellfire" to Jewish and Christian eschatology.

The Christian picture of Hell involves hierarchies of vicious devils exposing the damned to unimaginable tortures by physical pain, suffocation, fiery heat, and exposure to excrements. These ordeals represent specific punishments for the seven cardinal sins—pride, envy, wrath, sloth, avarice, gluttony, and lust. Hell is located far underground, with entrances through dark woods, volcanic craters, or the gaping mouth of Leviathan. The Book of Revelation mentions the lake that burns with fire and brimstone, the final destination of "the cowardly, the faithless, the polluted, murderers, fornicators, sorcerers, idolaters, and all liars." Less frequently, cold and ice are described as infernal instruments of torture.

The Roman Catholic faith includes also the concept of Purgatory, an intermediate state after death, during which venial sins may be expiated and fellowship may be restored with God. Christianity in some of its forms has elaborated the distinction between Purgatory, as a place of temporary punishment and purification, and Limbo, as a waiting place for persons such as heathens and unbaptized infants. The Christian teaching about Heaven, Hell, and Purgatory found an extraordinary and powerful expression in Dante's masterful poem *Commedia* (Divine Comedy).

The Islamic picture of Hell is very similar to that of the Judeo-Christian tradition from which it was derived. *Miraj Nameh*, the account of the Miraculous Journey of Muhammad mentioned earlier in this chapter, describes Muslim Hell, Gehenna, as Muhammad saw it during his visit with Archangel Gabriel. The gate to Gehenna is guarded by the reticent angel Malik, who made an exception during Muhammad's visit and broke his silence to greet him. Nature in Gehenna is ugly and dangerous; infernal spike trees bear poisonous fruit in the shape of demons. The doomed undergo cruel tortures and punishments: they are hung and strangled, their tongues are cut out, they are exposed to pus and boiling water, their bodies are roasted in fire and their skin is regenerated for more burning, and they suffer many other forms of agony, depending on the nature of their transgressions. The Islamic tradition also has an intermediate state for souls—barzakh (literally "barrier"), a place or condition in which both good and wicked souls dwell until the day of resurrection.

The Zoroastrian image of Hell is particularly shocking and revolting, as described graphically in the *Book of Arda Viraf* mentioned earlier. Hell is in the far north, in the depths of the earth, a dark place, foul and stinking, and teeming with demons. There the damned souls, "the followers of the lie," remain after death, in pain and misery, until the God of Darkness, Ahriman himself, is destroyed. The wicked are tortured by demons, vicious creatures (khrafstars), snakes, and scorpions. They are vexed by hunger and thirst, fed filth, flogged with darting serpents, repeatedly dismembered, and exposed to countless other gory and sordid torments. The reasons for these cruel punishments include sodomy, violation of menstrual taboos, adultery, and desecration of water and fire. According to the Zoroastrian religion, Hell is not an eternal punishment; the tortures will continue only until the victory of Ahura Mazda over Ahriman in the Cosmic Battle and subsequent renovation of the world (frashegird). The Zoroastrian religion also has an intermediate area, called hamestagan, for those who do not deserve either Heaven or Hell because the total weight of their good thoughts, good words, and good deeds is equal to that of the bad ones. These souls remain in a sort of limbo, a dwelling place of shadows without joy or torments.

The Greek Underworld, Tartarus or Hades, was an underground place of dreary darkness, described by Homer as "the hateful Chambers of Decay that fill the gods themselves with horror." The principal river of the Underworld was the stinking marshy Styx, across which the dead had to be ferried by Charon for a fee of a few coins. The dead in the Greek Underworld were anemic doubles, shadows that had to be revived with drafts of blood, mead, wine, and water in order to be able to speak. The guardian of the entrance to Hades was the three-headed, monstrous hound Cerberus.

Greek mythology featured archetypal figures experiencing eternal suffering of truly heroic proportions for offenses against gods. Those who had personally insulted Zeus were imprisoned in the bottomless pit of Tartarus and had to undergo agonizing torments. Sisyphus, who tried to trick death, was assigned to the deepest pit of Hades, rolling incessantly a heavy boulder up a hill. Tantalus, who attempted to test omniscience of the gods by serving them his dismembered son Pelops as a meal, was placed up to his neck in a pool of clean water, below a large throng of fresh grapes and was vexed forever by thirst and hunger, unable to reach either of them. Ixion, who tried to seduce Hera, was crucified on a fiery wheel that incessantly whirled through Hades. Prometheus, the Titan who stole fire from Zeus and gave it to people together with the knowledge of crafts and technology, was chained to a rock in the mountains of Caucasus and periodically attacked by Zeus' eagle, which pecked at and fed on his liver.

The Nordic Underworld, Niflheim or Helheim, was situated below one of the roots of the World Tree, Yggdrasil, and was ruled by the fierce and ruthless goddess Hel. It was a cold, dark, and misty world of the dead, situated north of the Void (Ginnungagap) in which the world was created. Niflheim, also called the World of Darkness, was divided into several sections, one of which was Náströnd, the shore of corpses. There a north-facing castle was filled with the venom of serpents, in which murderers, adulterers, and perjurers suffered torments, while the dragon Nidhogg sucked the blood from their bodies. Niflheim contained a well, Hvergelmir, from which flowed many rivers. Courageous warriors who fell in battle did not go to Helheim but to the god Odin, to Valhalla, the Hall of the Slain. Images of cold hells are not exceptional in world mythology. They existed in medieval Christianity and are also part of the Tibetan Underworld. Dante used the medieval image of the cold hell for the lowest circle of Hell and portrayed Satan in the middle of the earth sitting in a pool of his frozen blood.

Numerous types and levels of Hell exist in Hinduism and Buddhism. Like the various Paradises, they are not places where the deceased stay forever but are merely transitional stages in the cycle of birth, death, and rebirth. The hells in Buddhism are viewed as a creation of the mind, filled with self-deception and egocentrism, and the tortures experienced there are at least as multiform, diabolic, and ingenious as those described in other traditions. Besides the hell realms where the punishments involve physical pain and suffocation, Buddhist mythology describes hot hells with walls of fire, rivers of molten iron, and searing volcanic lava. Cold hells are vividly described also—sinners are tortured by freezing cold and ice and suffer painful frostbites.

The duration of passage through these hells reflects the amount of evil karma that has to be consumed. In the infamous Avichi Hell (literally "no space"), the wrongdoers suffer horrendous tortures for countless kalpas (Brahmanic eons). When they emerge from Hell, they degrade into animals, such as dogs or jackals, covered with sores and scabs. Buddhist hells feature judges deciding the fate of the deceased. For example, Emma-O, a figure from one of the Japanese Buddhist hot hells, judges with the help of two severed heads; the red one reports to him all the bad deeds of the deceased and the white one all the good deeds. He judges the souls of men, while his sister judges the souls of women. The Chinese Buddhist hells have four or sometimes ten infernal judges.

The Aztec Underworld, Mictlan, was a region of utter darkness ruled by the terrible Lord of the Dead, Mictlantecuhtli. His face was covered by a mask in the form of a human skull, his black, curly hair was studded with star-like eyes, and a human bone protruded from his ear. In the Aztec tradition it was not the conduct of the deceased that determined one's fate after death but the occupation and the manner of death. Those of the dead who were not selected for one of the Paradises were subjected in Mictlan to a series of magical trials where they had to pass through nine hells before reaching their final resting place. These hells were not places to which the wicked went for punishment but were regarded as necessary points of transition in the cycle of creation, because in the cosmic process of the Aztec tradition, all created things inevitably plunged into matter and returned back to light and to their creator.

I described the underworlds of native cultures as experienced by the shamans in their initiation crises and during their later journeying. In this chapter I have also referred to various underworlds in discussing the archetypal figures representing death and rebirth and their stories. (see Chapter 3). The most elaborate descriptions of the posthumous journey of the soul, including the scenes of judgment, can be found in the so-called "books of the dead." These famous eschatological texts are explored at some length in the following chapter.

6
THE BOOKS OF THE DEAD: MANUALS FOR LIVING AND DYING

Mors certa, hora incerta.
Death is certain, the hour uncertain.
– *Ars moriendi*

KNOWLEDGE of the transcendental realities obtained in holotropic states of consciousness inspired special texts in many parts of the world that described the posthumous journey of the soul. This chapter explores the most famous of these "books of the dead," ancient documents dedicated to the problems of death and dying. The oldest is the so-called Egyptian Book of the Dead, or *Pert Em Hru*, literally "Manifestation in the Light" or "Coming Forth by Day," a collection of illustrated Egyptian papyri and inscriptions decorating the walls of pyramids and tombs. The Tibetan Book of the Dead is probably the most famous such text and is known as the *Bardo Thödol*, or "liberation by hearing on the afterdeath plane." The Mesoamerican examples of eschatological literature include Toltec and Aztec material from the preserved screenfold codices, *Codex Borgia* and *Codex Borbonicus*. Also notable is the Mayan Book of the Dead, as reconstructed from the pictures and texts on the funeral vases of the so-called *Ceramic Codex*. These examples are discussed in detail below, followed by a review of the medieval European eschatological texts known as *Ars moriendi*.

When the ancient books of the dead first came to the attention of Western scholars, they were seen as fictitious accounts of the posthumous journey of the soul, wishful fabrications of people who were unable to accept the grim reality of death and impermanence. These texts were relegated to the same category as fairy tales—imaginary creations of human fantasy that had definite artistic beauty, but no relevance for everyday life. However, deeper study revealed that they had served as guides in mysteries of death and rebirth and in deep spiritual practice, and it became quite evident that the books of the dead fairly accurately described the experiences of the initiates, spiritual seekers, and practitioners. This new perspective suggested that these texts may have been originally presented by the priests as manuals for the dying simply to obscure their real function, a clever disguise to protect their esoteric message from the uninitiated.

Modern consciousness research brought unexpected new insights to bear on this question. Thanatological studies of life-threatening and near-death situations showed that such experiences actually manifested many of the features depicted in the eschatological texts and mythologies of ancient and preindustrial cultures. This process of startling discoveries continued when systematic study of the experiences observed in psychedelic sessions, in powerful non-drug forms of psychotherapy, and in spontaneously occurring psychospiritual crises revealed that many were also strikingly similar to those described in the ancient books of the dead (Leary, Alpert and Metzner 1964, Masters and Houston 1966, Grof 1975).

Researchers discovered to their great surprise that during visionary journeys their clients experienced the same kind of material that was featured prominently in the ancient books of the dead: psychospiritual death and rebirth, divine judgment, encounters with various blissful and wrathful deities, memories from previous incarnations, and visits to abodes of the Beyond—celestial realms, paradisean gardens, and infernal regions. The specific symbolism of these experiences was drawn from many different mythologies of the world, not necessarily the subject's own cultural heritage. It often involved mythological figures, realms, and motifs about which the respective individuals had no intellectual knowledge.

It became obvious that these experiences were manifestations of the collective unconscious as described by C. G. Jung (see Chapter 3), and that the books of the dead were actually maps of the deep territories of the psyche, which in holotropic states became available for conscious experience. The potential to experience these deep contents of the unconscious is present in each of us. Even so, many people never experience these realms, nor have any awareness of their existence until the time of biological death, when they are catapulted into this territory.

However, for some people this experiential domain opens up during their lifetime in a variety of situations—psychedelic sessions, powerful forms of experiential psychotherapy and self-exploration, systematic spiritual practice, participation in shamanic rituals, or during spontaneous psychospiritual crises. Thus it becomes possible to enter and traverse these ordinarily hidden territories of the psyche and gain intimate knowledge of them before biological death. As mentioned in the earlier discussion of death and rebirth in shamanism, rites of passage, and the ancient mysteries (Chapters

1-3), this experiential preparation of training for death, or "dying before dying," has profound consequences. Individuals are liberated from the fear of death, their attitude toward their mortality is changed, and their actual experience of dying at the time of the biological demise is radically modified. Once fear of death is eliminated, a person's way of being in the world is transformed. Consequently there is no fundamental difference between the preparation for death and the practice of dying, on the one hand, and spiritual practice leading to enlightenment, on the other. This is why the ancient books of the dead could be used in both situations.

Thanks to the findings of modern consciousness research during the last four decades, we can do more than simply outline the content of the books of the dead and review the information amassed by scholars who analyzed these texts. We can now compare this information with the observations from thanatology and other areas of ongoing investigation (such as psychedelic studies, experiential psychotherapy, field anthropology, and comparative religion) and so demonstrate the relevance of these ancient texts for contemporary readers.

Manifestation in the Light: The Egyptian Book of the Dead

One of the most famous funerary texts is the so-called Egyptian Book of the Dead or *Pert Em Hru*. Its English name is a misnomer, since it suggests a comprehensive and coherent work associated with a specific author, or at least a definite historical period. In actuality, *Pert Em Hru* is a vast and heterogeneous collection of texts, including spells and incantations, prayers, hymns, litanies, and magical formulas, as well as mythological stories and instructions for mummification and other procedures performed with or for the deceased. These texts originated in different parts of Egypt and different historical eras and, in their totality, they span a time period of almost five millennia.

The title "Egyptian Book of the Dead" is derived from a literal translation of the name given by Egyptian tomb-robbers to every roll of inscribed papyrus they found with the mummies—"Kitab al-Mayitun," or "book of the dead person." The original Egyptian title *Pert Em Hru* is usually translated as "manifestation in the light" or "coming forth by day." From this large body of funerary texts, the ancient scribes made specific selections for certain prominent individuals, brought these passages together into a comprehensive story, and provided them with rich illustrations. These were thus *ad personam* narratives, describing the posthumous journey of the individual involved. Instead of a standard and uniform text, the "Egyptian Book of the Dead," we have many individualized unique and original stories that bear the names of the deceased, such as those conveyed by the inscriptions and paintings on the walls of the tombs of the pharaohs Seti or Thutmes, or by the papyri of Ani, Hunefer, or Anhai, which are on display in the British Museum in London.

These funerary texts were originally written only for kings and were inscribed on the walls of certain pyramids, such as those erected in the honor of the pharaohs Cheops, Chephren, and Mykerinos in Sakkara. Both the pyramids and the pharaohs for whom they were built were related to the Sun God Ra. These so-called Pyramid Texts were produced between 2350 and 2175 B.C. and are the oldest written records not only in Egypt, but also in the entire human history. However, the material they contain points to sources that are even more archaic—the preoccupation with Afterlife and belief in the Beyond that led to the practice of mummification can be found in Egypt since 3100 B.C.

From about 1700 B.C., the practice of writing funerary texts was extended from the pharaohs to members of nobility and other famous persons. These more recent texts took the form of scrolls, which were put into the wooden coffins with the mummies or were painted on the sides of these coffins. For this reason, they are referred to as the Coffin Texts. The most famous of these funerary texts, such as the papyri of Ani, Hunefer, and Anhai, came from the city of Thebes. The first two papyri originated in the fifteenth century B.C., at the peak of the history of Thebes, while the last one dates from the eleventh century, the time of this city's decline. The Sun God Amon Ra, a principal figure of *Pert Em Hru*, was the state deity of Thebes.

From the first to the last, the texts of *Pert Em Hru* manifest the Egyptians' unalterable belief in the immortality of the soul, resurrection, and life after death. However, since the Egyptian funerary texts span a period of almost five thousand years, this message is not consistent and coherent like that of their Tibetan counterpart, the *Bardo Thödol*. Even such a conservative society as ancient Egypt would undergo significant cultural changes in the course of several millennia. In addition, various Egyptian cities had their preferences with regard to principal deities, and serious differences, conflicts, and power struggles occurred between the priests of Heliopolis, Memphis, Thebes, and Hermopolis. Furthermore when ancient Egyptians adopted new gods, they typically refused in their conservatism to give up the old ones. The old deities then continued to exert their influence, which further complicated the situation.

Despite their great complexity, one can discern two major ideological streams in the Egyptian funerary texts, personified by the deities Ra and Osiris. In many of them, the central theme is the diurnal-nocturnal journey of the Sun God Ra. He emerged daily in the east from behind Manu, the mountain of sunrise, traveling in the Manjet boat, the Barque of Millions of Years, and began traversing the Egyptian sky. Ra was accompanied on his triumphant journey by a retinue of other deities. During the day, he crossed the sky, giving heat, light, and life to the earth. At sunset, the sun boat entered an opening in the mountains of the west. There the Sun God and his crew boarded another barque, the Mesektet boat, and embarked on their night journey through the netherworld Tuat. The Tuat, as it was envisioned by ancient Egyptians, was a gloomy and treacherous place, divided into twelve portions, usually called arrits (halls) or sekhets (fields). Each division corresponded to one hour of the night, the period which the Sun God needed to traverse it. The geography and population of the Tuat was very complex. All the arrits had gates with specific gatekeepers, watchers, and heralds, and each of them had its own characteristic scenery, recognizable inhabitants, and unique dangers. As Ra passed along the infernal river, the various gods and demons, who inhabited each portion, came forward to haul his boat, because no wind could penetrate the Tuat. They were directed by the goddess of the hour who opened the gate leading into the next hour.

Ra and his companions struggled through places of blazing fire, where heat, fumes, and vapors destroyed nostrils and mouths. Many hideous beings and fantastic creatures threatened them as they passed. The most dangerous of these perils was Osiris' brother Seth in the form of Apep, a gigantic snake attempting to devour the solar disk just before sunrise.

Those Egyptians who worshipped Ra as their principal deity believed that after physical death they would join him and his divine retinue and travel with them in the solar barque. Their principal text was *Am Tuat* or The Book of What is in the Tuat, written by the priests of Amen-Ra. This book asserted the absolute supremacy of the Sun God in the realms of the dead and showed that all the gods of the dead throughout Egypt rendered him homage. The *Am Tuat* provided information about the portions of the Tuat and its many halls and gates for the followers of Amen Ra. It also gave them the names of the beings who guarded the portions and the necessary magic formulae and power words.

The second theme that permeated the texts of *Pert Em Hru* came from an even older tradition of the ancient mortuary god Osiris. Osiris was one of four divine siblings, the children of Geb, the god of the earth, and Nut, the goddess of the sky. He had two sisters, Isis and Nephthys, and a brother Seth. Osiris was also the husband of his sister Isis, and Nephthys was married to Seth. Seth plotted against Osiris, and he succeeded in killing him and hacking his body in many pieces. He then gave the fragments to the four winds and dispersed them all over the Nile Delta. With the help of Nephthys's son, the jackal-headed god Anubis, Isis and Nephthys were able to find all the scattered pieces of their brother's body; they collected them and reassembled them in a rawhide.

They then resurrected Osiris by using the eye of the falcon-headed god Horus, the child whom Isis managed to conceive by the dead Osiris. Horus later assumed the role of a formidable avenger of his father. After a long and hard struggle, Horus defeated Seth and castrated him. The death and resurrection of Osiris was for the Egyptians an important mythological foundation for the belief in survival after death and for the process of psychospiritual death and rebirth. The battle between Horus and Seth then became a metaphor for the cosmic battle between the forces of light and darkness or of good and evil.

Seth was often cast in a very negative role, as a vicious and treacherous archenemy of his brother Osiris. However, not all versions of the story are as extreme, and some explain Seth's animosity toward his brother. Nephthys was married to Seth, but her loyalties were to Osiris. Seth, being the god of aridity, was unable to father children, and the marriage remained childless. With the help of alcohol and disguised as Isis, Nephthys managed to seduce Osiris and conceived with him the son Anubis. Osiris also took over the kingdom, which he and Seth had jointly inherited. In this context, Seth's hostility toward Osiris appears justified or at least understandable.

According to the Egyptian eschatological lore, the worshippers of Osiris began their posthumous journey in the same way as the followers of Ra—by boarding the solar boat. However, they used it only as a means of transportation to the Underworld; their final destination was the kingdom of Osiris. To qualify for it, they had to pass divine judgment in the Hall of Maat, the goddess of justice. They were escorted to the hall by the jackal-headed god Anubis, who was an important funerary deity, the herald of death, and inventor of the embalming procedure. In the earlier stages of the posthumous journey, Anubis supervised embalming and performed the Opening of the Mouth ceremony on the mummy, a procedure making it possible for the deceased to perceive the realms of the Beyond.

The divine trial began under the supervision of a pantheon of deities with the recitation of the "negative confession," during which the deceased affirmed that he or she had committed no sins. This was followed by the "weighing of souls," presided over by the ibis-headed god Thoth in the role of an impartial judge. Thoth, a mysterious self-begotten deity, was considered the inventor of speech, of the sacred hieroglyphic alphabet, and also of mathematics, engineering, magic, and divination. In the middle of the Hall of Maat, by a large balance decorated with the goddess' statuette, Anubis stood and weighed the heart of the deceased against an ostrich feather, the symbol of the goddess Maat and of supreme justice. The heart was considered to be the seat of conscience and of intelligence responsible for actions; the feather symbolized the cosmic ethical order. If both scales were not in perfect balance, the deceased was devoured by Amemet, the Devourer of Souls, a hybrid monster who was part lion, part crocodile, and part hippopotamus. The doomed individual became one of the inhabitants of the dismal regions of the Underworld. If the deceased passed the judgment, he or she was brought and introduced to Osiris by the falcon-headed sky god Horus.

The followers of Osiris who successfully passed the judgment and were received by him into his kingdom enjoyed blissful existence in Sekhet Hetepet, or Happy Fields, a paradisean replica of the Nile Valley. There they enjoyed eternal life and mingled freely with gods and other spirits of the deceased, feasting on the "Bread of Eternity," and drinking the "Beer of Everlasting Life." They spent time talking and singing with friends and playing draughts. The deceased were expected to cultivate the fields and keep the irrigation canals of Osiris, but the agricultural work was easy and yielded extraordinarily rich harvests. This duty could also be taken over by the ushabti figures that had been placed in their tombs.

The Book of the Gates was the principal text of the followers of Osiris and was compiled to prove that, despite the assertions of the priests of Amen-Ra, Osiris, the ancient god of the dead, was still the supreme lord of the Underworld. This text, the most complete version of which was found inscribed on the alabaster sarcophagus of Pharaoh Seti I (around 1375 B.C.), consisted of two parts. The first was a series of texts and pictures describing the journey in the solar barque to the kingdom of Osiris, the judgment of the dead, the life of the beatified in Sekhet Hetepet, and the punishment of the wicked and the foes of the Sun God and of Osiris. The second part contained a series of texts and pictures representing the magical ceremonies that were performed in very ancient times to make the Sun God rise every day.

In the mystical tradition of Egypt, the experience of death and rebirth was not necessarily bound to the time of the biological demise. In the sacred temple mysteries of Isis and Osiris, initiates were given the opportunity to confront death long before old age or disease forced them to do so. Undergoing voluntarily the process of psychospiritual death and rebirth, they were able to conquer death and discover their own immortality. As mentioned at the beginning of this chapter, initiatory procedures of this kind not only helped neophytes overcome fear of death, but also profoundly changed their way of being in the world. The ancient Egyptians saw deep parallels between the adventures of the Sun God during his diurnal-nocturnal journey, the states associated with biological death, and the experiences of neophytes in the sacred mysteries. Modern consciousness research has shed new light on the connections and interrelations between these three situations and shifted ancient Egyptian eschatological beliefs from the world of primitive superstition to the domain of transpersonal psychology.

An essential part of the Egyptian eschatological practices was the technology of embalmment and the rituals associated with it. The earliest known mummies come from the Thinite Period (3200–2780 B.C.). The practice was already well established by 2400 B.C., when the Pyramid Texts were composed. Embalming existed until the fourth century A.D. when it was discontinued because of Christian influence.

Many passages of *Pert Em Hru* show that the Egyptians were deeply afraid of the decomposition of the body and exerted great effort to prevent it. They believed that the physical body was an important constituent of the human personality and that its integrity was essential for their well-being in the Afterlife. The deceased's *ka* or protective genius, represented by statues of the deceased that were placed by the mummy in the tomb, was seen as the transcendent part of a human being that emerged from the body at death and traveled to the West to meet his heavenly double. Subsequently, *ka* dwelt in Heaven, but at the same time also beside the mummy in the tomb and had to be nourished by the family to survive. Occasionally, the tomb was also revisited by *ba*, usually translated as soul—the part of a human that came into existence at the moment of death. Ba was usually represented as a falcon-headed man.

No other culture in human history has shown such determined and enduring effort to prevent and reverse the consequences of death. The Egyptians combined many practices over thousands of years to address the problem of death and dying, including their technology of embalming, magical rituals, and monumental architecture. The experiential counterpart of these efforts was the institution of the mysteries of Isis and Osiris, which provided for the initiates the technology and the context for the induction of profound experiences of psychospiritual death and rebirth.

Liberation by Hearing on the Afterdeath Plane: The Tibetan Book of the Dead

Many religions and cultures feature elaborate mythologies with vivid descriptions of the deities and demons, as well as complex scenery of various archetypal realms, but none match the rich and meticulous iconography of Tibetan Buddhism. This material found its expression in the Tibetan Book of the Dead or the *Bardo Thödol*, which offers detailed accounts of a fantastic array of blissful and wrathful deities and other archetypal inhabitants of the afterdeath plane. These figures are described with astonishing precision as to their general appearance, specific characteristics, symbolic attributes, and associated colors.

The *Bardo Thödol* is a funerary text of much more recent origin than its Egyptian counterpart and has incomparably more inner consistency and congruence. Unlike *Pert Em Hru*, it is well-defined and homogenous, and its author and approximate time of origin are known. While clearly based on much older oral material, the *Bardo Thödol* was first written down in the eighth century A.D. by the Great Guru Padmasambhava. This legendary spiritual teacher introduced Buddhism into Tibet and laid the foundations for Vajrayana, a unique amalgam of Buddhist teachings and elements of an ancient indigenous tradition called Bön that had been Tibet's principal religion before Padmasambhava's arrival. According to the Tibetan Buddhist tradition, Padmasambhava used his extraordinary spiritual powers to tame the ferocious local Bön deities and transform some of them into fierce protectors of Buddhism.

Not much is known with certainty about the pre-Buddhist religion (Bön) of Tibet. However, preoccupation with the continuation of life after death seemed to be one of its dominant features, as it included elaborate rituals to ensure that the soul of the dead person was conducted safely to the Beyond. Sacrificed animals, foods, drinks, and various precious objects accompanied the deceased during the posthumous journey. When a king or a high nobleman died, the funeral rites were particularly elaborate. In these cases the sacrifice included immolation of selected human companions; the ceremonies involved many priests and court officials and lasted several years. Besides insuring the happiness of the deceased in the Beyond, these rites were also expected to benefit the well-being and fertility of the living. (When a king died, the rites were seen as benefiting the entire society.) The original Bön had significant animistic and shamanistic components, and some of its other characteristic features included the cult of local gods, especially mountain and warrior deities, and the use of trance states for oracular activities.

After Buddhism arrived in Tibet, both of these religious systems coexisted and, in spite of their separate nature and differences, they shared rich cross-fertilization. In their extreme forms, it is relatively easy to distinguish genuine Buddhism and the Bön religion. However, in practice the two have been so closely combined that for many people they fused into a single belief system. The non-Buddhist elements are particularly prominent in the esoteric Chöd practice, a terrifying ritual of deliberate sacrifice of oneself to local demons in a charnel ground, as performed by certain ascetic yogis. The name Chöd, meaning literally "cut-off," refers to cutting of the ego and the defilements that support it by offering one's body, mind, and all attachments to the most hungry and fearsome beings.

The influence of the Bön religion is also easily recognizable in the remarkable *Bardo Thödol*. As a guide for the dying and the dead, the *Bardo Thödol* is a manual to help the departed recognize, with the assistance of a competent lama, the various stages of the intermediate state between death and subsequent rebirth and to attain liberation. The states of consciousness associated with the process of death and rebirth belong to a larger family of intermediate states or bardos:

1. Natural bardo state of the intrauterine existence (Chenay Bardo)
2. Bardo of the dream state (Milam Bardo)
3. Bardo of ecstatic equilibrium during deep meditation (Samten Bardo)

4. Bardo of the moment of death (Chikhai Bardo)
5. Bardo of the karmic illusions following death (Chönyid Bardo)
6. Bardo of the inverse process of sangsaric existence while seeking rebirth (Sidpa Bardo)

Although The Tibetan Book of the Dead is ostensibly written as a guide for the dying, it has additional levels of meaning. According to the Buddhist teachings, death and rebirth do not happen only at the time of biological demise and subsequent beginning of another lifetime, but in every moment of our existence. The states described in the *Bardo Thödol* can also be experienced in meditative states during systematic spiritual practice. This important text is thus simultaneously a guide for the dying, for the living, and for serious spiritual seekers. It is one of a series of instructions for six types of liberation: liberation through hearing, liberation through wearing (certain amulets), liberation through seeing, liberation through remembering, liberation through tasting, and liberation through touching.

The instructions for the different types of liberation were formulated by Padmasambhava and written down by his wife. Padmasambhava later buried these texts in the Gampo hills of central Tibet, as was customary with many texts and sacred objects, called termas or "hidden treasures." He gave the transmission of power to discover them to his twenty-five principal disciples. The texts of the *Bardo Thödol* were later found by Karma Lingpa, who belonged to the Nyingma tradition and was an incarnation of one of these disciples. They have been used throughout centuries by serious students of this teaching as important guides to liberation and illumination.

The *Bardo Thödol* describes the experiences that one encounters at the time of death (Chikhai Bardo), during the period of facing the archetypal visions and karmic illusions following death (Chönyid Bardo), and in the process of seeking rebirth (Sidpa Bardo). Traditionally, upon death and for a period of forty-nine days thereafter, this text is chanted by teachers or lamas to instruct the spirit of the deceased regarding what to expect in the Bardo state and how to use the experiences for liberation.

Chikhai Bardo: The Bardo of the Moment of Death

The Chikhai Bardo details the experiences associated with the moment of death. The most characteristic feature of this state is a sense of losing touch with the familiar world of polarities and entering a realm of unreality and confusion. The logical and ordered world that we know from everyday life starts to dissolve and is replaced by a sense of uncertainty as to whether one is attaining enlightenment or becoming insane. The *Bardo Thödol* discusses the experiences heralding imminent death in terms of the different elements of the body. The process starts with experiences of heaviness, intense physical pressures, and progressive loss of touch with the physical world. In this situation, one takes refuge in the mind and tries to reach reassurance that it is still functioning. This is described as "earth sinking into water." In the next stage, the operations of the mind cease to be fluid, and the circulation of thoughts is disturbed. Now the only way to relate to the world is through emotions, to think of somebody one loves or hates. The feelings of clammy cold are replaced by fiery heat. The *Bardo Thödol* refers to this experience as "water sinking into fire." Next the vivid emotions dissolve, and attention moves away from the objects of love and hatred; one's entire being seems to be blown into atoms. This experience of "fire sinking into air" creates a state of openness for the following encounter with cosmic luminosity.

At the actual moment of death, one has an overwhelming vision of *Dharmakaya*, or the Primary Clear Light of Pure Reality. All of existence suddenly appears in absolute totality, shining as a timeless unborn light. All dualities are transcended—agony and ecstasy, good and evil, beauty and ugliness, burning heat and chilling cold—all coexist in one undifferentiated whole. In the last analysis, the Dharmakaya is identical with the experiencer's own consciousness, which has no birth and death and is by its very nature the Immutable Light.

According to the *Bardo Thödol*, if one recognizes this truth of consciousness and has been prepared by systematic practice to surrender one's individuality to the enormity of this experience, this situation offers a unique opportunity for instant spiritual liberation. Those who let themselves be deterred and shy away from the Dharmakaya will have another chance immediately after death when the Secondary Clear Light dawns upon them. If they also miss this opportunity for a complete dissolution of their individuality, the force of their karma draws them relentlessly into a complicated sequence of spiritual adventures with an entire pantheon of blissful and wrathful deities, during which their consciousness becomes progressively more separated from the liberating light as they are approaching another rebirth. These experiences are described in the second and third bardos, as summarized below.

Chönyid Bardo: The Bardo of Experiencing Reality

The experiences in the Chönyid Bardo consist of successive visions of a rich panoply of divine and demonic presences that one encounters during the journey from the moment of death to the time of seeking rebirth. During the first five days of this bardo the glorious images of the five primordial Buddhas (Dhyani Buddhas) appear in their blissful aspects, enveloped in brilliant light of different colors, attended by male and female Bodhisattvas. These peaceful deities are Vairocana (Buddha Supreme and Eternal), Akshobhya (Immovable Buddha), Ratnasambhava (Buddha of Precious Birth), Amitabha (Buddha of Infinite Light), and Amoghasiddhi (Buddha of Unfailing Success).

The Dhyani Buddhas are the five principal modes of energy of Buddha-nature, fully awakened consciousness; they embody five qualities of wisdom. Everything that is part of existence—living beings, places, or events—can be described in terms of one of them. For this reason, they are known as the five families. The five primordial Buddhas are also called *Tathagatas* or *Jinas*. Tathagata means literally "thus gone" or "he who has become one with the essence of what is," and Jina translates as "victorious."

The five Tathagatas appear individually on the first five consecutive days of the Chönyid Bardo. On the sixth day, they all appear simultaneously with their attendants, together with the four wrathful Door-Keepers and their female *shaktis* or *dakinis*, with the Buddhas of the six realms into which one can be reborn (*lokas*), and with a number of additional divine figures—forty-two deities altogether. The unprepared are bewildered by this experience, since there seems to be no escape from the situation. The five Tathagatas fill all the space and all the directions, and the four gates are guarded by the Four Door-Keepers.

The radiances of the Tathagatas contrast sharply with the luring, dull, and illusory lights representing the six lokas. The six major emotions that attract us to the individual realms of rebirth are karmically determined: fear and terror for the realm of gods (*devaloka*), violent anger for the realm of the wild beasts (*tiryakaloka*), egotism for the realm of humans (*manakaloka*), attachment for the realm of hungry ghosts (*pretaloka*), and jealousy for the realm of warrior gods (*asuraloka*). The rebirth in Hell (*narakaloka*) is described in the *Bardo Thödol* as a "result of the influence of the illusions of one's propensities."

On the seventh day, five Knowledge-Holding Deities from the paradisean realms appear with their dakinis, innumerable heroes and heroines, celestial warriors, and faith-protecting deities. During the next period, between the eighth and fourteenth days, the Wrathful Deities emerge. The demonic figures which manifest between the eighth and twelfth days, as terrifying as they might seem, are in actuality the dark aspects of the transcendental Buddhas. On the thirteenth day the *Kerimas* manifest, the Eight Wrathful Ones, and the *Htamenmas*, terrifying zoomorphic deities. They have the heads of various animals—a lion, tiger, black fox, wolf, vulture, dark red cemetery bird, crow, and an owl. On the fourteenth day a rich array of deities comes forth, including the Four Female Door-Keepers with animal heads, some other powerful zoomorphic goddesses, and the yoginis.

For the unprepared and uninitiated, the wrathful deities are a source of abysmal awe and terror. However, those who are familiar with these images from their previous studies and who are prepared by intensive spiritual practice are able to recognize them as essentially empty images of their own mind and can thus merge with them and attain Buddhahood.

Sidpa Bardo: The Bardo of Seeking Rebirth

Those who have missed the opportunity for liberation in the first two bardos must face this last stage of the intermediate state. After having fainted from fear in the Chönyid Bardo, they now awaken in a new form—the bardo body. The bardo body differs from the gross one we know from everyday life and has many remarkable qualities: it is not composed of matter, it is endowed with the power of unimpeded motion, and it can penetrate through solid objects.

Those who exist in the form of bardo body can appear and disappear at will and reach any place on earth instantaneously, including the sacred cosmic mountain Mt. Meru. They can change size and shape and replicate their form, manifesting simultaneously in more than one location. At this point, one might seem to be in command of miraculous karmic powers. Here the *Bardo Thödol* issues a serious warning against becoming attached to these forces. (As we will see later in this book, some of the claims concerning the bardo body, however incredible they might seem, have been confirmed by modern thanatological research.)

The emotional quality of the experiences in this bardo—the degree of happiness or misery one feels—depends on the karmic record of the person involved. Those who have accumulated much bad karma are tormented by frightening events, such as flesh-eating demons or *rakshasas* brandishing menacing weapons, terrible beasts of prey, and raging elemental forces of nature. They can encounter clashing and crumbling rocks, angry overflowing seas, roaring fires, or ominous crevices and precipices. Those who have accumulated karmic merit experience various delightful pleasures, while those with neutral karma face colorless dullness and indifference.

The scene of judgment culminates the experiences in the Sidpa Bardo and determines which one of the six realms of existence (lokas) the dead will be assigned to. The judge of the dead is a deity called Dharma Raja (King of Law) or Yama Raja (King of Death); he is the wrathful aspect of Chenrazee, the national protector deity of Tibet. His head and body, as well as his pavilion and his court, are adorned with human skulls, heads, and hides. Underfoot he treads a mara figure, symbolic of maya, the illusory nature of human existence. He holds in his right hand a sword, a symbol of spiritual power, and in his left hand the Mirror of Karma, in which are reflected all the good and evil deeds of the judged.

The balance is attended by Shinje, a monkey-headed deity, and two figures stand beside it, each holding a sack of pebbles—the Little White God (white pebbles) and the Little Black God (black pebbles). Following the instructions of Yama Raja, they place white or black pebbles on the scale according to the karmic merits or debits of the judged. A council of deities sitting in the Court of Judgment, many of them animal-headed, ensures impartial justice and the regularity of the procedure. According to the result of the weighing, the dead are assigned to one of the six realms of existence.

The realm of the gods (devaloka) is described as a state of existence filled with endless delights and pleasures. Mythology describes heavenly and paradisean realms with gorgeous gardens, splendid palaces, brilliant gems and precious metals. This realm can be experienced in life by a consciousness suffused with loving kindness and compassion. In everyday existence, it manifests by being born into a loving, affluent family with access to spiritual scriptures and practice. When awareness is lacking, this domain is expressed as pride in the ego and one's separate identity, and the transient pleasures of worldly rank and wealth.

The realm of the jealous gods (asuraloka) is a domain entirely governed by jealousy and envy. Here the purpose of life is to function, survive, and win in the atmosphere of intrigues. On the archetypal level, it is the world of the titans, angry warrior demigods, who are in constant battle with the gods. In everyday life, it is expressed as the world of international diplomacy, military leaders, and politicians. One is born into this realm as a result of intense jealousy.

The realm of the hungry ghosts (pretaloka) is inhabited by the *pretas*, pitiful creatures with insatiable appetite. Their large, extended bellies demand satiation, but their tiny mouths are the size of pinholes, so the hungry ghosts can never be satisfied. This realm is characterized by tremendous longing for gathering possessions and material gains. However, even as we gather the fruits of our desire and possess them, we are unable to enjoy them, and we are left feeling more hungry and more deprived. As in addiction, our satisfaction does not last, and a fleeting experience of pleasure leads to further endless searching. This is the suffering that is associated with greed.

In the realm of Hell (narakaloka) one is exposed to extreme tortures, each of which represents in the last analysis the forces operating in our own psyche. The Eight Hot Hells consist of fields and mountains of red-hot metal, rivers of molten iron, and claustrophobic space permeated with fire. The extreme opposite occurs in the Eight Cold Hells, where all is frozen and covered with ice and snow. Those who committed impious acts motivated by violent anger are sent to the hot Hells; the cold Hells are for those whose acts resulted from selfish motives and pride. Additional tortures abound in this realm: being hacked or sawed to pieces, strangled with nooses, pierced by spikes, and exposed to crushing pressures. This realm also includes the horrible Avitchi Hell, where those who used sorcery to destroy their enemies or those who deliberately neglected to fulfill Tantric vows endure immeasurable tortures for ages.

The animal realm (tiryakaloka) is characterized by a dull way of life: mere surviving on a simple and uncomplicated level, where a sense of security alternates with episodes of fear. Anything irregular or unpredictable is perceived as threatening and becomes a source of confusion and paranoia. The animal realm is characterized by the absence of humor—the animals can experience pleasure and pain, but the sense of humor or irony is missing in their life.

The human realm (manakaloka) is a domain where pleasure and pain are balanced. Like the realm of the hungry ghosts (pretaloka), there is incessant passion to explore and seek pleasure. However, this loka also shares with the animal realm (tiryakaloka) the tendency to operate in such a way that one creates a safe and predictable situation. An important characteristic of the human realm is a sense of territoriality inspiring the invention of clever and cunning tools for self-protection and defeat of others. This leads to a world of tremendous success and achievement. However, when this process lacks conscious awareness, it results in a dangerous situation where people lose control of their lives. The advantage of this realm is that it offers the best conditions for achieving liberation.

Tibetan spiritual practice cultivates the awareness necessary to enter each of these experiential realms without entrapment. The essential strategy in approaching all domains of existence, whether they involve the challenges of everyday life, encounters with radiant and wrathful deities, or adventures in the various lokas, consists in realizing that all are ultimately products of our own mind, and that all forms are actually empty.

When the lights of the six lokas are dawning on the person at this stage of the bardo journey, an attempt can be made to close the door of the womb and prevent an unfavorable reincarnation. The *Bardo Thödol* suggests several strategies for this purpose. For example, one can contemplate one's tutelary deity or meditate on the clear light; additional possibilities are to realize the essential emptiness of all samsaric apparitions or to focus on the chain of good karma.

One of these methods is particularly interesting, since it seems to predate by many centuries Sigmund Freud's discovery of the Oedipus complex. The *Bardo Thödol* suggests that to avoid a particular reincarnation, one can try to avoid the strong feelings experienced at this time toward one's future parents, who are perceived as naked bodies engaged in sexual intercourse. In agreement with modern depth psychology, these emotions take the form of attraction to the parent of the opposite sex and repulsion or anger toward the parental figure of one's own gender.

If all the opportunities for liberation have been missed, one is irresistibly maneuvered by vivid illusions and incarnation into a new body, and rebirth will inevitably follow. With proper guidance, the unfortunate individual still has one hope left: the possibility of some influence concerning the choice of the womb into which he or she will be born. With the right environment and support, the new life might offer opportunities for spiritual practice and better preparation for the next journey through the bardo states.

The description of the tortures experienced in the Sidpa Bardo reflects the influence of the Bön religion. Note the comparison of the following passage from the *Bardo Thödol* to the description of a typical shamanic crisis (see the initiation of the Avam-Samoyed shaman in Chapter 1):

> The Lord of Death will place round thy neck a rope and drag thee along; he will cut off thy head, tear out thy heart, pull out thy intestines, lick up thy brain, drink thy blood, eat thy flesh, and gnaw thy bones; but thou will be incapable of dying. Even when thy body is hacked to pieces, it will revive again. The repeated hacking will cause intense pain and torture.

The descriptions of the various figures and events of the Sidpa Bardo also closely resemble those of the visionary scenes of the Egyptian *Pert Em Hru*. For example, the encounter with the world of horrifying rakshasas, menacing monsters, and dangerous forces of nature is reminiscent of the treacherous ordeals in the Tuat. There are also striking parallels between the scenes of judgment: the weighing of the good and bad deeds of the deceased with the assistance of the monkey-headed Shinje and various other zoomorphic deities echoes the events and characters in the Hall of Maat. Furthermore the usually ibis-headed Thoth has in some texts the form of a baboon. Variations on the theme of judgment of the dead can also be found in Chinese and Japanese Buddhist, Zoroastrian, and Christian eschatological mythology.

I mentioned earlier the similarity between the experiences in psychedelic sessions and those depicted in the books of the dead. Harvard researchers Timothy Leary, Richard Alpert, and Ralph Metzner found the parallels between these two situations so striking that they called their first book describing their experiments with LSD *The Psychedelic Experience: A Manual Based on the Tibetan Book of the Dead* (Leary, Alpert, and Metzner 1964). They also attempted to guide their subjects in the LSD sessions by reading passages from the *Bardo Thödol* to them.

Death and Rebirth of Quetzalcoatl: The Nahuatl Book of the Dead

Quetzalcoatl, an extremely complex and multifaceted Nahuatl (Aztec) deity, was by far the most important archetypal symbol of death and rebirth in the pre-Columbian world. Although he was artistically rendered in many different ways, Quetzalcoatl appeared most frequently in the form of a plumed serpent, symbolizing the union of the earthly and the spiritual elements of human nature. His name was a composite of two Nahuatl words: *quetzal*, a rare exotic bird of brilliant green color, and *coatl*, a serpent.

Another name for Quetzalcoatl was Precious Twin, an allusion to his identification with the planet Venus and its two aspects as Morning Star and Evening Star. He was also known as Ehecatl (the God of Wind), Lord of Dawn, Lord of the Land of the Dead, and by many other names. In the Mayan culture, he was referred to as Kukulcan.

Quetzalcoatl was born of the goddess Coatlicue, whose principal function was to solidify the transcendent spirit into the tangible material world. When the Sun took her for his bride, all the powerful generative and destructive forces of nature came into being, and Quetzalcoatl was the fruit of this union. Thus a trinity was formed of great balance and harmony: the Sun, as the male generative power, Coatlicue representing the Earth, and Quetzalcoatl associated with the planet Venus. While Coatlicue embodied primarily the forces that entrap the spirit in the material world, Quetzalcoatl symbolized the possibility of redeeming matter and reconnecting with the spiritual aspect of the world. The mysterious process through which this was possible was beautifully described in the myth about Quetzalcoatl's fall and penance, a profound story of annihilation, transformation, and rebirth.

The principal myth of Quetzalcoatl is an esoteric story of deep spiritual meaning, expressing an important universal truth. It describes Quetzalcoatl as a wise, good, and pure ruler of the City of Gods, which was established after the creation of the Fifth Sun. His heavenly rival and polar opposite, Tezcatlipoca, or Smoking mirror, engineered his downfall by intoxicating him with a drink of pulque. Under its influence, Quetzalcoatl committed incest with his sister Xochiquetzal, the goddess of love and beauty. After regaining sobriety, he realized what had happened and imposed severe penance upon himself. He first disposed of all his material riches and spent four days in a stone coffin. Then he traveled to the celestial shore of divine waters where he built a large pyre. Having donned his feathers and mask, he threw himself into the flames. As he was burning, all the rare birds gathered to watch him turn into ashes. Eight days later, his heart rose like a flaming star. After his physical form died and was consumed by fire, Quetzalcoatl underwent a journey through Mictlan, the Underworld and the land of the dead, accompanied by his twin Xolotl in the form of a dog.

Quetzalcoatl's journey through the Underworld began in the East, the Place of Burning, where he climbed on the pyre and was burnt to death. His ashes were scattered by the wind and transformed into a flock of beautiful birds. His heart or spiritual essence did not die in the fire but was resuscitated from his ashes and began its complex journey. In this form he first passed through the South, the Place of Thorns—the realm of cutting, dismembering, and decapitating. In the West, he traveled by two pyramid temples; the first temple was the abode of dead warriors and the second harbored women who had died in childbirth. Here Quetzalcoatl disappeared in the open throat of the earth dragon Cipactli and subsequently emerged in two forms—a red and a black one. The North was the darkest and lowest region of the subterranean world, the realm of the Dead. Here the red Quetzalcoatl was sacrificed by the black one and then, as the black one, he immolated himself. Transformed into a hummingbird, Quetzalcoatl then ascended in the eastern sky as the Morning Star, the Lord of Dawn.

The story of Quetzalcoatl's penance, death, dramatic journey through the Underworld, and transformation is the main content of the famous *Codex Borgia*, a Nahuatl screenfold filled with religious and ritualistic symbolism. The experiences that Quetzalcoatl undergoes during his underground journey are similar to descriptions found in the *Bardo Thödol*. During his descent into the chthonic Realm of the Dead, he encounters an entire pantheon of tzitzimimes, demons of darkness, and of wrathful deities threatening to destroy him. He also meets many peaceful deities, who are nourishing, protective, and supportive. As he passes through the regions of the Underworld, he is divided into two Quetzalcoatls, and his dark twin brother Xolotl is allied with his rival, Tezcatlipoca. After disintegrating into his physical, emotional, mental, and spiritual components, Quetzalcoatl transcends all the opposites and during his transformation into Venus achieves a state of spiritual wholeness. This state has been represented in Tibet and many other cultures by the sacred symbol of the mandala. The *Borgia Codex* contains some of the finest mandalas of all times.

During his journey through the Underworld Mictlan, the Land of the Dead, Quetzalcoatl succeeds in obtaining from Mictlantecuhtli, Lord of the Dead, the bones of a man and a woman and escapes with them after undergoing many trials and tribulations. When he redeems them with his own blood, the couple is able to start inhabiting the world. After this accomplishment, Quetzalcoatl ascends to Heaven and is transformed as the Lord of Dawn into the planet Venus, the Morning Star. He then repeats this journey as this astronomical body, first appearing in the western sky as the Evening Star, then disappearing underground, and finally reappearing in the eastern sky as the Morning Star to reunite with the rising sun.

The Quetzalcoatl myth is thus an expression of the universal theme of death and resurrection, sin and repentance. Since Quetzalcoatl, as one of the four sons of the supreme Creator, was already divine when he succumbed to mortal sin, the story clearly describes the perennial motif of all great religions: the incarnation of the pure spiritual principle into gross matter and the agonizing redemption of matter by spirit. Quetzalcoatl's journey through the Underworld and his celestial ascent represent a major Mesoamerican archetypal blueprint for the posthumous journey of the soul and for the initiatory death-rebirth experience.

This is reminiscent of the Egyptian *Pert Em Hru*, where the experiences of the deceased person and the initiate in the mysteries of Isis and Osiris were closely related to the diurnal/nocturnal journey of the Sun God through the Underworld. But while the Egyptian version made the astronomical association exclusively with the sun, linking death with sunset and rebirth with sunrise, the Mesoamerican version featured Venus and its different phases. It ascribed to Venus the role of mediator between night and day and between good and evil and also portrayed Venus as an agent facilitating transcendence of opposites within human nature. The importance of Venus for Mesoamerica is not entirely surprising, since in that latitude it shines with incredible brilliance and appears as large as a snowball in the dawn sky.

The myth of Quetzalcoatl played a very important role in the history of Mexico. For pre-Hispanic cultures, Quetzalcoatl/Kukulkan was also a legendary culture hero, who mysteriously appeared and shared with them his divine wisdom as an enlightened ruler. He provided divine guidance for his people, founded their religion, and taught them the arts of civilization. When he suddenly vanished without traces, his disappearance was as enigmatic as his arrival. For many years, Mesoamerican people eagerly expected his return. According to the legend, Quetzalcoatl had unusual physical features, including a white complexion and a beard. As the story goes, Hernando Cortez fit this description. This similarity played into the hands of the conquistadores, as many Mesoamericans perceived Cortez as the incarnation of Quetzalcoatl. Since the myth of Quetzalcoatl was the basic religious theme common to all Mesoamerica, the conquistadores' victory was all the more assured.

Adventures of the Hero Twins: The Mayan Book of the Dead

The ancient Mayan civilization was quite sophisticated and had a rich cultural heritage, but much of its literary legacy has been lost. This was partially due to the climate of Central America, an unfortunate combination of heat and moisture that accelerated the degradation of easily perishable documents. However, the Spanish invaders were mostly responsible, because they deliberately destroyed enormous amounts of literary treasures—especially the so-called "codices," accordion-like bark paper screenfolds with rich and colorful illustrations. They presented a wealth of information about various aspects of Mayan life, and unfortunately only a few of them escaped the Spaniards' ravaging. No codices exist from the Classical Period (before A.D. 900), and only four survived from the Post-Classical Period (from A.D. 900 to the Spanish conquest in the sixteenth century).

The Mayans lived with sharp awareness of death. Short life expectancy, high infant mortality, and the combination of warfare and sacrificial rituals made death an ever-present reality in their everyday life. Much of Mayan ritual and art was dedicated to posthumous existence, from the soul's entrance into the Underworld, Xibalba, to a

Mayan Hero Twins. Drawing after a Mayan vase depicting the Hero Twins, Hunahpu and Xbalanque, whose resourcefulness helped them to vanquish the Xibalba lords. The bat hovering overhead recalls their ordeal in the House of Bats, where Hunahpu was decapitated.

final rebirth and apotheosis. Mayan mythology and funerary art described death as an intricate journey. Its important stages and challenges were depicted on coffins, wall paintings, pottery, jades, and other objects, which accompanied the deceased during the great transition.

In spite of this keen interest in death and dying, no Mayan eschatological texts comparable to the Egyptian or Tibetan Book of the Dead have survived from the Classical Period. However, Mayologist Michael Coe identified a well-defined group of funerary vessels, which he designated as "codex-style ceramics," because their style was very similar to that of the Mayan codices. He concluded that the artists who created these masterpieces were the same as those who painted the bark accordion scrolls (Coe 1978). Heart surgeon and archaeologist Francis Robicsek, a scholar who had studied the Mayan funeral vases extensively, went one step farther. He became convinced that these vases not only resembled the codices, but placed in proper sequence they actually *were* codices (Robicsek 1981).

To support this assumption, Robicsek visited many Mayan archeological sites, as well as institutional and private collections worldwide. Together with anthropologist-hieroglyphist Donald M. Hales, he made the first complete study of the Mayan codex-style ceramics, which encompassed all known examples. The two scholars realized that many of the vases fell into groups, each of which represented a single underworld myth or tale. They were able to suggest a tentative sequence of funerary ceramics, which together represent the "Mayan Book of the Dead," although its stories with accompanying illustrations are scattered on individual funeral vases and are not parts of a comprehensive and coherent text comparable to the *Bardo Thödol.*

The codex style as a technique for decorating vases was used during the Late Classic Period, probably around the turn of the 8th century A.D. This period marked the greatest economic and political prosperity of the Mayan city-states, and the artists of this time created some of the best works of pre-Columbian art. The scenes depicted on the vases of the Mayan "ceramic codex" are extremely rich and complex and are painted in a combination of white, black, red, and Maya blue colors. Some represent underworld lords and ladies with their attendants, the Hero Twins, palace ceremonies, sacrificial scenes, warfare, hunts, and ritual ballgames. Others depict a rich array of mythological inhabitants of Xibalba.

Various anthropomorphic, zoomorphic, and skeletal beings are prominently featured in this spectrum of fantastic figures, as well as an entire menagerie of chthonic creatures—the Great Bearded Dragon, the mysterious shape-shifting Cauac, the Vision Serpent of Bloodletting, the Principal Bird Deity, the Celestial Monster, and the scaly toad-like Uinal. Some of the many animals represented on these vases include jaguars, jaguar-dogs, spider monkeys, bats, rabbits, vultures, moan-birds, serpents, turtles, toads, fish, fireflies, and scorpions. Certain figures are wearing sacrificial scarves and holding triadic bowls, which contain enucleated eyes, bones, and severed hands.

The rich pantheon of Xibalba also includes a large group of death gods. Many of the Xibalban underworld lords are shown with very old, toothless human faces and some combine male and female characteristics. Their breath and farts are so foul and pungent that they appear in the form of huge visible scrolls. They often wear as jewelry enucleated eyes or disembodied bones. Named for various causes of death, such as disease, old age, sacrifice, and war, the underworld lords are often represented with bony bodies, distended bellies, and black marks signifying decay. The Mayologists refer to them sometimes by their Mayan names, sometimes by capital letters.

Xibalba was a terrifying and dismal place, which in many ways resembled the Egyptian Tuat, the Sidpa Bardo of the Tibetan Book of the Dead, and the underworlds of the shamanic cultures. Filled with the stench of decaying corpses and rotting blood, it was the source of diseases that plagued humanity. The word "Xibalba" is derived from *xib*, meaning "fear, terror, trembling with fright." Like the Middle World (the world of everyday life), Xibalba had landscapes and architecture, including temples and palaces of the Lords of Death. In general, the Underworld of the Maya Classical Period bore great similarity to that of the *Popol Vuh*, the famous epic of the Quiche Maya Indians of Guatemala, with one significant exception. The images on funeral vases of the ceramic codex indicate that it was a watery environment or was in some important way associated with water. As in Greek mythology, death and the passage through the Mayan Underworld involved crossing of a body of water. Entering Xibalba was often represented as a canoe trip or as sinking under water; other aquatic symbols were used, including various kinds of fish, rows of shells, water lilies, and alligator-like creatures.

While some of these images are clearly related to myths and legends that are now lost, many others seem to reflect the famous mythological story of the Hero Twins, who underwent drastic ordeals during their visit to the Underworld and ultimately experienced death and rebirth. The description of their adventures constitutes an important part of the *Popol Vuh*. This document was created shortly after the conquest by an anonymous Guatemalan Indian, but is clearly based on a much older oral tradition. The *Popol Vuh* chronicles kings and the wars they fought among themselves and with their neighbors. Its most distinct mythological theme is perpetual effort of the gods of ancient America to evolve a living thing that will have the capacity of knowing and worshipping its maker.

The most relevant section of the epic describes the victorious encounter of the Hero Twins with the lords of the Underworld, the rulers of Xibalba. The story begins when the father of the twins Hun-Hunahpu and his companion Vucub-Hunahpu are lured to the Underworld by the Xibalba lords to play ball. After their defeat, they are killed and decapitated; the Underworld lords then hang Hun-Hunahpu's head on a calabash tree as a warning. The tree, previously barren, immediately bears fruit, which is hailed as miraculous. When a maiden named Xquic comes to look at the fruit, Hun-Hunahpu's skull spits into her hand and makes her pregnant. The young woman then returns to the surface of the earth and gives birth to the Hero Twins Hunahpu ("Hunter") and Xbalanque ("Infant Jaguar)."

When the twins grow up into beautiful youths, they discover the rubber ball, which was used by their father, along with some accessories needed to play the game. They begin to practice rigorously and with great determination. After acquiring extraordinary skills, they decide to descend to Xibalba to avenge their father's death. In the Underworld, the Xibalba lords subject Hunahpu and Xbalanque to a series of difficult ordeals. The twins successfully overcome all the dangers in the House of Gloom, the House of Knives, the House of Cold, the House of Jaguars, and the House of Fire. However, in the House of Bats they almost meet defeat when a bat pulls off Hunahpu's head. The Xibalba people take the head and hang it in the ballcourt as a trophy.

Xbalanque calls the animals, and the turtle takes the shape of Hunahpu's head. Xbalanque then bounces the ball (turtle) far over the court, where a rabbit is stationed with the task to steal the ball and bound off with it, encouraging the Xibalba people to run after him. Xbalanque uses this diversion and rescues Hunahpu's real head; Hunahpu is restored to life, and the game ends in a tie. During the next test, the twins willingly jump into the flames of a great fire, knowing that by then their prowess has won them immortality. Five days later, they rise from the dead and perform miracles in the guise of ragged fishermen. They burn houses and make them reappear, then cut themselves to pieces and return to life looking younger and more beautiful then before. When the Xibalba lords ask the same for themselves, the twins sacrifice them and do not bring them back to life.

In the written version of *Popol Vuh*, the Hero Twins are taken into Heaven and become the Sun and the Moon. Mayologist J. Eric S. Thompson argued that this version reflected a distortion and degeneration of the original story due to Spanish influence and suggested that in the oral tradition the twins were changed into Sun and Venus. These celestial bodies were considered in the Mayan mythology to be brothers, whereas the feminine Moon was seen as the Sun's wife. This correction would make Hunahpu into the Mayan equivalent of Quetzalcoatl. It is also likely that the original oral version of *Popol Vuh* placed much greater emphasis on the spiritual aspect of the transformation of the twins.

Although the *Popol Vuh* itself was put into writing after the conquest, the legends describing the birth, life, death, and rebirth of Hunahpu and Xbalanque are remnants of an important mythic cycle from the Classic Period. The adventures of the Hero Twins reveal the Mayan concept of the soul's journey through death and subsequent rebirth and provide important information for defeating death and achieving resurrection. The story thus conveys an important message of universal relevance: it suggests that the kings, the nobles, and possibly all human beings assume at death the identity of one of the legendary twins and partake in his experiential adventures.

The incomplete evidence of the Mayan Ceramic Codex thus seems to indicate that one of the Mesoamerican archetypal patterns for the posthumous journey of the soul and possibly also for the sacred initiation of death and rebirth was closely related to the themes of *Popol Vuh*. It portrays the transformation process of death and rebirth as a series of difficult ordeals and experiences that occur in chthonic realms, with their characteristic protagonists. The theme of the ritual ballgame is a particularly interesting and mysterious aspect of this symbolism, as the ballgame was an important aspect of everyday life in Mesoamerican cultures and may have offered the opportunity to act out the myth of the Hero Twins during one's lifetime.

Strong evidence exists that in pre-Columbian cultures the knowledge of the eschatological realms was not limited to the information derived from actual near-death experiences. Much of it very likely came from visionary states induced by various psychedelic plants and by the ritual practice of bloodletting. Modern ethnobotanists have identified many psychedelic plants that are still used by various aboriginal groups in Central America. Among the most well known are the sacred mushrooms (*Psilocybe mexicana*), known to the Indians as teonanacatl or "Flesh of the Gods," the Mexican cactus peyote (*Lophophora williamsii*), the morning glory seeds (*Ipomoea violacea*) called by the natives ololiuqui, and *Salvia divinatorum*, also known as diviner's sage.

In the highland area of Guatemala, as well as southern Mexico and El Salvador, archaeologists have long been unearthing mysterious stone figures with an umbrella-like top, dating from 1000 B.C. to A.D. 500. Most are about a foot tall, and research conducted several decades ago showed that they represent psychedelic mushrooms. Similar mushroom representations occur in the illustrations of various pre-Columbian codices. Thanks to combined efforts of mycologists Gordon Wasson and Roger Heim, ethnobotanist Richard Schultes, and chemist Albert Hofmann, the mushrooms have been identified as *Psilocybe coerulescens* and its close relatives; and their psychoactive alkaloids, psilocin and psilocybin, have been isolated, chemically identified, and prepared in pure form (Schultes and Hofmann 1979). Ritual use of magic mushrooms, which had a long history in various pre-Columbian cultures, is also very common in contemporary Mexico, particularly among the Mazatec, Zapotec, and Mixtec Indians.

According to archaeological discoveries, ritual use of peyote is more than 3,000 years old. Ever since the arrival of the first Europeans in the New World, peyote use has provoked violent attacks by the Christian Church. Like psychedelic mushrooms, it was condemned by the Spanish missionaries as "satanic trickery" and was subjected to severe suppression and persecution. Even so, peyote is still used in modern Mexico among the Huichol, Cora, and Tarahumara Indians. In the last hundred years, peyote rituals have also spread among various tribes of North America. Paintings on ancient vessels reveal that peyote was administered among the ancient Mayans in the form of ritual enemas, and evidence also suggests that peyote was used in Central America, together with the magic mushrooms, as a premedication for sacrifice.

It is also likely that ancient Mesoamerican cultures, including the Mayans, used for ritual purposes certain varieties of toads (genus Bufo), whose skin secretions contain tryptamine derivatives with proven or alleged psychedelic properties, such as 5-methoxy-*N,N*-dimethyltryptamine and bufotenine. This assumption is based on many iconographic representations of toads in Mesoamerican art, as well as mythological references.

Pre-Columbian cultures also practiced ritual bloodletting. This practice can be traced back to the Late Pre-Classic Period, and its imagery also pervades Classic Mayan art. Bloodletting was a powerful mind-altering method that induced visionary experiences through massive loss of blood and subsequent shock. Originally seen as an occasional act of personal penance, it was later recognized as an important and widespread ritual practice, particularly among the Mayans. Bloodletting was basic to kingship, mythology of the world order, and public rituals of all kinds. In the visions induced by this procedure, the Mayans came into contact with the world of gods and also with their ancestors, who were expected to appear in their visions.

Ritual bloodletting opened up an experiential realm that was not ordinarily accessible before the time of biological death. The Mayans used the symbol of the Vision Serpent for the experiences induced by blood loss and shock. This symbol represented the contact between the everyday world of human beings and the supernatural realms. Many Mayan paintings and reliefs depict scenes of bloodletting, as well as vision serpents symbolizing the inner experiences induced by it. Bleeding was usually achieved by using lancets made of stingray spines, flint, or obsidian to wound the tongue, earlobes, and genitals. The lancet was perceived as a sacred object with enormous power; it was personified in the form of the Perforator God. The Mayans saw the blood drawn from different parts of the body as necessary sustenance for the gods.

The ritual ballgame was the central theme in the internecine confrontation between the Hero Twins, Hunahpu and Xbalanque, and the death gods ruling the Underworld Xibalba. The Mayan version of the game, pok-ta-pok, as described in the *Popol Vuh*, played a critical role in pre-Columbian mythology of death and rebirth, as well as in sacrificial rituals. Like its Aztec counterpart, it has been for many centuries a subject of fascination for scholars and many members of the general public visiting the Mayan archaeological sites. While the exoteric aspects of this game—the layout and architecture of the ballcourts and the technical elements of the play—are well known, its full esoteric meaning and spiritual symbolism have remained shrouded in mystery. The ritual ballgame was clearly deeply connected with death and sacrifice, two areas with which the Mayan culture was obsessed.

The Mayan ballgame was a dangerous sport that required skillful manipulation of a heavy rubber ball, about a foot in diameter. The players wore protective garments on their legs and arms, the parts of the body that took most of the painful blows. Teams of one to four players competed in controlling the ball without touching it with their hands and directing it toward markers or rings. The objective of the game was to make the ball pass through the stone ring attached high on the wall of the ballcourt, or at least to hit the marker. It was very difficult to actually drive the ball through the

Sacrifice in the Ballcourt. A line drawing after a sculpture from the Great Ballcourt in Chichen Itza depicts the culmination of the ballgame: the victorious players decapitate the defeated ones. The ball is represented as a belching skull; six snakes and an elaborate tree sprouting from the victim symbolize the fertility and life energy that this sacrifice will bring. (Chichen Itza, Yucatan, Mexico, Mayan Post Classic period, A.D. 900-1200)

opening; even the legendary players succeeded only a few times in their lifetime. The play was extremely popular, as attested by the number of ballcourts disseminated throughout Central America.

While the challenges of the game, the potential for a disabling blow from the heavy rubber ball, and the accompanying gambling created part of the excitement, it was most likely the close mythological connection with death and sacrifice that was responsible for its spellbinding nature and popularity. The ballgame was a gladiatorial combat that tested the strength of a captive or a slave and his desire to avoid death. Losers were sacrificed, and their hearts were offered to the gods. Some of the ballcourts even had racks for exhibiting the skulls of the less fortunate players.

The deeper symbolism of the ballgame suggests that the winner, like the Hero Twins who in the *Popol Vuh* defeated the lords of Xibalba, had the capacity to triumph over death. When played by royalty, the Mayan rulers might have dressed as the Hero Twins, enacting thus the roles of demigods whom they emulated. The defeat of the opposition by the kings dressed as warriors or deities was then recast in stone as a victorious combat with death and with the dark forces of the Underworld.

Many images on the codex-style vessels emphasize the importance of the themes of death and resurrection in Mayan mythology and religion. In the *Popol Vuh*, the ordeals of the Hero Twins are followed by rebirth, divinization of the brothers, and their transformation into celestial bodies. In Mayan visual art, the representations of the triumphant ending of the spiritual journey—rebirth and resurrection—were generally represented much less frequently than its challenges and ordeals. This latter aspect may be more heavily featured because most of the objects carrying the images were found in the tombs, and their purpose was to prepare the deceased for the vicissitudes of the passage. Regardless, many paintings and sculptures represent extraordinary examples of the rebirth theme. These artifacts portray young lords being born from a cracked skull or a turtle carapace and emerging from water lily blossoms. The lotus was a powerful spiritual symbol in pre-Columbian cultures, as in India and Egypt. On Mayan ceramics it also symbolizes a watery environment—a river, a pond, a lake, or a sea. On a deeper level, it stands for the mythological primeval lake under the earth, the source of all life. The Lacandon Mayans still have a creation myth in which the creator deity makes first a water lily from which then the gods are born. The lotus, which originates in the mud, emerges through water, and opens up to the sun, is a very fitting symbol of spiritual rebirth. It also represents ancestry, the Underworld, life, death, and resurrection, and appears in association with the Mayan calendar.

Often the underworld scenes on Mayan vases show the Infant Jaguar in specific relations to a fantastic and mysterious entity, the Cauac Monster. The Cauac has very strange, almost freakish characteristics: it can vary greatly in size and shape from one vessel to another and has the propensity to split, cleave, and produce bizarre extensions of itself. Besides representing a monster, the Cauac can also serve as a sacrificial altar or as a description of a location—a cave-like setting for various activities. Francis Robicsek has shown that the relative positions of the Infant Jaguar and the Cauac depicted on Maya vases can be arranged into a meaningful sequence and suggested that they might be related to the movements of a celestial body (Robicsek 1981). However, closer inspection shows that this sequence very likely reflects biological birth, with the Cauac as a stylized representation of the delivering uterus. This seems to confirm the findings of modern consciousness research, which link the experiences of psychospiritual death and rebirth to reliving of the birth trauma.

For ancient Mayans, the myth of the Hero Twins and their visit to the Underworld with subsequent rebirth and deification provided an optimistic model for their own posthumous journey, as well as their initiatory experience of psychospiritual death and rebirth. The thematic and symbolic parallels between this Mayan eschatological mythology, on the one hand, and the Egyptian *Pert Em Hru* and the Tibetan *Bardo Thödol*, on the other, are highly significant. On another level, an additional important common denominator for all texts is that much of the knowledge they convey was mediated by holotropic states of consciousness induced by psychedelics and by powerful non-drug techniques. This commonality provides an important bridge to modern consciousness research and makes the information conveyed by Mayan funeral art relevant for our time.

Ars Moriendi: The Art of Proper Dying and Living

While many people in the West have heard of the Tibetan Book of the Dead and the Egyptian Book of the Dead, it is generally less known that an extensive body of literature and associated visual art related to problems of death and dying also exists in the European cultural tradition. This material is usually referred to as *Ars moriendi* or the "Art of Dying." Toward the end of the Middle Ages, the works belonging to this genre were among the most popular and widespread literary forms in many European countries, particularly Austria, Germany, France, and Italy.

Intense interest in death and dying in medieval times resulted from the general uncertainty of human existence during this period of history. Death was ever present in everyday life in the cities and villages. The mortality rate was astronomical—people were dying by the tens of thousands in various wars and battles, in mass epidemics of infectious diseases such as plague and syphilis, during travels through dangerous territories, in the course of long episodes of famine, and from the unhygienic conditions of living.

People often witnessed the deaths of their relatives, neighbors, and friends. During the outbreak of pestilence a quarter, a third, or even a half of an entire population could be exterminated. Funeral corteges and processions with corpses were standard features of daily life. Mass burials, burning of cadavers, public executions, as well as immolations of heretics and alleged witches and Satanists in *autos-da-fe*, were conducted on a large scale. According to some estimates, the number of the people accused of witchcraft and killed by the Holy Inquisition alone exceeded three million.

The all-pervading presence of death and the far-reaching corruption and disintegration of the social, political, and religious fabric in medieval Europe provided the context that inspired the *Ars moriendi* literature. Both the mystical and the scholastic tradition contributed to the development of this eschatological genre, and many outstanding theologians considered its topic worthy of significant time and energy. However, the message of *Ars moriendi* was not limited to sick, old, and dying people concerned primarily with biological demise. Like the Egyptian *Pert Em Hru* and the Tibetan *Bardo Thödol*, the European eschatological writings addressed not only the issues related to death, but also the basic problems of human existence.

Ars Vivendi, or Art of (Proper) Living

The extensive body of literature referred to as *Ars moriendi* falls into two broad categories. The first deals primarily with the significance of death in life and should be called more appropriately *Ars vivendi*, or "Art of (Proper) Living." It emphasizes the importance of the right attitude toward death for everyday life and describes a strategy of existence that leads to salvation. The second category then focuses more specifically on the experiences of death and dying, as well as the management of dying people and the emotional and spiritual support for them in their final days and hours.

A recurrent theme of many works in the category of *Ars vivendi* is contemplation of death (*contemplatio mortis*) that leads to the contempt for the world and for secular pursuits (*contemptus mundi*). In many different forms this literature conveys a strong reminder that life oriented exclusively toward material goals is futile and wasted: such an attitude is based on deep ignorance, possible only for those who are not aware that everything in the material world is impermanent and who have not accepted the sovereign role and paramount importance of death in all life.

The basic problem of human existence is best described by the Latin saying "mors certa, hora incerta" (death is certain, the hour uncertain). The greatest certainty in life is that we will die; the greatest uncertainty is the time when death will strike us. The awareness of death is the beginning of all wisdom; it introduces into human life constant vigilance and a tendency to avoid harmful behavior. Our main concern should not be to live long, to extend our life at all cost and by all possible means; but to live correctly, in accordance with the divine law. Since we do not know when death will strike us, we should live every moment of our lives as if it were our last.

This does not necessarily mean living in constant anxiety and anticipation of death. The more useful interpretation is to reduce the degree to which we waste time and energy in the pursuit of multiple external goals which cannot bring true satisfaction, and focus instead on the fullest possible experience of the gift of life as manifested in the present moment. A parable from the *Ars moriendi* lore which illustrates this attitude was one of the favorite teaching stories of Joseph Campbell, the greatest mythologist of the twentieth century:

> A man pursued by a vicious tiger falls into a deep precipice and manages to interrupt his fall by grabbing onto the branches of a shrub growing on a little knoll. As he slowly loses his strength, he notices a wild strawberry in a patch of grass near his face, reaches it with his tongue, and lets it slowly dissolve in his mouth. Did it taste good!

The works concerning the contempt of the world portrayed the impermanence and futility of all worldly pursuits in many symbolic images, metaphors, and parables. Their favorite targets were the powerful, rich, famous, and otherwise influential personages of the time. The members of the religious hierarchy—the bishop, cardinal, and pope—and representatives of secular power—the judge, military leader, Duke, King, and Caesar—appeared with great frequency. Depicting individuals who had achieved the highest goals in the material world and showing their despair at the moment of death was devastating proof of the deep truths contained in the succinct statements used in *Ars moriendi* to show the ultimate futility of all material strivings: *Vanitas vanitatum, omne est vanitas* (vanity of vanities, all is vanity), *Memento mori* (remember death), *Sic transit gloria mundi* (this is how passes the glory of the world), and *Memento, homo, quia pulvis es, et in pulverem reverteris* (Remember, man, that thou art dust and to dust shalt thou return).

The strongest argument for the contempt of material existence was the contemplation of the ugliness of death, which included realistic descriptions of the human body in various stages of putrefaction and decomposition. In certain forms of meditation, medieval monks were asked to visualize their own death and identify with their bodies as they were gradually reduced to rotting flesh, skeletons, and finally dust. Modern consciousness research has shown that exercises of this kind are much more than pathological indulgence in morbid topics. Deep acceptance of one's physicality, including the worst that biology has to offer, leads to the realization that we are more than our bodies. This understanding is a prerequisite to transcendence of the body and to spiritual opening. The basic message of the *Ars vivendi* thus was that we should not strive for worldly pleasures, power, and riches, since all these turn into sadness at the time of death. Instead, we should focus our attention on transcendental realities.

The theme of death, which was so powerfully expressed in a prosaic form in the literature on the contemplation of death and the contempt of the world, was also expressed in many *Memento mori* poems reminding people of their mortality. Especially interesting were polemic poems (*Streitgedichte*), in which philosophical and religious problems of life and death were presented in argumentative dialogues between man and death, world and man, life and death, soul and body, or the dying and the devil. In the poems called *Vado mori* (I am walking to die), dying representatives of various social groups or symbolic personifications of different human character traits shared their feelings and reflections. These poems were in many ways predecessors to the texts used in the dances of death (*danses macabres, Totentänze*), fascinating medieval manifestations of mass psychology, which are discussed later in this chapter.

The main objective of the *Ars moriendi* literature was to emphasize the futility of a life strategy dominated exclusively by the pursuit of secular goals and based on obtaining happiness from external achievements, such as money, material possessions, sensual pleasures, power, and fame. The texts used various means to demonstrate that such an orientation was unfulfilling and useless. Only spiritually oriented life could bring peace of mind and true satisfaction. In their efforts to divert people from menial and ultimately self-defeating ambitions and turn them toward God, the artists of *Ars moriendi* used the theme of death and impermanence as the ultimate teaching device. In the large body of literature, visual art, and music of *Ars moriendi*, we can detect three distinct and popular themes:

- The Triumph of Death
- The Dance of Death
- The Three Quick and the Three Dead

The Triumph of Death

If we mistakenly confuse who we are with what we have and see our acquisitions and possessions as an integral part of our personal identity, we will face a profound existential crisis at the time of our biological demise. The imminence of death confronts us mercilessly with the harsh reality that we cannot take any of our material possessions and worldly attributes with us. Naturally we have known this intellectually all along, but we have usually repressed the full emotional impact of this painful fact until we face this final moment of truth when denial is no longer possible.

At this moment we realize that what our society taught us about private property is actually a fallacy. We never really own anything; we only use it as long as we are alive. Nowhere is this truth more evident than with regard to land, which will be here for eons, long after we are all gone, as stated so powerfully in one version of the 1854 Treaty Oration, attributed by some sources to Chief Seattle. Moreover, when we are facing death, all the time we have spent seeking and pursuing false securities and sources of happiness in the material world now appears to have been wasted. We realize that by always orienting ourselves toward future achievements, we have never lived in the present and, in a sense, never really fully lived at all. The larger the scope of various existential crutches we have managed to accumulate, the more we have to let go of, and the harder the process of dying will be for us.

Many people have already achieved what we only fantasize about in our wildest dreams: the powerful, the rich, and the famous. We see clearly that their fabulous acquisitions, achievements, and power have not made them happy. And yet we tend to fool ourselves and believe that it would be different for us. The *Ars moriendi* literature focuses on this category of prominent and illustrious people, and the texts and images attempt to show that the glory of the world is of little value when we are facing death and that material attachments can actually represent a serious impediment and complication. The message is clear: external achievements failed to make the depicted individuals happy when they were alive and were not able to protect them against the ultimate crisis at the time of death.

The Grim Reaper is a great equalizer and does not differentiate. He does not shy away from wealth, fame, or power and takes away people of all walks of life, professions, and social classes. The texts of *Ars moriendi* abound with descriptions of dying kings, great military leaders, and popes or other representatives of the secular power or the Church. This literature portrays Death as the absolute ruler of everything: whatever is alive and exists will sooner or later die and be annihilated. The paintings, drawings, woodcuts, etchings, and sculptures inspired by *Ars moriendi*, which depict the final moments of the rich and powerful and the triumph of death, form an important chapter in the European history of art.

The basic dilemma of human existence—the need to find meaning in life against the background of death and impermanence—was graphically illustrated in the medieval picture of the Staircase of Life. This image represented the process of aging as ascending a staircase and getting older with each step. The top of the staircase symbolized the prime time of life and the remaining years were portrayed as a gradual descent on the same staircase. In a poignant contrast, the newborn baby in a cradle and the deceased person in a tomb occupied corresponding places on the opposite sides of the picture, forming a mirror image to each other. This powerful allegory suggested that this harsh reality of our existence must be considered as part of any intelligent adaptation to the process of life.

The same theme was expressed in a somewhat different way in the picture of the Wheel of Life, which showed Death towering over the globe as the absolute ruler of the world. Under this skeletal figure, a horizontal rotating wheel represented the course of human life. Each person entered this wheel as a small baby, grew older as it rotated, and fell off dead at the same place where he or she entered. A famous painting by Hans Baldung-Grien, *Three Ages of Woman*, represents very succinctly yet another variation on the same theme. It juxtaposes the image of the same woman in three periods of her life—as a little baby, a young beauty, and an old crone. Death in the background stands in the form of the Grim Reaper holding an hourglass counting the remaining days of life.

The most powerful and masterful depiction of the inescapable power of death is the sixteenth century painting by Pieter Brueghel the Elder, entitled *The Triumph of Death*. It illustrates the medieval concept of equality of all in death: king, bishop, knights, monks, soldiers, and peasants are attacked by death and defeated without any distinction. The unrelenting nature of death is convincingly conveyed by the artist's brilliant idea to portray it in the form of huge armies of skeletons outnumbering and overpowering their helpless victims. The atmosphere of horrifying catastrophes, such as fires, shipwrecks, and executions, completes the picture.

Dance of Death. Scenes from *La danse macabre des hommes* (the Dance of Death of Men), printed by Guyot Marchant, Paris, 1486, and from *La danse macabre des femmes* (the Dance of Death of Women), printed by Antoine Verard, Paris, 1486.

Bride and Prostitute. From *La danse macabre des femmes* (The Dance of Death of Women)

Pope and Emperor. From *La danse macabre des hommes* (the Dance of Death of Men)

Doctor and Lover. From *La danse macabre des hommes* (the Dance of Death of Men)

Astrologer and Bourgeois. From *La danse macabre des hommes* (the Dance of Death of Men),

Brueghel's masterpiece is as powerful in its totality as it is in every detail. One detail of this large canvas shows, for example, two figures representing secular and religious authority—the king and the bishop—at the time of their deaths. None of their earthly power is of any use at this moment. The skeletons casually claim their bodies and collect the gold and silver that these powerful figures have collected during their lifetimes. Another detail shows death in the form of a host of skeletons descending on a gay party of people pursuing the joys of life. While a gambler is trying to hide under the table and two lovers are trying to escape this world of terror by attending to each other, a resilient soldier is making a futile attempt to resist the unrelenting power of death.

The Dance of Death (Danse macabre, danza de la muerte, Totentänz)

While the representations of the Triumph of Death show the universal overwhelming power of death as the ultimate and undisputed ruler of everything that is alive, the theme of the Dance of Death focuses on the dynamic aspect of death. In this portrayal, Death encounters people in countless forms and contexts and sweeps them into its intoxicating frenzy. The theme of the Dance of Death was not only described in literature and portrayed in art, but also acted out in grotesque allegoric processions involving many thousands of participants and spectators. Large crowds of people in bizarre costumes and strange masks wandered through medieval towns dancing to the sounds of loud, penetrating music. The frantic dance of the living and the dead represented the all-conquering power, inevitability, and impartiality of Death. Plague epidemics killing people by the thousands gave these processions an apocalyptic background of extraordinary power.

The Dance of Death was a popular mass phenomenon and found its expression in literature, poetry, drama, and visual arts. It originated in the late thirteenth and early fourteenth centuries in France, where it was known as *danse macabre*; however, many other European countries had their local equivalents, such as the German *Totentanz* or the Spanish *danza de la muerte*. The concept, anticipated in the poems of *Vado mori* (I am walking toward my death), seems to have crystallized and gained momentum as a result of the Black Death in the mid-fourteenth century. The fourteenth century song "Ad mortem festinamus" (we are hurrying toward death) provides an early example of this motif in music, and toward the end of that century, a dramatized version was performed in a church in Normandy.

The earliest known example of the fully developed Dance of Death is a series of paintings that was formerly in the Paris graveyard Cimetière des Innocents. In this series, the whole hierarchy of church and state, from Pope and Emperor to child, clerk, and hermit, formed a dance configuration, the living alternating with skeletons and corpses who are escorting the living to the grave. This stern reminder of the inevitabil-

Orchestra of the Dead. Woodcut by Michael Wolgemut.
(From Hartmann Schedel's *Liber Chronicarum,* Nüremberg, 1493)

ity of death and exhortation to repentance was destroyed in 1669, but its reproduction survived in the woodcuts of the Paris printer Guyot Marchant, and the explanatory verses have also been preserved. A collection of woodcuts by the German painter Hans Holbein the Younger from the first half of the fifteenth century is another famous series of powerful illustrations depicting various themes of *Ars moriendi.*

The theme of the Dance of Death had a profound impact on the cultural life of Europe for a several centuries. Its motifs appeared in literature, poetry, caricatures, paintings, and sculptures, as well as music, pantomime, and ballet. Many prominent cultural figures were attracted and inspired by the Dance of Death, such as Johann Wolfgang von Goethe and Franz Liszt. The dance craze reached truly epidemic proportions in many European countries and was by far the most dramatic manifestation of the medieval preoccupation with death, because of its unusual psychological power transcending the barriers of sex, age, and social class. The dance emphasized the terrors of death to frighten sinners into repentance. By emphasizing the impartiality of death and social equality, it also served as a mockery of the pretenses of the rich and powerful.

The Three Quick and the Three Dead

A powerful medieval teaching tale of death and impermanence is the story of three young persons and three corpses. Three young and rich noblemen are riding in a hunt through the countryside with their retinue. At one point they discover three coffins with corpses in different stages of decay and decomposition. To their surprise, the corpses start talking and convey to them an unpleasant and distressing message about the truth, from which the aristocrats have been trying to escape by pursuing worldly pleasures: "We once were what you are now, and the time will come when you become what you see here." The most famous rendition of this theme in visual art is the large fresco in Camposanto de Pisa attributed usually to Francesco Traini, which shows the three corpses in their coffins communicating with the three noblemen. The same painting also portrays a party of their rich friends engaged in sorrow-free feasting and entertainment. In the background, devils are claiming the people who did not lead proper life and are transporting them to Hell.

The Art of Dying and the Attacks of Satan

The second major category of medieval works dealing with death is the literature on *Ars moriendi* in the narrower sense, including texts focusing on the actual experience of dying and on the art of guiding and supporting dying individuals on their last journey. As in the case of the texts of *Ars vivendi*, the ideas expressed in these works profoundly influenced not only literature and philosophy, but also the painting and sculpture of the time. The beginning of this literary genre can be traced back to the end of the fourteenth century, when the mortality rate reached critical dimensions, and it became physically impossible for the priests to visit personally all the seriously ill people and prepare them for dying.

Under these circumstances, many people died without clerical assistance and thus, as the Christian Church saw it, "in the middle of their sins." As a result, many concerned representatives of the clergy became interested in disseminating information to help people prepare for death while they were still alive. Dominican and Franciscan monks especially preached and taught about death and the last affairs of human beings. Originally, *Ars moriendi* was conceived as a pastoral manual for young priests to prepare them for work with dying individuals. Later, when the number of the priests was insufficient to meet the increasing demand, the texts were translated into popular

Attacks of Satan. According to medieval Christian belief, at the time of death the diabolic forces made their last desperate attempt to divert the soul from its way to heaven. These pictures portray the "attacks of Satan" by temptation through vanity, avarice, and impatience. (Xylographic Dutchblock-book edition of *Ars moriendi,* c. 1471)

languages to make them understandable and available for lay people.

Certain parts of these texts were deeply influenced by orthodox Christian doctrines. These portions focus on specific questions which the officials of the Church considered important for the dying and which, according to them, required specific answers. Other parts contain passages of great interest to thanatologists and transpersonal psychologists because they discuss the states of consciousness experienced by the dying to prepare them for various difficulties and challenges of the posthumous journey of the soul. Special sections also contain various instructions for the family members and other persons assisting the critically ill. These describe how to treat and guide individuals facing death during the last hours and days of their lives to ease their transition into the Beyond.

The number of such medieval death manuals seems at first truly overwhelming. However, many are actually variations on several original sources. In any case, several basic lines of thought and certain recurrent themes can be extracted from this part of the literature on *Ars moriendi*. As mentioned earlier, some of the texts are of a relatively formal nature, based on a rigid and codified system of specific questions addressed to the dying, which required prescribed answers. A standard set of concrete instructions and admonitions was also included, along with model prayers to Christ, Mary, and Archangel Michael. This aspect of the care for the dying was most directly influenced by traditional Christian beliefs and was an immediate outgrowth of orthodox doctrines.

Much more interesting from a modern point of view are other parts of the texts which, although also colored by traditional Christian symbolism, focus on the actual experiential aspects of dying. Among these, the phenomena usually referred to as the attacks of Satan (*die Anfechtungen Satans*) deserve special attention. These were specific challenges, which the dying typically experienced during the holotropic states of consciousness occurring in their last hours. The authorities of the Christian Church interpreted these difficult experiences as resulting from the devil's last minute desperate attempts to divert the souls from their way to Heaven by interfering at this most critical and strategic time.

Most of the manuals distinguished and discussed five major "attacks of the devil:"

- serious doubts regarding faith;
- desperation and agonizing qualms of conscience;
- impatience and irritability due to suffering;
- conceit, vanity, and pride, and
- greed, avarice, and other worldly concerns and attachments.

In addition, some texts add unwillingness to surrender to the process of dying.

Rich man, Old Man, Merchant, and Farmer. From *Imagines Mortis* by Hans Holbein the Younger. (Printed by J. Frellon, Lyons, 1547)

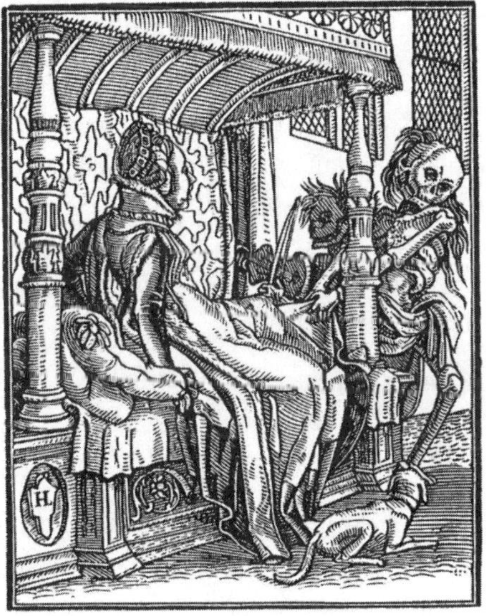

Emperor, Abbot, Duchess, and Nun. From *Imagines Mortis* by Hans Holbein the Younger. (Printed by J. Frellon, Lyons, 1547)

These attempts of the devil were then counteracted by divine interventions and influences that gave the dying a foretaste of Heaven, a sense of being subjected to divine judgment, a feeling of obtaining higher help, and a joyful promise of redemption. I have discussed earlier in this chapter similar passages from the Egyptian and Tibetan Books of the Dead, which describe death, the divine judgment, abodes of the Beyond, and rebirth in another lifetime.

Most medieval manuals agreed that the goal of this preparation for biological demise was to engender in the person facing death the right disposition and the right attitude toward dying. They particularly cautioned against instilling false hope in the moribund person. Open and honest confrontation with death was seen as absolutely crucial, and avoiding one's predicament was considered a major danger and pitfall for the dying person. Some of the manuals explicitly stated that it was less objectionable and harmful if the helpers evoked fear in the dying individual that later proved unsubstantiated than if they allowed him or her to use denial and therefore die unprepared.

The approach to the dying advocated in *Ars moriendi* was thus diametrically opposed to the practices that until recently have dominated modern Western medicine. In our hospitals, the attending physicians and other medical personnel often tried to conceal from the patients the diagnosis and prognosis of serious diseases, because they were afraid of the emotional reaction of the patient to the dismal news. The same attitude and strategy was also frequently shared by the family members. In our Spring Grove Program described in Chapter 13, we often encountered situations when the medical personnel and the relatives conspired and exerted great effort to hide the reality of the situation from the patient. Despite much progress in this area, this type of approach is not unusual even today.

7
CULTURAL PERSPECTIVES ON THE NATURE OF REALITY AND CONSCIOUSNESS

The greatest obstacle to discovery is not ignorance—
it is the illusion of knowledge.
– Daniel J. Boorstin, author and Librarian of Congress

THE BELIEF SYSTEMS of preindustrial cultures made the psychological situation of dying people easier compared to the typical experience of dying in today's Western technological civilization. People of earlier cultures typically believed in survival of consciousness after death, spiritual realities, ancestral realms, and reincarnation. The conclusion that immediately occurs to an educated Westerner is that this psychological advantage was because people in earlier societies had misconceptions about the nature of reality. Their speculations about life after death, the posthumous journey of the soul, and the Beyond were nothing else than products of fear and wishful self-deception. If such beliefs were simply naive, the greater difficulty modern people have in facing death would be the price they pay for their more advanced and mature knowledge of the universal scheme of things. In that case, we might prefer to courageously face the grim reality of our existence and bear the emotional consequences of knowing the truth. However, closer examination of the existing evidence shows that what may at first sight seem like childish superstitions of preindustrial cultures can in fact be supported by the findings of modern consciousness research.

The understanding of human nature and of the cosmos shared by modern technological countries differs significantly from the world views found in the ancient and preindustrial cultures. To some extent, this is a natural and expected consequence of historical progress. Over the centuries, scientists from different disciplines have systematically explored the material world—from the realm of subatomic particles to other galaxies—and accumulated an impressive amount of previously unavailable information. Given the tremendous technological advance of printing to preserve and disseminate this information, generations of scientists have vastly complemented, corrected, and replaced earlier concepts about the world of matter. However, the most striking and surprising difference between the two world views is not the relative amount and accuracy of data about material reality, but the fundamental disagreement concerning the human psyche and the sacred or spiritual dimension of existence.

Holotropic States and the Nature of Reality

Modern consciousness research has shown that the most important factor responsible for the difference between these two cultural perspectives is not the superiority of materialistic science over primitive superstition, but our profound ignorance with regard to holotropic states. The only way the monistic materialistic world view of Western science can be maintained is by suppressing or misinterpreting large amounts of evidence generated by the studies of human consciousness, whether the source of this information is history, anthropology, comparative religion, or various areas of modern research, such as parapsychology, thanatology, psychedelic therapy, sensory deprivation, experiential psychotherapies, or work with individuals in psychospiritual crises ("spiritual emergencies").

Systematic exposure to various forms of holotropic states, an essential component of the ritual and spiritual life of ancient and aboriginal cultures, inevitably leads to an understanding of the nature of reality and of the relationship between consciousness and matter that is fundamentally different from the belief system of technological societies. I have yet to meet a single Western academician who, after extensive inner work involving holotropic states, continues to subscribe exclusively to the scientific world view taught currently in Western universities. As a result of such experiences, the understanding of the psyche, consciousness, human nature, and the nature of reality typically moves in the direction of the great Eastern spiritual philosophies and the mystical world view. This shift is entirely independent of the educational background, IQ, and specific area of expertise of the individuals involved. Thus the difference in opinion regarding the possibility of survival of consciousness after death reflects the amount of experience with holotropic states.

Ancient and preindustrial cultures held holotropic states in high esteem, experienced them regularly in socially sanctioned contexts, and spent much time and energy developing safe and effective techniques of inducing them. These experiences represented the main vehicle for the ritual and spiritual life of these cultures and mediated direct contact with the world of deities and demons, archetypal domains, nature, and the cosmos. Holotropic states were also used to diagnose and heal diseases, cultivate intuition, and serve as sources of artistic inspiration. Other uses were more practical, such as locating game and following its movements or finding lost people and objects. (According to anthropologist Victor Turner, group participation in rituals contributes to tribal bonding and tends to create a sense of deep connectedness ("communitas") (Turner 1974)). Furthermore, holotropic experiences, spontaneous or resulting from rigorous spiritual practice, represented also the single most important source of the world's great religions.

Under the influence of the Scientific and Industrial Revolution, Western societies rejected holotropic states and the revelations they provided and even outlawed some of the means and contexts for inducing them, simply because the perspectives acquired from such states conflicted with rational thinking. In the modern era, anything associated with these states has been seen as an embarrassing leftover from the Dark Ages or as a legacy from humanity's infancy, which scientific progress has discredited and outgrown. Mainstream psychiatrists have tended to pathologize holotropic states and have spent much time trying to develop effective ways of suppressing them when they occur spontaneously. Native cultures are seen as "primitive," and their ritual and spiritual practices as products of immature magical thinking or even psychopathology. This perspective has profoundly influenced the attitude of materialistic scientists toward religion, since visionary experiences played a critical role in the spiritual history of humanity.

Gautama Buddha, meditating in Bodh Gaya under the Bo tree, had a dramatic visionary experience of Kama Mara, the master of the world illusion, who tried to distract him from his spiritual quest. Kama Mara first used his three beautiful and seductive daughters—Desire, Fulfillment, and Regret—in an effort to divert Buddha's interest from spirituality to sex. When this failed, he brought in his menacing army to instigate the fear of death in Buddha and prevent him from reaching enlightenment. Buddha successfully overcame these obstacles and experienced illumination and spiritual awakening. In his meditation, Buddha also envisioned a long chain of his previous incarnations and experienced what he felt was a profound liberation from karmic bonds.

In the Judeo-Christian tradition, the Old Testament describes many visionary experiences, including Yahweh talking to Moses from within the burning bush and Daniel's vision of the four beasts and the future Messiah. Other relevant passages are the account of Joshua's powerful experience of "the captain of the host of the Lord" (the angel who gave him instructions how to capture Jericho), and the prophet Isaiah's apparition of "God high and lifted up." The New Testament describes Jesus' experience of the temptation by the devil during his stay in the desert. Similarly, Saul's blinding vision of Jesus on the way to Damascus, St. John's apocalyptic revelation in his cave on the island Patmos, Ezekiel's observation of the flaming chariot, and many other episodes clearly are transpersonal experiences in holotropic states of consciousness. The Bible provides many other examples of direct communication with God and with the angels. In addition, the descriptions of the temptations of St. Anthony and of the visionary experiences of other Desert Fathers and saints are well-documented episodes of Christian history.

The Islamic text *Miraj Nameh* describes the "miraculous journey of Muhammad," a powerful visionary experience during which Archangel Gabriel escorted Muhammad through the seven Muslim Heavens, Paradise, and Hell (*Gehenna*). During this visionary visit to Heaven, Muhammad experienced an "audience" with Allah. In a state described as "ecstasy approaching annihilation," he received from Allah a direct communication. His prophetic visions, in which Archangel Gabriel proclaimed him the "Messenger of God," continued for nearly twenty years. Muhammad's followers memorized his visions and later wrote them on palm leaves, rocks, and bones. The collected work became the basis for the *suras* of the Qur'an and for the Muslim faith.

Mainstream psychiatrists usually interpret any visionary experiences, including those of the founders of religions, their saints, and prophets, as manifestations of serious mental diseases, although there is no medical explanation to support this position. In this context no distinction is made between a mystical or spiritual experience and a psychotic experience—both are seen as products of a pathological process of unknown etiology. In rejecting religion, mainstream psychiatry does not differentiate between primitive folk beliefs or the fundamentalists' literal interpretations of scriptures and sophisticated mystical traditions and Eastern spiritual philosophies based on centuries of systematic introspective exploration of the psyche. Psychiatric literature contains numerous articles and books that discuss what would be the most appropriate clinical diagnoses for many of the great figures of spiritual history (Vondrá□ek and Holub 1993).

Modern clinicians typically see famous religious personages of the stature of Buddha, Jesus, Ramakrishna, and Sri Ramana Maharshi as suffering from schizophrenia or some other form of psychosis, because they interpret the visionary experiences of these spiritual teachers as hallucinations and their ideas as delusions. In the same vein, St. John of the Cross has been labeled "hereditary degenerate," St. Teresa of Avila called a "severe hysterical psychotic," and Muhammad's mystical experiences attributed to epilepsy. Similarly, traditionally educated anthropologists have argued whether shamans should be diagnosed as schizophrenics, ambulant psychotics, epileptics, or hysterics. The famous psychoanalyst Franz Alexander, known as one of the founders of psychosomatic medicine, wrote a paper in which even Buddhist meditation is described in psychopathological terms and referred to as "artificial catatonia" (Alexander 1931). The most favorable official academic judgment so far regarding mysticism was the statement of the Committee on Psychiatry and Religion of the Group for the Advancement of Psychiatry entitled "Mysticism: Spiritual Quest or Psychic Disorder?" This document, published in 1976, conceded that mysticism might be a phenomenon that lies somewhere between normalcy and psychosis.

Religion and spirituality have been extremely important forces in the history of humanity and civilization. If visionary experiences of the founders of religions, saints, and prophets were simply products of pathological processes afflicting the brain, it would be difficult to explain why countless millions of ordinary people found such experiences inspiring and allowed them to shape their lives, to say nothing of the profound influence religious ideas have had on human history throughout centuries. And, if we consider the extraordinary artistic creations inspired by the great religions of the world, from breathtaking paintings, sculptures, and sacred music of all ages to Hindu temples, Muslim mosques, and Gothic cathedrals, it is preposterous to think about them as honoring hallucinations and delusions of psychotic individuals. Ritual and spiritual life played a pivotal role in every single ancient or preindustrial culture. The current approach of Western psychiatry and psychology thus pathologizes not only the spiritual but also the cultural life of all human groups throughout centuries. According to this mind-set, the only sane and normal group would be the educated elite of the Western industrial civilization, which shares the materialistic and atheistic world view.

How could religion have so profoundly influenced world history if ritual and spiritual life were based on psychotic hallucinations, delusions, and entirely unfounded superstitions and fantasies? To exert such a powerful effect, religion clearly must reflect a very deep and authentic aspect of human nature, however problematic and distorted its expressions of this genuine core may be. Fortunately, consciousness research conducted over the last fifty years has generated a rich array of fascinating data, which provide new insights into spirituality, in general, and into the problem of eschatological literature and survival of consciousness after death, in particular.

Evidence for Spiritual Dimensions of Reality and Posthumous Survival of Consciousness

Modern studies of holotropic states have revolutionized the understanding of consciousness and of the human psyche, at least for those researchers who can examine the available evidence with an open mind. Unfortunately, many academicians have an unshakeable a priori commitment to the existing paradigm and so are immune to any facts that challenge their beliefs. This attitude characterizes fundamentalist religions, but unfortunately is not limited to them. True science is open to unbiased investigation of any existing phenomena. With this in mind, let us now briefly review the experiences and observations that bring supportive evidence for the existence of the spiritual dimensions of reality and the possibility of survival of consciousness after death.

This material falls into two large categories. The first includes experiences that do not fit current conceptual frameworks and consequently require that the model of the human psyche used in psychiatry and psychology be vastly revised and expanded. These anomalies represent a critical challenge to the monistic materialistic philosophy of Western science and its understanding of the nature of consciousness and its relationship to matter. Results from such experiences offer convincing evidence for the existence of the spiritual dimensions of reality and for the legitimacy of spiritual pursuits because they show that the basic tenets of the mystical world view are well founded and consistent with the research data. By undermining the assumption that consciousness is an epiphenomenon of matter, these findings lend credence to the possibility that consciousness survives biological demise but do not provide direct evidence for the belief in Afterlife.

The second category of observations from holotropic states includes phenomena specifically related to the problem of survival of consciousness after death. Here belong apparitions and various events associated with dying and death, near-death experiences (NDEs), experiential sequences suggesting the possibility of reincarnation, and communications with deceased beings. While these findings do not constitute definitive proof for continuation of consciousness and existence beyond the point of biological demise, they make this concept possible or even plausible. If nothing else, the existence of such transpersonal experiences shows that the beliefs in survival of consciousness, posthumous journey of the soul, abodes of the Beyond, and reincarnation are more than unfounded wishful fantasies.

In the next chapter, I outline the expanded cartography of the psyche based on research of holotropic states. In addition to the biographical-recollective level and the individual unconscious, this new map includes two transbiographical domains: perinatal and transpersonal. These realms of the psyche are the sources of numinous experiences which have provided the inspiration for great religions and mystical traditions of the world and continue to ignite, spur, and inform the spiritual quest. After outlining this cartography, essential for the understanding of spirituality, I then discuss in subsequent chapters the experiences that are directly relevant to the problem of survival of consciousness after death.

Lascaux Shaman. A mysterious scene from the crypt of the Lascaux temple cave features a supine figure with an erect penis, most likely a shaman in trance. From right to left appear an eviscerated bull with a spear penetrating his body, a bird effigy on a pole, and a rhinoceros.

Famous Cavern near the Sanctuary in Eleusis. According to legend, this was the entry into the Underworld which Hades used when he abducted Persephone.

Model of the Eleusinian Sanctuary during the Roman Period. The *telestrion* (or main hall, where the mysteries took place) is viewed from beyond the fortification wall; to the right, the Greater Propylaea and the Lesser Propylaea.

Death God with Mushroom. Detail of a leaf from an Aztec codex, which dates from the years immediately after the conquest. The God of Death Mictlantecuhtli stands over a person eating a psychoactive ("magic") mushroom. *(Codex Magliabecchi,* Mexico*)*

Bloodletting Ritual Honors Heir's Birth. A Mayan limestone lintel shows Bird Jaguar and his wife Lady Balam-Ix performing a bloodletting ritual on the occasion of the birth of Bird Jaguar's son and heir. Bird Jaguar is perforating his penis and his wife her tongue. (Yaxchilan, Chiapas, Mexico, Mayan Late Classic Period, A.D. 770)

Heart Offering. A Mayan monument shows a ballplayer offering the heart of the sacrificed victim to the sun god, Cozumel. (c. A.D. 1000)

Sequence of Infant Jaguar Scenes. This composite drawing by Mayologist Francis Robicsek shows that the relative positions of the Infant Jaguar God to the Cauac Monster depicted on Mayan vases can be arranged into a meaningful sequence. Robicsek suggested that this might reflect movements of a celestial body. However, this pattern is more likely related to biological birth, thus confirming the findings of modern consciousness research that link the experiences of psychospiritual rebirth to the reliving of the birth trauma.

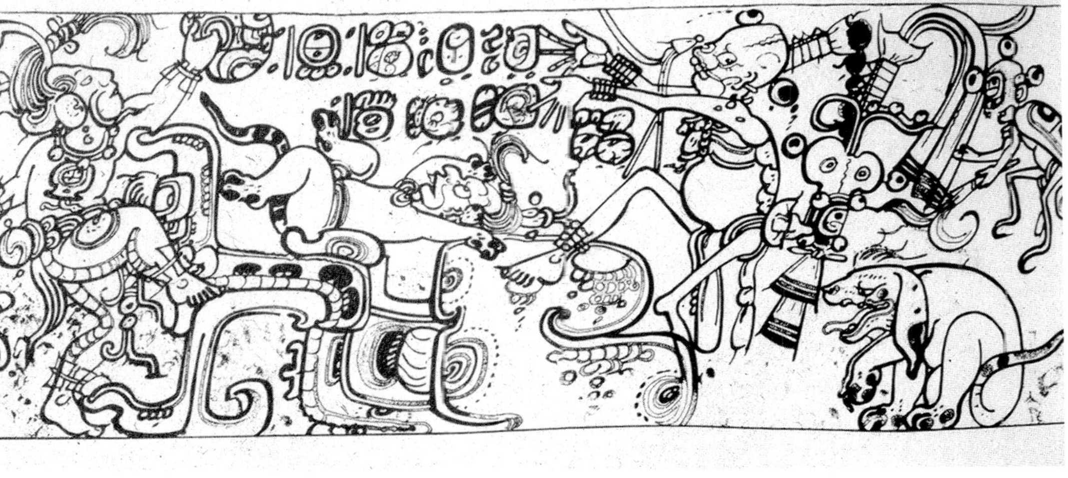

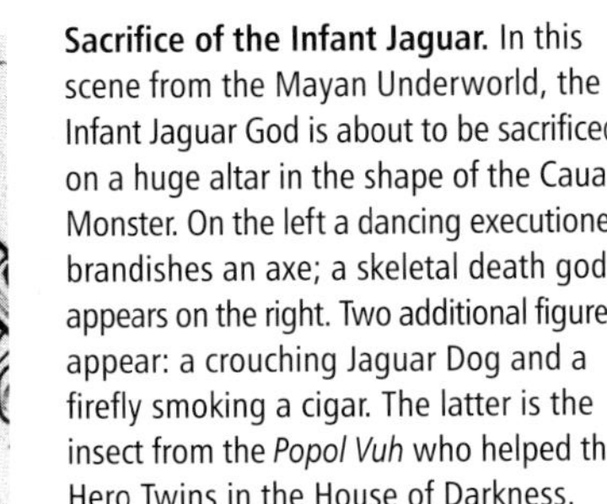

Sacrifice of the Infant Jaguar. In this scene from the Mayan Underworld, the Infant Jaguar God is about to be sacrificed on a huge altar in the shape of the Cauac Monster. On the left a dancing executioner brandishes an axe; a skeletal death god appears on the right. Two additional figures appear: a crouching Jaguar Dog and a firefly smoking a cigar. The latter is the insect from the *Popol Vuh* who helped the Hero Twins in the House of Darkness. (Funeral vessel, Mayan Late Classic period, A.D. 600-800)

Mayan Scene of Death and Rebirth. This tripod plate shows Hun Hunahpu, father of the Hero Twins, wearing a headdress of quetzal feathers as he emerges from a cracked turtle-shell carapace decorated by a skull. Attending the reborn are his sons, Hunahpu and Xbalanque. (Late Classic Period)

Pre-Columbian Mushroom Effigy. Large numbers of ceramic and stone sculptures representing mushrooms and mushroom deities dating from 1,000 B.C. to A.D. 500 have been found in southern Mexico, Guatemala, and San Salvador. This terra cotta portrays celebrants dancing around a mushroom effigy, possibly representing the World Tree, the axis mundi. Colima, Mexico, 200 B.C.–A.D. 100.

Quetzalcoatl, God of Life and Death, as the Plumed Serpent. This sculpture portrays the powerful Mesoamerican symbol of psychospiritual death and rebirth. The name *Quetzalcoatl* is a composite of two Nahuatl words: *quetzal,* a colorful, parrot-like bird, symbolizes the spiritual element in human beings; *coatl,* the snake, refers to their earth-bound nature. (Aztec, 14th–16th century)

Judgment in the Sidpa Bardo. Yama Raja, flanked by the Defender and the Accuser, judges deceased Tibetans. The karmic balance is attended by the monkey-headed Shinje and two assistants, while various animal-headed deities function as impartial judges. Issuing from the court, on either side of the Judge, are the six Karmic Pathways leading to the Six Buddhas of the lokas, the realms into which one can be reborn. At the bottom of the painting are various scenes depicting the tortures experienced in the eight hot hells and eight cold hells. At the top of the picture, in the center, presiding over all, is Dorje Chang, the Divine Guru of the Red-Hat School of Padma Sambhava, the ever-living spiritual source that continues to emanate all the esoteric doctrines underlying the Bardo Thödol.

Citipati Dyad. Two skeletal figures represent death in its dancing form. In the background is a carnal ground, the end of existence (a place where carnivorous animals search for corpses). The Citipati are portrayed as a dyad, since death always involves polarity and dualism. They play a very important role in Tibetan ritual dances. (Tibetan thangka, 19th century)

Allegory of Time: The Great Staircase of the World. Symbolic representation of the fatal trajectory of human life and the impermanence of incarnate existence. The steps depict consecutive stages of life beginning at birth, culminating in the prime of life, and ending in old age and death. The infant cradle on the left forms a sharp contrast to the coffin that appears on the right as its mirror image (Isaac, Jasparde, d. 1654).

Wheel of Life. The basic dilemma of human existence—the difficult task to find meaning in life against the relentlessness of death and impermanence—is graphically illustrated in this image of the Wheel of Life. Death towers over the globe as the absolute ruler of the world. Under him a horizontal rotating wheel symbolizes the course of human life. Each person enters this wheel as a small baby, grows older as the wheel rotates, and falls off dead at the same place where he or she entered. (Anonymous)

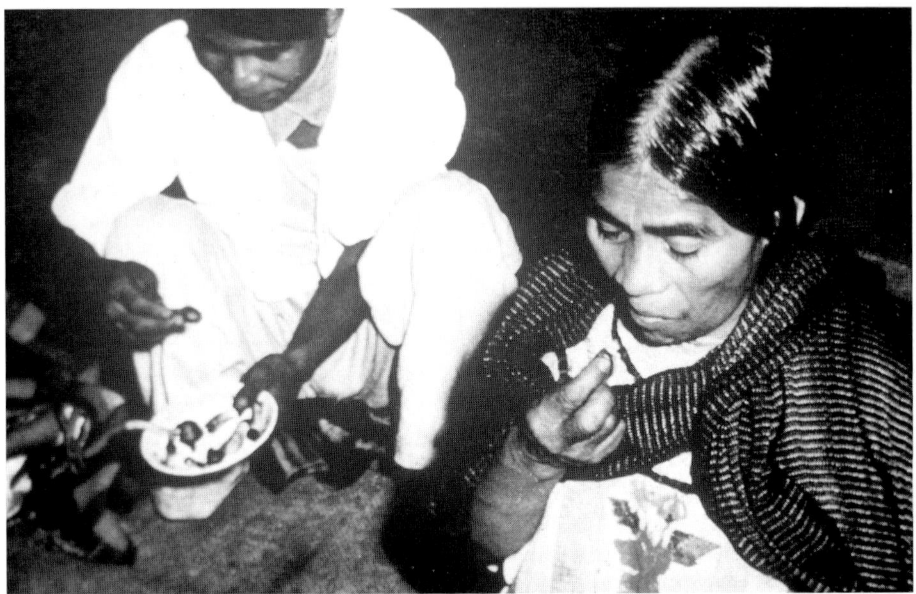

Maria Sabina, the Mazatec curandera, who invited Gordon Wasson and his wife Valentina Pavlovna to her sacred ceremony (velada) and introduced them to psychedelic ("magic") mushrooms.

Gordon Wasson in his New England office with a pre-Columbian mushroom effigy.

Stanislav Grof during his 1973 visit to Gordon Wasson's house in Danbury, Connecticut.

Pioneers of psychedelic therapy with cancer patients: Aldous Huxley, the author of *Brave New World* and *Island*, and Laura Archera Huxley, author of *This Timeless Moment.*

Albert Hofmann in his Basel laboratory at the time when he discovered LSD.

Members of the Spring Grove staff during the visit of German psychedelic researcher Hanscarl Leuner. From left to right: Stanislav Grof, Karen Leihy, Bob Leihy, Hanscarl Leuner, Sanford Unger, and Bill Richards.

Albert Hofmann with psychedelic researcher Walter Pahnke and music therapist Helen Bonny in front of the newly built Maryland Psychiatric Research Center during his 1970 visit.

Shamanic Themes Featured in Experiences from Holotropic Breathwork. (Artist: Tai Hazard)

Right: ***Guided by the Ravens to the Doorway beyond Space and Time.***

Below: ***Dismembered by the Leopard while being held by the Spirit Guide.***

8
DIMENSIONS OF CONSCIOUSNESS: NEW CARTOGRAPHY OF THE HUMAN PSYCHE

There is one spectacle grander than the sea,
that is the sky; there is one spectacle grander than the sky,
that is the interior of the soul.
– Victor Hugo, *Les Misérables*

EXPERIENCES and observations of holotropic states cannot be explained in terms of the conceptual framework used by academic psychiatry and psychology, which is limited to postnatal biography and to the Freudian individual unconscious. These new data represent a critical conceptual challenge for monistic materialism and the Newtonian-Cartesian paradigm dominating academic science. To explore meaningfully the problem of survival of consciousness after death, we need an incomparably larger and more encompassing image of the human psyche and a radically different understanding of consciousness.

In the early years of my psychedelic research, I sketched a vastly expanded cartography of the psyche that seems to meet this challenge. While the source of this map was my clinical work with psychedelics, its general relevance was later confirmed by our observations from the practice of Holotropic Breathwork, where no substances are used. This new model of the psyche has also been independently confirmed by results from other areas of consciousness research, experiential psychotherapies, and work with individuals undergoing spontaneous psychospiritual crises. In its present form, this expanded cartography is based on observations from sessions with many thousands of clients, trainees, and participants in experiential workshops (Grof 1980 and 2000, Grof and Grof 1990).

The new map of the psyche shares with academic psychology and psychiatry the *biographical-recollective domain* and the Freudian *individual unconscious*. However, while in the mainstream conceptual framework these two regions represent the totality of the psyche, the new cartography is vastly expanded. It contains two large and important additional domains which are transbiographical in nature; they lie beyond (or beneath) the realm of conscious and unconscious contents related to postnatal biography. I call the first of these two new domains *perinatal*, which reflects its close connection with biological birth, and the second *transpersonal*, or reaching beyond the personal identity as it is usually defined.

The expanded cartography of the psyche in its present form is not entirely new. Although it emerged independently from my own research, it represents a synthesis of the perspectives of various schools of depth psychology known from the history of psychoanalysis. It includes some of Freud's original concepts, as well as important revisions proposed by famous psychoanalytic renegades. For example, in his pioneering book *The Trauma of Birth*, Otto Rank described the existence of the perinatal unconscious and emphasized its importance for psychology and psychotherapy (Rank 1929). Psychoanalysts Fodor Nandor and Lietaert Peerbotle independently confirmed Rank's ideas about the psychological importance of the trauma of birth and of prenatal dynamics (Nandor 1949, Peerbolte 1975).

Wilhelm Reich discovered the powerful energies stored in the psyche and in the body responsible for what he called the "character armor" (Reich 1949). He discussed the important role such energies play in a wide range of phenomena, from psychoneuroses and psychosomatic disorders to sociopolitical movements (Reich 1961, 1970). Another of Freud's followers, Sandor Ferenczi, seriously considered in his essay "Thalassa" the possibility that the deep unconscious harbored memories of life in the primeval ocean (Ferenczi 1968). C. G. Jung introduced by far the most radical revision with his discovery of the collective unconscious and its governing principles, the archetypes (Jung 1959). The concept of the collective unconscious was also an integral part of Roberto Assagioli's psychosynthesis (Assagioli 1976). The ideas of these pioneers of depth psychology had to be significantly modified in the light of the observations from holotropic states before they could be integrated into the new cartography (Grof 1985).

Postnatal Biography and the Individual Unconscious

The biographical-recollective domain consists of memories from infancy, childhood, and later life. Since this aspect of the psyche is well known from traditional psychiatry, psychology, and psychotherapy, it does not require much discussion. In fact, the model of the psyche used in academic circles is limited exclusively to this domain and to the Freudian individual unconscious. As described by Freud, the unconscious is closely related to postnatal biography in that it contains material that we have forgotten or actively repressed. But the description of the biographical level of the psyche in the new cartography is not identical with the traditional one. Research with holotropic states has revealed certain aspects of the dynamics of the biographical realm that remained hidden to researchers using only verbal psychotherapy.

In therapy using holotropic states, unlike those based on verbal exchange, people do not merely remember emotionally significant events or reconstruct them indirectly from narratives, free associations, or transference distortions. Typically the original emotions, physical sensations, and even sensory perceptions are experienced in full age regression. This means that during the reliving of an important trauma from infancy or childhood, the person actually has the body image, the naive perception of the world, sensations, and the emotions corresponding to the age he or she was at that time. The authenticity of this regression is evident in many different ways; for instance, wrinkles in the face of regressed individuals temporarily disappear, giving them an infantile expression, and their postures, gestures, and behavior become childlike. Deeply regressed people commonly salivate like babies and suck on their thumbs.

Another significant difference in the biographical material that emerges in holotropic states, as compared with verbal psychotherapies, is that it often involves reliving and integrating traumas primarily of a physical nature—not just the usual emotional psychotraumas discussed in psychotherapeutic literature. Many people participating in psychedelic therapy or Holotropic Breathwork, as well as those undergoing spontaneous psychospiritual crises, have relived operations, accidents, and children's diseases. Insults associated with suffocation seem especially important, such as episodes of near-drowning, diphtheria, whooping cough, aspiration of a foreign object, or attacks involving strangling. This material emerges into consciousness quite spontaneously and without any programming.

As the memories of these bodily traumas surface into consciousness, their full impact becomes very apparent. Not only are they physically damaging; bodily traumas also have a strong psychotraumatic impact and play an important role in the psychogenesis of emotional and psychosomatic problems. Physical traumas are regularly instrumental in the development of such disorders as asthma, migraine headaches, psychosomatic pains, phobias, sadomasochistic tendencies, depression, and suicidal tendencies (Grof 1985, 2000). Reliving and integrating such traumatic memories can have very far-reaching therapeutic effects. This observation contrasts sharply with the position of academic psychiatrists and psychologists, who do not recognize the enormous emotional impact and importance of physical traumas.

COEX Systems

Another important insight from studying the biographical level of the psyche during holotropic states of consciousness was the discovery that emotionally relevant memories are not stored in the unconscious as a mosaic of isolated imprints, but in the form of complex dynamic constellations. I have coined for these memory aggregates the name *COEX systems*, or "systems of condensed experience." This concept is of such theoretical and practical importance that it deserves special notice. A COEX system consists of emotionally charged memories from different periods of life that resemble each other in the quality of emotion or physical sensation that they share. Each COEX system has a basic theme, or common denominator, that permeates all its layers. The individual layers then contain memories of events from different periods of the person's life that represent variations on this basic theme. The number and the nature of the COEX constellations vary considerably from one person to another.

For example, the layers of a particular system can contain all the major memories of humiliating, degrading, and shaming experiences that have damaged the patient's self-image and self-esteem. In another COEX system, the common denominator can be anxiety experienced in various shocking and terrifying situations or claustrophobic and suffocating feelings evoked by oppressive and confining circumstances. Another common motif is one of rejection and emotional deprivation that damages the ability to trust men, women, or people in general. Other typical examples are situations that have generated profound feelings of guilt and a sense of failure, events that have resulted in a conviction that sex is dangerous or disgusting, and encounters with indiscriminate aggression and violence. Particularly important are COEX systems that contain memories of situations endangering life, health, and integrity of the body.

Before I discovered the perinatal and transpersonal domains of the psyche, my understanding of psychology was limited to the narrow biographical model I had inherited from my teachers, particularly my Freudian analyst. Thus in the early stages of my psychedelic research when I first discovered the existence of COEX systems, I perceived them as principles governing the dynamics of the biographical-recollective level of the unconscious. This notion was further supported by observations from the initial psychedelic sessions of a therapeutic series (particularly when lower dosages were used) because the biographical material often dominated the picture. As my experience with holotropic states became richer and more extensive, I saw that the roots of the COEX systems reached much deeper.

My present understanding is that each COEX constellation is superimposed over and anchored in a particular aspect of the trauma of birth; in other words, a COEX constellation is psychodynamically connected to the experiences the fetus has in one of the stages of delivery. The experience of biological birth is so complex and rich in emotions and physical sensations that it contains in a prototypical form the elementary themes of most conceivable COEX systems. However, a typical COEX constellation reaches even further, and its deepest roots consist of various forms of transpersonal elements, such as past-life experiences, Jungian archetypes, conscious identification with various animals, and others.

I now see the COEX systems as general organizing principles of the human psyche. This concept resembles to some extent C. G. Jung's ideas regarding "psychological complexes" (Jung 1960) and Hanscarl Leuner's notion of "transphenomenal dynamic systems" (*tdysts*) (Leuner 1962), but it has many distinguishing features. The COEX systems play a crucial role in our psychological life: they can influence the way we perceive ourselves, other people, the world, and how we feel and act. They are the dynamic forces behind our emotional and psychosomatic symptoms, difficulties in relationships with other people, and irrational behaviors (Grof 1975, 2000).

According to the nature of the emotional charge, COEX systems may be negative (because they contain memories of specific traumatic events and unpleasant experiences) or positive (comprising pleasant aspects of personal history). People who are tuned into negative COEX systems perceive themselves and the world in a generally pessimistic way. They experience depression, anxiety, guilt, or some other form of emotional distress, depending on the nature and content of the COEX systems involved. In addition, they also show a variety of psychosomatic symptoms derived from physical aspects of the experiences registered in the corresponding COEX systems. Those individuals who are influenced by positive COEX systems generally experience a state of emotional well-being and optimal functioning and are capable of enjoying themselves and the world.

Inner Radar Function of Holotropic States

Holotropic states tend to engage an "inner radar" process, a very important and remarkable feature that is extremely useful in charting the experiential territories of the psyche. This process brings into awareness the contents from the unconscious that have the strongest emotional charge, are most psychodynamically relevant at the time, and most readily available for conscious processing. This extraordinary feature of holotropic states has also proved to be of invaluable help for the process of psychotherapy (Grof 2000).

In psychotherapy that relies on verbal means, the clients present in their free associations or narratives a rich array of information, and the therapist must evaluate it by deciding what is important, what is irrelevant, where the client is blocking, and so on. The main problem with this approach is that there are many schools of psychotherapy and very little agreement concerning the psychological processes, including the most fundamental issues. The various schools of psychotherapy have widely divergent views regarding the main motivating forces and psychodynamic mechanisms of the human psyche, the causes and meaning of symptoms, the nature of effective therapeutic mechanisms, and psychotherapeutic techniques.

Without general agreement on these fundamental theoretical issues, many interpretations made during verbal psychotherapy are arbitrary and questionable—they always reflect the personal bias of the therapist, as well as the specific views of his or her school. Holotropic states save the therapist such problematic decision-making and eliminate much of the subjectivity and professional idiosyncrasy of the verbal approaches. Once the client enters a holotropic state, the material for processing is chosen quite automatically. As long as the client keeps the experience internalized, the primary role of the therapist is to accept and support what is happening, whether or not it is consonant with any preconceived theoretical concepts and expectations.

This "inner radar" function of holotropic states has made it obvious that the memories of physical traumas carry a strong emotional and physical charge and play an important role in the genesis of emotional and psychosomatic disorders. This automatic selection of emotionally relevant material has also spontaneously guided the process of self-exploration of my clients from postnatal biography to the perinatal and transpersonal levels of the unconscious, transbiographical domains not recognized and acknowledged by academic psychiatry and psychology.

The Perinatal Domain of the Psyche

When our process of deep experiential self-exploration moves beyond the level of memories from childhood and infancy and reaches back to birth, we start encountering emotions and physical sensations of extreme intensity, often surpassing anything we previously considered humanly possible. At this point, the experiential content becomes a strange mixture of the themes of birth and death, involving sensations of a severe, life-threatening confinement and a desperate and determined struggle to free ourselves and survive. Because of the close connection between this domain of the unconscious and biological birth, I have chosen to name it *perinatal*, a Greek-Latin composite word where the prefix *peri*, means "near" or "around," and the root *natalis* signifies "pertaining to childbirth."

Academic psychiatry generally denies the possibility that biological birth has a strong psychotraumatic impact on the child. The cerebral cortex of the newborn is not fully "myelinized'—its neurons are not completely covered with protective sheaths of the fatty substance myelin. This is usually presented as an obvious reason why the experience of birth is psychologically irrelevant and why it is not recorded in memory. The absurdity of this perspective is quite evident in many respects. To deny that the brain of the newborn can record the memory of birth and, at the same time, attribute great psychological significance to memories of nursing, violates elementary logic.

Furthermore this position conflicts not only with daily observations from experiential psychotherapy, but also with comparative anatomy and physiology, as well as prenatal research (Grof 1985, 2000).

The amount of emotional and physical stress involved in childbirth clearly surpasses that of any postnatal trauma in infancy and childhood discussed in psychodynamic literature, with the possible exception of extreme forms of physical abuse. Various schools of experiential psychotherapy have amassed convincing evidence that biological birth is the most profound trauma of our life and an event of paramount psychospiritual importance. This primal event is recorded in our memory in miniscule details down to the cellular level, and it profoundly affects our psychological development. Because birth represents an actually or potentially life-threatening situation, it creates a deep liaison between birth and death in our unconscious. The memory of birth is an important source of fear of death; this explains why reliving birth in the process of psychospiritual death and rebirth can free us from such fear and transform our way of living.

The rich and complex material originating on the perinatal level of the unconscious appears in holotropic states in four experiential patterns or blueprints. In my early research, it soon became obvious that these characteristic combinations of emotions, physical feelings, and images were closely related to the experiences of the fetus and the newborn during the consecutive stages of the biological birth process. For this reason, I coined for them the name "Basic Perinatal Matrices" or BPMs. In the following text, I briefly describe these matrices in the sequence that corresponds with the phases of delivery during actual childbirth. However, in psychedelic therapy and in Holotropic Breathwork sessions this chronological order is usually not followed, and individual matrices can occur in many different sequential patterns.

The Experience of Cosmic Unity or the "Amniotic Universe" (BPM I)

This important perinatal experience is related to the primal union of the fetus with the mother during advanced pregnancy, the situation where the two organisms form a symbiotic unity. When no noxious stimuli interfere, the conditions for the fetus are close to ideal; they provide a sense of protection, security, and satisfaction of all needs. The basic characteristics of this experience are absence of the subject-object dichotomy, transcendence of time and space, exceptionally strong positive emotions (peace, tranquility, serenity, bliss), and feelings of sacredness (numinosity). This state of *oceanic ecstasy* is typically associated with profound insights of cosmic relevance.

The imagery associated with this matrix combines fetal elements with oceanic and cosmic motifs: floating in the sea, identifying with various aquatic animals, or drifting in interstellar space as, for instance, an astronaut walking in space. Positive intrauterine experiences can also be associated with archetypal visions of Mother Nature—safe, beautiful, and unconditionally nourishing, like a good womb. Mythological images from the collective unconscious that often appear in this context portray various celestial realms and paradises as described in mythologies of different cultures. Reliving episodes of intrauterine disturbances brings about the sense of dark and ominous threat and feelings of being poisoned. Sequences of this kind can be associated with archetypal visions of frightening demonic entities or with a sense of insidious, all-pervading evil.

The Experience of Cosmic Engulfment and "No Exit" or Hell (BPM II)

The experience of cosmic engulfment is related to the very onset of biological delivery, when the original equilibrium of intrauterine existence is disturbed, first by chemical changes and later by muscular contractions. This stage of the process is usually associated with an overwhelming feeling of increasing anxiety and a sense of imminent vital threat. The source of the approaching danger cannot be clearly identified, and people in this predicament frequently tend to interpret the immediate environment or the whole world in paranoid terms. They often feel poisoned or experience evil influences coming from secret organizations, inhabitants of other planets, and evil magicians. They can also sense noxious energies, toxic gases, and life-threatening radiation or feel influenced by some diabolical machine or other insidious device.

The sense of anxiety usually intensifies with the sensation of a maelstrom sucking the individual and his or her entire world relentlessly toward its center. A frequent variation of this theme of universal engulfment is that of being swallowed and incorporated by a terrifying archetypal monster. Another form of the same experience is the journey of descent into the Underworld and an encounter with various dangerous creatures or entities. These are well-known motifs from the shamanic lore, mythology of the hero's journey, and spiritual scriptures (Jung 1956, Campbell 1968) and are discussed more fully in earlier chapters of this book.

The experience of cosmic engulfment typically culminates in a situation of hopeless entrapment and imprisonment. This experiential pattern corresponds to the fully developed first clinical stage of delivery, when uterine contractions encroach on the fetus and cause its total constriction. In this stage the uterine cervix is still closed, and the way out is not yet available. In holotropic states this experience is characterized by loss of perception of colors and striking darkness of the visual field. One feels caged, trapped in a claustrophobic world, and experiences incredible psychological and physical tortures.

Because one's sense of linear time is lost during this state, the torments seem eternal, and their intensity invokes the atmosphere of Hell. The terror revolves around three topics—insanity, death, and never coming back. Under the influence of this matrix, human life and existence in general seem completely meaningless and utterly futile. The most common symbolism that accompanies this experiential pattern involves images of Hell from various cultural frameworks. This pattern is further typified by its unique emphasis on the role of the victim and the fact that the situation seems inescapable and eternal—no way out either in space or in time. Many famous mystics, such as St. Teresa of Avila and St. John of the Cross experienced agonizing torments which had many characteristics of BPM II; this matrix underlies what is known in spiritual literature as the "dark night of the soul" (Bache 1985, 1991a).

BPM II is also importantly connected with existential philosophy and the "Theater of the Absurd." Individuals influenced by it are selectively blinded and unable to see anything positive in their lives and in human existence in general. The connection to the divine dimension seems irretrievably severed and lost. Through the prism of this matrix, life appears devoid of any purpose, a meaningless farce, "waiting for Godot." Existential philosophy seems to offer the only true and relevant description of existence. In this respect, it is noteworthy that Jean Paul Sartre's work was deeply influenced by a badly managed and unresolved mescaline session dominated by BPM II (Riedlinger 1982). Samuel Beckett's preoccupation with death and birth and his tortured relationship with his mother also reveal strong perinatal influences (Knowlson 2004).

The Experience of Death-Rebirth Struggle (BPM III)

The BPM III pattern correlates with the second clinical stage of delivery. In this phase, the uterine contractions continue, but the cervix is now wide open. The fetus is gradually propelled through the birth canal and experiences crushing pressures, struggle for survival, and often a high degree of suffocation. In the terminal phases of delivery, the fetus may intimately contact a variety of biological material, such as blood, mucus, fetal liquid, urine, and even feces. From the experiential point of view this pattern is rather complex and has several important facets: the atmosphere of a titanic fight, sadomasochistic sequences, intense sexual arousal, scatological elements, and the motif of purifying fire (pyrocatharsis).

The *titanic aspect* of BPM III is quite understandable, considering the enormity of the forces operating during the final stage of childbirth. When we encounter this facet of the third matrix we experience overwhelming streams of incredibly intense energy rushing through the body and building up to explosive discharges. At this point, we might identify with raging elements of nature, such as volcanoes, electric storms, earthquakes, tidal waves, or tornadoes. The experience can also portray the enormous energies of the technological world in the form of tanks, rockets, spaceships, lasers, electric power plants, or even thermonuclear reactors and atomic bombs. The titanic experiences of BPM III can reach archetypal dimensions and portray battles of gigantic proportions, such as the cosmic clash between the forces of Light and Darkness, angels and devils, or the gods and the Titans.

Aggressive and sadomasochistic aspects of this matrix reflect the biological fury of the organism whose survival is threatened by suffocation, as well as the introjected destructive onslaught of the uterine contractions. Facing this aspect of BPM III, we might experience cruelties of astonishing proportions, manifesting in scenes of violent murder and suicide, mutilation and self-mutilation, massacres of various kinds, and bloody wars and revolutions. These sequences often take the form of torture, execution, ritual sacrifice and self-sacrifice, bloody man-to-man combats, and sadomasochistic practices.

The experiential logic of the *sexual aspect* of the death-rebirth process is not as immediately obvious. The human organism seems to have an inbuilt physiological mechanism that translates inhuman suffering, and particularly suffocation, into a strange kind of sexual arousal and eventually into ecstatic rapture, as illustrated by the experiences of the martyrs and of flagellants described in religious literature. Additional examples occur in the material from concentration camps, from the reports of prisoners of war, and from the files of Amnesty International. The connection between sex and death is notably evident in the well known phenomenon that men dying of suffocation on the gallows typically have an erection and even ejaculate.

Sexual experiences that occur in the context of BPM III are characterized by enormous intensity of the sexual drive, by their mechanical and unselective quality, and their exploitative, pornographic, or deviant nature. They depict scenes from red light districts and from the sexual underground, extravagant erotic practices, and sadomasochistic sequences. Equally frequent are episodes portraying incest and episodes of sexual abuse or rape. In rare instances, BPM III imagery can involve the gory and repulsive extremes of criminal sexuality—erotically motivated murder, dismemberment, cannibalism, and necrophilia. Such extreme experiences are more likely in high-dose psychedelic sessions of individuals who are reliving an extremely difficult and life-threatening birth. On this level of the psyche, sexual arousal is inextricably connected with highly problematic elements: vital threat, extreme danger, anxiety, aggression, self-destructive impulses, physical pain, and ordinarily repulsive biological material. This connection forms a natural basis for the development of the most important types of sexual dysfunctions, variations, deviations, and perversions.

The *demonic aspect* of BPM III can present specific problems for the experiencers, as well as therapists and facilitators, because of the uncanny and eerie characteristics of the manifestations involved. Despite the often frightening nature of such experiences, it is crucial that they be supported and worked through in a therapeutic context. The most frequent motifs are scenes from the Sabbath of the Witches (*Walpurgis Night*), satanic orgies and Black Mass rituals, and temptation by evil forces. The common denominator connecting this stage of childbirth with the themes of the Sabbath or with the Black Mass rituals is the peculiar experiential amalgam of death, deviant sexuality, pain, fear, aggression, scatology, and distorted spiritual impulse that they share. This observation seems to have great relevance for the recent epidemic of experiences of satanic cult abuse reported by clients in various forms of regressive therapy.

The *scatological aspect* of the death-rebirth process has its natural biological basis in situations during the final phase of the delivery when the fetus comes into close contact with various forms of biological material—blood, vaginal secretions, urine, and even feces. However, the nature and content of these experiences by far exceed what the newborn might have actually experienced during birth. In the extremes, experiences of this aspect of BPM III can involve such scenes as heaps of offal, gross sewage systems, and piles of excrement, or repulsive images of putrefaction—an intimate and shattering encounter with the worst aspects of biological existence.

As it nears resolution, the experience of BPM III becomes less violent and disturbing. The prevailing atmosphere is one of extreme passion and driving energy of intoxicating intensity, with imagery that portrays exciting explorations and conquests of new territories, hunts of wild animals, extreme sports, and adventures in amusement parks. These experiences are clearly related to activities that involve "adrenaline rush"—car racing, bungee jumping, challenging circus performances, dangerous movie stunts, and acrobatic diving.

At this time, we can also encounter archetypal figures of deities, demigods, and legendary heroes representing death and rebirth. We may have visions of Jesus, his torment and humiliation, the Way of the Cross, and crucifixion, or even actually experience full identification with his suffering. Even though we may not be familiar with the corresponding mythologies, we can experience resurrection of the Egyptian god Osiris, or death and rebirth of the Greek deities Dionysus, Attis, or Adonis. The experience can portray Persephone's abduction by Pluto, the descent into the Underworld of the Sumerian goddess Inanna, or the ordeals of the Mayan Hero Twins of the *Popol Vuh*.

Just before the experience of psychospiritual rebirth, the *element of fire* is often encountered, either in its ordinary everyday form or in the archetypal form of purgatorial fire (*pyrocatharsis*). We may feel that our body is on fire, have visions of burning cities and forests, and identify with the victims of immolation. In the archetypal version, the burning seems to radically destroy whatever is corrupted in us and prepare us for spiritual rebirth. A classical symbol of the transition from BPM III to BPM IV is the legendary bird Phoenix who dies in fire and rises resurrected from the ashes.

The pyrocathartic motif is a somewhat puzzling aspect of BPM III, since its connection with biological birth is not as direct compared to some of the other symbolic elements. The biological counterpart of this experience might be the explosive liberation of previously blocked energies in the final stage of childbirth or the over-stimulation of the fetus with indiscriminate "firing" of the peripheral neurons. Interestingly, this encounter with fire has its experiential parallel in the delivering mother who at this stage of delivery often feels that her vagina is on fire. This enormous release of previously pent-up energy can also find its expression in images of atomic explosions or in the archetypal motif of the boon-bestowing "jinni" liberated from the confining vessel.

Several important characteristics of this experiential pattern distinguish it from the previously described no-exit constellation (BPM II). The situation in BPM III does not seem hopeless. The subject is not helpless but rather is actively involved. The suffering seems to have a definite direction and goal. In religious terms, this situation is closer to the concept of Purgatory than Hell. In addition, subjects do not play exclusively the role of helpless victims. They are observers and can also identify with both perspectives at the same time, to the point where they hardly distinguish whether they are the aggressor or the victim. While the no-exit situation of BPM II involves sheer suffering, the experience of the death-rebirth struggle (BPM III) represents a strange mixture of agony and ecstasy. In contrast to the oceanic ecstasy of the good womb, this state can be called *volcanic* or *Dionysian ecstasy*.

The Death-Rebirth Experience (BPM IV)

This experiential pattern is related to the third clinical stage of delivery. The agonizing process of the birth struggle culminates, the propulsion through the birth canal is completed, and the process of delivery ends with explosive relief and relaxation. After the umbilical cord is cut, physical separation from the mother is complete, and the newborn starts his or her new existence as an anatomically independent organism. During this transition, suffering and agony culminate in an experience of total defeat and annihilation on all imaginable levels—physical, emotional, intellectual, moral, and transcendental. This stage is usually referred to as the "ego death" and seems to involve instantaneous destruction of all previous reference points of the individual. In the addiction circles, this experience is known as "hitting bottom," an important turning point in the lives of many alcoholics and drug addicts.

If the experience of emerging into the world at the time of biological birth was not obfuscated by heavy anesthesia, the sense of total annihilation is followed by visions of blinding white or golden light, peacock designs, and rainbow spectra. The feelings of liberating decompression and expansion culminate in a sense of psychospiritual rebirth. The archetypal domain at this point typically features Great Mother goddesses and blissful deities of various cultures appearing in brilliant light. The universe is perceived as indescribably beautiful and radiant; one feels cleansed and purged. In religious terms, this experience could be described as redemption, salvation, second birth, or union with God. This type of rapture associated with extraordinary insights of cosmic relevance can be referred to as *epiphanic* or *Promethean ecstasy*.

The Transpersonal Domain of the Psyche

In addition to perinatal matrices, research with holotropic states has added a second major experiential domain to mainstream psychiatry's cartography of the human psyche: the *transpersonal*, meaning literally "beyond the personal" or "transcending the personal." Experiences on this level involve transcending the usual boundaries of the body/ego and the limitations of three-dimensional space and linear time, which restrict our perception of the world in the ordinary state of consciousness. Transpersonal motifs can appear in holotropic states in various combinations with perinatal elements or independently of them. The transpersonal realm is the source of a wide range of anomalous phenomena, presenting serious challenges not only to current conceptual frameworks of psychology and psychiatry, but also to the monistic materialistic philosophy of modern science.

Transpersonal experiences are best defined by describing how they differ from everyday experience. In the ordinary or "normal" state of consciousness, we experience ourselves as material objects contained within the boundaries of our skin and operating in a world with Newtonian characteristics. The American writer and philosopher Alan Watts referred to this experience of oneself as identifying with the "skin-encapsulated ego" (Watts 1961). Under ordinary circumstances, our perception of the environment is restricted by the physiological limitations of our sensory organs and by physical characteristics of the environment.

For example, we cannot see objects separated from us by a solid wall, ships that are beyond the horizon, or the surface of the other side of the moon. If we are in Prague, we cannot hear what our friends are talking about in San Francisco. We cannot feel the softness of the lambskin unless the surface of our body is directly contacting it. In addition, we can only experience vividly and with all our senses events that occur in the present moment. We can recall the past and anticipate future events, fantasize about them, or try to use various methods to predict them. However, this kind of relationship with the past and future is very different from the immediate and direct sensory perception of what is happening in the present. In transpersonal experiences such limitations do not apply; any of them can be transcended.

Types of Transpersonal Experiences

Transpersonal experiences can be divided into three large categories. The first involves primarily transcending the usual spatial barriers, or the limitations of the skin-encapsulated ego. Typical examples are merging with another person into a state that can be called "dual unity," assuming the identity of another person, or identifying with the consciousness of an entire group of people (e.g., all mothers of the world, the entire population of India, or all the inmates of concentration camps). In extreme cases, a person may even experience an extension of consciousness so enormous that it seems to encompass all of humanity, the entire human species. Experiences of this kind have been repeatedly described in the spiritual literature of the world.

In a similar way, one can transcend the limits of the specifically human experience and identify with consciousness of various animals, plants, or even assume a form of consciousness associated with inorganic objects and processes. In rare instances, it is possible to experience consciousness of the entire biosphere, of our planet, or the entire material universe. Incredible as it may seem to a Westerner subscribing to the world view formulated by materialistic science, these experiences suggest that everything that we can experience in our everyday state of consciousness as an object has, in holotropic states, a corresponding subjective representation. It is as if everything in the universe has its objective and subjective aspect, the way it is described in the great spiritual philosophies of the East. For example, in Hinduism all phenomenal worlds are seen as divine play of Absolute Consciousness or Brahman (*Lila*), in Taoism all elements of material reality are described as transformations of the Tao, and so on.

The second category of transpersonal experiences is characterized primarily by overcoming temporal rather than spatial boundaries, i.e., by transcendence of linear time. We have previously discussed the possibility of vivid reliving of important memories from infancy, childhood, birth, and prenatal existence. In holotropic states, this historical regression can continue farther and involve what appears to be authentic experiential identification with the sperm and the ovum at the time of conception on the level of cellular consciousness. But the experiential travel back in time does not stop even here and can continue to episodes from the lives of one's human or animal ancestors, or even those that seem to be coming from the racial and collective unconscious as described by C. G. Jung. Very frequently, the experiences that seem to be happening in other cultures and historical periods are associated with a sense of personal remembering. People then talk about the reliving of memories from their past lives. As we will see later, these observations throw new light on the problem of reincarnation and karma, a concept of extreme spiritual and cultural importance, which has been summarily dismissed by materialistic science.

The content of the transpersonal experiences described thus far reflects various aspects of the material world and events happening at specific points of space and time.

These experiences involve elements of the everyday familiar reality—other people, animals, plants, and materials. This content is not especially surprising, but the manner in which we apprehend it is very significant: we are able to witness or experientially identify with something that is not ordinarily accessible to our senses, something that is considered not humanly possible to experience. We know that pregnant whales exist in the world, but we should not be able to have an authentic experience of being one. We accept that the French Revolution happened, but we should not be able to have a vivid experience of actually being there and dying on the barricades of Paris. We know that many things occur in the world in distant places, but usually we cannot experience something that is happening in remote locations without the mediation of technology, such as computers, satellites, and television. We may also be surprised to find consciousness associated with lower animals, plants, and with inorganic nature.

The third category of transpersonal experiences is even stranger. Here consciousness seems to extend into realms and dimensions that the Western industrial culture does not consider "real," such as numerous visions of archetypal beings and mythological landscapes, encounters or even identification with deities and demons of various cultures, and communication with discarnate beings, spirit guides, suprahuman entities, extraterrestrials, and inhabitants of parallel universes. In its farthest reaches, individual consciousness can identify with cosmic consciousness or the Universal Mind known under many different names—Brahman, Buddha, the Cosmic Christ, Keter, Allah, the Tao, the Great Spirit, Anima Mundi, and many others. The ultimate of all experiences appears to be identification with the Supracosmic and Metacosmic Void, the mysterious and primordial emptiness and nothingness that is conscious of itself and is the ultimate cradle of all existence. It has no concrete content yet contains all there is in a germinal and potential form.

The transpersonal realm is so extraordinary and fantastic that people who have not experienced it and are not culturally prepared for it refuse to believe that it exists. The brilliant writer and philosopher Aldous Huxley, astonished by what had emerged from the deep recesses of his psyche during his mescaline and LSD experiences, wrote this remarkable testimony:

> Like the giraffe and the duckbilled platypus, the creatures inhabiting these remoter regions of the mind are exceedingly improbable. Nevertheless they exist, they are facts of observation; and as such, they cannot be ignored by anyone who is honestly trying to understand the world in which he lives (Huxley 1959).

Scientific and Philosophical Challenges Presented by Transpersonal Experiences

Transpersonal experiences have many strange characteristics that shatter the most fundamental metaphysical assumptions of the Newtonian-Cartesian paradigm and of the monistic materialistic world view. Researchers who have studied and/or personally experienced these fascinating phenomena realize that the attempts of mainstream science to dismiss them as irrelevant products of human fantasy and imagination or as hallucinations—erratic products of pathological processes in the brain—are naive and inadequate. Any unbiased study of the transpersonal domain of the psyche must conclude that it critically challenges not only psychiatry and psychology, but also the philosophy of Western science and the popular belief system of industrial civilization.

Although transpersonal experiences occur in the process of deep individual self-exploration, they cannot be interpreted simply as intrapsychic phenomena in the conventional sense. On the one hand, they appear on the same experiential continuum as the biographical and perinatal experiences and are obtained from within the individual psyche in the process of introspection. Yet they also seem to tap directly, without mediation of the senses, into sources of information that are clearly far beyond the conventional reach of the individual. Somewhere on the perinatal level of the psyche, a strange rearrangement occurs: what was previously deep intrapsychic probing starts yielding experiences of different aspects of the universe-at-large obtained by extrasensory means. Some people have compared this to an "experiential Moebius strip," since it is impossible any more to distinguish internal from external experience.

These observations indicate that information about the universe can be obtained in two radically different ways. Besides the conventional possibility of learning through sensory perception and analysis and synthesis of the data, we can also explore various aspects of the world by directly identifying with them in a holotropic state of consciousness. Each of us thus appears to be a microcosm containing the information about the entire macrocosm. In mystical traditions, this principle is expressed by such phrases as: "as above, so below" or "as without, so within." In the past, this basic tenet of esoteric schools, such as Tantra, the Hermetic tradition, Gnosticism, and Kabbalah, has seemed an absurd confusion of the relationship between the part and the whole, a violation of Aristotelian logic. More recently this claim has received unexpected scientific support, with the discovery of the principles operating in optical holography (Talbot 1991).

During transpersonal episodes of embryonic existence, the moment of conception, and elements of cellular, tissue, and organ consciousness, people often gain medically accurate insights into the anatomical, physiological, and biochemical aspects of the processes involved. Similarly, ancestral, racial and collective memories and past incarnation experiences frequently provide very specific details about architecture, costumes, weapons, art forms, social structure, and religious and ritual practices of the relevant cultures and historical periods, or even concrete historical events previously unknown to the person. Those who experience phylogenetic sequences (i.e., stages of evolutionary development of a species) or identification with existing life forms not only find them unusually authentic and convincing, but often acquire extraordinary insights concerning animal psychology, ethology, specific habits, or unusual reproductive cycles. In some instances, such experiences are accompanied by archaic muscular innervations uncharacteristic of humans or even such complex behaviors as enactment of courtship dances of the corresponding species.

The scientific and philosophical challenges associated with such observations are further augmented by the mythological dimension of transpersonal experience. Episodes correctly reflecting the material world often appear on the same continuum and intimately interwoven with elements from the mythological world, which the Western industrial civilization does not consider to be ontologically real. These experiences involve deities and demons from various cultures, abodes of the Beyond such as heavens and paradises, and legendary or fairy-tale sequences. For example, we can experience communication with Jesus, Virgin Mary, or the Devil; have a shattering encounter with the Hindu goddess Kali; or identify with the dancing Shiva. We can also visit various mythological realms, such as the paradise of the Aztec rain god Tlaloc, the Sumerian Underworld, Shiva's Heaven, or one of the Buddhist hot hells. Even these episodes can impart accurate new information about religious symbolism and mythical motifs that were previously unknown to the person involved.

These types of experiences support C. G. Jung's concept that besides the Freudian individual unconscious we can also gain access to the collective unconscious that contains the cultural heritage of all humanity (Jung 1959). Although these mythic elements are accessed intrapsychically, in a process of introspection, they have objective existence, are ontologically real. To distinguish transpersonal experiences from imaginary products of individual fantasy, Jungians refer to this domain as "imaginal." French scholar, philosopher, and mystic, Henri Corbin, who first used the term *mundus imaginalis*, was inspired in this regard by his study of Islamic mystical literature (Corbin 2000). Islamic theosophers call the imaginal world (where everything existing in the sensory world has its analogue) *alam a mithal*, or the "eighth climate," to distinguish it from the "seven climates," regions of traditional Islamic geography. The imaginal world possesses extension and dimensions, forms and colors, but these are not perceptible to our senses as they would be when they are properties of physical objects. However, this realm is in every respect as fully ontologically real and susceptible to consensual validation by other people as the material world perceived by our sensory organs.

These conclusions are drawn from daily observations made over a period of fifty years of researching holotropic states of consciousness. However, the data are so revolutionary and incredible that it is unrealistic to expect that a few generalizations would suffice to override the deeply culturally ingrained world view of readers who are unfamiliar with the transpersonal dimension and who cannot relate such information to their personal experience. I myself had the opportunity to observe closely and hear the accounts of many thousands of people experiencing holotropic states. Yet it was decades before I could fully absorb the impact of the cognitive shock involved. The most convincing evidence for the validity of the astonishing and incredible new data did not come from extensive observation of others, but from my own deep personal experience.

Detailed case histories illustrating the nature of transpersonal experiences and the extraordinary insights and new knowledge they provide are available elsewhere (Grof 1975, 1988, 1992). These sources discuss at length the various types of transpersonal experiences, including many examples of how these experiences yield accurate new information about other people, animals, plants, inorganic materials and processes, and mythological realms. Those who are interested in personally verifying such observations can attend Holotropic Breathwork workshops with some of the many hundreds of certified facilitators worldwide who have completed the Grof Transpersonal Training. The necessary information is available at our website (www.holotropic.com).

The existence and nature of transpersonal experiences violate some of the most basic assumptions of mechanistic science. They imply such seemingly absurd notions as relativity and arbitrary nature of all physical boundaries, non-local connections in the universe, communication through unknown means and channels, memory without a material substrate, non-linearity of time, or consciousness associated with all living organisms, and even inorganic matter. Many transpersonal experiences involve events from the microcosm and the macrocosm, realms that cannot normally be reached by unaided human senses, or from historical periods that precede the origin of the solar system, formation of planet earth, appearance of living organisms, development of the nervous system, and emergence of *Homo sapiens*. In all these experiences, we can access entirely new information that by far surpasses anything obtained by conventional means. The study of consciousness that can extend beyond the body, William Roll's "theta consciousness" or the "long body" of the Iroquois, is extremely important for the issue of existence after death, since it is this aspect of human personality that would likely survive death (Roll 1974).

Traditional academic science describes human beings as highly developed animals and biological thinking machines. Experienced and studied in the everyday state of consciousness, we appear to be Newtonian objects made of atoms, molecules, cells, tissues, and organs. However, transpersonal experiences in holotropic states clearly show that each of us can also manifest the properties of a field of consciousness that transcends space, time, and linear causality. The complete new formula, remotely reminiscent of the wave-particle paradox in modern physics, thus describes humans as paradoxical beings who have two complementary aspects: they can show properties of Newtonian objects and also those of infinite fields of consciousness. The appropriateness of each of these descriptions depends on the state of consciousness in which these observations are made. Physical death then seems to terminate the aspect of us described by one half of this definition, while the other comes into full expression.

Research of holotropic states clearly reveals another astounding paradox concerning the nature of human beings. In a mysterious and yet unexplained way, each of us contains the information about the entire universe and all of existence, has potential experiential access to all its parts, and in a certain sense is the whole cosmic network. At the same time, from another perspective, each of us is also an infinitesimal part of the universe, a separate and insignificant biological entity. The new cartography of the psyche reflects this paradox and portrays the individual human psyche as being essentially commensurable with the entire cosmos and the totality of existence. As implausible as this idea might seem, it can be fairly easily reconciled with new revolutionary developments in various scientific disciplines usually referred to as the new or emerging paradigm. Modern science has thus brought unexpected supportive evidence for the answer that the ancient Indian Upanishads give to the question about our true nature: "Thou Art That" (in Sanskrit *Tat tvam asi*)—you are commensurable with the cosmic creative principle and with all there is.

According to materialistic science, any memory requires a material substrate, such as the neuronal network in the brain or the DNA molecules of the genes. However, it is impossible to imagine any material medium for the information conveyed by the various forms of transpersonal experiences described above. This information clearly has not been acquired during the individual's lifetime through the conventional channels, i.e., by sensory perception, but seems to exist independently of matter—contained in the field of consciousness itself, or in some other types of fields that cannot be detected by our scientific instruments. The observations from the study of transpersonal experiences are supported by evidence from other areas of study. Challenging the basic metaphysical assumptions of Newtonian-Cartesian thinking, scientists such as Heinz von Foerster and Rupert Sheldrake seriously explore such possibilities as "memory without a material substrate" (von Foerster 1965) and "morphogenetic fields" (Sheldrake 1981, 1990).

By far the most radical attempt of this kind is the work of the world renowned system theorist Ervin Laszlo. Many of the puzzling features of transpersonal experiences and similar "anomalous phenomena" from various disciplines can be illuminated by

Laszlo's theory (Grof 2005). In an intellectual tour de force, Laszlo has explored a wide range of paradoxical observations and paradigmatic challenges, for which these disciplines, including transpersonal psychology, had no explanations (Laszlo 1994, 2003). Drawing on advances from hard sciences and mathematics, he has offered an interdisciplinary solution to many of the baffling enigmas of Western science. The basis for Laszlo's solution is his "connectivity hypothesis," which has as its main cornerstone the existence of the "akashic field" (Laszlo 2004). Laszlo describes it as a sub-quantum field, which holds a holographic record of all the events that have happened in the phenomenal world since the beginning of time.

To understand the mystics' claim that each individual is commensurate or identical with the entire universe, we must realize that it applies to the world of information and not to the world of matter (understood in the sense of Newtonian-Cartesian science as an assembly of indestructible particles). We are not observing here Galileo Galilei's admonition to limit our scientific exploration only to those aspects of the world that can be measured and weighed. We ignore the taboo against including subjective data and instead draw conclusions from what each human being can experience. The statements which materialistic science has made about the measurable and weighable aspects of reality remain valid in their own right, but they are not relevant to the observations and conclusions summarized in this book.

I firmly believe that the expanded cartography of the psyche discussed in this chapter is critically important for any serious approach to such phenomena as shamanism, rites of passage, mysticism, religion, mythology, parapsychology, and psychedelic experiences. Above all, it offers revolutionary new perspectives on many of the subjects explored in this book, such as near-death experiences, survival of consciousness after death, the posthumous journey of the soul, reincarnation, and many others. This new model of the psyche is not just a matter of academic interest—it has deep and revolutionary implications for the understanding of emotional and psychosomatic disorders, including functional psychoses, and offers new and revolutionary therapeutic possibilities (Grof 1985 and 2000, Grof and Grof 1989 and 1990).

9
CONSCIOUSNESS ON THE THRESHOLD OF DEATH

You grieve for those that should not be grieved for.
The wise grieve neither for the living nor the dead.
Never at any time was I not.
Nor thou, nor these princes of men.
Nor will we ever cease to be hereafter.
For the unreal has no being and the real never ceases to be.
–Bhagavad-Gita

THE RESEARCH of certain specific aspects of dying and death conducted at the end of the nineteenth and beginning of the twentieth centuries was motivated primarily by the interest in phenomena suggesting the possibility of survival of consciousness after death. Most studies were not concerned with the experiences and behavior of dying people themselves but instead focused primarily on the extrasensory and visionary experiences and physical phenomena that coincided with or were otherwise related to the deaths of certain individuals

Early Research: Physical Portents, Apparitions, and Deathbed Visions

Early researchers collected numerous accounts of relatives, friends, and acquaintances who reported seeing visions of a dying person at or around the time of that person's death. A large study conducted by a group of Cambridge academicians in the second half of the nineteenth century demonstrated that such visions occurred with statistically high frequency during a period of twelve hours around the death of the envisioned individual (Sidgewick 1894). Many early studies also focused on unexplained physical events occurring at the time of death, such as watches stopping and starting, bells ringing, paintings or photographs falling off walls, and other incidents that seemed to announce a person's death (Bozzano 1948).

Initial work also concerned reports that individuals approaching death often had visions of their dead relatives, who seemed to welcome them to the next world. These deathbed visions were very authentic and convincing and often induced a state of euphoria in the dying person that seemed to ease his or her transition from life to death. These visions could not be easily explained in psychopathological terms and dismissed as hallucinations, since they were observed in individuals with clear consciousness who were not delirious, disoriented, and confused. However, these phenomena in and of themselves were not particularly interesting for the researchers, since the dying could have easily constructed such images from memories.

Early researchers therefore focused on an important subgroup of subjects usually referred to as "Peak in Darien" cases. This idea was conceived by Frances Power Cobbe in 1877 and later developed and elaborated by James Hyslop, William Barrett, and Harnell Hart (Cobbe 1877, Hyslop 1908, Barrett 1926, Hart 1959). This concept is based on the belief that spirits of dead relatives come to aid the dying, ease their transition, and take them to another world. The "Peak in Darien" concept thus implies that dying persons see only persons who are already dead. Thus, if a patient saw an apparition of a dead person about whose death he or she was not informed, this was then seen as strong supportive evidence for survival after death.

More relevant for our purpose is an extensive study of the deathbed observations of physicians and nurses conducted by Karlis Osis and his co-workers (Osis 1961). Instead of testing a specific narrow hypothesis, Osis recorded a wide range of phenomena occurring in dying individuals and analyzed the patterns recorded in his data. His study was based on a large survey: 10,000 questionnaires covering various aspects of deathbed observations were sent out, half of them to physicians and the other half to nurses. Detailed analyses were conducted on the 640 questionnaires that were returned. Although the number of respondents was relatively small, those who did return the questionnaires reported a large number of cases—a total of 35,540 deathbed observations.

Osis found that about 10% of dying patients appeared to be conscious in the hour preceding death. Surprisingly enough, according to the physicians and nurses in the sample, fear was not the dominant emotion in these individuals. The caretakers reported their patients more frequently experienced discomfort, pain, and even indifference. Furthermore, about one in twenty dying persons actually showed signs of elation. Another unexpected finding was a high incidence of visions with a predominantly nonhuman content: approximately ten times more frequent than one would expect in a comparable group of healthy persons.

Some of these visions more or less fit traditional religious concepts and represented Heaven, Paradise, or the Eternal City. Others were secular images of indescribable beauty, such as landscapes with gorgeous vegetation and exotic birds. According to the authors, most of these visions were characterized by brilliant colors and bore a close resemblance to psychedelic experiences induced by mescaline or LSD. Less frequent were horrifying visions of devils and Hell or other frightening experiences, such as being buried alive. The main focus of this study was on visions that involved human beings—visions of close relatives usually represented dead persons, whereas visions of non-relatives usually represented living persons.

Osis was able to support Barrett's and Hyslop's hypotheses that dying individuals predominantly envision dead persons who often claim to aid the individual's transition into post-mortem existence. He also confirmed the apparitional nature of these visions, since a large majority of patients experienced them in a state of clear consciousness. Their mental functioning was not disturbed by sedatives, other medication, or high body temperatures; and only a small proportion had a diagnosed illness that might be conducive to hallucinations, such as brain injury, cerebral disorders, mental disease, and uremia. Most dying individuals were fully conscious, with adequate awareness and responsiveness to the environment. This study also demonstrated the relative independence of the basic characteristics of these visions from physiological, cultural, and personality variables. The roots of this type of experience seemed to go beyond the personality differences between the sexes, beyond physiological factors such as clinical diagnosis and type of illness, and beyond educational level and religious background.

Pioneering Studies of Near-Death Experiences

Experiences associated with sudden vital emergency or clinical death are especially pertinent to consciousness research. Many descriptions of such experiences can be found in autobiographical accounts, novels, and poetry; but until the 1960s this area was surprisingly neglected by psychiatrists and psychologists. The first study of near-death experiences was not conducted by a psychiatrist or psychologist but by a Swiss geology professor from Zürich, Albert Heim. Heim was renowned for his studies of the Alps and for his book on mountain-forming processes. Having had several near-fatal accidents himself, Heim was very interested in subjective experiences of dying.

Over several decades, he collected accounts from survivors of situations involving serious vital threats. The persons who volunteered their reports were soldiers wounded in wars, masons and roofers who had fallen from heights, workers who had survived disasters in mountain projects and railway accidents, and a fisherman who had nearly drowned. However, the most important part of Heim's study was based on numerous reports made by Alpine climbers who had fallen off cliffs and been subsequently rescued, including three of his professional colleagues. Heim first presented his findings before the Swiss Alpine Club on February 26, 1892. His paper was subsequently published under the title, "Notizen über den Tod durch Absturz" (Remarks on Fatal Falls) in the yearbook of the Swiss Alpine Club (Heim 1892).

In this study Heim concluded that the subjective experiences of near death in about 95% of the victims were strikingly similar and showed only slight variations. It did not seem to make much difference whether the precipitating situation was a fall from a cliff, a fall from ice or snow, or a fall into a ravine or waterfall. Even the subjective perceptions of those individuals who had been run over by a wagon, crushed by machines, shot on the battlefield, or experienced near drowning, basically followed the same pattern. Practically all persons who faced death in accident situations developed a similar mental state, in which there was no pain or despair, grief, or overwhelming anxiety—emotions that tend to paralyze individuals in instances of lesser dangers that are not acutely life-threatening. Instead, mental activity at first became enhanced and accelerated, rising to a "hundred-fold velocity and intensity." Then the individuals experienced feelings of calm and profound acceptance. The perception of events and anticipation of the outcome were unusually clear, without disorientation or confusion. Time became greatly expanded, and individuals acted with lightning rapidity and on the basis of accurate reality testing of their situation. This was followed in many cases by a sudden review of the victim's entire past. Finally the person facing the threat of death often heard heavenly music and had an experience of transcendental beauty.

I will illustrate Heim's description of life-threatening situations with two subjective reports included in his original paper. The first is an account of his own mountaineering accident, which occurred when he was climbing in the Swiss Alps and fell off a glacial sheet, dropped about sixty-six feet, and landed on a border of snow:

> As soon as I began to fall I realized that now I was going to be hurled from the crag, and I anticipated the impact that would come. With clawing fingers, I dug into the snow in an effort to brake myself. My fingertips were bloody but I felt no pain. I heard clearly the blows on my head and back as they hit each corner of the crag and I heard a dull thud as I struck below. But I first felt pain some hours afterward. The earlier-mentioned flood of thoughts began during the fall. What I felt in five to ten seconds could not be described in ten times that length of time. All my thoughts and ideas were coherent and very clear, and in no way susceptible, as are dreams, to obliteration.
>
> First of all, I took in the possibilities of my fate and said to myself: "The crag point over which I will soon be thrown evidently falls off below me as a steep wall, since I have not been able to see the ground at the base of it. It matters a great deal whether or not snow is still lying at the base of the cliff wall. If this is the case, the snow will have melted from the

wall and formed a border around the base. If I fall on the border of snow I may come out of this with my life, but if there is no more snow down there, I am certain to fall on rubble and at this velocity death will be quite inevitable. If, when I strike, I am not dead or unconscious I must instantly seize my small flask of spirits of vinegar and put some drops from it on my tongue. I do not want to let go of my alpenstock; perhaps it can still be of use to me." Hence I kept it tightly in my hand.

I thought of taking off my glasses and throwing them away so that splinters from them might not injure my eyes, but I was so thrown and swung about that I could not muster the power to move my hands for this purpose. A set of thoughts and ideas then ensued concerning those left behind. I said to myself that upon landing below I ought to, indifferent to whether or not I were seriously injured, call immediately to my companions out of affection for them to say "I'm all right!" Then my brother and three friends could sufficiently recover from their shock so as to accomplish the fairly difficult descent to me. My next thought was that I would not be able to give my beginning university lecture that had been announced for five days later. I considered how the news of my death would arrive for my loved ones and I consoled my thoughts.

Then I saw my whole past life take place in many images, as though on a stage at some distance from me. I saw myself as the chief character in the performance. Everything was transfigured as though by a heavenly light and everything was beautiful without grief, without anxiety, and without pain. The memory of very tragic experiences I had had was clear but not saddening. I felt no conflict or strife; conflict had been transmuted into love. Elevated and harmonious thoughts dominated and united the individual images, and like magnificent music a divine calm swept through my soul. I became ever more surrounded by a splendid blue Heaven with delicate roseate and violet cloudlets. I swept into it painlessly and softly and I saw that now I was falling freely through the air and that under me a snowfield lay waiting. Objective observations, thoughts, and subjective feelings were simultaneous. Then I heard a dull thud and my fall was over.

The second example from Heim's paper is, according to him, a classical presentation of subjective experiences occurring during sudden accidental falls. This account is from a theology student who was involved in a train disaster with the collapse of the Münchenstein Bridge in 1891:

> Near the Birs Bridge, I felt a sudden strong shock that ensued from our erratic progress. But at the same moment, the train stopped in the middle of the fastest run. The shock threw the riders up to the roof. I looked backwards, unable to see what had happened. From the powerful metallic crashing that resounded up ahead, I presumed that there had been a collision. I opened the door and intended to go out. I noticed that the following car had lifted itself upwards and threatened to tumble down on me. I turned in my place and wanted to call to my neighbor at the window: "Out the window!" I closed my mouth as I bit my tongue sharply.
>
> Now there took place, in the shortest possible times, the ghastliest descent that one can imagine. I clung spasmodically to my seat. My arms and legs functioned in their usual way, as if instinctively taking care of themselves and, swift as lightning, they made reflex parries of the boards, poles, and benches that were breaking up around and upon me. During the time I had a whole flood of thoughts that went through my brain in the clearest way. The thoughts said, "The next impact will kill me." A series of pictures showed me in rapid succession everything beautiful and lovable that I had ever experienced, and between them sounded the powerful melody of a prelude I had heard in the morning: "God is almighty, Heaven and Earth rest in His hand; we must bow to His Will."
>
> With this thought in the midst of all the fearful turmoil, I was overwhelmed by a feeling of undying peace. Twice more the car swung upwards; then the forward part suddenly headed perpendicularly down into the Birs, and the rear part that I was in swung sideways over the embankment and down into the Birs. The car was shattered. I lay jammed in and pressed under a heap of boards and benches and expected the near car to come crashing down on my head; but there was sudden quiet. The rumbling noise stopped. Blood dripped from my forehead, but I felt no pain. The loss of blood made me light-headed. After a short struggle I worked my way out of the heaps and fragments and through a window. Just then I formed, for the first time, a conception of the immensity of the disaster that had taken place…

Heim concluded his paper by stating that death through falling is subjectively a very pleasant death. Those who have died in the mountains have, in their last moments, reviewed their individual pasts in states of transfiguration. Elevated above corporeal pain, they experienced noble and profound thoughts, glorious music, and feelings of peace and reconciliation. They fell in a magnificent blue or roseate Heaven, and then everything was suddenly still. According to Heim, fatal falls are much more "horrible and cruel" for the survivors than for the victims. It is incomparably more painful in both the feeling of the moment and subsequent recollection to see another person fall than to fall oneself. In many instances spectators were deeply shattered and incapacitated by paralyzing horror and carried a lasting trauma away from this experience while the victim, if he or she was not badly injured, emerged free of anxiety and pain. Heim illustrated his point with his personal experience of seeing a cow falling, which was still painful for him, while his own misfortune was registered in his memory as a powerful and even ecstatic transfiguration—without pain and without anguish—just as it actually had been experienced.

Autobiographical accounts and descriptions in fiction and poetry confirm that persons experiencing vital danger and those actually approaching death typically have episodes of unusual states of consciousness. These experiences are qualitatively different from our everyday consciousness and do not lend themselves easily to verbal descriptions. To convey the flavor and dimensions of such experiences it is therefore necessary to refer to accounts of individuals who are both very introspective and articulate. An excellent such description comes from C. G. Jung's autobiography, *Memories, Dreams, Reflections* (Jung 1961). Early in 1944 Jung broke his foot, and then suffered a heart attack. While Jung hung on the edge of death and received oxygen and camphor injections, he had a series of profound visionary experiences. The following is a condensed version of his detailed account of this state:

> It seemed to me that I was high up in space. Far below I saw the globe of the earth, bathed in a gloriously blue light. I saw the deep blue sea and the continents. Far below my feet lay Ceylon, and in the distance ahead of me the subcontinent of India. My field of vision did not include the whole earth, but its global shape was plainly distinguishable and its outlines shone with a silvery gleam through that wonderful blue light. In many places the globe seemed colored, or spotted dark green like oxidized silver. Far away to the left lay a broad expanse—the reddish-yellow desert of Arabia; it was as though the silver of the earth had there assumed a reddish-gold hue.
>
> Then came the Red Sea, and far, far back—as if in the upper left of a map—I could just make out a bit of the Mediterranean. My gaze was directed chiefly toward that. Everything else appeared indistinct. I could also see the snow-covered Himalayas, but in that direction it was foggy or cloudy. I did not look to the right at all. I knew that I was on the point of

departing from the earth. Later I discovered how high in space one would have to be to have so extensive a view—approximately a thousand miles! The sight of the earth from this height was the most glorious thing I had ever seen.

After contemplating it for a while, I turned around. I had been standing with my back to the Indian Ocean, as it were, and my face to the north. Then it seemed to me that I made a turn to the south. Something new entered my field of vision. A short distance away I saw in space a tremendous dark block of stone, like a meteorite. It was about the size of my house, or even bigger. It was floating in space, and I myself was floating in space. I had seen similar stones on the coast of the Gulf of Bengal. They were blocks of tawny granite, and some of them had been hollowed out into temples. My stone was one such gigantic dark block. An entrance led into a small antechamber.

To the right of the entrance, a black Hindu sat silently in lotus posture upon a stone bench. He wore a white gown, and I knew that he expected me. Two steps led up to this antechamber, and inside, on the left, was the gate to the temple. Innumerable tiny niches, each with a saucer-like concavity filled with coconut oil and small burning wicks, surrounded the door with a wreath of bright flames. I had once actually seen this when I visited the Temple of the Holy Tooth at Kandy in Ceylon; the gate had been framed by several rows of burning oil lamps of this sort.

As I approached the steps leading up to the entrance into the rock, a strange thing happened: I had the feeling that everything was being sloughed away; everything I aimed at or wished for or thought, the whole phantasmagoria of earthly existence, fell away or was stripped from me—an extremely painful process. Nevertheless something remained; it was as if I now carried along with me everything I had ever experienced or done, everything that had happened around me. I might also say: it was with me, and I was it. I consisted of all that, so to speak. I consisted of my own history, and I felt with great certainty: this is what I am. "I am this bundle of what has been, and what has been accomplished."

In this case the visionary quality and mythical nature of Jung's account could be attributed to his unusual personality and professional interests. A second example comes from an individual of very different character and profession: the German actor Curt Jurgens, who died a clinical death during a complicated surgical operation conducted in Houston, Texas, by Dr. Michael DeBakey. To replace the defective aorta with a plastic tube, the surgeon had to remove the heart from circulation. During this operation Curt Jurgens was dead for several minutes. The following is the account of his unusual experiences during this time from Jean-Baptiste Delacour's *Glimpses of the Beyond* (Delacour 1974):

> The feeling of well-being that I had shortly after the Pentothal injection did not last long. Soon a feeling that life was ebbing from me rose up from the subconscious. Today I like to say that this sensation came at the moment my heart stopped beating. Feeling my life draining away evoked powerful sensations of dread. I wanted to hold onto life more than anything, yet it was impossible for me to do so. I had been looking up into the big glass cupola over the operating room. This cupola now began to change. Suddenly it turned a glowing red. I saw twisted faces grimacing as they stared down at me. Overcome by dread, I tried to struggle upright and defend myself against these pallid ghosts, who were moving closer to me.
>
> Then, it seemed as if the glass cupola had turned into a transparent dome that was slowly sinking down over me. A fiery rain was now falling, but though the drops were enormous, none of them touched me. They splattered down around me, and out of them grew menacing tongues of flames licking up about me. I could no longer shut out the frightful truth: Beyond doubt, the faces dominating this fiery world were faces of the damned. I had a feeling of despair, of being unspeakably alone and abandoned. The sensation of horror was so great it choked me, and I had the impression I was about to suffocate.
>
> Obviously I was in Hell itself, and the glowing tongues of fire could be reaching me any minute. In this situation, the black silhouette of a human figure suddenly materialized and began to draw near. At first I saw it only indistinctly amid the flames and clouds of reddish smoke, but quickly it became clearer. It was a woman in a black veil, a slender woman with lipless mouth and in her eyes an expression that sent icy shudders down my back. When she was standing right face to face with me, all I could see were two black, empty holes. But out of these holes, the creature was nonetheless staring at me. The figure stretched out her arms toward me, and, pulled by an irresistible force, I followed her. An icy breath touched me, and I came into a world filled with faint sounds of lamentation, though there was not a person in sight.
>
> Then and there I asked the figure to tell me who she was. A voice

> answered: "I am Death." I summoned all my strength and thought: "I'll not follow her any more, for I want to live." Had I betrayed this thought? In any event, she moved closer to me and put her hands on my bare breast so that I would again be under the spell of her magnetic force. I could feel her ice-cold hands on my skin, and the empty eye sockets were fixed immovably on me. Again I concentrated all my thoughts on living, so as to escape death in this womanly guise. Before entering the operating room, I had embraced my wife. Now the phantom of my wife came to rescue me from Hell and lead me back to earthly existence.
>
> When Simone [his wife] appeared on the scene, the woman with the black veil departed soundlessly, on her lipless face a dreadful smile. Death could avail nothing against Simone, all radiant with youth and life. I felt only freshness and tenderness as she led me back by the hand along the same way that just before had been under the dark figure's spell. Gradually, gradually we left the fearful realm of shadows behind us and approached the great light. This luminousness guided us on, and finally became so bright that it began to blind me, and I had to close my eyes.
>
> Then suddenly a severe, dull pain set in, threatening to tear apart my chest cavity. I clutched Simone's hand harder and harder after my sudden return to consciousness. I found Simone sitting on my bed wearing a white nurse's uniform. I just had the strength to muster a weak smile. It was all I could do to utter one word: "Thanks." With this word I concluded a fearful but still fascinating journey into the afterworld, one I shall never forget as long as I live.

A major contribution to the near-death literature was a fascinating study carried out by David Rosen, psychiatrist from the Langley Porter Neuropsychiatric Institute in San Francisco. Rosen conducted follow-up interviews of six of the eight people who had survived suicidal jumps off the Golden Gate Bridge and one of the two survivors who had jumped off the San Francisco Bay Bridge (Rosen 1975). Rosen not only attempted to obtain information that would help clarify the magical attraction that Golden Gate Bridge has for suicidal people, but he also recorded and analyzed the nature of the subjective experiences during the falls and the long-term effects of this event on the survivors' lives.

All survivors, during and after their jumps, experienced mystical states of consciousness characterized by losing the sense of time and space and by feelings of spiritual rebirth and unity with other human beings, the entire universe, and God. As a result of their intimate encounter with death, some of them had a profound religious conversion; others described a reconfirmation of their previous religious beliefs. One of the survivors denied any suicidal intent altogether. He saw the Golden Gate Bridge as "golden doors" through which he would pass from the material world into a new spiritual realm. He claimed that his jump off the bridge was fulfilling a spiritual need and had more to do with parapsychology than with psychology or psychopathology.

When Rosen examined the lives of the survivors after their suicidal attempts, he discovered lasting beneficial changes in their emotional states, thinking, and behaviors. The most striking aspect of this transformation was a powerful upsurge of spiritual feelings, resulting in religious conversions or reinforcement of preexisting religious beliefs. A sense of spiritual rebirth was associated with a new way of perceiving and being in the world. The most significant practical consequences of this new orientation toward life were fewer self-destructive tendencies, more vitality, and joyful affirmation of human existence. One of the survivors described it this way:

> I was refilled with a new hope and purpose in being alive. It is beyond most people's comprehension. I appreciate the miracle of life—like watching a bird fly—everything is more meaningful when you come close to losing it. I experienced a feeling of unity with all things and a oneness with all people. After my psychic rebirth, I also feel for everyone's pain. Surviving reconfirmed my belief and purpose in my life. Everything was clear and bright—I became aware of my relationship with my creator.

Along with Mt. Mihara, a volcano in Japan, the Golden Gate Bridge is the world's leading suicide location. At least 1,200 people have been seen jumping or have been found in the water since the bridge opened in 1937, and the suicidal attempts continue at a rate of one every two weeks (Friend 2003). The bridge seems to have a magical attraction for people who contemplate suicide, perhaps because its name combines three powerful transcendental symbols—gold, gate, and bridge. In my experience suicide represents a tragic confusion between the ego death that would lead to psychospiritual rebirth and physical death, between egocide and suicide (Grof 1985, 2000).

The subjective accounts of the survivors in Rosen's study are very similar to Heim's material and also to reports of near-death experiences from other sources. The major difference is the emphasis on the transcendental phase, with the element of struggle and resistance notably absent. Also, the reliving of memories and the life-review are truncated or altogether absent. Rosen related these differences to the volitional nature of suicide, as compared to the unexpected and involuntary character of accidents. Individuals anticipating suicide would have faced the resistance to the termination of their life before they arrived at the decision to end it. Similarly some of the life review and final reckoning could well have happened earlier.

In the early near-death research, efforts to understand the mechanism of experiences associated with death and to formulate a theoretical framework for their interpretation were even scarcer than descriptive and phenomenological studies. Edward Clarke, author of the classical study of near-death experiences entitled *Visions: A Study of False Sight*, written when he was dying, considered a global reference to impaired functioning of the brain to be a satisfactory explanation for the changes of consciousness observed in dying individuals (Clarke 1878). Others referred to a more specific mechanism—cerebral anoxia—and pointed to the similarity between near-death experiences and various abnormal phenomena observed in high altitudes, during anesthesia, in experimental subjects in hypoxic chambers, and other situations involving lack of oxygen. Karlis Osis (1961) and Russell Noyes (1971) found interesting parallels between visionary experiences of the dying and the states induced by psychedelic drugs. This observation, although of great theoretical significance, does not really contribute to our understanding of the experience of dying. As we have seen earlier, psychedelic experiences are themselves very complex phenomena, which represent a serious challenge to current conceptual frameworks and have not yet been adequately explained.

Such explanations address at most only one aspect of near-death phenomena—the physiological or biochemical trigger of these experiences—and do not say anything about their specific content and deeper psychological significance. Two psychoanalytic studies have made serious attempts to apply basic psychoanalytic concepts to the study of near-death experiences. In the first of these papers, Oskar Pfister used as a basis for his speculations the study conducted by Albert Heim, described earlier in this chapter (Pfister 1930). In addition to Heim's observations collected during twenty-five years following his own near-fatal fall, Pfister had at his disposal a letter from Heim describing many details of his experience that were not mentioned in the original paper.

The rich data obtained from Heim enabled Pfister to familiarize himself with the general nature of near-death experiences. However, for a deeper psychodynamic assessment and interpretation of these phenomena, he needed the survivors' free associations to the specific manifest content. Such analysis was made possible with information volunteered by a casual travel acquaintance, a man who had been nearly killed in a wartime trench thirteen years before meeting Pfister. This person was able to describe the fantasies he had had in that situation and offer free associations to their content. On the basis of this material, Pfister drew tentative theoretical conclusions about the psychodynamic mechanisms of the shock thoughts and fantasies of an individual in mortal danger.

In *Beyond the Pleasure Principle*, Freud expressed the idea that the living organism would be annihilated by the energy-charged external world if it were not equipped with a special protective apparatus that functions as a stimulus barrier (Freud 1975). Pfister found this concept most useful for understanding the mechanism of near-death experiences. According to him, shock fantasies save the individual from excessive emotional trauma and function as a mechanism protecting him or her from losing waking consciousness and plunging into sleep or fainting. This mechanism would thus be a counterpart of the function that dreams play in protecting sleep. Where the danger is mild, an individual will react with paralysis and speechlessness. However, extreme danger results in high activation and stimulation of thought production. Several protective mechanisms occur in this phase. One of these is the illusion that the danger can be coped with effectively; another is the ability to register all the accompanying feelings. According to Pfister, the derealization so frequently observed in this situation also serves a protective function, because it involves a denial of the situation or its relevance when it is not possible anymore to cope realistically with the danger.

Under those circumstances, reality orientation breaks down, and regressive fantasies enter in. Some of the recollections that are part of the frequently observed life review are memories of a comforting nature, allusions to dangerous situations in the past that had a happy ending, or free fantasies. Déjà vu experiences or flight into anticipation of the future can also be seen as denial of a grim reality situation. The extreme, of course, is escape into a transcendental experience of Heaven or paradise that, according to psychoanalytic concepts, is a regression into the oceanic bliss of prenatal existence. Pfister thus saw near-death experiences as manifestations of "a brilliant victory of wishful thought over dreadful facts and illusion over reality."

Another relevant psychoanalytic study of the process of dying was published by R. C. A. Hunter, who had the unique opportunity of analyzing the content of a near-death experience of a medical nurse with whom he was working in long-term psychoanalysis (Hunter 1967). He saw her in regular analytic sessions two hours prior to her accident and twenty-two hours after it. These circumstances thus permitted the early collection of her fantasies and remembered experiences, along with some of the accompanying free associations. His patient was a physically healthy thirty-four-year-old woman, the mother of three children. At the time of the accident, she did not seem pathologically depressed, and there was no reason to suspect that she had suicidal impulses. She was in analysis because of interpersonal problems with her husband. The near-fatal accident was unexpected and had an abrupt onset.

Her dentist took an X ray of a tooth that was causing her pain and diagnosed an abscess forming at its root; he prescribed aspirin-codeine and penicillin. She took a tablet of the antibiotic when she was driving home with her husband in rush-hour traffic. Twenty minutes later, as a result of her allergic reaction to penicillin, she developed laryngeal and glottal edema accompanied by a high degree of suffocation and eventual unconsciousness. She was given adrenaline and taken by ambulance to a nearby hospital, where she was put on oxygen, more adrenaline, and cortical steroids. She recovered fully within a short time, and the next day she was able to talk about her experience in an analytic session. The following is Hunter's account of her report:

> She had never before suffered from any allergic manifestations, nor was there a family history of allergy. Being a nurse, she was aware, however, of the occurrence of penicillin allergy, and when she took the tablet, the thought crossed her mind that she might be allergic to penicillin. In the car, when her breathing began to become difficult, she realized what was happening and she experienced frantic fear, which, however, soon passed. (She would never fear dying again, she said.) She felt intense sympathy for her husband. Then she felt guilty that she was putting him through this ordeal. She was ashamed. It felt to her now (*post hoc*) that it had been partly revenge, but really she had had no control over it. She remembered a "last violent reaction" in which she had fought desperately against death, but she was not afraid, and then she had given in, knowing she wanted it.
>
> She had then witnessed, in rapid succession, a great many scenes from her life. They seemed in retrospect to start from about the age of five. She remembered the impression of vivid color. She had seen a beloved doll that she had had and was struck by how bright blue the glass eyes were. There was also a picture of herself on her bright red bicycle on the equally bright green lawn. She was confident that her whole life was not pictorially represented, only some scenes from her childhood, and she emphasized that it was all ecstatically happy.
>
> Her next memory was of a state of "bliss" and of "ecstasy." There was a picture of the Taj Mahal in which she was deeply, idyllically engrossed. It was a picture that she must have seen on several occasions—the usual one taken from the end of the lily pond in front. It was colored, the pond and lily pads blue and green, the minarets and the dome a very lovely gold and cream. She became aware of people trying to wake her up and felt resentful and irritated. She wanted to be left alone with her beautiful dream of the Taj Mahal. Then she became aware of an oxygen mask and the fact that an intravenous was running. She reluctantly regained consciousness to find herself in the emergency out-patient department of a hospital.

Analyzing her experience, Hunter was surprised by the similarity of her account to that published by Pfister. In both the recognition of danger is followed by a brief fear reaction, denial of the threat, and then a review from the victim's earlier life of unusually happy or ecstatic scenes. Hunter suggests on the basis of his observations that it is important to distinguish between death as a state and the experience of dying. While death may have many idiosyncratic meanings for different individuals, the process of suddenly and unexpectedly dying may move through certain definable and predictable stages. The content of these experiences is, however, colored by established personality patterns.

Hunter saw the life review that occurred in his patient as a denial or negation of the life-threatening situation. The sequence of regressive joyful memories and screen memories imparted a pleasant quality to the experience that actually masked an unpleasant affect. In Hunter's interpretation, the vision of the Taj Mahal had an idiosyncratic psychodynamic meaning for the patient. Not only did it help her negate and transcend the mortal danger, it also reflected her wishful fantasies toward her husband, as the Taj Mahal is a mausoleum built by an adoring husband for a beloved wife. On a deeper level of regression, according to Hunter, the pool and the dome suggested intrauterine and breast fantasies.

Russell Noyes, professor of psychiatry at the University of Iowa, reviewed several subjective accounts of individuals facing death and analyzed them from the psychiatric and psychodynamic point of view (Noyes 1972). He discovered striking uniformity, typical patterning, and characteristic experiential sequences underlying the seemingly rich and multiform content of individual accounts. According to Noyes, the descriptions of near-death and death experiences break down into three successive stages: resistance, life-review, and transcendence. The degree to which these individual stages are represented in a particular account can vary considerably, and in a particular case one of them might be missing entirely. However, these stages appear frequently and consistently enough to warrant such a division.

The initial stage of resistance involves recognizing danger, followed by fear of it or struggle against it, and finally acceptance of death. The realization that death is imminent precipitates a brief though violent struggle, often accompanied by marked anxiety. The individual oscillates between the need for active mastery and an urge for passive resignation. As long as even a slight chance of survival remains, the person's awareness of, and alertness to the dangerous situation are greatly enhanced. Under these circumstances the energy available for both physical and mental activity can be enormously increased. Disorganizing panic is delayed but may emerge with full strength as soon as the immediate danger has passed.

The remarkable acceleration of mental processes occurring in an individual facing death or serious injury often results in a fully conscious, sustained, and complex series of thoughts and even effective life-saving activity. This can be illustrated by Albert Heim's account of another accident, where such extraordinary activation of his mental resources saved him from extensive physical damage:

> In the summer of 1881, I fell between the front and rear wheels of a wagon traveling between Aosta and St. Remy and for a fleeting moment I was still able to hold onto the edge of the wagon. The following series of thoughts went through my mind: "I cannot manage to hold on until the horse comes to a stop; I must let go. If I simply let go, I will fall on my back and the wheel will travel forward over my legs. Then at least a fracture of the knee-cap or shinbone will be unavoidable; I must fall upon my stomach and the wheel will pass over the backs of my legs.
>
> If I will then tense the muscles, they will be a protective cushion for the bones. The pressure of the street will be somewhat less likely to break a bone than the pressure of the wheel. If I am able to turn myself to the left, then perhaps I can sufficiently draw back my left leg; on the other hand, turning to the right would, by the dimensions of the wagon, result in both legs being broken under it." I know quite clearly that I let myself fall only after these lightning-fast, wholly precise reflections, which seemed to imprint themselves upon my brain. Thereupon through a jerk of my arm, I turned myself to the left, swung my left leg powerfully outward, and simultaneously tensed my leg muscles to the limit of their strength. The wheel passed over my right ham, and I came out of it with a slight bruise (Heim 1892).

Individuals who are dying in a more gradual manner feel as though their will to live sustains them and are afraid that if they yield, they will die. At the point of surrender, fear subsides, and the person develops a feeling of serenity and tranquility. When death becomes certain, its advent is faced with inner calmness. Usually the stage of life review immediately follows the shift from active mastery to passive surrender. At this point the self splits from its bodily representation, an event that can precipitate "out-of-body experiences." Individuals can actually see their bodies approaching death, but there is no more fight against impending death. Death as a reality is negated, and the self becomes a witness watching this scene with detached interest.

The review of life that occurs at this time usually takes the form of a stream of memories that follow in rapid succession and appear to encompass the individual's entire past. The unrolling of this life film is sometimes retrogressive, moving from the time of the accident back into childhood, sometimes progressive, repeating the actual chronological sequence of events. Often pleasant emotions accompany this review; less frequently the review may engender a negative and painful affect. On occasion the life review is of a panoramic instead of sequential nature—in this case important memories from different periods of life appear simultaneously as part of a single continuum.

The stage of life review can be illustrated by an excerpt from a letter written by Admiral Beaufort, in which he describes his own near-drowning accident. When he was a youngster on board ship in Portsmouth harbor, he fell into the water. Unable to swim, he soon became exhausted and temporarily sank below the surface before he was rescued. His account was published in W. Munk's book, *Euthanasia or Medical Treatment in Aid of an Easy Death* (Munk 1887):

> All hope fled, all exertion had ceased, a calm feeling of the most perfect tranquility superseded the previous tumultuous sensations—it might be called apathy, certainly not resignation, for drowning no longer appeared to be an evil. I no longer thought of being rescued, nor was I in any bodily pain. On the contrary, my sensations were now of rather a pleasurable cast, partaking of that dull but contented sort of feeling, which precedes the sleep produced by fatigue. Though the senses were thus deadened, not so the mind; its activity seemed to be invigorated in a ratio which defies a description, for thought rose after thought with a rapidity of succession that is not only indescribable, but probably inconceivable, by anyone who has not himself been in a similar situation.
>
> The course of these thoughts I can even now in a great measure retrace—the event which had just taken place, the awkwardness that had produced it, the bustle it must have occasioned, the effect it would have on a most affectionate father, and a thousand other circumstances minutely associated with home were the first series of reflection that occurred. They then took a wider range—our last cruise, a former voyage and shipwreck, my school, the progress I had made there and the time I had misspent, and even all my boyish pursuits and adventures.
>
> Thus traveling backwards, every past incident of my life seemed to glance across my recollection in retrograde succession; not, however, in mere outline as here stated, but the picture filled up every minute and collateral feature; in short, the whole period of my existence seemed to be placed before me in a kind of panoramic review, and each act of it seemed to be accompanied by a consciousness of right or wrong, or by some reflec-

> tion on its cause or its consequences; indeed, many trifling events which had been long forgotten, then crossed into my imagination, and with the character of recent familiarity.

According to Noyes, this return to memories of the past may result from the sudden loss of future time orientation. Aging persons approaching the end of their lives tend to withdraw their investment in the future and turn toward reminiscences of the past. Similarly, individuals who are suddenly confronted with the termination of their lives may experience an increased investment in their pasts. This narrow focusing of vital energy on past events might be related to the intensity and vividness of the emerging early memories. Noyes pointed out the existential significance of this final life review and emphasized the unique perspective upon life that it brings.

At the moment of death, an individual's existence becomes a completed and unalterable pattern. Throughout history death has been recognized as a climactic moment for this very reason; it represents the last opportunity to attain or defend the aims held highest. Dying individuals undergoing this final review passionately affirm the transcendent meaning of their existence and integrate it into the universal order, which they embrace. This can be seen as a powerful assertion of the dying person's spiritual aspirations. In many instances the visionary experiences of some are so gratifying that they actually desire to die and stay forever in the transcendental realms; such persons are often resentful or even hostile when they are revived and awakened to everyday reality.

Usually the stage of transcendence evolves naturally from the life review. Individuals surveying their existence from the point of view of good and evil can see it from an increasingly distant perspective and may arrive at a point where they view their lives in their entireties and in complete detail. Finally even this limitation is overcome, and dying individuals experience what has been referred to as mystical, transcendental, cosmic, or religious consciousness, or what Abraham Maslow called a "peak experience" (Maslow 1964). In some instances the life review does not occur, and the individual suddenly confronted with death moves directly into the phase of transcendence.

In 1966, Walter Pahnke conducted comparative literary research of transcendental experiences of mystics and religious teachers through the ages (Pahnke 1966). He modified William James's and Walter Stace's criteria (James 1929, Stace 1960) and defined the following characteristics as the most important common denominators of a "peak experience:"

- A sense of unity (inner and outer)
- Strong positive emotion
- Transcendence of time and space
- Sense of sacredness (numinosity)
- Paradoxical nature
- Objectivity and reality of the insights
- Ineffability
- Positive aftereffects

As this list shows, during a peak experience, we have a sense of overcoming the usual fragmentation of the mind and body and feel that we have reached a state of unity and wholeness. We also transcend the ordinary distinction between subject and object and experience an ecstatic union with humanity, nature, the cosmos, and God. In the process we feel intense joy, bliss, serenity, and inner peace. In a mystical experience of this type, we have a sense of leaving ordinary reality, where space has three dimensions and time is linear. We enter a metaphysical, transcendent realm where these categories no longer apply. In this state, infinity and eternity become experiential realities. The numinous quality of this state has nothing to do with previous religious beliefs but rather reflects a direct apprehension of the divine nature of reality.

Descriptions of peak experiences are usually full of paradoxes. The experience can be described as "contentless, yet all-containing;" it has no specific content, but contains everything in a potential form. We may sense that we are simultaneously everything and nothing. While our personal identity and the limited ego have disappeared, we feel that we have expanded to the point where our being encompasses the entire universe. Similarly we may perceive all forms as empty, or emptiness as being pregnant with forms. We can even reach a state in which we see that the world exists and does not exist at the same time.

The peak experience can convey what seems to be ultimate wisdom and knowledge in matters of cosmic relevance, which the Upanishads describe as "knowing That, the knowledge of which gives the knowledge of everything." The knowledge imparted by the experience is ineffable; the very nature and structure of our language seem to be inadequate to describe it. Yet the experience can profoundly positively influence our system of values and strategy of existence. The situations associated with clinical death have all the characteristics described by Pahnke's mystical categories. These episodes of unusual states of consciousness can be accompanied by perceptual changes, in particular by vivid imagery.

Renaissance of Interest in Near-Death Experiences

In the 1970s, the books *On Death and Dying* by Elisabeth Kübler-Ross and *Life Af-*

ter Life by Raymond A. Moody marked a new era in the study of phenomena associated with death (Kübler-Ross 1969, Moody 1975). While Kübler-Ross focused more on clinical work with dying people, Moody's international bestseller explored the phenomenology of the near-death experiences (NDEs). Several aspects of Moody's work made his book a very special contribution to the study of the death experience: his combined background in psychology and medicine, the fact that he personally interviewed the survivors, and his objective approach uncolored by sensationalism.

Moody collected material from 150 persons divided into three categories. Some persons had been resuscitated after having been thought, adjudged, or pronounced dead by their doctors. The second category involved individuals who, in the course of accidents, severe injuries, or diseases, had a very close confrontation with physical death. The third category consisted of persons who described their experiences of dying to other people present at their deathbeds.

Moody personally interviewed over fifty persons in the first two categories in great detail and found far-reaching similarities among individual reports. He was able to isolate some basic characteristics of the death experience that occurred quite constantly. Some significantly overlapped with the experiential themes described earlier in the section on perinatal and transpersonal experiences. For example, many of the accounts included descriptions of passage through a dark enclosed place, referred to as a funnel, cave, tunnel, cylinder, valley, trough, or sewer, followed by encounters with divine light. Although the birth process was not specifically mentioned by Moody, the allusions to it seem obvious, such as sliding down head first, passing through a tunnel with concentric circles, staying in an enclosed space, lacking air and experiencing breathing difficulties, encountering scatological elements, and others.

Individuals on the threshold of death often reported hearing extraordinary sounds similar to those described in the Tibetan Book of the Dead and to those occurring in psychedelic sessions. Some were unpleasant noises, such as loud clicks, roaring, ringing, buzzing, whistling, or banging. Others were beautiful and soothing sounds—celestial chimes or majestic music of transcendental nature, often accompanied by feelings of peace and tranquility. Many of the NDE survivors complained about the ineffability of the experience and the inadequacy of our language to convey its extraordinary nature. Some described how, during a comatose state or after physical death, they heard statements and even entire discussions about their condition made by doctors, nurses, and relatives. On occasion, the accuracy of such perceptions could be corroborated by subsequent investigation.

Out-of-body phenomena were some of the most common characteristics of near-death experiences. These could take different forms. Some individuals experienced themselves as amorphous clouds, energy patterns, or pure consciousness. Others felt that they had a body, but one that was permeable, invisible, and inaudible to those in the material world. Some people reported fear, confusion, and a tendency to return to the physical body. Others described ecstatic feelings of timelessness, weightlessness, peace, serenity, and tranquility. While certain individuals felt concerned about the fate of their physical bodies, others were totally indifferent. Some perceptions were completely lacking: smells, temperature, and bodily sensations. By contrast, hearing and seeing were enhanced almost to the point of having no limitations.

Many dying individuals mentioned in Moody's study reported encounters with other beings, such as dead relatives or friends, "guardian spirits," or spirit guides. Visions of the "Being of Light" were especially common—an apparition of unearthly, radiant, and brilliant light that somehow showed certain personal characteristics—love, warmth, compassion, and a sense of humor. The communication with this divine being occurred without words, through an unimpeded transfer of thoughts. In the context of this encounter or outside of it, the dying individual often experienced a partial or total review of his or her life, which almost always involved vivid colors and a three-dimensional, dynamic form. The message from this experience seemed to be the understanding that the most important values in human life were learning to love other people and acquiring higher knowledge.

Some accounts spoke of reaching some absolute border or limit, where the decision had to be made as to whether to return or to continue the journey to the Beyond. In some instances, this frontier had a purely abstract form; in others it was represented by some symbolic obstacle or frontier—a door or a gate, a body of water, a gray mist, a fence, or a line. The attitudes toward coming back seemed to change during the process of dying. The first few moments after death were often characterized by a desperate desire to get back into the body and regrets over one's demise. This attitude typically changed into unwillingness to return after a certain depth had been reached and especially after the encounter with the Being of Light. Some individuals attributed their return to their own decision to do so, while others felt that they were sent back by the Being of Light or were brought back by love or the needs and prayers of others, regardless of their own wishes. Sometimes survivors did not remember how or why they returned.

Moody focused particularly on the problems people had when they tried to communicate their experiences to others. Often they found it extremely difficult to adequately describe such a profoundly significant event. Moody suggested that the reason so little was known of these relatively frequent episodes was precisely because they were so hard to describe. To complicate matters further, people listening to these accounts were often unable to comprehend them and sometimes were hampered by a condescending or derisive attitude. For instance, only one physician in Moody's entire sample had any familiarity at all with near-death experiences.

As a result of their experiences, survivors of the near-death situations and of clinical death emerged with new concepts of death and different attitudes toward it. Many lost their fear of death and even developed positive feelings about it, but not in the sense of desiring death or having suicidal tendencies. The survivors' doubts about the possibility of existence after death were dissipated, and continuation of consciousness beyond the point of physical demise became an experiential fact for them.

One of the most important aspects of Moody's study is his discussion of how people's lives were changed by their near-death experiences. Most felt that their lives significantly broadened and deepened as a result. They developed serious interest in ultimate philosophical and spiritual issues, and started pursuing quite different values in life. Existence suddenly appeared very precious, and they put much more emphasis on fully experiencing the present moment—on the here and now—than on ruminating about the past or fantasizing about the future. Their sense of the relative importance of the physical body and consciousness changed dramatically. A few survivors even developed psychic abilities.

These findings agree fully with Walter Pahnke's conclusions regarding the consequences of mystical experiences that occur spontaneously or during religious practice, without the association with vital emergency (Pahnke 1963). One of Pahnke's categories describing mystical consciousness includes lasting positive changes in feelings, attitudes, and behavior following the experience. These changes appear identical to those described by Moody. Russell Noyes reports similar conclusions in his analysis of several near-death and clinical death experiences (Noyes 1972). Temporary or lasting changes of this kind are very common in people who have had an intimate experiential encounter with death, whether it occurs in real life—in an accident, suicidal attempt, serious disease, or operation—or in a symbolic form. For example, a well-integrated spontaneous mystical experience, psychedelic session, participation in a powerful rite of passage, or spiritual emergency can have similar positive effects.

Despite the many similarities between Moody's findings and the observations we made during our work with terminal cancer patients, certain fundamental differences deserve special notice. Moody emphasized the lack of mythological elements in the near-death experiences he had observed, as well as in the resulting new concepts of death. He dismissed what he called the "the cartoonist's Heaven of pearly gates, golden streets, and winged, harp-playing angels, or Hell of flames and demons with pitchforks." He also suggested that the NDEs were always of a positive nature (Moody 1975).

When Moody's *Life After Life* was published, my book *The Human Encounter with Death*, coauthored with Joan Halifax (Grof and Halifax 1977), was in the process of being published. Moody and I were thus able to compare our respective findings, and I pointed out to him the differences in our observations. In our study at the Maryland Psychiatric Research Center, described in Chapters 13 and 14, specific archetypal images of divine beings and demonic presences appeared as frequently as the Divine without any form. We also witnessed frightening NDEs and some others that were outright hellish. Curt Jurgens's experience, described earlier, illustrates such an episode. In his sequel to *Life After Life*, Moody acknowledged that more recently he had encountered NDEs with such elements as the realm of confused ghosts and "cities of light" (Moody 1977). In later years, it became clear that frightening NDEs are fairly common, and they have since attracted considerable theoretical interest (Greyson and Bush 1992, Bache 1996).

Raymond Moody's book *Life After Life* generated great interest in near-death experiences both in the general population and in professional circles and inspired an entire generation of investigators—Kenneth Ring, Michael Sabom, Bruce Greyson, Phyllis Atwater, Barbara Harris Whitfield, and many others—to explore these fascinating phenomena. These researchers have shown that NDEs occur in about one-third of the people who encounter various forms of life-threatening situations, such as serious illness, car accident, near-drowning, heart attack, or cardiac arrest during a surgical operation. In some cases, similar effects can be induced simply by a strong sense of imminent death or even an expectation of death.

NDEs have also been induced experimentally. James Whinnery, a chemistry professor at West Texas A&M University, exposed experimental subjects, fighter pilots, and students in various aviation medical courses to intense gravitational forces in a giant centrifuge to simulate the extreme conditions of aerial combat maneuvering. He collected data from over 15 years of acceleration-research experience and more than 700 episodes of loss of consciousness caused by increased gravitation (G-LOC) that occurred in both fighter aircraft and during simulation experiments. Whinnery showed that under extreme g-forces, fighter pilots and experimental subjects lose consciousness and have a near-death experience (Whinnery 1997).

Basic Characteristics of Near-Death Experiences

NDEs can occur regardless of gender and age (including children). These episodes seem to happen with the same frequency in people of all socioeconomic groups, educational levels, sexual orientations, spiritual beliefs, religious affiliations, and life experiences. The phenomenology of NDEs shows significant variations, and no two experiences are identical. However, thanatologists have been able to define and describe certain characteristic features that are usually present in various combinations, including out-of-body experiences, life-review sequences, episodes of passing through tunnels toward light, ecstatic or rapturous feelings, and, less often, distressing sensations. Certain near-death experiences have all these experiential elements, but in most cases some are missing.

The most extraordinary aspect of NDEs is the occurrence of "veridical" out-of-body experiences (OBEs), a term used when disembodied consciousness is capable of accurate extrasensory perception of the surroundings. Thanatological studies have repeatedly confirmed that people who appear unconscious to external observers, including those who are clinically dead, can have OBEs during which their consciousness continues to perceive the environment. In these situations people are able to observe their bodies and the rescue procedures from above and "travel" freely to other parts of the same building or various remote places. Independent research has repeatedly confirmed the accuracy of observations made by disembodied consciousness (Ring and Valarino 1998, Sabom 1982 and 1998).

Such experiences are strikingly reminiscent of the descriptions of the bardo body found in the Tibetan Book of the Dead. According to the *Bardo Thödol*, after having fainted from fear in the Chönyid Bardo, the dying person awakens in the Sidpa Bardo in a new form—the bardo body. The bardo body differs from the gross body of everyday life: it is not composed of matter and has many remarkable qualities, such as the power of unimpeded motion and the ability to penetrate through solid objects. Those who exist in the form of bardo body can travel instantaneously to any place on earth and even to the sacred cosmic mountain Mt. Meru. Only two places are not accessible to this form: the mother's womb and Bodh Gaya, clear references to leaving the bardo state at the time of conception or enlightenment (Evans-Wentz 1957).

An extensive study conducted by Ken Ring and his colleagues has added a fascinating dimension to these observations: people who are congenitally blind for organic reasons and have never been able to see anything their entire lives can see the environment when their consciousness is disembodied during emergencies. The veracity of many of these visions has been confirmed by consensual validation (Ring and Valarino 1998, Ring and Cooper 1999). Various aspects of the environment accurately perceived by disembodied consciousness of the blind subjects ranged from details of electrical fixtures on the ceiling of the operation room to the surroundings of the hospital observed from a bird's eye view. Modern thanatological research has thus confirmed an important aspect of classical descriptions of OBEs, which can be found in spiritual literature and philosophical texts of all ages.

The occurrence of veridical OBEs is not limited to near-death situations, vital emergencies, and episodes of clinical death. Such experiences can emerge in sessions of powerful experiential psychotherapy (such as primal therapy, rebirthing, or Holotropic Breathwork), in the context of experiences induced by psychedelics, particularly the dissociative anesthetic Ketalar (ketamine), and also spontaneously—either as isolated episodes in the life of the individual, or repeatedly as part of a crisis of psychic opening or some other type of spiritual emergency.

Robert Monroe, the foremost researcher of OBEs, had spontaneous experiences of out-of-body travel himself over a period of many years (Monroe 1971, 1985, 1994). He developed electronic laboratory techniques for inducing OBEs and founded a special institute in Faber, Virginia, to conduct systematic studies of them. Other controlled clinical studies have also demonstrated the authenticity of OBEs, including experiments by the well-known psychologist and parapsychologist Charles Tart with Ms. Z. at the University of California in Davis (Tart 1968) and perceptual tests conducted by Karlis Osis and D. McCormick with Alex Tanous (Osis and McCormick 1980).

Life review, another important aspect of NDEs, is a replay or even reliving of one's life in its entirety or as a mosaic of separate events. Life review proceeds with extraordinary speed and can be completed within seconds of clock time. Some of David Rosen's subjects experienced complete life review within the three seconds that it takes to fall from the railing of the Golden Gate Bridge to the water's surface. The direction of the sequence of events varies. In some instances, the replay begins with birth, follows the actual course of life, and ends in the life-threatening situation. In others, time seems to roll back from the situation of vital threat toward childhood, infancy, and birth. (There are even some indications that individuals whose life review unfolds in such a way that it moves away from the accident suffer surprisingly little damage.) Yet another possibility is a "panoramic life review," in which one's life appears in its entirety, without the element of linear time.

A major and fairly consistent feature of near-death experiences is a sense of passing through a dark tunnel or funnel and moving toward a source of brilliant golden or white light of supernatural beauty and distinctly numinous quality. Many NDE survivors, as well as thanatologists studying these experiences, have pointed out that the passage through the tunnel toward light seems to be closely related to similar experiences in holotropic states engaging the perinatal level. This experience could thus represent an accelerated replay of the birth process as part of the life review. In this context the experience of traveling through a tunnel reflects an archetypal pattern that characterizes the transition from prenatal life to postnatal life, as well as the passage from incarnate to discarnate existence.

Hence the vicissitudes of the struggle in the birth canal during biological delivery could be instrumental in separating and alienating us from the connection with the numinous dimensions of reality and our true identity, which is divine. In Alan Watts' words, the emotional and physical suffering involved in this process would forge the "taboo against knowing who we are" and force us to identify with the "skin-encapsulated ego" (Watts 1961). A passage through the tunnel in the opposite direction, as it happens in the experience of psychospiritual death and rebirth, in near-death situations, and at the time of biological demise would then reconnect us with the numinous dimensions of reality and our transpersonal identity. In the paintings of people undergoing deep regressive therapy this experiential template is usually portrayed either as an hourglass or as a spiral, depending on the point of view.

The divine radiance that we encounter as we are emerging from the tunnel has definite personal characteristics and even a sense of humor. It can communicate telepathically, i.e., ask questions and give answers without the use of words and likewise receive questions and answers from humans. People who have experienced this luminescent entity describe it as a "Being of Light, "Supreme Being," or God. This encounter is often combined with the review and moral evaluation of one's life, where the person has the sense of being judged or of judging oneself in the context of the higher cosmic order. The emphasis in this ethical evaluation seems to be on one's ability to love and help others. This observation represents empirical validation of another recurring theme found in eschatological mythologies of many religions, the scene of the divine judgment that the soul of the deceased encounters during its posthumous journey.

Most NDEs also are accompanied by unusually strong positive feelings that can reach the level of ecstatic rapture or "peace that passeth all understanding." Such feelings can be associated with visions of celestial realms, paradisean gardens, beautiful natural sceneries, exquisite bird songs, and heavenly music. However, contrary to Moody's original findings, not all NDEs are pleasurable and comforting. As mentioned previously, thanatological literature contains many references to frightening, painful, distressing, and even hellish NDEs (Grey 1985, Irwin and Bramwell 1988, Greyson and Bush 1992, Ring 1994, Bache 1996).

According to Greyson and Bush, distressing NDEs fall into three categories. The first and most common has the same general features as the pleasurable version—an out-of-body experience and rapid movement through a tunnel or void toward light—but the individual feels overwhelmed and out of control and is frightened as a result. The second, less common type of distressing NDE is characterized by an acute awareness of nonexistence or of being completely alone, forever lost in a meaningless void. In this type of experience, people sometimes receive a totally convincing message that the material world, including themselves, never really existed. The third and rarest type of frightening NDE involves hellish imagery such as ugly or foreboding landscapes, demonic beings, loud and annoying noises, frightening animals, and various beings in extreme distress (Greyson and Bush 1992). Barbara Rommer added yet a fourth type, an NDE with a negative life review and an experience of judgment by a higher power which is not loving and supportive, but guilt-provoking and emotionally devastating (Rommer 2000).

Many survivors report that they have received some extraordinary illuminating knowledge or wisdom concerning existence, the universal scheme of things, or meaning of life—the type of experience that the Upanishads referred to as "Knowing That, the knowledge of which gives Knowledge of Everything." Less frequently the information can be of a concrete and specific nature, such as disclosure of family secrets concerning adoption, parentage, or deceased siblings, specific features of one's ancestors, and others. In some instances, NDEs include visions portraying the self-destructive course that humanity is pursuing and alarming images of the future that awaits us if we do not change. On rare occasions, NDEs can predict specific future events. The best known example of such an occurrence is the case of Dannion Brinkley:

> In September 1975, Dannion Brinkley was talking on the phone during a thunderstorm. A bolt of lightning hit the phone line and electrocuted him; as a result of it, his heart stopped and he died. When he came back to life in the morgue twenty-eight minutes later, Brinkley had an incredible story to tell about the NDE experience he had had at the time when he was clinically dead. He described a passage through a dark tunnel and his visit to a crystal city and a "cathedral of knowledge." There thirteen angels shared with him one hundred seventeen revelations about various future events, ninety-five of which have already come true. Among them was the prediction of the Chernobyl accident, of the war in the Middle East, and of the upcoming presidency of "an actor, whose initials would be R. R. and who would project the image of being a cowboy to the rest of the world" (Brinkley, Perry, and Moody 1995).

Many accounts of NDEs refer to what appears to be a "point of no return." This threshold may take a concrete form—a fence, body of water, cliff, or some other type of barrier—or involve simply a strong sense of an invisible but nevertheless compelling obstruction. Reaching this limit is associated with a convincing feeling that continuing beyond this point would mean physical death and would make return into one's body impossible. The decision not to continue and return to the body reflects the individual's sense of unfinished business or an important mission remaining in life. It can also be strongly influenced by emotional reactions of surviving children, spouses, parents, or other relatives, who are attached to the individual and are unable to let go. This emotional pressure to return has its opposite in the "welcoming committee," apparitions of deceased relatives and friends, who are welcoming the individual in crisis and inviting him or her to join them in the Beyond.

Several researchers have described lasting aftereffects of NDEs (Ring 1984, Atwater 1988, Sutherland 1992), including increased zest for life, a tendency to live more fully in the present, and less time spent ruminating about the past or fantasizing about the future. Such changes might be associated with a less accepting attitude toward clocks, schedules, time pressures, and the hastiness of modern life. People definitely display less interest in material possessions and goals and instead shift their focus toward learning, self-actualization, and service to others. Consumption of cigarettes, alcohol, and drugs tends to decline considerably. Particularly surprising is the observation that NDE survivors are frequently unable to wear watches and have problems with electrical conductivity, such as shorting out computers and erasing credit cards (Morse 1992).

A greater capacity to love other people, animals, nature, and life in general is a very common consequence of NDEs. These experiences tend to engender spirituality of a non-denominational, non-sectarian, universal, and all-encompassing nature, one that resembles the spirituality of mystics and has very little to do with church affiliation and organized religions. Essential aspects of this new spiritual orientation are lack of fear of death, confidence about life after death, and belief in reincarnation. The sense of personal identity tends to shift from the persona and the body/ego to that of an immortal being, consciousness, or soul. This shift is often accompanied by a sense of planetary citizenship and a strong inclination to participate in activities seen as beneficial for the future of humanity. Increase of intuition, sensitivity, and ESP are some additional aftereffects of NDEs.

Near-Death Experiences and the Nature of Consciousness

Attempts to provide biological explanation for NDEs have proved unsuccessful and unconvincing. Some authors have suggested that NDEs are caused by drugs administered to the patients at the time of crisis, such as anesthetics and morphine. However, NDEs can occur in situations where no such drugs are administered—even cases where there is only expectation of death, but no physiological emergency whatsoever. With the exception of the dissociative anesthetic ketamine, the effects of these drugs are also completely different than the phenomenology of NDEs. The same is true for endorphins, morphine-like substances produced by the body, which some authors referred to as causes of NDEs. Others have attributed the experiences to anoxia; this explanation is equally implausible for the same reasons as the pharmacological theories. Not all NDEs are associated with anoxia. Furthermore, lack of oxygen causes progressive confusion and muddling of cognitive functions, the antithesis of the clarity and expansion of consciousness that characterize NDEs.

Peter Fenwick, the renowned British neuropsychiatrist, summed up his serious doubts that NDEs can be explained by physiological and chemical changes in the brain in the following way:

> I am absolutely sure that such experiences are not caused by oxygen shortages, endorphins, or anything of that kind. And certainly none of these things would account for the transcendental quality of many of these experiences, the fact that people feel an infinite sense of loss when they leave them behind... What is also quite clear is that any disorientation of brain function leads to a disorientation of perception and reduced memory. You cannot normally get highly structured and clearly remembered experiences from a highly damaged or disoriented brain (Fenwick and Fenwick 1995).

Michael Sabom, a cardiologist known in the thanatological circles for his book *Recollections of Death* (Sabom 1982), makes the most convincing argument that NDEs do not result from disturbances of the brain functions. In his more recent work, *Light and Death: One Doctor's Fascinating Accounts of Near-Death Experiences* (Sabom 1998), he presents the extraordinary case of Pam Reynolds. Pam underwent a rare surgical operation because of a giant aneurysm of the basilar artery at the base of her brain. The size and location of the aneurysm required a daring surgical procedure known as hypothermic cardiac arrest or "standstill."

When Pam's body temperature was lowered to sixty degrees, her heartbeat and breathing stopped. She was also "brain-dead" by all three criteria used to determine brain death: her electroencephalogram was flat, her brain-stem response to acoustically evoked potentials was absent, and there was no blood flow through her brain. Interestingly, while she was in this state, she had the deepest NDE of all the fifty people participating in Michael Sabom's Atlanta study. Her remarkably detailed veridical out-of-body observations were later verified to be very accurate. Her case is considered to be one of the strongest examples of veridical NDEs, because of her ability to describe unique surgical instruments and procedures used by the medical team while she was clinically dead and brain-dead.

The existing psychological theories of NDEs are equally unconvincing as the biological ones. Suggestions that NDEs are wish-fulfilling pleasurable fantasies protecting the individual from suffering and the threat of destruction (Pfister 1930, Hunter 1967, Noyes and Kletti 1972) cannot explain the occurrence of frightening and unpleasant

NDEs. The idea that they reflect one's religious upbringing and cultural conditioning is just as unsatisfactory, because there is absolutely no correlation between religious beliefs and NDEs (Grosso 1981, Sabom 1982, Ring 1984). And the clearly paradigm-breaking phenomenon of veridical OBEs represents a formidable challenge and mortal blow to current biological and psychological theories.

References to the similarity between NDEs and psychedelic experiences, particularly those originating on the perinatal level, are very appropriate and interesting. In our program of psychedelic therapy with terminal cancer patients conducted at the Maryland Psychiatric Research Center in Baltimore, we observed several patients who had first psychedelic experiences and later actual NDEs when their disease progressed (e.g., a cardiac arrest during an operation). These patients reported that both situations were very similar and described the psychedelic sessions as invaluable experiential training for dying (see the case history of Ted in Chapter 14).

However, the similarity between these two categories of experiences hardly supports a simple chemical explanation for NDEs. Psychedelic states are themselves extremely complex and present formidable theoretical challenges. OBEs with confirmed extrasensory perception of the environment undermine the basic metaphysical assumption of monistic materialistic science, which sees consciousness as an epiphenomenon, a function which somehow mysteriously emerges out of the complexity of neurophysiological processes in the brain. OBEs make it absolutely clear that consciousness is capable of doing things that the brain cannot possibly perform. These observations indicate that consciousness is at least an equal partner of the brain, if not supraordinated to it.

The OBEs occurring in near-death situations are especially relevant to the problem of survival of consciousness after death, since they demonstrate that consciousness can operate independently of the body. If consciousness were nothing else than a product of neurophysiological processes in the brain, it could not possibly detach itself from the body and from the brain, become autonomous, and be able to perceive the environment without mediation of the senses. Yet this is precisely what occurs in many well-documented cases of OBEs. Naturally, people who have had OBEs in near-death situations and returned to give us their reports might have come very close to death, but for whatever reason did not cross the point of no return. However, if consciousness can function independently of the body during one's lifetime, it may well be able to do likewise after death.

10
THE MYSTERY OF KARMA AND REINCARNATION

"It is no more surprising to be born twice than to be born once."
– Voltaire, French writer and philosopher

AMONG THE MOST INTERESTING and controversial transpersonal phenomena are experiences featuring episodes from different historical periods and countries, associated with a convincing feeling of *déjà vu* and *déjà vécu*—a strong sense of personal remembering that one has already seen or experienced these events in another lifetime. People who have such experiences often refer to them as memories from previous incarnations and see them as proof or at least indication of a previous life. Past life memories are clearly directly relevant to the problem of survival of consciousness after death. They also provide fascinating insights into the belief in karma and reincarnation, which has been independently developed and held by many religious and cultural groups in different parts of the world.

The concept of karma and reincarnation represents the cornerstone of Hinduism, Buddhism, Jainism, Sikhism, Zoroastrianism, the Tibetan Vajrayana Buddhism, and Taoism. Similar ideas occur in such geographically, historically, and culturally diverse groups as various African tribes, native Americans, pre-Columbian cultures, the Hawaiian Kahunas, practitioners of the Brazilian Umbanda, the Gauls, and the Druids. In ancient Greece, several major schools of thought subscribed to this concept, including the Pythagoreans, the Orphics, and the Platonists. The Essenes, the Pharisees, the Karaites, and other Jewish and semi-Jewish groups also adopted the concept of karma and reincarnation, and it formed an important part of the Kabbalistic theology of medieval Judaism. Other groups adhered to this belief, including the Neo-Platonists and Gnostics.

Concepts similar to reincarnation and karma existed also among the early Christians. According to St. Jerome (A.D. 340-420), reincarnation was given an esoteric interpretation that was communicated to select elite. Origen (A.D. 186-253), one of the greatest Church Fathers of all times, was the most famous Christian thinker who speculated about the pre-existence of souls and world cycles. In his writings, particularly his book *De Principiis* (On First Principles) (Origenes Adamantius 1973), Origen asserted that certain scriptural passages could only be explained in terms of reincarnation. His teachings were condemned by the Second Council of Constantinople, convened by the Emperor Justinian in A.D. 553, and became a heretical doctrine. The Constantinople Council decreed: "If anyone assert the fabulous pre-existence of souls and shall submit to the monstrous doctrine that follows from it, let him be anathema!" However, some scholars believe that they can detect traces of his teachings in the writings of St. Augustine, St. Gregory, and even St. Francis of Assisi.

Sholem Asch, a twentieth century Hassidic scholar, describes the problem of past life experiences in mythological language:

> Not the power to remember, but its very opposite, the power to forget, is a necessary condition of our existence. If the lore of the transmigration of souls is a true one, then these souls, between their exchange of bodies, must pass through the sea of forgetfulness. According to the Jewish view, we make the transition under the overlordship of the Angel of Forgetfulness. But it sometimes happens that the Angel of Forgetfulness himself forgets to remove from our memories the records of the former world; and then our senses are haunted by fragmentary recollections of another life. They drift like torn clouds above the hills and valleys of the mind, and weave themselves into the incidents of our current existence (Asch 1967).

Certainly we need more than a poetic reference to ancient mythology to validate the concept of reincarnation. Careful study of the amassed evidence is absolutely necessary to make any valid conclusions. For the Hindus, Buddhists, and many other religious and cultural groups, as well as knowledgeable consciousness researchers, reincarnation is not a matter of belief, but an empirical issue, based on very specific experiences and observations. According to Christopher Bache, the evidence in this area is so rich and extraordinary that scientists who do not think the problem of reincarnation deserves serious study are "either uninformed or bone-headed" (Bache 1991b). Colin Wilson, author of many books on psychology, philosophy and mysticism, is even more emphatic: "The sheer volume of evidence for survival after death is so immense that to ignore it is like standing at the foot of Mount Everest and insisting that you cannot see the mountain."

This issue is highly important, since beliefs regarding reincarnation have great ethical impact on human life. Given the present global crisis, anything that could mitigate the senseless bloodshed and increase the chances of the human race to survive deserves serious attention. In view of the theoretical and practical importance of the problem of karma and reincarnation and its highly controversial nature, the existing evidence must be carefully and critically examined.

Spontaneous Past Life Memories in Children: Research by Ian Stevenson

Important supportive evidence for reincarnation can be drawn from numerous cases of small children who remember and describe their previous lives in other bodies, other places, and with other people. These memories usually emerge spontaneously shortly after these children begin to talk and often are associated with various complications, such as certain "carry-over pathologies" involving phobias, strange reactions to certain people, or various idiosyncrasies. Access to these memories usually disappears between the ages of five and eight.

Many cases of this kind have been described by child psychiatrists and psychologists. Ian Stevenson, professor of psychology at the University of Virginia in Charlottesville, VA, has conducted meticulous studies of over 3,000 such cases and reported them in his books *Twenty Cases Suggestive of Reincarnation, Unlearned Languages,* and *Children Who Remember Previous Lives* (Stevenson 1966, 1984, and 1987). Only the strongest cases are included in these works, and even these total several hundred. The others were eliminated because they did not meet his strict criteria and high standards—cases in which, for instance, the family of the child benefited financially, in terms of social prestige, or public attention. In some other problematic cases, he found a connecting person who could have been the psychic link. Additional reasons for exclusion were inconsistent testimony, cryptomnesia (the appearance of images in memory that seem to be original creations), witnesses of questionable character, or indication of fraud.

Stevenson's findings were quite remarkable. Although in all the reported cases he had eliminated the possibility that the information could have been obtained through conventional channels, he was able to confirm by independent investigation the stories the children were telling about their previous lives, often with incredible details. In some cases, he actually took the children to the village which they remembered from their previous life. Although they had never been there in their current lifetime, they were familiar with the topography of the village, were able to find the home they had allegedly lived in, recognized the members of their "family" and the villagers, and knew their names. To illustrate the remarkable nature of Stevenson's material, I present here the story of Parmod Sharma, one of his most interesting cases. This condensed version of the case of Parmod Sharma was originally published in Chris Bache's book *Lifecycles: Reincarnation and the Web of Life* (Bache 1991b).

The Case of Parmod Sharma

Parmod Sharma was born on October 11, 1944, in Bisauli, India. His father was Professor Bankeybehary Lal Sharma, a Sanskrit scholar at a nearby college. When Parmod was about two and a half, he began telling his mother not to cook meals for him anymore, because he had a wife in Moradabad who could cook. Moradabad was a town about ninety miles northeast of Bisauli. Between the ages of three and four, Parmod began to speak in detail of his life in Moradabad. He described several businesses he had owned and operated with other members of his family, particularly a shop that manufactured and sold biscuits and soda water, which he called "Mohan Brothers," run by the Mehra family. He insisted that he was one of the Mehra brothers and that he also had a business in Saharanpur, a town about a hundred miles north of Moradabad.

Parmod tended not to play with the other children in Bisauli but preferred to spend time alone, building models of shops complete with electrical wiring. He especially liked to make mud biscuits, which he served his family with tea or soda water. During this time, he provided many details about his shop: its size and location in Moradabad, what was sold there, and his activities connected to it, such as his business trips to New Delhi. He even complained to his parents about the less prosperous financial situation of their home compared to what he had been used to as a successful merchant.

Parmod's uncle had been temporarily stationed as a railroad employee in Moradabad when Parmod was very young. Because of Parmod's interest in biscuits, his uncle had brought him biscuits from the "Mohan Brothers" shop. The biscuits had the shop's name embossed on them, and although Parmod could not yet read, the biscuits might have stimulated associations for him. Interestingly, Parmod's mother said that Parmod did not recognize the biscuits. His uncle had not been in Moradabad when Parmanand (one of the Mehra brothers who had died prematurely) was alive, nor did he have any personal acquaintance with any of the Mehra brothers.

Parmod had a strong distaste for curd, which is quite unusual for an Indian child, and on one occasion even advised his father against eating it, saying that it was dangerous. Parmod said that in his other life he had become seriously ill after eating too much curd one day. He had an equally strong dislike for being submerged in water, which could have related to his report that he had previously "died in a bathtub." Parmod said that he had been married and had had five children—four sons and one daughter. He was anxious to see his family again and frequently begged his parents to take him back to Moradabad to visit them. His family always refused the request, though his mother did persuade him to begin school by promising to take him to Moradabad when he had learned to read.

Parmod's parents never investigated or tried to verify their son's claims, perhaps because of the Indian belief that children who remembered their previous lives died early. News of Parmod's statements, however, eventually reached the ears of a family in Moradabad named Mehra, whose circumstances matched many of the details of Parmod's story. The brothers of this family owned several businesses in Moradabad, including a biscuit and soda shop named "Mohan Brothers." The shop had been named after the eldest brother, Mohan Mehra, and had originally been called "Mohan and Brothers," later shortened to "Mohan Brothers." This shop had been started and managed by Parmanand Mehra until his untimely death on May 9, 1943, eighteen months before Parmod was born.

Parmanand had gorged himself on curd, one of his favorite foods, at a wedding feast and had subsequently developed a chronic gastrointestinal illness followed later by appendicitis and peritonitis from which he had died. Two or three days before his death, he had insisted, against his family's advice, on eating more curd, saying that he might not have another chance to enjoy it. Parmanand had blamed his illness and impending death on overeating curd. As part of his therapy during his appendicitis, Parmanand had tried a series of naturopathic bath treatments. While he had not in fact died in a bathtub, he had been given a bath immediately before his death. Parmanand left a widow and five children—four sons and one daughter.

In the summer of 1949, the Mehra family decided to travel to Bisauli to meet Parmod, who was a little under five years old at the time. When they arrived, however, Parmod was away and no contact was made. Not long thereafter, Parmod's father took him to Moradabad to explore his son's compelling remembrances first hand. Among those who met Parmod at the railway station was Parmanand's cousin, Sri Karam Chand Mehra, who had been quite close to Parmanand. Parmod threw his arm around him weeping, calling him "older brother" and saying "I am Parmanand." Parmod had not used the name Parmanand before this meeting. Indians commonly call a cousin "brother" if the relationship is a close one, as had been the case for Parmanand and Karam. The intensity and genuineness of the emotions this reunion generated alone seemed very significant—at least equally as important a piece of evidence as verifying and corroborating external objects and events.

Parmod then proceeded to find his way to the "Mohan Brothers" shop on his own, giving instructions to the driver of the carriage, which brought them from the station. Entering the shop, he complained that "his" special seat had been changed. In India it is customary for the owner of a business to have an enclosed seat—a *gaddi*—located near the front of the store where he can greet customers and direct business. The location of Parmanand's gaddi had in fact been changed some time after his death. Once inside, Parmod asked: "Who is looking after the bakery and soda water factory?" This had been Parmanand's responsibility. The complicated machine, which manufactured the soda water, had been secretly disabled in order to test Parmod. However, when it was shown to him, Parmod knew exactly how it worked. Without any assistance, he located the disconnected hose and gave instructions for its repair.

Later at Parmanand's home, Parmod recognized the room where Parmanand had slept and commented on a room screen that he correctly observed had not been there in Parmanand's day. He also identified a particular cupboard that Parmanand had kept his things in, as well as a special low table, which had also been his. "This is the one I used to use for my meals," he said. When Parmanand's mother entered the room, he immediately recognized her as "Mother" before anyone else present was able to say anything. He also correctly identified Parmanand's wife and acted somewhat embarrassed in front of her. She was, after all, a full grown woman and he was only five, though apparently possessing at least some of the feelings of an adult husband. When they were alone, he said to her: "I have come, but you have not fixed *bindi*," referring to the red dot worn on the forehead by Hindu wives. He also reproached her for wearing a white sari, the appropriate dress for a Hindu widow, instead of the colored sari worn by wives.

Parmod correctly recognized Parmanand's daughter and the one son who was at the house when he had arrived. When Parmanand's youngest son later came home from school, Parmod correctly identified him as well, using his familiar name, Gordhan. In their conversation, Parmod would not allow the older Gordhan to address him by his first name, but insisted that he call him "Father." "I have only become small," he said. During this visit, Parmod also correctly identified one of Parmanand's brothers and a nephew.

Parmod showed a striking knowledge for other details of Parmanand's world. While touring the Victory Hotel which the Mehra brothers owned in Moradabad, Parmod commented on the new sheds that had been built on the property. The Mehra family confirmed that these had indeed been added after Parmanand's death. Entering the hotel, Parmod pointed out a cupboard and said: "These are the *almirahs* I had constructed in Churchill House." Churchill House was the name of a second hotel the Mehra brothers owned in Saharanpur, a town about a hundred miles north of Moradabad. Shortly after Parmanand's death, the family had in fact decided to move these particular cupboards, which Parmanand had built for Churchill House, to the Victory Hotel.

On a visit to Saharanpur later that fall, Parmod spontaneously identified a doctor known to Parmanand in that city. "He is a doctor and an old friend of mine," he said. During that visit, he also recognized a man named Yasmin who, as he insisted, owed him (Parmanand) some money. "I have not got some money back from you," he said.

At first, Yasmin was reluctant to acknowledge the loan, but after being reassured that the Mehra family was not going to press for repayment, he admitted that Parmod was quite right about the debt.

Why do such children remember their previous lives? According to Stevenson, the specific circumstances of death play a key role, particularly those involving a shock that "can possibly break through the amnesia." This is congruent with the fact that the most vivid memories usually involve events immediately preceding death and leading up to it. Stevenson points out that these children are not able to say anything about events that occurred in the setting of their former personalities' lives after their death. This is an important factor in determining whether they are unconsciously reconstructing the details of this life by telepathically reading the minds of those who knew the deceased, or possess these details as genuine memories.

Possibly the strongest evidence in support of the reincarnation hypothesis is Ian Stevenson's two-volume set entitled *Reincarnation and Biology: A Contribution to the Etiology of Birthmarks and Birth Defects* (Stevenson 1997). On 2,265 small-print pages, illustrated with charts and graphic photographs, including some from autopsy reports, Stevenson presents his unique and convincing biological support for reincarnation. He shows that about 35% of the children who claim to remember previous lives have unusual birthmarks, strange physical abnormities, or rare birth defects that correspond closely to a wound, often fatal, or scar on the body of the deceased person the child remembers being. Stevenson conducted a meticulous study of 210 such children, including 49 cases in which he was able to obtain medical documents, usually a postmortem report. In cases where the deceased person was identified, he found close correspondence between the birthmarks and/or birth defects on the child and the wounds on the deceased person. With this major meticulously researched and documented opus, Stevenson made it much more difficult for his critics to challenge the reality of this phenomenon.

In evaluating this evidence, it is important to emphasize that Stevenson's cases are not taken only from "primitive," "exotic" cultures with an a priori belief in reincarnation, but also from Western countries, including Great Britain and the United States. His research meets high standards and has received considerable esteem. In 1977 the *Journal of Nervous and Mental Diseases* devoted almost an entire issue to this subject. More recently Stevenson's work was reviewed in the *Journal of the American Medical Association* (JAMA 2004).

Spontaneous and Evoked Past Life Memories in Adults

Unprompted, vivid reliving of past life memories occurs most frequently during spontaneous episodes of holotropic states of consciousness ("spiritual emergencies").

However, various degrees of remembering—from strong déjà vu experiences in specific locations to vivid flashbacks—can also happen in more or less ordinary states of consciousness in the middle of everyday life. Academic psychiatry and current theories of personality are based on the monistic materialistic world view and subscribe to the "one-timer view." Traditional professionals are aware of the existence of past life experiences, but consistently treat them as symptoms of psychosis and thus as indications of serious psychopathology.

Past life experiences can be elicited by a wide variety of techniques that mediate access to deep levels of the psyche, such as meditation, hypnosis, psychedelic substances, sensory isolation, bodywork, and various powerful experiential psychotherapies (primal therapy, rebirthing, or Holotropic Breathwork). Such episodes often appear spontaneously in sessions with therapists who are not trying to induce them, in some cases even happening to those who do not believe in them, catching these people completely off-guard. The emergence of karmic memories typically is also completely independent of the subject's previous philosophical and religious beliefs. Furthermore, such experiences occur on the same continuum with accurate memories from adolescence, childhood, infancy, birth, and prenatal period that can be reliably verified. Often past life experiences emerge in connection with the perinatal matrices, either simultaneously with various fetal elements, as a deeper level of the same experience, or alternating with them (Grof 1988, 1992).

Past incarnation memories resemble in many ways ancestral, racial, and collective memories. However, they usually have very strong emotional charge, and the subject identifies deeply with the protagonist. The sense of his or her personal identity completely shifts to a different person, place, time, and context. An essential aspect of these experiences is a convincing sense of remembering or reliving something that happened once before to the same person, to the same unit of consciousness. This feeling of déjà vu and déjà vécu is very basic—comparable to the experiential quality in everyday life that helps us distinguish our memories of actual events from our daydreams and fantasies. It would be very difficult, for instance, to convince a person who is telling us about a memory of something that happened last week or last month that the event did not really happen and is just a figment of his or her imagination.

Past incarnation experiences usually involve previous lifetimes of one or more other persons. In rare instances, various animals can play the role of protagonists in these sequences. The individual then feels that he or she became "karmically imprinted" on a scene of being killed by a tiger, trampled to death by a wild elephant, gored by a frenzied bull, or bitten by a venomous snake. Episodes of this kind are similar to other types of karmic scenes in their lasting impact on the individual but lack the reciprocity of repetition in subsequent incarnations. They thus resemble situations where the psychological effect transcending individual incarnations involves impersonal causes. Typical examples of such situations would be bitterness and envy associated with a painful and disabling disease, deformity, or crippling injury; and the anxiety and agony experienced in connection with accidental death under a rockslide, in swamps or quicksand, or during a volcanic eruption or fire.

Karmic experiences fall into two distinct categories characterized by the quality of the emotions involved. Some reflect highly positive connections with other persons—deep friendship, passionate love, spiritual partnership, teacher-disciple relationship, blood bonds, or life-and-death commitment. More frequently they involve intensely negative emotions and cast subjects into various internecine past life situations characterized by agonizing physical pain, murderous aggression, or inhuman terror. Intense anguish, bitterness and hatred, insane jealousy, insatiable vengefulness, uncontrollable lust, or morbid greed and avarice are additional emotional features of this latter category.

Many individuals who have experienced negative karmic experiences are able to analyze the nature of the destructive bond between the protagonists of such sequences. They realize that all these distinctly different emotional qualities, such as murderous passion, insatiable desire, consuming jealousy, or mortal anguish—when intensified beyond a certain point—actually begin to resemble each other. At a certain state of high biological and emotional arousal, all the extreme affective qualities converge and attain metaphysical dimensions. According to these insights, when two or more individuals reach this universal "melting pot" of passions and instincts, they become imprinted by the totality of the situation that caused them, irrespective of the particular role which they played in it.

In situations of extreme emotional intensity, the sadistic arousal of the torturer and the inhuman pain of the tortured increasingly resemble each other. Similarly, the rage of the murderer merges with the anguish and suffering of the dying victim. This emotional fusion seems to be instrumental in karmic imprinting, rather than a specific role in the experiential sequence. According to the insights of the people who have had past life experiences, whenever two individuals get involved in a situation where their emotions reach this state, they will repeat the same pattern in their future lives, but in alternating roles, until they reach the level of awareness necessary to resolve this karmic bond.

Sophisticated subjects familiar with spiritual literature equate this state of undifferentiated emotional arousal which generates karmic bondage with the Buddhist concept of *trsna* (tanha), or "thirst of flesh and blood," the force that drives the cycle of death and rebirth and is responsible for all human suffering. Others report insights regarding the deep similarity between this state and the strange experiential mixture characterizing the final stages of biological birth (BPM III), where physical pain, murderous aggression, vital anguish, extreme sexual arousal, demonic tendencies, and scatological elements merge into a strange, inextricable amalgam with religious fervor. Biological birth thus seems to represent a potential station of transformation, where the intangible "morphogenetic fields" of the karmic record (known in the spiritual literature as the "akashic record") enter the biopsychological life of the individual.

To reach a complete resolution of a karmic pattern and bond, the individual must experience fully all the painful emotions and physical sensations involved in a destructive past incarnation scene. The event must be transcended emotionally, ethically, philosophically, and spiritually before the person can rise above it entirely, forgive and be forgiven. Such a full liberation from a karmic pattern and the bondage involved is typically associated with a sense of paramount accomplishment and triumph that is beyond any rational comprehension, along with an overwhelming feeling that one has waited for this moment and worked for centuries to achieve this goal. At this point the person typically experiences ecstatic rapture and overwhelming bliss. In some instances, the individual sees a rapid replay of his or her karmic history and has clear insights as to how this pattern repeated itself in different variations through ages and has contaminated lifetime after lifetime. Several subjects speak to the experience of a cleansing "karmic hurricane" or "cyclone" blowing through their past and tearing their karmic bonds in all the situations involving the pattern which they have just resolved. A beautiful description of Buddha's experience of liberation from karmic bonds can be found in the Pali Canon (*Tipitaka*), a collection of early texts that forms the doctrinal foundation of Theravada Buddhism.

Past incarnation episodes are very common in deep experiential psychotherapy, and they have great therapeutic potential. They also have far-reaching theoretical significance, because several of their aspects represent a serious challenge to the mechanistic and materialistic world view. Since insufficient factual knowledge is one of the main sources of the current skepticism regarding reincarnation and karma, I will describe certain specific features of past life experiences which deserve serious attention in this regard. These should be exceptionally interesting to any researcher of consciousness and of the human psyche. As we will see, there are important reasons to assume that past life experiences are authentic phenomena *sui generis*, with major implications for psychology and psychotherapy because of their heuristic and therapeutic potential.

The first extraordinary characteristic of karmic experiences is that they often contain accurate information about various historical periods, cultures, and even specific events, which the individual could not have acquired through the ordinary channels. In some instances, the accuracy of such information can be objectively verified, sometimes with remarkable details. Another noteworthy feature is their deep connection with various emotional, psychosomatic, and interpersonal problems. The theme of karmic memories often shows such an intimate and specific relationship with the subject's psychopathological symptoms and difficulties in the present lifetime that there can be little doubt that the experiences represent a critical factor in the genesis of these problems.

Current psychiatry attributes pathogenic significance only to traumatic events from postnatal history. Observations of karmic experiences significantly extend the range of possibilities—the time of the traumatic events seems to make little difference. Sequences from ancient Egypt, Nazi Germany, or Czarist Russia can be just as significant factors as episodes from prenatal life, birth, infancy, and childhood in the present life of the individual. On the positive side, full reliving and integration of these past life experiences has remarkable therapeutic potential. Consequently a therapist who does not support the spontaneous emergence of these experiences in his or her clients and refuses to work with them is depriving these individuals of a powerful mechanism for healing and personality transformation.

The most convincing evidence for the special status of reincarnation memories is their association with extraordinary synchronicities. In many instances my clients who had experienced karmic sequences identified the karmic partners featured in them as being specific persons from their present life—parents, children, spouses, boyfriends and girlfriends, and other important figures. When they completed reliving the karmic scene and reached successful resolution, they felt that the respective interpersonal partners had been so deeply part of their experience that they themselves had to feel something similar and might have been influenced by the experience. When I became sufficiently open-minded to try to verify these insights, I discovered to my great surprise that they were often accurate. The persons whom my clients had denoted as their partners in the karmic sequences experienced dramatic positive changes in their own feelings toward my clients at exactly the same time when the process was completed. This extraordinary synchronistic liaison between the events in the session and the changes in the attitudes of the "karmic partners" could not be explained by linear causality. Often these other individuals were hundreds or thousands of miles away, and they had no knowledge of my client's experience. Furthermore, the changes they experienced were produced by an entirely independent sequence of events, such as having a deep transformative experience of their own, receiving some information that entirely changed their perception of the subject, or being influenced by some other independent development in their environment. The timing of these synchronistic happenings was often remarkable; in some instances they were minutes apart. This aspect of past life experiences, suggesting nonlocal connections in the universe, is similar to the phenomena described by Bell's theorem in quantum-relativistic physics (Bell 1966, Capra 1982).

Supporting Evidence for the Authenticity of Past Life Memories

The criteria for determining the authenticity and veracity of past life memories are essentially the same that we use for memories of what happened last week, last month, or ten years ago. We must retrieve these memories with as much detail as possible and obtain independent evidence for at least some of them. (Even our current memories, however, cannot always be corroborated.) Naturally past life memories are more difficult to verify. They do not always contain specific information that can be readily confirmed. Also, since the episodes are much older and involve other countries and cultures, any supporting evidence is more difficult to obtain. Most evoked past life memories do not permit the same degree of verification as Stevenson's spontaneous memories, which are typically more recent and contain much specific information. However, in rare cases, the circumstances allow verification of induced past life memories in remarkable detail, as illustrated below by two cases from my collection. In these cases the most unusual aspects of the narrative could be verified by historical research.

The Case of Karl

Karl's experiences of karmic memory started to emerge during sessions of primal therapy. The material continued to surface and completed itself in sessions of Holotropic Breathwork during our month-long seminar at the Esalen Institute.

At an early stage of his therapy when Karl was reliving various aspects of his birth trauma, he started experiencing fragments of dramatic scenes suggestive of a foreign country in another century. The scenes involved powerful emotions and physical feelings and seemed to have some deep and intimate connection to his life, yet none of them made any sense in terms of his present biography. He had visions of tunnels, underground storage spaces, military barracks, thick walls, and ramparts that appeared to be parts of a fortress situated on a rock overlooking an ocean shore. This was interspersed with images of soldiers in a variety of situations. He felt puzzled, since the soldiers seemed to be Spanish, but the scenery looked more like Scotland or Ireland.

As the process continued, the scenes became more dramatic and involved—many represented fierce combat and bloody slaughter. Although surrounded by soldiers, Karl experienced himself as a priest and at one point had a very profound vision that included a Bible and a cross. At this point, he saw a seal ring on his hand and could clearly recognize the initials that it bore. Being a talented artist, he decided to document this strange process, although he did not understand it at the time. He produced a series of drawings and some very powerful and impulsive finger paintings. Certain images depicted different parts of the fortress, others scenes of slaughter, and a few his own experiences, including being gored by a sword, thrown over the ramparts of the fortress, and dying on the shore. He also drew the seal ring with the initials.

As he was recovering bits and pieces of this story, Karl was finding more and more meaningful connections with his present life. He was discovering that many emotional and psychosomatic symptoms, as well as problems in interpersonal relationships that he had at that time in his everyday life, were clearly related to his inner process and involved the mysterious past event. A turning point came when Karl suddenly decided on an impulse to spend his holiday in Western Ireland. After his return, when he was viewing for the first time the images that he had shot on the Western coast of Ireland, he realized that he had taken eleven consecutive pictures of the same scenery that did not seem particularly interesting. He took a map and reconstructed where he had stood at the time and in which direction he had been shooting. He realized that the place which had attracted his attention was the ruin of an old fortress called Dún an Óir, or Forte de Oro (Golden Fortress).

Suspecting a connection with his experiences from his inner exploration, Karl decided to study the history of Dún an Óir. He discovered to his enormous surprise that at the time of Walter Raleigh, the fortress was taken by the Spaniards and then besieged by the British. Walter Raleigh negotiated with the Spaniards and promised them free egress from the fortress, if they would open the gate and surrender to the British. The Spaniards agreed to these conditions, but the British did not hold their promise. Once inside the fortress, they slaughtered all the Spaniards mercilessly and threw them over the ramparts to die on the ocean beach.

Despite this absolutely astonishing confirmation of the story that he laboriously reconstructed in his sessions, Karl was not satisfied. He continued his library research until he discovered a special document about the Battle of Dún an Óir where he learned that a priest accompanied the Spanish soldiers and was killed together with them. The initials of the name of the priest were identical with those that Karl saw in his vision of the seal ring and depicted in one of his drawings.

The Case of Renata

The story of Renata, a neurotic patient who received LSD therapy for her cancerophobia, involves one of the most unusual coincidences I have encountered during my psychedelic research. The phenomena here are ambiguous in that they manifest characteristics of both ancestral and past incarnation experiences. This example shows clearly the complexity of this area of research.

In the advanced stage of Renata's therapy, we observed an unusual and unprecedented sequence of events. Four of her consecutive LSD sessions consisted almost exclusively of scenes from a particular period of Czech history—she experienced several episodes that occurred in Prague during the seventeenth century. This time was a crucial period for the Czechs. After the disastrous battle of White Mountain in 1621, which marked the beginning of the Thirty Years' War in Europe, the country ceased to exist as an independent kingdom and came under the hegemony of the Hapsburg dynasty for 300 years.

In an effort to destroy the feelings of national pride and defeat the forces of resistance, the Hapsburgs sent out mercenaries to capture the country's most prominent noblemen. Twenty-seven outstanding members of the nobility were arrested and beheaded in a public execution on a scaffold erected on the Old Town Square in Prague. During her historical sessions, Renata had an unusual variety of images and insights concerning the architecture of the period, typical garments and costumes, as well as weapons and various utensils used in everyday life. She was also able to describe many of the complicated relationships existing at that time between the royal family and the vassals. Renata had never specifically studied this period, and I had to consult special references to confirm the information she reported.

Many of her experiences concerned various periods in the life of a young nobleman, one of the twenty-seven members of the aristocracy beheaded by the Hapsburgs. In a dramatic sequence, Renata finally relived with powerful emotions and in considerable detail the actual events of the execution, including this nobleman's intense anguish and agony. In all these scenes, Renata experienced full identification with this individual. She was not certain what these historical sequences signified or how they were related to her present personality. She finally concluded that she must have relived events from the life of one of her ancestors, although this possibility conflicted with her personal beliefs and philosophy.

As a close witness of this emotional drama, I shared Renata's bewilderment and confusion. Trying to decipher this enigma, I chose two different approaches. On the one hand, I spent much time trying to verify the historical information involved and was increasingly impressed by its accuracy. On the other, I tried to apply the psychoanalytic approach to the content of Renata's stories to see if I could understand them in psychodynamic terms as a symbolic disguise for her childhood experiences or elements of her present life situation. But despite my concerted efforts, the experiential sequences did not make any sense from this point of view. I finally gave up on this problem when Renata's LSD experiences moved into new areas. Focusing on other more immediate tasks, I stopped thinking about this peculiar incident.

Two years later, when I was already in the United States, I received a long letter from Renata with the following unusual introduction: "Dear Dr. Grof, you will probably think that I am absolutely insane when I share with you the results of my recent private search..." In the text that followed, Renata described how she had happened to meet her father, whom she had not seen since her parents' divorce when she was three years old. After a short discussion, her father invited her to have dinner with him, his second wife, and their children. After dinner, he told her that he wanted to show her the results of his favorite hobby, which she might find interesting.

During World War II, the Nazis ordered every family in the occupied countries to submit its pedigree demonstrating the absence of persons of Jewish origin for the last five generations. Forced to work on the family genealogy by existential necessity, Renata's father became absolutely fascinated by this procedure. After he had completed the required five-generation pedigree for the German authorities, he continued his research out of personal interest and traced the history of his family back through the centuries, thanks to the relatively complete system of birth records kept in the archives of parish houses in European countries. With considerable pride, Renata's father pointed to a large and carefully designed ramified pedigree of their family and showed her that they were descendants of one of the noblemen executed after the battle of White Mountain.

After having described this episode in the letter, Renata expressed how happy she was to have obtained this independent confirmation of her "gut feeling" that her ancestral memory was authentic. She saw this as a proof that highly emotionally charged memories could be imprinted in the genetic code and transmitted through centuries to future generations. After my initial amazement regarding this most unusual coincidence, I discovered a rather serious logical inconsistency in Renata's account. During her historical LSD sessions she had re-experienced the terminal anguish of the nobleman during his own execution. However, physical death terminates the possibility of further genetic transfer; it destroys the biological hereditary line. A dead person cannot procreate and "genetically" pass the memory of his terminal anguish to future generations.

Before completely discarding the information contained in Renata's letter as supportive evidence for her experiences, several facts deserve serious consideration. None of the remaining Czech patients, who had a total of over two thousand sessions, had ever even mentioned this historical period. In Renata's case, four consecutive LSD sessions almost exclusively contained historical sequences from this time. It is practically impossible that this could have been merely a meaningless coincidence. The absence of a conventional pathway for biological transfer of this information and the independent confirmation of Renata's experiences by her father's genealogical quest suggest a situation that characterizes past life experiences. In any case, it is hard to imagine any plausible explanation of this astonishing coincidence that would not violate some basic assumptions of traditional Western science.

The extraordinary characteristics of past life experiences have been repeatedly confirmed by independent observers. This raises a very interesting question: Does the existence of these experiences constitute a definitive "proof" that some essential part of us survives death and reincarnates as the same separate unit of consciousness, the same individual soul? Despite all the extraordinary evidence discussed earlier, the answer to this question has to be negative. To assume survival of individual consciousness over many lifetimes is just one possible interpretation of the existing evidence, essentially a theory made on the basis of the above observations. This is basically the same situation that researchers encounter daily in other scientific disciplines: they amass large amounts of data and observations and look for theories that would make them comprehensible within a coherent conceptual framework.

A basic rule in modern philosophy of science is that a theory should never be confused with the reality which it describes—"the map should never be confused with the territory" (Korzybski 1933, Bateson 1972). The history of science clearly shows that more than one theory always exists that seems able to account for the available data. The situation in reincarnation research is not any different. In the study of past life phenomena, as in any other area of exploration, we must separate facts of observation from the theories that try to make sense of them. For example, we all know that if we drop an object, it falls; this is an obvious and indisputable fact, something we observe all the time. However, over the centuries Aristotle, Newton, Einstein, and quantum physicists have offered entirely different theories as to why gravity happens, and many more are likely to be proposed in the future.

Any serious researcher who is sufficiently open-minded and interested to check the existing evidence can verify the existence of past life experiences, with all their remarkable characteristics. It is also clear that there is no plausible explanation for these phenomena within the conceptual framework of mainstream psychiatry and psychology. However, interpreting the existing data is a much more complex and difficult matter. The popular understanding of reincarnation as a repeated cycle of life, death, and rebirth of the same individual is a reasonable conclusion from the available evidence, one that is certainly far superior to the attitude of most traditional psychologists and psychiatrists. These professionals are either remarkably unfamiliar with the existing research data or pointedly ignoring them, preferring instead to rigidly adhere to established ways of thinking, much like religious fundamentalists.

While the observations suggestive of reincarnation are very impressive, some alternative interpretations of the same data can certainly be imagined. Naturally no alternative will be congruent and compatible with the monistic materialistic paradigm of Western science. In the Hindu tradition, the belief in reincarnation of separate individuals is seen as a popular and unsophisticated understanding of reincarnation. In the last analysis, there is only one being that has true existence and that is Brahman, or the creative principle itself. All separate individuals in all the dimensions of existence are just products of infinite metamorphoses of this one immense entity. Since all the divisions and boundaries in the universe are illusory and arbitrary, only Brahman really incarnates. All the protagonists in the divine play of existence are different aspects of this One. When we attain this ultimate knowledge, we are able to see that our past incarnation experiences represent just another level of illusion or maya. From this perspective, to see these lives as "our lives" requires perception of the karmic players as separate individuals and reflects ignorance concerning the ultimate unity of everything.

Sri Ramana Maharshi, echoing the renowned Hindu philosopher Shankara, expressed the paradoxical relationship between the creative principle and the elements of the material world in a very succinct way:

The world is illusory
Brahman alone is real;
Brahman is the world.

Use of Hypnosis to Verify Past Life Experiences

Interesting experimental work has been conducted with hypnotic techniques in an effort to obtain verifiable data about reincarnation. The objections against this kind of research emphasize the danger of suggestion. However, a strong case can be made for information that comes from a skilled use of hypnosis and is verifiable. Helen Wambach regressed 750 subjects into various past lives and used a detailed sociological questionnaire to collect specific information about costumes, food, weapons, money, and other aspects of the periods involved. She often found verification for even the smallest details. Interestingly, she maintained the balance of male and female subjects in her studies, except during wartime when women were more numerous than men. Famous personalities were not more frequent; in fact, she found not a single case of a famous historical person. Most were lives in poverty, boring, and without color (Wambach 1979).

Tibetan Practices Relevant to the Problem of Reincarnation

Tibetan spiritual literature describes some interesting phenomena suggesting that certain highly developed human beings are able to gain far-reaching knowledge related to the process of reincarnation. This includes the possibility of exerting influence on the time of one's death, predicting or even directing the time and place of one's next incarnation, and maintaining consciousness through the intermediate states between death and next incarnation (bardos). Conversely, accomplished Tibetan monks can apply various clues received in dreams, meditation, and through other means to locate and identify the child who is the reincarnation of the Dalai Lama or another tulku. The child is then exposed to a test where he must identify correctly from several sets of similar objects those that belonged to the deceased. Some aspects of this practice could, at least theoretically, be subjected to rather rigorous testing following Western scientific standards. His Holiness the Dalai Lama has shown great openness for similar experiments when he granted his permission to test the effects of the Tibetan practice of tummo, which can lead within a short period of time to an astonishing increase of body temperature of many degrees (Benson et al. 1982).

11
MESSAGES AND VISITS FROM THE BEYOND

There is little doubt that if attention is directed to occult phenomena the outcome will very soon be that the occurrence of a number of them will be confirmed; and it will probably be a very long time before an acceptable theory covering these new facts can be arrived at.
– C.G. Jung, *Memories, Dreams, Reflections*

Apparitions of deceased persons and communication with them may occur in the context of near-death experiences and deathbed visions, as described in Chapter 9. However, such apparitions are not restricted to situations of dying and death; they can emerge spontaneously in everyday situations or be triggered by ingestion of psychedelics, experiential methods of psychotherapy, or meditation. Of course the relevance of such experiences as research data has to be critically evaluated. A private experience of this kind can easily be dismissed as a wishful fantasy or hallucination. Some additional factors are required to qualify these experiences as valid research material. At a minimum, those apparitions that seem to satisfy some strong need of the percipient must be distinguished from others where any personal motivation of this kind cannot be found.

Some apparitions have certain characteristics that make them especially interesting or even challenging for researchers, as in cases where apparitions of persons unknown to the subject are later identified through photographs and verbal descriptions. Other notable and relatively common situations involve apparitions that are witnessed collectively or by many different individuals over long periods of time, as it is the case in "haunted" houses and castles. In some instances, the apparitions can have distinguishing bodily marks accrued around the time of death unbeknownst to the percipient.

Examples Involving Extraordinary Synchronicities and Verifiable Information

Of particular interest are those cases where the deceased conveys some specific and accurate new information that can later be verified or those where this event is linked with an extraordinary synchronicity. I have observed several extraordinary instances of this kind in psychedelic therapy and in Holotropic Breathwork, and I have summarized three examples below that illustrate the nature of such observations.

The first example comes from the LSD therapy of a young depressed patient, Richard, who had made repeated suicidal attempts. In one of his LSD sessions, Richard had a very unusual experience involving a strange and uncanny astral realm. This domain had an eerie luminescence and was filled with discarnate beings that were trying to communicate with him in a very urgent and demanding manner. He could not see or hear them; however, he sensed their almost tangible presence and was receiving telepathic messages from them. I wrote down one of these messages that seemed very specific in the hope that I might verify it later.

The message asked Richard to contact a couple in the Moravian city of Kromeríz and inform them that their son Ladislav was doing all right and was well taken care of. The message included the couple's name, street address, and telephone number; all of these data were unknown to me and to my patient. This experience was extremely puzzling; it seemed to be an alien enclave in Richard's experience, totally unrelated to his problems and the rest of his treatment. After some hesitation and with mixed feelings, I finally decided to do what certainly would have made me the target of my colleagues' jokes, had they found out. I went to the telephone, dialed the number in Kromeríz, and asked if I could speak with Ladislav. To my astonishment, the woman on the other side of the line started to cry. When she calmed down, she told me with a broken voice: "Our son is not with us any more; he passed away, we lost him three weeks ago."

The second illustrative example involves a close friend and former colleague of mine, Walter N. Pahnke, a member of our psychedelic research team at the Maryland Psychiatric Research Center in Baltimore. Walter was deeply interested in parapsychology, particularly in the problem of consciousness after death, and worked with many famous mediums and psychics, including our mutual friend Eileen Garrett, President and Founder of the Parapsychology Foundation. In addition, he was also the initiator of the LSD program for patients dying of cancer, discussed in Chapters 12-15.

In the summer of 1971, Walter and his wife Eva took their children for a vacation in a cabin situated right by the ocean in Maine. One day he went scuba diving by himself and did not return. An extensive and well-organized search failed to find his body or any part of his diving gear. Under these circumstances, Eva found it very difficult to accept and integrate his death. Her last memory of Walter was when he was leaving the cabin, full of energy and in perfect health. It was hard for her to believe that he was no longer part of her life and to start a new chapter of her existence without any sense of closure for the preceding one.

Being a psychologist herself, Eva qualified for an LSD training session for mental health professionals offered through a special program in our institute. She decided to have a psychedelic experience with the hope of getting some more insights and asked me to be her sitter. In the second half of the session, she had a very powerful vision of Walter and carried on a long and meaningful dialogue with him. He gave her specific instructions concerning each of their three children and released her to start a new life of her own, unencumbered and unrestricted by a sense of commitment to his memory. It was a very profound and liberating experience.

Just as Eva was questioning whether the entire episode was just a wishful fabrication of her own mind, Walter appeared once more for a brief period of time and asked Eva to return a book that he had borrowed from a friend of his. Eva had no previous knowledge of this book. Walter proceeded to give her the name of the friend, the room where it was, the name of the book, the shelf, and the sequential order of the book on this shelf. Following the instructions, Eva was actually able to find and return the book.

The third example involves Kurt, a psychologist participating in our three-year professional training program. In the course of his training, he had witnessed a wide variety of transpersonal experiences from Holotropic Breathwork sessions of his colleagues. He also had had some powerful perinatal experiences and a few glimpses of the transpersonal realm himself. However, he continued to be very skeptical about the authenticity of these phenomena, constantly questioning whether or not they were ontologically real. Then in one of his Holotropic Breathwork sessions, he experienced an unusual synchronicity that convinced him that he might have been too conservative in his approach to human consciousness. A brief account of this episode follows.

Toward the end of his breathwork session, Kurt had a vivid visionary encounter with his grandmother, who had been dead for many years. He had been very close to her in his childhood, and he was deeply moved by the possibility that he might be really communicating with her again. Despite his deep emotional involvement in the experience, he continued to maintain an attitude of professional skepticism about the encounter. Naturally he had had many real interactions with his grandmother while she was alive and theorized that his mind could have easily created an imaginary encounter from these old memories. However, this meeting with his dead grandmother was so emotionally profound and convincing that he simply could not dismiss it as a wishful fantasy. He decided to seek proof that the experience was real, not just his imagination. He asked his grandmother for some form of confirmation and received the following message: "Go to Aunt Anna and look for cut roses." Still skeptical, he decided on the following weekend to visit his Aunt Anna's home. Upon his arrival, he found his aunt in the garden, surrounded by cut roses. He was astonished. The day of his visit just happened to be the only day of the entire year that his aunt had decided to do some radical pruning of her roses.

Experiences of this kind are certainly far from definitive proof that astral realms and discarnate beings actually exist. However, such astonishing synchronicities clearly suggest that this fascinating area deserves serious attention of consciousness researchers. Belief in the existence of astral realms and in the possibility of communicating with the deceased is very likely based on experiences similar to those that I have just described.

Evidence from Spiritism and Trance Mediumship

Of special interest is the quasi-experimental evidence for survival of consciousness after death that comes from a highly controversial source—that of spiritism and mental or trance mediumship. Although some of the professional mediums (including the famous Eusapia Palladino) have been caught cheating, others (such as Mrs. Piper, Mrs. Leonard, and Mrs. Verall) have withstood all the tests and gained the high esteem of careful and reputable researchers (Grosso 1981). The best media are able to accurately reproduce the deceased's voice, speech patterns, gestures, mannerisms, and other characteristic features.

On occasion, the received information is unknown to any of the present persons or even to any living person whatsoever. Uninvited "drop-in" entities have also suddenly intruded, and in some cases their identities have been confirmed later. In other instances, relevant messages have been received in "proxy sittings," where a distant and uninformed party has sought information in lieu of a close relative or friend of the deceased. In the cases of "cross correspondence," bits and pieces of a comprehensive message have been conveyed through several mediums.

Some of the spiritistic reports considerably stretch the mind of an average Westerner, let alone a traditionally trained scientist. For example, the extreme form of spiritistic phenomena, the "physical mediumship," includes telekinesis and materializations, upward levitation of objects and people, projection of objects through the air, manifestation of ectoplasmic formations, and sudden appearance of writings or objects ("apports"). In the Brazilian spiritist movement, media perform psychic surgeries using their hands or knives allegedly under the guidance of the spirits of deceased people. These surgeries do not require any anesthesia, and the wounds close without sutures.

Events of this kind have been repeatedly studied and filmed by Western researchers of the stature of Walter Pahnke, Stanley Krippner, and Andrija Puharich.

My wife Christina and I had the rare opportunity to witness a remarkable performance of Luiz Gasparetto, a Brazilian psychologist and member of the Spiritist Church, when he was a guest faculty at one of our month-long seminars at the Esalen Institute. Luiz had the reputation of channeling the spirits of great painters and painting in their style. He was able to paint in complete darkness. However, for his Esalen performance the otherwise darkened room was partially illumined by dim red light. This provided enough light so that spectators could watch him work, but not enough light for Luiz to distinguish colors through the ordinary channels.

Listening throughout the entire session to Vivaldi's *Four Seasons* (which he found particularly inspiring), Luiz produced with astonishing speed one remarkable painting after another, each in the style of a different famous painter—van Gogh, Picasso, Gauguin, Rembrandt, Monet, Manet, and many others. He used both his hands, at times painting two pictures simultaneously, one with each hand. Much of the time he did not even look at the paper. He actually painted one Manet portrait under the table, upside down and with his right foot, without looking at all. Luiz's stunning performance lasted a little over an hour. When he stopped painting, the floor around him was covered with large paintings, twenty-six of them altogether. In spite of the red light in the room, which normally makes it impossible to distinguish colors, Luiz was able to choose appropriate tones for all the paintings.

People in the room started to move, eager to come closer and inspect the paintings. However, it was obvious that Luiz's process was not yet finished. He sat for a while in quiet meditation and then announced: "There is a spirit here, who calls himself Fritz Pearls; he wants to have his portrait painted by Toulouse-Lautrec." He then produced a painting of the legendary South African therapist and founder of Gestalt practice, who had spent the last years of his life at Esalen. It was not only a very accurate portrait of Fritz, but it bore all the unmistakable characteristics of Toulouse-Lautrec's style.

Luiz finished the painting but gave no indication that the performance was over. After a brief moment of reflection, he said: "There is another spirit here; her name is Ida Rolf. She would also like to have her portrait made, not the way she looked before she died, but when she was forty years old." Ida Rolf was another Esalen legend and idol. A German biochemist, she had developed a famous technique of bodywork that carried her name. She had lived for many years in an Esalen house, about one-and-a-half miles from the main premises, which became our residence after Ida had left Esalen.

The portrait of Fritz showed him as people remembered him or knew him from his photographs. The portrait of Ida was artistically very interesting and showed a middle-aged female figure, but there was no way to assess its accuracy. Nobody in the Esalen community had any idea what Ida Rolf had looked like at the age of forty, since she was already old when she had arrived at Esalen from Germany. Dick Price, the co-founder of Esalen, was fascinated by Luiz's performance, but particularly by his portraits of the two people from the Esalen history whom Luiz had not previously known. Dick subsequently spent much time and effort to obtain from Germany Ida's photograph at age forty. The photograph that finally arrived bore a striking resemblance to Ida's "portrait from the Beyond," and provided very convincing evidence for Luiz's extraordinary psychic gifts.

Moody's Psychomanteum and the Interdimensional Transcommunication

Raymond Moody describes an interesting and innovative procedure for connecting with the deceased in his book *Reunions: Visionary Encounters with Departed Loved Ones*. Moody's inspiration for this project came from an ancient Greek underground complex (psychomanteum) that offered visitors the opportunity to see apparitions of their dead relatives and friends on the surface of water filling a large copper kettle. In the preparatory phase of his research, Moody conducted a systematic review of literature on crystal-gazing, scrying, and similar phenomena. He then used a large mirror and black velvet drapes to create a special environment which, according to him, could facilitate visionary encounters with the deceased loved ones. Moody reported instances in which the apparitions actually emerged from the mirror and freely moved around the room as three-dimensional holographic images (Moody 1993).

An approach known as instrumental transcommunication (ITC) is an especially fascinating and incredible development in attempts to communicate with spirits of discarnate people. ITC, which involves modern electronic technology, originated in 1959 when Swedish portrait painter, filmmaker, and amateur ornithologist Friedrich Jürgenson was recording the sounds of passerine birds in a quiet forest. Jürgenson also picked up human voices on his tape recorder, allegedly belonging to dead persons. Some of these voices supposedly talked directly to him in an effort to communicate. Inspired by this event, Latvian psychologist Konstantin Raudive conducted a systematic study and recorded over 100,000 multilingual paranormal voices, which he identified as messages from the Beyond (Raudive 1971). Interestingly, Thomas Alva Edison is alleged to have worked for many years on a machine that could communicate with the spirit world. However, Edison died in 1931 before he had a chance to publish any of his notes.

More recently a worldwide network of researchers, including Ernest Senkowski, George Meek, Mark Macy, Scott Rogo, Raymond Bayless, and others, has coordinated a group effort to establish "interdimensional transcommunication" (Senkowski 1994).

This group claims to have received many paranormal verbal communications and pictures from the deceased through electronic media—tape recorders, telephones, FAX machines, computers, and TV screens. Among the spirits communicating from the Beyond are supposedly some of the former researchers in this field, such as Jürgenson and Raudive, who have died and are now trying to make contact from the other side. In addition, a discarnate entity who calls himself "the Technician" designs electronic circuits for optimal interdimensional communication with the Beyond and transmits this information to earthbound researchers (Senkowski 1994). In a recent lecture, Mark Macy also described his communications with nine angelic beings, obtained by the technology of interdimensional transcommunication (Macy 2005).

Like the observations from thanatological investigation of near-death experiences and the rich material of past life experiences in children and adults, research data concerning communication with discarnate entities and astral realms cannot be considered a "proof" of survival of consciousness after death. However, they certainly belong in the category of "anomalous phenomena," events for which the current scientific paradigms have no reasonable explanation.

12
THE HISTORY OF PSYCHEDELIC THERAPY WITH THE DYING

The last rites should make one more conscious
rather than less conscious, more human
rather than less human.
– Aldous Huxley, author of *Island* and *Brave New World*

MY OWN EXPERIENCE with dying individuals is closely related to the development of psychedelic therapy with *d*-lysergic acid diethylamide (LSD-25), *N,N*-dipropyltryptamine (DPT), and 3,4-methylenedioxyamphetamine (MDA). While this treatment modality results directly from modern pharmacological and clinical research, it resembles procedures practiced by many native cultures. The roots of psychedelic therapy reach far back in human history and prehistory to healing ceremonies of several ancient civilizations and even further to shamanic rituals. The notion that psychedelic therapy could alleviate the suffering of cancer patients in modern times came independently from several different sources. This chapter summarizes some of the major contributions to this field of work.

Ethnomycological Research by Gordon and Valentina Pavlovna Wasson

Valentina Pavlovna Wasson, a pediatrician of Russian origin, first suggested that psychedelic substances could be useful in the therapy of individuals dying of incurable diseases. The contribution that Valentina and her husband Gordon Wasson made to psychedelic history is fascinating and deserves notice. Gordon Wasson was the most unlikely person to become involved with anything related to psychedelics; he was a successful New York banker and vice-president of J.P. Morgan Trust Company. The story begins in 1927, when he and his young wife were on their belated honeymoon in the Catskill Mountains. During one of their strolls in the forest Valentina Pavlovna collected wild mushrooms and insisted on preparing them for dinner.

As a typical Anglo-Saxon, Gordon was a mycophobe (a term he later coined for people who believe that the only edible mushrooms are found in the supermarket and who refer to any kind of wild mushrooms as "toadstools"). He was horrified at the prospect of eating wild mushrooms and tried unsuccessfully to dissuade her. Valentina, a mycophile (the term Gordon used for Eastern European mushroom enthusiasts), prevailed and prepared a delicious dinner with wild mushrooms as the main ingredient. Gordon very reluctantly tasted her dish and liked it very much. The next morning, when he discovered to his great surprise that both he and Valentina were still alive and well, he experienced a dramatic conversion from a mycophobe to a mycophile.

This experience awakened in him a profound lifelong interest in mushrooms, and he became a world-famous amateur ethnomycologist. Gordon and Valentina then spent twenty years studying the role mushrooms had played in human history, archaeology, comparative religion, folklore, and mythology. This extensive research culminated in their joint colossal, lavishly produced work, *Mushrooms, Russia, and History* (Wasson and Wasson 1957), in which the Wassons concluded that mushroom worship was a significant component of preliterate humanity's religious life in most of Eurasia and the Americas. They were particularly fascinated by the ritual use of the psychoactive mushroom *Amanita muscaria* by shamans of the Finno-Ugrians and other far-north Eurasian peoples.

This interest led them eventually to the discovery of ritual use of "magic" mushrooms in pre-Hispanic cultures and in contemporary Central America. After three field trips to Mexico, they discovered Maria Sabina, the Mazatec *curandera* (or medicine woman), who was using in her healing ceremonies psychoactive mushrooms known in Mesoamerica as teonanacatl, or the Flesh of Gods. In June 1955 the Wassons and their friend, New York photographer Allan Richardson, became the first Westerners allowed to participate in Maria Sabina's mushroom ritual or *velada*. *Mushrooms, Russia and History* gave the first account of the Wassons' encounter with Maria Sabina and their experience with magic mushrooms.

The Wassons were deeply impressed by the powerful effects of the mushrooms that they had experienced in Maria Sabina's velada. In 1957 Valentina Pavlovna gave an interview about the history of their discovery and her own experience after ingesting teonanacatl, which was published in Baltimore's *This Week* magazine (Wasson 1957). In this interview she suggested that if the active agent could be isolated and produced in sufficient quantities, it could become a vital tool in the study of the human psyche. She also stated that as the drug became better known, medical uses would be found for it—perhaps to treat alcoholism, narcotic addiction, mental disorders, and terminal diseases associated with severe pain.

Valentina did not have to wait long for her extraordinary intuitive prediction to come true. Roger Heim, a famous French mycologist whose aid the Wassons sought, identified the teonanacatl mushrooms botanically as *Psilocybe mexicana* and its congeners; he sent samples to the laboratories of the Swiss pharmaceutical company Sandoz for chemical analysis. In a brilliant chemical tour de force, Albert Hofmann, the world-famous discoverer of LSD, was able to identify two active alkaloids responsible for the effect of the Psilocybe mushrooms: psilocybin and psilocin. Sandoz produced large quantities of dragées of the two new psychedelics and made them available for laboratory and clinical research.

As described below, several years later a team of researchers working in Baltimore independently tested the validity of Valentina Pavlovna's suggestion. A group of psychiatrists and psychologists at the Maryland Psychiatric Research Center, who were not familiar with her article in *This Week*, launched a series of systematic controlled studies of psychedelic therapy with LSD, a drug closely related to psilocybin, for exactly the same indications that Valentina Wasson had predicted—alcoholism, narcotic drug addiction, neuroses, and terminal cancer patients (Grof 1980). I myself was very surprised to discover the newspaper clipping with Valentina's interview in Gordon Wasson's library during a 1974 visit to his New England home.

Contributions of Aldous Huxley

The next stimulus for using psychedelics with dying individuals did not come from a physician or a therapist, but from the writer and philosopher Aldous Huxley. After his own personal experiences with LSD and mescaline, Huxley became fascinated by religious and mystical experiences, as well as death and dying. In 1955 he used this knowledge when his first wife Maria was dying of cancer. Trained in the use of hypnosis, Huxley eased her final hours by using hypnotic induction in a very special way. While she was in the trance state, he instructed her to return to ecstatic experiences that she had spontaneously experienced on several occasions during her earlier life. Huxley's explicit goal was to ease her experience of dying by guiding her toward mystical states of consciousness as her death approached. Huxley later used the memory of this extraordinary process in his novel *Island* as an inspiration for a moving passage describing the death of Lakshmi, one of the main protagonists (Huxley 1963).

In a letter to Humphry Osmond, a psychiatrist and pioneer in psychedelic research who had introduced him to LSD and mescaline, Huxley wrote: "My own experience with Maria convinced me that the living can do a great deal to make the passage easier for the dying, to raise the most purely physiological act of human existence to the level of consciousness and perhaps even of spirituality." For those who are familiar with the effects of psychedelic drugs and with Huxley's personal history, there is no doubt that "soma" in his *Brave New World* and the "moksha medicine" in Island are psychedelic substances similar in their effects to LSD, mescaline, and psilocybin. In Huxley's vision "moksha" gives inhabitants of the island mystical insights that free them from the fear of death and enable them to live more fully.

In another letter to Humphry Osmond written as early as February 1958, Huxley was quite explicit about his idea of using LSD with dying individuals: "...yet another project—the administration of LSD to terminal cancer cases, in the hope that it would make dying a more spiritual, less strictly physiological process." According to his second wife Laura, Aldous mentioned on several occasions that "the last rites should make one more conscious rather than less conscious, more human rather than less human." In 1963 when he himself was dying of cancer, Huxley demonstrated the seriousness of his vision. Several hours before his death he asked Laura to give him 100 micrograms of LSD to facilitate his own dying. This moving experience was later described in Laura's book, *This Timeless Moment* (Huxley 1968, see Appendix). Despite his unique personal example, Huxley's recommendation had no influence on medical researchers for several years.

Eric Kast's Studies of the Analgesic Properties of LSD

The next major contribution to psychedelic therapy with the dying came from a rather unexpected source, unrelated to Huxley's pioneering idea and efforts. In the early 1960s, Eric Kast of the Chicago Medical School studied the effects of various drugs on the experience of pain in the quest for an effective and reliable analgesic. He became interested in LSD as a possible candidate because of certain peculiarities of its effect on humans. In some users LSD produced a marked distortion of the body image and alterations of body boundaries. Furthermore, it also seemed to interfere with the ability to concentrate and maintain selective attention on a particular physiological sensation. Kast postulated that the simple visual impressions of individuals who were under the influence of LSD might take precedence over sensations of pain or concerns related to survival. Both the effect of LSD on the body image and its interference with selective focus on significant input seemed worth exploring in terms of their potential for altering the perception of physical pain.

Kast and Collins conducted a study comparing the hypothetical analgesic properties of LSD to those of two established and potent narcotic drugs, dihydromorphinone (Dilaudid) and meperidine (Demerol) (Kast 1963, Kast and Collins 1964). Their group of fifty individuals suffering from severe physical pain included thirty-nine patients with various types and stages of cancer, ten patients with gangrenes of feet or legs, and one with severe herpes zoster (shingles). The statistical analysis of this comparison indicated that the analgesic effect of LSD proved superior to both Dilaudid and Demerol. In addition to pain relief, some individuals developed a striking disregard for the gravity of their personal situations. They frequently talked about their impending death with an emotional attitude that would be considered atypical in our culture. Yet it was quite obvious that this new perspective was beneficial in view of the situation they were facing.

In a later study of 128 individuals with metastatic cancer, Kast explored some of his earlier findings in more detail (Kast 1964). This time he focused not only on the effects of LSD on pain but also on some additional parameters: emotional changes, sleep patterns, and attitudes toward illness and death. Considering that there was no psychotherapeutic emphasis and the patients were not even informed that they had been given LSD, the results were quite remarkable. About two to three hours after the administration of 100 micrograms of LSD, many patients experienced a dramatic alleviation of pain that lasted an average of twelve hours. Pain intensity for the whole group (not necessarily for every single patient) was decreased for a period of three weeks. For ten days after the session, Kast observed improvement of sleep and noticed that the patients were less concerned about their illness and impending death.

In 1966, Kast published another paper in which he paid more explicit attention to the influence of LSD on the religious and philosophical experiences and ideas of the patients (Kast 1966). The group he studied consisted of eighty persons suffering from terminal malignant disease, with estimated life expectancies of weeks or months, each of whom had been fully informed of the diagnosis. In contrast to earlier studies, the LSD sessions were terminated by an intramuscular injection of 100 milligrams of chlorpromazine upon the appearance of fear, panic, unpleasant imagery, or the desire to rest. The beneficial influence of a single administration of 100 micrograms of LSD on physical pain, mood, and sleep patterns was similar to the preceding studies. In addition, Kast described a variety of changes in the patients that made their situation more tolerable. He noticed improved communication both between the observer and the patients and among the patients themselves. This enhanced their morale and self-respect and created a sense of cohesion and community among them. Quite significant was the occurrence of "happy, oceanic feelings" lasting up to twelve days following the administration of LSD.

Kast also reported some qualitative results that were not reflected by his numerical data and graphs, namely that the philosophical and religious beliefs of his patients were changed, as well as their attitudes toward dying. Despite some limitations in Kast's experimental protocol, the historical value of his pioneering effort is unquestionable. He not only discovered the analgesic value of LSD for patients with intractable pain, but also brought forth experimental evidence for Aldous Huxley's suggestion that the administration of LSD to persons suffering from cancer might ease their encounter with death. Kast concluded the last of his studies by observing that LSD is not only capable of improving the lot of dying individuals by making them more responsive to their environment and family, but also enhances their ability to appreciate the nuances and subtleties of everyday life. It gives them aesthetic satisfaction and "creates a new will to live and a zest for experience, which, against a background of dismal darkness and preoccupying fear, produces an exciting and promising outlook" (Kast 1966).

Psychedelic Therapy Research by Cohen and Fisher

The encouraging results of Kast's studies inspired Sidney Cohen, a prominent Los Angeles psychiatrist, friend of Aldous Huxley, and one of the early pioneers in LSD research, to start a program of psychedelic therapy for patients dying of cancer. Unfortunately the results of his study and the details of his treatment procedure have never been published. In a 1965 article Cohen expressed his feelings about the potential of psychedelic therapy for the dying, based on his pilot experiments with a small group of patients (Cohen 1965). He stated that his own work confirmed Kast's findings that LSD had a beneficial effect on severe physical pain and suggested that LSD might one day provide a technique for altering the experience of dying. Cohen clearly appreciated the significance of this research endeavor: "Death must become a more human experience. To preserve the dignity of death and prevent the living from abandoning or distancing themselves from the dying is one of the great dilemmas of modern medicine."

Cohen's co-worker, Gary Fisher, later published a paper on the personal and interpersonal problems of the dying, in which he emphasized the significance of transcendental experiences, whether spontaneous, resulting from various spiritual practices, or induced by psychedelic drugs (Fisher 1970). As a result of such experiences the individual ceases to be concerned about his or her own physical demise and sees it instead as a natural phenomenon in the cycling of the life force. This acceptance drastically alters a person's life-style; the individual no longer reacts with panic, fear, pain, and dependency to the changes that are occurring. Rather, he or she is willing and eager to share this new knowledge with close family members and friends. Fisher discussed the use of LSD therapy within the framework of a research project in which this drug was compared with an experimental analgesic and only one hour was allowed to prepare patients for the session. In spite of this limitation, he observed dramatic results in terms of pain reduction, psychological aftereffects, and adjustment of the patients to their impending deaths.

Psychedelic Psychotherapy at the Psychiatric Research Institute in Prague

Another series of observations that was later integrated into comprehensive psychedelic therapy for the dying originated in the Psychiatric Research Institute in Prague, Czechoslovakia, where I was principal investigator in a research program studying the effects of LSD- and psilocybin-assisted psychotherapy. In the 1960s our team conducted experiments with psychiatric patients to explore the potential of these substances for personality diagnostics and psychotherapy. This research involved intense psychological work and a series of therapeutic sessions with medium dosages of LSD or psilocybin. This approach was initially based in theory and practice on Freudian psychoanalysis. However, over the course of years our research approach was substantially modified and became an independent therapeutic procedure that included work on birth-related (perinatal) and transpersonal material, in addition to biographical psychodynamic issues.

It soon became obvious that when psychotherapy was combined with administration of psychedelics, all our patients, irrespective of their diagnostic categories, sooner or later transcended the realm of postnatal biography and of the individual unconscious. The process of their experiential self-exploration spontaneously moved into realms that lay far beyond the narrow boundaries of the psyche as defined by Freud. To our surprise and often with intellectual consternation, we witnessed phenomena that had been described through millennia in many ancient and preindustrial cultures of the world in the context of shamanic procedures, various mystical traditions, temple mysteries, and rites of passage. The most common and important of these phenomena were experiences of death and rebirth, often followed by feelings of cosmic unity. This profound encounter with one's own impermanence and mortality was very complex and had biological, emotional, intellectual, philosophical, and spiritual dimensions.

These experiences seemed to have very beneficial effects on the emotional and psychosomatic symptoms of my clients, including those that had not previously responded to any conventional therapies. After these episodes of psychospiritual death and rebirth and especially after the experiences of oneness with the universe, clients almost immediately showed dramatic improvements of various psychopathological conditions. These observations revealed the existence of powerful therapeutic mechanisms as yet unknown to Western psychiatry and psychology, with a healing and transformative potential clearly far superior to anything that conventional psychotherapy or pharmacotherapy had to offer.

Many individuals who experienced psychospiritual death and rebirth independently reported that their attitude toward dying and their concept of death underwent dramatic changes. Fear of their own physiological demise diminished, they became open to the possibility of consciousness existing after clinical death, and they tended to view the process of dying as an adventure in consciousness rather than the ultimate biological disaster and personal defeat. Two individuals suffering from severe thanatophobia (whose primary problem was pathological fear of death) were among those who experienced these striking changes. As we conducted this research, we repeatedly witnessed an astonishing process that closely resembled the initiation practices in the ancient mysteries of death and rebirth and often involved experiential sequences similar to those described in the Tibetan or Egyptian Books of the Dead.

The reports of changed attitudes toward death were so frequent and profound that it seemed important to test their practical relevance. It was obvious that such deep changes in one's attitude toward death could be very beneficial for dying individuals, particularly those with chronic, incurable diseases. I therefore decided to conduct LSD sessions with several patients diagnosed with cancer. These pilot observations indicated that the alleviation of the fear of death I had observed in my psychiatric patients, most of whom were young and physically healthy, could also occur in individuals for whom the issue of death was of immediate relevance. At this point, the Prague group began seriously discussing the possibility of working systematically with dying people, and I designed a research program using serial LSD sessions with terminal cancer patients.

Early Psychedelic Research at Spring Grove State Hospital

These plans were interrupted during my 1965 visit to the United States, when I was offered a scholarship by the Foundations' Fund for Research in Psychiatry in New Haven, Connecticut, to spend a year in Baltimore, Maryland, as Clinical and Research Fellow at the Johns Hopkins University. My host and new boss, Dr. Joel Elkes, head of Henry Phipps Psychiatric Clinic at Johns Hopkins, invited me to start a program of psychedelic therapy. Unfortunately, shortly before my arrival in Baltimore, Maimon Cohen and his colleagues published the results of their research indicating that LSD was among the substances that could cause structural changes in the chromosomes of white blood cells (Cohen, Marinello, and Back 1967). Their paper was discovered by sensation-hunting journalists, who launched a hysterical media campaign threatening LSD users that their self-experimentation could have deleterious effects on future generations.

The journalists who initiated and fueled this media campaign conveniently overlooked the fact that Cohen's paper described an experiment conducted in a test tube (in vitro) and not with human beings, and that Cohen had earlier reported similar chromosomal structural changes in experiments involving many other commonly used substances, including aspirin, caffeine, and tetracycline antibiotics. They also made unsubstantiated extrapolations from this one in vitro experiment and talked about mutagenic, teratogenic, and carcinogenic effects of LSD and the catastrophic consequences the use of this substance might have for posterity. All these claims turned out to be false, disproved by future research. But the adverse publicity created a national hysteria that proved detrimental for LSD research, already severely negatively affected by unsupervised mass experimentation with psychedelics by the young generation.

Under these circumstances, Dr. Elkes decided not to implement his plan to start a new LSD project at Johns Hopkins. By an extraordinary coincidence, the only project of LSD psychotherapy in the United States that had survived the severe administrative and legal measures aimed to curb the widespread, unsupervised self-experimentation with psychedelics happened to be stationed at Spring Grove State Hospital in Baltimore. Due to the new circumstances, Dr. Elkes suggested a change in the program of my fellowship; instead of creating a new research project at Johns Hopkins, I would have a part-time teaching appointment at the university and join the Spring Grove team to participate in their research projects.

When I attended my first staff meeting at Spring Grove, I was greatly surprised to discover that most of the discussion revolved around the great promise LSD psychotherapy might hold for alleviating the emotional and physical suffering of cancer patients. The research team had initially become interested in this area in 1963 when a group of Spring Grove psychiatrists, psychologists, and social workers had been exploring the effects of a brief course of LSD-assisted psychotherapy on the drinking behavior, psychological condition, and social adjustment of alcoholics. In a parallel study, the therapeutic potential of this new treatment had been tested in a group of neurotic patients. The post-session and follow-up evaluations, based on clinical interviews as well as a battery of psychological tests (the Minnesota Multiphasic Personality Inventory or MMPI, Shostrom's Personal Orientation Inventory or POI, the Rorschach Ink Blot Test, and others), showed that depression and anxiety were the symptoms that most readily responded to psychedelic therapy.

Case History of Gloria

While these studies with alcoholics and neurotics were well under way, a tragic development directed the attention of the research team to the emotional needs of cancer patients. One of the staff members, Gloria, a woman in her early forties, was diagnosed with breast carcinoma. The tumor was already in a very advanced stage when it was discovered. Gloria had to undergo radical mastectomy, and subsequent biopsy revealed inoperable metastases in her liver. Although still ambulatory, she was in severe physical and emotional distress. Gloria was fully aware of her condition and her prognosis and shared her feelings of despair with other staff members. Sid Wolf, psychologist and member of the therapeutic team, suggested that a high-dose LSD session might alleviate Gloria's anxiety and depression as it had so frequently for alcoholic patients.

The Spring Grove team decided to try an LSD session, fully aware that Gloria's emotional condition differed from the depression and anxiety in alcoholics in that it was a reaction to serious physical discomfort and an incurable life-threatening disease. After discussions with Gloria's husband and her physician and with the approval of all concerned, a course of psychedelic therapy was initiated with Sidney Wolf in the role of guide or "sitter." In his work with Gloria, Sid followed the format used by the Spring Grove team in the treatment of psychiatric patients. The preparation for the session lasted approximately a week. The daily interviews conducted during this time focused on personal history and current interpersonal relationships. In the last session preceding the administration of LSD, the therapist clarified for the client any important issues related to the effects of the substance and gave all the necessary instructions for the session. The primary objective of this procedure was to facilitate the occurrence of a deep spiritual experience ("psychedelic peak experience") in the context of brief but intensive psychotherapy.

In the morning on the day of the session, Gloria ingested 200 micrograms of LSD. She spent most of the day lying on the couch in the treatment suite with eyeshades and headphones, listening to high fidelity stereophonic music. Sid remained with her from about an hour before she took the substance until late in the evening. In the first five hours, he changed music and checked with her briefly at regular intervals. Later in the session, he talked with her and helped her integrate the experience. The outcome of this pioneering experiment was extraordinary and more than fulfilled the expectations of the research team. The quality of Gloria's remaining days was profoundly improved as a result.

Shortly after the LSD session, Gloria went on a vacation with her husband and children. Upon her return, two weeks after the session, she completed the following retrospective report:

> The day prior to LSD, I was fearful and anxious. I would at that point have gratefully withdrawn. By the end of the preparatory session, practically all anxiety was gone; the instructions were understood and the procedure clear. The night was spent quietly at home; close friends visited and we looked at photograph albums and remembered happy family times. Sleep was deep and peaceful. I awakened refreshed, and with practically no fear. I felt ready and eager. The morning was lovely—cool and with a freshness in the air. I arrived at the LSD building with the therapist. Members of

the department were around to wish me well. It was a good feeling.

In the treatment room was a beautiful Happiness rosebud, deep red and dewy, but disappointingly not as fragrant as other varieties. A bowl of fruit, moist, succulent, also reposed on the table. I was immediately given the first dose and sat looking at pictures from my family album. Gradually, my movements became fuzzy and I felt awkward. I was made to recline with earphones and eyeshades. At some point the second LSD dose was given to me. This phase was generally associated with impatience. I had been given instructions lest there be pain, fear, or other difficulties. I was ready to try out my ability to face the unknown ahead of me and to triumph over my obstacles. I was ready, but except for the physical sensations of awkwardness and some drowsiness, nothing was happening.

At about this time, it seems, I fused with the music and was transported on it. So completely was I one with the sound that when particular melody or record stopped, however momentarily, I was alive to the pause, eagerly awaiting the next lap of the journey. A delightful game was being played. What was coming next? Would it be powerful, tender, dancing, or somber? I felt at these times as though I were being teased, but so nicely, so gently. I wanted to laugh in sheer appreciation of these responses, regardless of where I had just been, how sad or awed. And as soon as the music began, I was off again. Nor do I remember all the explorations.

Mainly I remember two experiences. I was alone in a timeless world with no boundaries. There was no atmosphere; there was no color, no imagery, but there may have been light. Suddenly I recognized that I was a moment in time, created by those before me and in turn the creator of others. This was my moment, and my major function had been completed. By being born, I had given meaning to my parents' existence.

Again in the void, alone without the time-space boundaries. Life reduced itself over and over again to the least common denominator. I cannot remember the logic of the experience, but I became poignantly aware that the core of life is love. At this moment I felt that I was reaching out to the world—to all people—but especially to those closest to me. I wept long for the wasted years, the search for identity in false places, the neglected opportunities, the emotional energy lost in basically meaningless pursuits.

Many times, after respites, I went back, but always to variations on the same themes. The music carried and sustained me. Occasionally, during rests, I was aware of the smell of peaches. The rose was nothing to the

> fruit. The fruit was nectar and ambrosia (life); the rose only a beautiful flower. When I finally was given a nectarine it was the epitome of subtle, succulent flavor.
>
> As I began to emerge, I was taken to a fresh windswept world. Members of the department welcomed me, and I felt not only joy for myself, but for having been able to use the experience these people who cared for me wanted me to have. I felt very close to a large group of people. Later, as members of my family came, there was a closeness that seemed new. That night, at home, my parents came, too. All noticed a change in me. I was radiant, and I seemed at peace, they said. I felt that way too. What has changed for me? I am living now, and being. I can take it as it comes. Some of my physical symptoms are gone—the excessive fatigue, some of the pains. I still get irritated occasionally and yell. I am still me, but more at peace. My family senses this and we are closer. All who know me well say that this has been a good experience.

Five weeks after this session, Gloria suddenly developed ascites (accumulation of serous fluid in the abdominal cavity) and had to be rehospitalized; she died quietly three days later. The result of Sidney Wolf's endeavor was so encouraging that the Spring Grove staff decided to explore further the potential of psychedelic therapy for alleviating the suffering of patients dying from cancer. A group of open-minded surgeons at Baltimore's Sinai Hospital expressed interest in this procedure, offered their cooperation, and agreed to refer patients to us for LSD therapy. Following Gloria's session, Sandy Unger, a psychologist who had played an important role in launching the Spring Grove studies of alcoholics and neurotics, conducted LSD sessions with three more cancer patients.

Walter Pahnke's Initiative and Role in the Spring Grove Program

The next important phase in the development of the Spring Grove program of psychedelic therapy with cancer patients was closely associated with Walter N. Pahnke, who joined the Spring Grove team in the fall of 1967. In Chapter 11 I mentioned his tragic death in the context of describing the psychedelic session of his wife Eva. Walter was a psychiatrist who entered psychedelic history in 1962, when he conducted his famous Good Friday experiment in Boston University's Marsh Chapel to investigate the potential of psychedelic substances to facilitate mystical experiences. He administered psilocybin to a group of Protestant divinity students under controlled conditions and was able to show that, compared to the control subjects, those who had received psilocybin experienced to a greater extent the phenomena reported by the mystics (Pahnke 1963).

Walter was a graduate of Harvard Medical School, and he had also a doctoral degree in comparative religion and a degree in divinity. His educational background made him thus ideally suited for this type of work: because of his combined training in medicine, psychology, and religion he was uniquely qualified to conduct psychedelic therapy with dying patients. Walter was instrumental in moving the cancer project from its fledgling stage to a systematic pilot study and eventually to an extensive research program. With unusual energy, enthusiasm, and devotion, he assumed the leading role as principal investigator in the project. He was able to obtain the necessary financial support from the Mary Reynolds Babcock Foundation to launch a research program exploring the value of LSD therapy in terminal cancer patients.

In July 1971, Walter's life and work were drastically terminated by a tragic accident when he was vacationing with his wife and children in his summer cabin in Maine. Besides his passion for consciousness research, Walter had many other interests and hobbies which he pursued with equal enthusiasm and energy. In all of these, he radiated unusual *joi de vivre* and *élan vital.* Among others, he was known as a daredevil skier and motorcycle driver. Shortly before his Maine vacation he had added scuba diving to the list of his hobbies. His cabin was located on the ocean shore and provided an ideal opportunity to pursue his new interest. A novice in this sport, Walter was using second-hand diving equipment that he had purchased from a friend of his, and without a marker, he ventured into the Atlantic Ocean for a "brief dive before lunch." He did not return, and his body and diving equipment have never been recovered. The nature of this accident has remained a mystery, despite the concerted and collective effort of many people, including the Coast Guard, several renowned psychics, and others.

Walter's demise was a great loss for the Spring Grove team, both personally and professionally. I had worked with Walter in the cancer study from its inception, and after his death I assumed medical responsibility for the project as my primary research activity and interest. My objective was not only to complete this research and accumulate enough data, but also to formulate a theoretical framework that would account for some of the dramatic changes occurring as a result of LSD therapy. At this stage of research, it was necessary to carefully analyze the data from LSD sessions of normal volunteers, psychiatric patients, and dying individuals, and to formulate a comprehensive theory of LSD therapy based on a new model of the unconscious. The next chapter discusses in detail the comprehensive Spring Grove program of psychedelic therapy.

13
THE SPRING GROVE PROGRAM

What is soundless, touchless, formless, imperishable,
Likewise tasteless, constant, odorless,
Without beginning, without end, higher than the great, stable—
By discerning That, one is liberated from the mouth of death.
– Katha Upanishad

THE SPRING GROVE PROGRAM began as a cooperative effort between the Research Unit of Spring Grove State Hospital in Catonsville, Maryland (a Baltimore suburb) and the Oncological Unit of Sinai Hospital in Baltimore. In 1969 the Spring Grove psychedelic research team moved into the Maryland Psychiatric Research Center that had been built between 1967 and 1969 on the premises of the hospital. This state-of-the-art facility, specially designed by the Spring Grove team for systematic study of holotropic states of consciousness, consisted of two treatment suites with closed circuit TV cameras, a large biochemical laboratory, special laboratories for studying sleep, dream, and hypnosis, a full-size sensory deprivation tank, and sensory overload department.

Between 1967 and 1974 more than one hundred persons dying of cancer participated in the Spring Grove program of psychedelic therapy. These individuals fell into four groups:

- patients who received LSD psychotherapy during the initial period of pilot experimentation (before the inception of the controlled studies and the introduction of the rating system);
- patients who volunteered for the controlled study of psychedelic therapy with LSD;
- patients who received as adjunct to psychotherapy dipropyltryptamine (DPT), a short-acting psychoactive substance with similar effects as LSD; and

- patients who had been assigned to the control groups in the main studies and were later offered psychedelic sessions when their role as control subjects ended.

Selection of the Patients

In the LSD and DPT studies Walter Pahnke and I functioned as a bridge between the Maryland Psychiatric Research Center and Sinai Hospital. We both spent one day a week in the Oncology Unit at Sinai, where we were present during the visits of clients in the outpatient clinic, participated in the grand rounds on the oncology ward, and attended staff conferences. Our purpose was to find, in cooperation with the oncologists and the nurses, those terminal cancer patients who seemed likely candidates for psychedelic treatment and invite them into our program. Typically these were patients with very poor prognoses, for whom all available medical treatments had been tried and had failed.

The primary psychological criteria for acceptance into the program were anxiety, depression, insomnia, emotional tension, and social withdrawal associated with the patient's malignancy. On the basis of Eric Kast's papers and observations from our pilot study, we also included among the indications intense physical pain that did not respond to analgesics, including administration of narcotics. Participation in the controlled study required a reasonable life expectancy of at least three months, since we were interested not only in the immediate treatment outcome but also in the duration of the positive results. Patients with shorter life expectancy were not denied treatment, but they were not included in the controlled study.

Contraindications of psychedelic therapy included major cardiovascular disorders, such as high blood pressure, advanced arteriosclerosis, or aneurysms and history of myocardial infarction, cardiac failure, or brain hemorrhage. The reason for these contraindications was not any direct pharmacological danger from psychedelic drugs per se but rather the propensity of these substances to elicit powerful emotions accompanied by increase of blood pressure that could cause cardiovascular complications. A history of epileptic seizures was considered to be another warning sign, because previous studies had suggested that, for persons with the history of epilepsy or epileptic disposition, psychedelics might trigger an epileptic seizure or, in rare instances, even status epilepticus, a rapid sequence of seizures that can be very difficult to control.

In the later stages of research we also included brain tumors, both primary and metastatic, among the physical contraindications. This was based on unsatisfactory results with several patients suffering from brain neoplasms who had been treated in the early stages of this research. These observations suggested that an anatomically intact brain was a necessary prerequisite for a successful psychedelic session and a good integration of the experience.

In general, psychedelic therapy proved to be physically very safe, considering the serious condition of most individuals in our study. In no cases did patients die during the session, or even in close connection with it. And yet one of the patients, Jesse, whose case history is described below, was so close to death that he died four days after his DPT session.

Other important considerations were the personality and psychological condition of the clients. A history of serious psychiatric problems that required hospitalization, such as schizophrenic reactions, manic episodes, or other types of psychotic disorders, deep depression with suicidal attempts, or borderline psychotic behavior, constituted contraindications for LSD treatment in the context of our Spring Grove program. (While I had previously treated patients with some of these conditions at the Psychiatric Research Institute in Prague, where I had my own ward with 18 beds staffed by nurses trained in work with holotropic states of consciousness, it would not have been wise under the circumstances in this case.) Work with these categories of patients brings the risk of flashbacks, prolonged reactions, and precipitation of transient psychotic episodes. Management of such complications requires a 24-hour facility with specially trained personnel, which our team did not have. The Maryland Psychiatric Research Center had only treatment suites, laboratories, and offices, but no hospital beds. In case of psychiatric emergency we would have had to rely on the locked wards of Spring Grove State Hospital—a facility with different philosophy, and a setting that was far from ideal. Furthermore, such a facility would also have needed the capability to address the specific needs of cancer patients, including possible emergencies.

When we found patients who met the above criteria and were interested in participating in the program, we scheduled them for special interviews in which we explained the nature of psychedelic treatment. We informed them that psychedelic therapy was an experimental form of therapy and discussed openly with them its potential benefits and risks. We also talked with the members of the patients' families or their significant others. When we reached agreement, we asked the patient to sign an informed consent form and accepted him or her into the program.

After the initial interviews, the patients were introduced to one of the therapists at the center, and the therapeutic work began. The course of psychedelic therapy consisted of three stages: an initial preparatory period, the psychedelic session itself, and a post-session period involving several interviews in which the therapist helped the client understand the experience, process the unconscious material that had emerged during the session, and facilitate the integration of the new insights and psychological changes into his or her everyday life.

Preparation for the Session

The preparation phase usually lasted eight to twelve hours and typically extended over a period of two to three weeks. Preparation consisted of a series of discussions in which we explored the patient's past history and present situation. Since a positive relationship and an atmosphere of basic trust are the most important factors in successful psychedelic therapy, we made a special effort during this phase to become acquainted and establish close rapport. The psychotherapeutic work focused on the patient's history and on the way various events, circumstances, and experiences had shaped his or her life. We explored the patient's interpersonal relationships and the unresolved issues with significant persons in his or her life—parents, siblings, partners, and children. Another important step in preparing for the session was to examine the patient's interactions and relationships with attending physicians and the hospital staff.

In many instances even a superficial look at the patient's immediate social network revealed significant distortion and confusion in communication with relatives, friends, attending physicians, and nurses. Denial, avoidance, guilt, passive-aggressive behavior, instilling of false hopes, and well-meant white lies often predominated and created a toxic and destructive atmosphere. Sometimes we encountered situations in which the staff and family members, as well as the patient, knew the diagnosis and the dismal prognosis and yet continued playing hide-and-seek in order to "protect" each other. Unless therapy succeeded in breaking through these vicious circles, the death of a patient usually left the relatives and sometimes even the hospital staff with feelings of deep distress, frustration, and guilt.

We discovered that it was essential for the best possible outcome of the session to deal with the skewed and dishonest communication in the patient's interpersonal field. Often the extremely distorted and painful interpersonal interactions could be rectified by several simple catalyzing interventions. We saw family members in various combinations, both with and without the patient, depending on the nature of the problems involved. We did all we could to create an opportunity for the patient and the relatives to discuss their feelings about each other, about the disease, and about the seriousness of the situation, including the imminence of death.

Each situation was unique, and there was no simple formula or technique for working with the family network. Our general strategy was to facilitate open and honest communication, help to resolve interpersonal conflicts, and reach agreement on important issues. We encouraged the family members to increase their interactions with the patient and with each other in as many areas and on as many levels as possible, in order to alleviate the psychological isolation so frequently experienced by individuals facing death. In this process family members often discovered their own fear of death, which was masked by their evasive maneuvers in approaching the dying relative. Similar distortions in communication were frequently found in the interactions between the medical staff, the dying individual, and the family members. In most instances, the medical personnel and the patient's family were relieved when they found out that the patient knew and accepted the diagnosis.

It proved very important to ascertain what the patient had been told concerning the diagnosis and prognosis and what his or her reaction to the disclosure was. Quite often we observed that the attending physicians and the family members did not inform the cancer patients about their diagnosis and did not want this issue to be discussed. While we did not indiscriminately disclose to the patients their diagnosis and prognosis and the imminence of death, we did not avoid discussions about these critical questions and answered honestly when the clients asked us directly. Although we often discussed problems of dying and death in great detail, our emphasis was not on death but on living as fully as possible during the remaining days. During this work, it became clear that our own emotional reactions played a critical role in this process. A therapist's own fear of death can severely inhibit the quality of communication and create a situation of fearful alienation for the dying individual. Our personal experiences of death and rebirth in psychedelic training sessions made it possible for us to engage in a more total and honest way with individuals who were facing the possibility of physical demise in the immediate future.

In no case did we present psychedelic therapy as a potential cure for cancer. When patients asked us if psychedelic treatment could cure cancer, we usually referred them to the literature suggesting that psychological factors might play an important role in determining the ability of the organism to defend itself against practically any disease. We also pointed out that emotions can influence the course of the pathological process and affect the outcome. Occasionally we discussed some of the hypotheses concerning the role of psychogenic factors in the etiology and course of cancer. This left open the possibility of exploring the psychosomatic aspects of cancer if the insights from the psychedelic session pointed in that direction. At the same time, this approach saved patients from disappointment when their efforts to heal themselves remained unsuccessful. It also protected us and our research from the wrath of the oncologists, who were all traditional and were convinced that cancer was a purely biological problem. They would have seen any discussions about the role of the psyche in this disease as unprofessional and would probably have discontinued the research.

The oncologist Carl Simonton and his wife Stephanie Matthews-Simonton were among the researchers emphasizing the role of psychological factors in the etiology, pathogenesis, and therapy of cancer during this time. They developed a method using guided imagery to mobilize the immunological defenses of the body to combat cancer, a program that was approved by the Surgeon General's Office in 1973 (Simonton, Creighton, and Simonton 1978). In one of our discussions about using psychedelic therapy in the treatment of cancer, Carl emphasized that we should explicitly suggest to our clients that psychedelic therapy might influence not just the psychological condition and pain, but the disease itself. He maintained that the belief that cancer is an incurable and fatal disease functions in a way similar to the witchdoctor's hex in some native cultures. According to him, the spell that this diagnosis casts on patients in our culture had to be broken for treatment to succeed. Unfortunately, we were working within a traditional medical context, and consequently we could not test the validity of Carl's suggestion.

Philosophical, Religious, and Spiritual Issues

Many of the discussions we had with our cancer patients focused on philosophical, religious, and spiritual issues. Such discussions are important in the context of psychedelic therapy with the dying for many reasons. The confrontation with one's own impermanence and physical demise can create or deepen interest in the spiritual and philosophical dimensions of existence. The concept of death, the attitude toward dying, and the quality of a dying person's remaining days and hours are profoundly influenced by his or her personal philosophy, spiritual orientation, and religious beliefs. Moreover, psychedelic experiences themselves often induce powerful mystical experiences, and exploring this area during the preparatory period can save much confusion during the session itself. This issue is of such paramount importance that it deserves to be explored at some length.

During the 1950s and 1960s, a period known as the "golden era of psychopharmacology," the fact that LSD and other psychedelic substance were able to trigger a broad range of spiritual experiences became the subject of heated scientific discussions. At the center of this controversy was the fascinating problem concerning the nature and value of this "instant" or "chemical" mysticism. These debates soon generated four different perspectives on this issue. The first was the position of hardcore materialistic scientists, who welcomed the observation that psychedelics were able to induce the experiences described by mystics. For these scientists this observation indicated that what the mystics consider revelations of numinous dimensions of reality were nothing but toxic artifacts, products of aberrant chemical processes in the brain. These experiences thus had no ontological value and belonged to the realm of science, not religion.

The second perspective painted an entirely different picture: since psychedelics had the power to induce mystical experiences, they were not ordinary chemicals but sacred substances. As sacraments psychedelics were connecting the users with normally invisible but ontologically real, numinous dimensions of reality. The proponents of this perspective essentially assumed the position of shamans and healers from native cultures, who make a similar distinction in regard to plants. Plants that have psychedelic effects are considered sacred, as reflected in the pre-Hispanic name for Mexican magic mushrooms—teonanacatl or "Flesh of Gods." These plant materials either mediate access to divine realities or are themselves deities. For shamans and members of societies that use psychedelic plants in their rituals, it would seem ludicrous to argue that their mystical experiences are not real or that they are inferior because they involve chemical compounds. In their opinion, these plants are the gifts from gods and are sacraments; they represent principal vehicles of their ritual and spiritual practice.

The third perspective acknowledged that psychedelic substances were able to induce experiences which were practically indistinguishable from those described by founders of religions, saints, prophets, and mystics of all ages. Walter Pahnke's Good Friday experiment brought convincing scientific evidence in this regard (Pahnke 1966). However, these experiences are not necessarily genuine or of equal spiritual value to those attained through meditation, fasting, devotional prayer, pious behavior, and lifetime of service to God, or those that occur spontaneously as a gift of divine grace. In this view, the ultimate decision about the value of mystical experiences induced by psychedelics should be made by spiritual teachers and religious figures, not scientists. Unfortunately, many notable spiritual teachers disagreed seriously on this issue.

One religious figure who denied any spiritual value to psychedelics was Meher Baba, the silent Indian saint called "The Compassionate One" and considered by his followers to be an avatar of our age, God in human form. In his pamphlet *God in A Pill*, he strongly expressed his opinion that psychedelic experiences had no place in the spiritual quest; he actually considered them to be pitfalls and detractions for the seekers: "No drug, whatever its great promise, can help one to attain the spiritual goal. There is no short-cut to the goal, except through the grace of the Perfect Master. LSD, mescaline, and psilocybin are superficial and add enormously to one's addiction to the deceptions of illusion, which is but the shadow of reality" (Meher Baba 1966).

The British historian of religion R.C. Zaehner expressed an equally negative reaction to "instant mysticism." In his books, *Mysticism Sacred and Profane* (Zaehner 1957) and *Zen, Drugs, and Mysticism* (Zaehner 1972), he examined and refuted the religious claims for mescaline which Aldous Huxley expressed in his *Doors of Perception* (Huxley 1959). He argued that from a Christian perspective it was sacrilegious to suppose that the use of drugs could produce "the same transports" as those recorded by Christian mystics. To complicate matters further, for those traditionally opposed to mysticism, even in its Christian form, the fact that the psychedelic experiences often take a Hindu or Buddhist form in which God appears not as a person, but as "an eternal and unconditional state of being" makes these experiences doubly suspect.

Many spiritual seekers of comparable caliber strongly disagree with these negative perspectives. Aside from the great Siberian, African, Native American, Mexican, and South American shamans, this group also includes Indian Brahmans and members of certain Sufi orders who use hashish as a sacrament. I myself have been honored to witness the psychedelic experiences of several Tibetan teachers and hear personal stories of sessions from others, including Lama Govinda. They all agreed that psychedelics are spiritual tools of awesome power, but warned that they must be used with utmost caution. Many years ago, I also personally gave LSD to Solon Wang, a prominent Buddhist scholar and diplomat from Chiang Kai-Shek's inner circle in Taiwan. After a lifetime study of Buddhism and rigorous practice that had failed to bring him the expected results, he had what he considered to be an absolutely authentic experience of nirvana in his first psychedelic session, which he later described in his book *The Multiple Planes of the Cosmos and Life* (Wang 1979).

Huston Smith, the world-famous scholar of comparative religion, has suggested the fourth perspective on the issue of "chemical mysticism.' During his lifetime Huston Smith has had profound psychedelic experiences, and so he speaks with an understanding that many other critics, including Meher Baba, are lacking. As expected from a person of his wisdom and stature, Huston Smith's perspective offers a convincing middle way in this argument. In his opinion, there is no doubt that psychedelic substances facilitate genuine mystical experiences. However, he strongly cautions that the value of these experiences and their impact on the individual's life critically depend on the larger context, the set and the setting. An experience that happens to a devout seeker after years of serious spiritual practice and religious studies would certainly be more valuable and influential than one that occurs to a totally unprepared and unsuspected guest in a party in Berkeley, where somebody throws a handful of sugar cubes laced with LSD into the fruit punch.

Discussion regarding mystical experiences induced by psychedelics must address the patient's religious beliefs and church affiliation. It is essential to talk openly about the conflicts that the dying individuals might have concerning their fundamentalist religious upbringing, traumatic experiences with priests, activities of the church to which they belong, and the role of God in their lives and in the world. Some of the issues that often emerge during these discussions concern the discrepancy between the ideals that organized religions propound and the reality of their actions in the world, particularly internecine wars between various creeds and all the atrocities they have perpetrated in the name of God.

To prevent misunderstanding and confusion, it is important to distinguish clearly between spirituality and religion. Many people in our culture do not know the fundamental difference between the two. Spirituality is based on direct experiences of normally invisible dimensions and domains of reality. It does not require a special place or an officially appointed person mediating contact with the Divine. The mystics do not need churches or temples; their bodies and nature serve as the context in which they experience the sacred dimensions of reality, including their own divinity. Rather than officiating priests, mystics need a supportive group of fellow seekers or the guidance of a teacher who is more advanced on the inner journey. Spirituality thus involves a special kind of relationship between the individual and the cosmos and is, in its essence, a personal and private affair.

Organized religion, however, is based on institutionalized group activity, which takes place in a designated location, a temple or a church, and involves a system of appointed officials who may or may not have had personal experiences with spiritual realities. Once a religion becomes organized, it often loses the connection with its spiritual source completely and becomes a secular institution that exploits human spiritual needs without satisfying them. Organized religions tend to create hierarchical systems focusing on the pursuit of power, control, politics, money, possessions, and other secular concerns. Under these circumstances, religious hierarchy as a rule discourages direct spiritual experiences in its members, because they foster independence and cannot be effectively controlled. In these cases, genuine spiritual life continues only in the mystical branches, monastic orders, and ecstatic sects of the religions involved.

For those patients who feel very uncomfortable about the spiritual aspects of psychedelic therapy, it is helpful to emphasize that spiritual experiences in psychedelic sessions as a rule do not assume an orthodox religious form. If they contain specific archetypal figures and domains, these can be drawn from any culture of the world, without regard to the individual's own cultural and religious background. Frequently, however, they transcend all secular and archetypal symbolism and have all the characteristics of what the Hindus call "nirvikalpa samadhi," experience of God without any form. They are thus universal, nondenominational, and all-encompassing.

Spiritual aspects of psychedelic sessions also frequently resemble what Einstein referred to as cosmic religion. This form of spirituality does not involve a personified godhead, a pantheon of intermediary saints, and formalized ritual procedures. The focus instead is on the awe and wonder one experiences when confronted with the creative forces of nature and the many mysteries of the universal design. Spiritual feelings are associated with such issues as the dilemmas and puzzles concerning the nature of time and space, origin of matter, life and consciousness, complexity of the universe and human existence, and the ultimate purpose underlying the process of creation.

If the psychedelic experiences are related to one of the great religions of the world, they manifest the characteristics described by the mystics of the respective creeds rather than reflecting or supporting the dogmas of their mainstream orthodoxy. They bring revelations about Christian mysticism rather than traditional Christianity, about Kabbalah or Hassidism rather than Orthodox Judaism, and about Sufism rather than the official Muslim faith. Often the psychedelic experiences involve elements totally alien to the individuals' own religious traditions, or are encountered in the framework of a different cultural area. Thus a Christian or a Muslim can have a past life episode and discover the law of karma, a Japanese Buddhist can identify with Jesus on the cross, or a Jew might experience a conversion to Hinduism or Tibetan Buddhism.

Final Pre-Session Interviews

Immediately before the session, after we had covered all the above issues, we scheduled a special interview to give the patients all the necessary information they needed before they took the substance involved. We explained the effects of psychedelics, talked about the healing potential of holotropic states of consciousness, and described the course of the session and all the necessary technical details. This was a very essential part of the preparation, since an average person living in industrial civilization has very little information about holotropic states of consciousness in general and those induced by psychedelic substances in particular. Even more problematic, he or she may have preconceptions that have been shaped by the media and anti-drug propaganda.

We described psychedelics as unspecific amplifiers or catalysts that make it possible to take a journey into one's own psyche and explore otherwise inaccessible deep recesses of the unconscious. In talking about the psychedelic experience, we found it helpful to liken it to a powerful "waking dream" or a vivid intrapsychic movie. We emphasized that it was important for the best outcome of the treatment that clients remain for most of the session in a reclining position, keeping their eyes covered by eyeshades and using headphones to listen to music. This helped keep the experience internalized and minimized confusion between the inner and outer worlds.

Another important step in the preparation phase was to inform the patients that their experience would very likely take them far beyond the boundaries of the narrow and superficial model of the psyche used by mainstream psychiatry and psychology. The high dosages of psychedelics used in the Spring Grove studies typically provided access not only to memories from infancy and childhood and the related domain of the individual unconscious, but also to memories of biological birth and prenatal life and to what we now call transpersonal experiences. The latter include experiential identification with other people, with animals and other life forms, as well as ancestral, racial, collective, karmic, phylogenetic, and archetypal episodes.

Traditional psychiatrists do not consider these transbiographical experiences to be normal constituents of the human psyche and see them as artifacts caused by an unknown pathological process and thus manifestations of serious mental disease. We assured the patients that this was a misconception. Modern consciousness research has shown that perinatal and transpersonal experiences are not only normal but also have extraordinary healing, transformative, and even evolutionary potential. We encouraged our patients to surrender to the experience, whatever direction it might take, face everything that might emerge in the session, experience it fully, and express it. To insure the maximum effect of the psychedelic substances, we discontinued all tranquillizing medication before the session. Prescribed antibiotic and hormonal medication were not interrupted, and the narcotics the patient was taking were available on demand.

We also met with the family members or significant others whom the patients wanted to include in the "family reunion" in the later hours of the experience. The purpose of this briefing was to help these individuals understand the nature of the psychedelic experience and explain to them how they could best support the patient, who would still be in a non-ordinary state of consciousness. We asked the relatives to bring photographs or works of art which had special meaning for the patient and to provide flowers and fruit for the room in which the session would take place.

The Psychedelic Session

We ran most of the psychedelic sessions in the Oncology Unit of Sinai Hospital because the patients referred to us by Sinai oncologists suffered from very advanced stages of cancer. Transporting them on the day of the session, particularly in the evening when they were still in a holotropic state of consciousness, would have been difficult and inconvenient. Given their serious physical condition, it also made sense to run the sessions in the hospital, where immediate medical help would be available, if necessary. After we had made the results of our study public and the news about the project had been spread by the media, we were able to include self-referred patients in earlier stages of their disease. We ran these later sessions in our treatment suites at the Maryland Psychiatric Research Center, which were ideally equipped for psychedelic therapy and had closed circuit TVs; most of these sessions could thus be videotaped.

When the session was conducted at Sinai, the patient was transferred on the preceding day into a private room. The stereophonic music equipment was also set up a day in advance, so that the patient could become accustomed to headphones and eyeshades, as both would be used for many hours on the day of the session. We tried to make this setting as comfortable and inviting as a hospital environment could be by using flowers, fragrant incense, paintings, little sculptures, beautiful drapes, and other similar props. On the morning of the session day, the hospital staff gave the patient the necessary routine care earlier than usual so that the session could begin as soon as we arrived.

After a short discussion with the patient regarding his or her momentary emotional condition and feelings about the session, we administered the psychedelic substance. The dosage of LSD ranged from 200 to 600 micrograms, depending on the patient's condition. LSD can generally be given orally, but in certain cases we preferred intramuscular administration—when we were concerned about inadequate absorption of the substance by the gastrointestinal system or possible nausea and vomiting (for example if cancer was located in the stomach or esophagus). In LSD sessions, there is a latency period of twenty to forty minutes between the administration of the drug and the onset of its effect, depending on the mode of application. We usually spent this time in relaxing discussions or looking at pictures and listening to quiet music.

If the psychedelic drug used in the session was DPT, it was always given intramuscularly. This substance is ineffective when ingested, because it is quickly deactivated in the gastrointestinal system. The dosage of DPT ranged between 90 and 150 milligrams, depending on the patient's physical condition, psychological defenses, and body weight. This was comparable in terms of its effect to the dosage range of LSD used in the parallel cancer study. Since the onset of the DPT effect is almost instant and frequently dramatic, the DPT patients were asked immediately after the injection to lie down and put on the eyeshades and headphones.

The Use of Music in the Sessions

As the patient began to feel the effect of the substance, he or she was encouraged to stay in a reclining position and use the eyeshades and headphones. This helped the individual focus on the internal phenomena that were beginning to unfold and avoid external distractions. From this point on, there was no difference between the approach with the LSD patients and those who were given DPT. We turned on the music and the session began. The choice of music for the session was made after a consultation with Helen Bonny, who was an experienced music therapist, as well as psychedelic therapist. For most of our patients, the music was a combination of classical pieces, selections of ethnic music from different countries of the world, and recordings from various spiritual traditions.

Internalizing the session by using the reclining position, eyeshades, headphones, and stereophonic music greatly intensifies and deepens the psychedelic experience. Music has several important functions in the session: it facilitates the emergence of deep emotions into consciousness, helps the patients let go of their psychological defenses, and provides a dynamic carrier wave, which takes the patients through difficult experiential impasses. Our clients frequently reported that the flow of their experience was interrupted when the records were being changed, and they eagerly or even anxiously waited for it to resume.

Our general strategy was to play music that supported the experience the patient was having at the time. In the most general sense, this meant following the trajectory of a typical psychedelic experience. At the beginning we played flowing and comforting music that gradually became more intense. Later in the session we shifted to powerful, dynamic, and evocative instrumental and orchestral music. Between the third and fourth hour in LSD sessions (earlier in DPT sessions)—a period that in many sessions brought an important turning point—we introduced what we called "breakthrough music." These were powerful pieces of music, usually with strong spiritual emphasis, in which full orchestra was combined with human voices. Following this period, the music gradually quieted down and became heartfelt and soothing. In the late hours of the session, we played quiet, timeless, flowing, and meditative music. It was important to choose the music with this general blueprint in mind. For example, it would have been inappropriate to play a soft and sweet violin solo at a time when the patient's experience culminated or, conversely, introduce powerful African drums during the late hours of the session when the patient was relaxed and in a meditative mood.

In addition to following these general guidelines, the therapists tried to respond as sensitively as possible to certain specific features of individual sessions. If the patient reported that the session was very sensual and erotic, or we inferred this from pelvic movements or other physical signs, we might, for example, play the final scene from Wagner's *Tristan and Isolde* or Rimsky-Korsakoff's *Sheherezade*. When we observed fist clenching and contractions of the jaw muscles or heard from the patient that the content of the experience was violent, we would support that mood with intense, dynamic music.

Similarly when the experiences focused on a particular country (e.g., India, China, Japan, or Russia) or a specific cultural group (e.g., Native Americans, gypsies), we found it useful to provide corresponding ethnic music. We generally avoided music that included words in languages that the patients understood because this tended to divert the attention from emotions and physical feelings to intellectual and cognitive processing at the expense of the depth of the experience. The function of music in psychedelic sessions was discussed in a special paper by two members of our staff, Helen Bonny and Walter Pahnke (Bonny and Pahnke 1972).

After the LSD had been administered, the patient spent ten to twelve hours (about half that time if DPT had been used) in the company of a therapist and a co-therapist, always a male-female dyad. If the course of the session was smooth, the main function of the therapists was to change the music and briefly check with the patients as they did so. They also kept detailed records of what they observed and what the patients said. In addition, the therapists took care of the patients' basic needs—taking them to the bathroom, bringing a glass of water or juice, providing an extra blanket, or handing them a tissue. Sometimes the experience became too overwhelming, and the patients removed the headphones and eyeshades. When this happened, the task of the therapists was to comfort and reassure them and remind them that it was important to keep the experience internalized. The general strategy was to convince the patients to return into their inner world as soon as possible.

Most talking took place before the session, in its termination period, and on the days following the session. During the session itself the primary emphasis was on experiencing and feeling. During the hours when the psychedelic experience was intense, verbal communication was kept at the absolute minimum. At regular intervals, usually when we were changing music, we removed the patient's headphones and made brief verbal contact to find out how the patient was feeling and if he or she needed anything. Whenever necessary, we reminded the patient that it was important to suspend psychological defenses and encouraged him or her to experience fully whatever was emerging from the unconscious and to express the emotions and physical energies associated with it.

Use of Supportive Physical Contact and Focused Bodywork

When the patients were experiencing unusually painful and frightening episodes, particularly from the preverbal period of their history, we often used supportive physical contact, which proved far more effective than verbal assurances. This form of intervention was based on the observation that there are two fundamentally different forms of trauma and that they require diametrically different approaches. The first, *trauma by commission*, results from external intrusions with damaging impact on the future development of the individual. Here belong such insults as physical or sexual abuse, frightening situations, destructive criticism, or ridicule. These traumas represent foreign elements in the unconscious that can be brought into consciousness, energetically discharged, and resolved.

Although this distinction is not recognized in conventional psychotherapy, the second form of psychotrauma, *trauma by omission*, differs radically from the first. It is caused by lack of positive experiences that are essential for healthy emotional development. The infant and toddler have strong primitive needs for instinctual satisfaction and security that pediatricians and child psychiatrists call *anaclitic* (from the Greek *anaklinein*, meaning to cling or lean upon). These involve the need to be held, caressed, comforted, played with, and be the center of the caregivers' attention. If these needs are not met, there are serious consequences for the future of the individual.

Many people have a history of emotional deprivation, abandonment, and neglect that resulted in serious frustration of the anaclitic needs. Offering a corrective experience in the form of nourishing physical contact is a very effective way of healing such early emotional trauma. For this approach to be effective, the individual has to be deeply regressed to the infantile stage of development. If that is not the case, the corrective measure does not reach the developmental level on which the trauma occurred. Depending on circumstances, this physical support can range from simple holding of the hand or touching of the forehead to extended comforting embrace.

When the pharmacological effects of the psychedelic substance were subsiding (five to six hours into the session if the psychedelic used was LSD; about three to four hours into the session when it was DPT), we suggested that the patient take off the eyeshades and headphones and engaged him or her in conversation. The purpose here was to get a brief account of the patient's experiences and assess how well the main issues confronted in the session were completed and integrated. If residual physical tensions or unresolved emotions were apparent, we offered the patient a specific form of focused bodywork designed to reach a better closure for the session.

The general strategy of the bodywork was to ask the clients to find area(s) of their bodies where they felt some discomfort—pain, tension, too much energy, nausea, or other uncomfortable physical feelings. Once they had identified and located the problem, we suggested that they focus their attention on that area and do whatever was necessary to intensify the existing sensations. We then helped them to intensify those feelings even further by appropriate external intervention and encouraged them to find a spontaneous response to this situation. It was important for this reaction not to reflect conscious choice but be fully determined by the unconscious process. The vocal response to this situation was not always something one would expect, such as growling, sighing, or screaming. Sometimes it took on a surprising form: baby talk, voice of an animal, gibberish, or talking in tongues. Similarly physical reactions did not include only tremors, coughing, and grimacing, but also complex movements that resembled animal behavior patterns or art forms of various cultures of the world. The sources of these extraordinary manifestations were clearly the phylogenetic memory banks and the collective unconscious.

Reunion with Relatives and Friends

The major effects of LSD lasted in most instances between six and ten hours; in rare instances, we stayed with the patient fourteen or more hours. The effects of DPT lasted for a considerably shorter time; four or five hours after administration, the DPT sessions usually terminated with a relatively fast return to the usual state of consciousness. As the patient started coming back to normal, we invited family members or significant others of the patient's choice to the treatment room for a "reunion." At this time, the patient's special state of consciousness frequently facilitated more open and honest communication and lead to unusually rewarding interaction.

The basic rule of these meetings was to be sensitive to the patients' state of mind and their needs—engage in discussion if they were social and communicative, spend time with them in silence when they felt introspective and pensive, be serious or jovial depending on their mood, and so on. At this time we also served dinner brought in from nearby restaurants. Respecting the patients' culinary preferences, we chose dishes that had interesting tastes, colors, and textures; among the favorites were Northern Chinese and Japanese cuisine. The overall intention was to create a situation that would connect the new positive feelings of the patients to everyday experiences and activities. After the visit came to a natural closure, we spent some more time with the patients alone before entrusting them to the hospital personnel. Patients in earlier stages of cancer who did the session at the Maryland Psychiatric Research Center spent the night there in the company of significant others of their choice. The treatment suites had homelike furniture and their own kitchenettes and bathrooms; they provided adequate comfort for the patients and their companions.

Clinical Work with Self-Referred Patients

Thus far I have described the psychedelic treatment procedure followed in the LSD and DPT controlled studies, where the therapists had to abide by the rigid requirements of the research design. The conditions of clinical work with cancer patients who were self-referred differed considerably from those governing the early pilot project and also from those followed in the LSD and DPT controlled studies. In the pilot project the major objective of therapeutic experimentation was to collect the first clinical impressions about the potential of psychedelic therapy in cancer patients. By the time we worked with the patients in the self-referred group, we already had considerable clinical experience with this treatment procedure. The goal of our exploration in this case was to learn what psychedelic therapy had to offer under conditions unrestricted by rigid methodology. In other words, we were trying to ascertain how this therapy should be conducted in order to reach its maximum potential.

There were several other important differences between the therapeutic work in this category and the two research programs. In the controlled studies, the patients were referred by surgeons and other physicians from the Oncology Unit of Sinai Hospital. These patients came into the program in the last stages of their illness, usually after all conventional medical approaches had been tried and had failed. Most of the patients in the self-referred category bypassed this routine selection process altogether. They were usually from places other than Baltimore and contacted us after the first results of the Spring Grove program had been presented at conferences, published in scientific journals, and discussed in the media. Several of these clients were in much earlier stages of their illness, and the work with them was generally easier and more rewarding. The rest of the patients in the self-referred category had originally been included in the LSD or DPT study but had been assigned to the control groups, which did not receive the psychedelic substance. After the time required for the follow-up, they were given the option of having a psychedelic session outside the research framework.

The amount of time spent with the dying individual and family members in the controlled studies was restricted by the research design. In the self-referred group it was up to us how much time we wanted to spend with the dying individuals and their families in the preparation process and in the interviews following the psychedelic session. Furthermore, both the therapist and co-therapist worked with the patient and the family from the first contact until the last meeting. This differed considerably from the LSD and DPT research projects, where the co-therapist (or nurse) usually entered the treatment process a day or two before the psychedelic session.

The drug-free interviews, as well as the psychedelic sessions, usually were conducted in one of the two special treatment suites at the Maryland Psychiatric Research Center. When the patients were from Baltimore, we tried to do most of the work in the comfortable and familiar settings of their homes. In the later stage of our work, we were fortunate to obtain permission to run even the psychedelic sessions in their homes. Therapeutic work in this context was a much deeper personal experience for us, as well as for the patients and their families. It became an invaluable source of in-depth learning about the psychological, philosophical, and spiritual aspects of dying and about the value of the psychedelic experience in the encounter with death.

Post-Session Interviews and Follow-Up

On the day following the session and later during that week, we met with the patients for follow-up interviews. In these meetings we discussed at length what had transpired during the session, advised the patients what they could do to facilitate a good integration of the experience, and helped them bring the new insights into their everyday life. The patients provided detailed written accounts of their experiences in sessions and after them. When the outcome of the psychedelic session was successful, no additional drug experiences were scheduled. If the result was not satisfactory, or if the patient's emotional condition worsened at a later date as the disease progressed, the psychedelic session was repeated.

Evaluation of the Therapeutic Results

The changes that we observed in cancer patients following psychedelic therapy were extremely varied, complex, and multidimensional. Some of them, such as alleviation of depression, tension, anxiety, sleep disturbance, and psychological withdrawal, were of a familiar nature; they could often be achieved by traditional forms of therapy. However, many others involved phenomena new to Western psychiatry and psychology and specific for psychedelic therapy, such as attenuation or even elimination of fear of death and radical changes in basic life philosophy and strategy, in spiritual orientation, and in the hierarchy of values. In addition to their influence on the emotional, philosophical, and spiritual aspects of the patients' existence, both LSD and DPT also often deeply influenced the experience of physical pain, even pain which had not responded to narcotic drugs.

Because of the complexity of these changes and the lack of specific and sensitive psychological instruments for some of them, objective assessment and quantification of the treatment results became a difficult task. This was further complicated by the physical and emotional condition of many cancer patients and their frequently negative attitude toward time-consuming and exhausting psychological testing, which limited the use of the existing research instruments. During the Spring Grove studies we experimented with different methods of evaluation and did not find a fully satisfactory solution to these problems.

As an example, I will briefly describe our methods of assessing the therapeutic outcome and our approach to data analysis for our controlled study of LSD psychotherapy, which included thirty-one cancer patients. More detailed information on the research methodology, quantitative data, itemized tables, and results of the statistical analysis is available in the original papers (Pahnke et al. 1970, Richards et al. 1972). According to the original research design, each patient was expected to complete several psychological tests before and after treatment. However, this turned out to be a rather unrealistic expectation. Such tests required a degree of concentration and perseverance that for many of these severely ill patients was simply not possible because of their physical pain and exhaustion. Consequently our primary evaluation tool became rating by external observers.

Walter Pahnke and Bill Richards developed a special instrument for this purpose: the Emotional Condition Rating Scale (ECRS). This scale made it possible to obtain values ranging from - 6 to + 6 reflecting the degree of the patient's depression, psychological isolation, anxiety, difficulty in medical management, fear of death, and preoccupation with pain and physical suffering. Ratings were made one day before and three days after the administration of the psychedelic substance by attending physicians, nurses, family members, therapists, and co-therapists. In later stages of research we also included a psychiatric social worker who functioned as an independent rater. In addition, the amount of narcotics required in the management of the patient was used as a criterion for assessing the degree of physical pain.

The effectiveness of the psychedelic treatment program was evaluated by performing tests of statistical significance on pre- and post-session ratings of the clinical condition. Computations were done separately for each of the individual subscales—depression, psychological isolation, anxiety, difficulty in medical management, fear of death, and preoccupation with pain and physical suffering—and also for the representatives of each of the six categories of raters: therapist, co-therapist, attending physician, nurse, closest family member, and independent rater. In addition, a composite index was obtained for each of the categories of distress by pooling the ratings of all the raters.

Therapeutic results in each of the categories were then assessed by comparing the individual composite indexes from before treatment to indexes made after treatment. For a rough assessment of the degree of improvement, a global index of the overall clinical condition was obtained for each patient by collapsing the data from all individual raters for all the clinical categories measured. This procedure made it possible to describe the condition of the patient with a single numerical index. Although this approach obscured the specifics of the clinical problems as well as the often surprising differences of opinion among individual raters, it was useful for comparing results in individual patients and expressing the degree of improvement in terms of percentages of the entire group. The results of the rating supported the clinical impressions of the often dramatic effects of LSD psychotherapy on the emotional condition and physical pain of cancer patients. The most pronounced therapeutic changes were observed in the areas of depression, anxiety, and pain, closely followed by those related to fear of death. The results were least impressive in the area of medical management.

"Dramatic improvement" was defined as an increase of four or more points in the global index and "moderate improvement" as a gain of two to four points. Patients who showed an increase of less than two points or an equivalent decrease were considered "essentially unchanged." According to this definition nine of the patients (29%) showed dramatic improvement following LSD psychotherapy, thirteen patients (42%) were moderately improved, and the remaining nine (29%) were essentially unchanged. Only two patients had a lower global index in the post-treatment period than before treatment; in both of them the decrease was negligible (-0.21 and -0.51 points respectively). As far as the demand for narcotics was concerned, the mean daily dose for the whole group showed a definite positive trend; however, the decrease did not reach a sufficient degree to be statistically significant. This finding seems to conflict with the ratings which indicate a highly significant decrease of pain, and this seeming discrepancy is analyzed further in Chapter 15.

The results of the DPT study were described and evaluated by Bill Richards, a psychologist and therapist at the Maryland Psychiatric Research Center who had participated in the cancer program since its inception in 1967. This project involved forty-five patients assigned randomly to the experimental or control group. Two independent raters used psychological scales to evaluate the patients and family members. Detailed analysis of the data and discussion of the results of the Spring Grove DPT study are presented in Bill Richards' doctoral dissertation (Richards 1975).

Although DPT psychotherapy brought quite spectacular positive results in individual cases, the clinical outcome for the entire experimental group did not show a sufficient degree of improvement to be statistically significant. Significant results and important trends occurred in certain individual scales, but generally this study did not demonstrate that DPT could successfully replace LSD in psychedelic therapy of cancer patients. This was consistent with the clinical impressions and feelings of psychedelic therapists at the Maryland Psychiatric Research Center, who almost unanimously preferred to work with LSD.

More interesting than the overall results of the study was Bill Richards' effort to detect the therapeutic value of the psychedelic peak experience, as described by Abraham Maslow (Maslow 1964). The occurrence of peak experiences was measured by the Psychedelic Experience Questionnaire (PEQ) developed by Pahnke and Richards. This questionnaire emphasized the basic categories of the peak experience: unity, transcendence of time and space, objectivity and reality, feelings of sacredness, deeply felt positive mood, and ineffability (for definition and description of these categories see Chapter 15). Responses were rated on a zero-to-five scale of intensity. Another source of data was the therapists' assessment of the patients' psychedelic experience. Bill Richards found that the data collected in the DPT study showed significantly better therapeutic results in patients who had a psychedelic peak experience compared to those who did not.

One important aspect of this work will necessarily elude even the most sophisticated methodology in all similar studies conducted in the future: the depth of the personal experience of those who are privileged to share the situation of dying with another human being and witness how the deep psychological crisis so frequently accompanying the encounter with death can be alleviated or even completely reversed by a psychedelic experience. Repeated participation in this extraordinary event is more convincing than numerical data and leaves no doubt in the mind of the psychedelic therapist that this work with the dying is worth pursuing.

14
PSYCHEDELIC CASE HISTORIES

The underlying theme that has remained constant
in almost everything I have written is
the intolerable nature of human reality when devoid of
all spiritual, metaphysical dimension.
–David Gascoyne, English poet and writer

PREVIOUS CHAPTERS have summarized the history of psychedelic therapy with cancer patients, described how it was conducted in the Spring Grove Program, and summarized our clinical results and observations in this area. This chapter presents seven case histories to provide more personal and intimate insights into this form of treatment. I have selected patients whose stories illustrate certain important aspects of psychedelic therapy—its effect on their emotional condition, on their attitude toward death, and on physical pain accompanying cancer.

- *Matthew* was a brilliant physician and a talented musician with a broad cultural background. Because of his medical background, he was fully aware of the problems he was facing, as were his close relatives. Communication in Matthew's family was very open and honest. Matthew's major problem in facing and accepting death was his pragmatic and atheistic orientation anchored in his traditional scientific background. His psychedelic session and the transformation he underwent illustrate that mystical experiences can occur in well-educated, skeptical, and scientifically oriented individuals with a materialistic world view.
- *Ted* was in many respects on the opposite side of the spectrum. His education was very limited, and he was fairly open to religious ideas. The interpersonal relations and communication in his family were skewed and dishonest and required much psychological work. Both Ted and his wife kept personal secrets,

including the information concerning his disease. Ted's three LSD sessions mediated powerful personal experiences of God and deep spiritual insights concerning cycles of death and rebirth. He became reconciled with his disease as a result and was able to come to terms with his mortality.

- *Jesse* was a person with traditional Christian religious beliefs who worked as an unskilled laborer. He was almost illiterate—even reading the daily newspapers and the Bible was an intellectual challenge for him. To our great surprise, he discovered and adopted in his psychedelic session a metaphysical system that included belief in reincarnation and resembled Eastern spiritual philosophies. The psychological power of his new vision was so great that it helped him overcome his excessive fear of death. Jesse was able to let go of his ravaged body, which had become infiltrated with multiple metastases, and relinquish his desperate, hopeless clinging to life.
- *Suzanne* volunteered for psychedelic therapy because of the excruciating pain associated with her cancer. Psychedelic therapy had a powerful positive effect on her in many important ways, but her main problem—the agonizing pain—remained the same and was not in the least alleviated. However, as a result of her psychedelic experiences, she lost her fear of palliative surgery, which eventually brought her the relief she had been seeking.
- Conversely, *John's* case illustrates the capricious and often surprising effect psychedelic therapy can have on pain, even pain that resists high doses of narcotics. He received a relatively low dose of DPT, and his experiences lacked the profundity that we had seen in the sessions of many other patients. After what seemed at first to be an unsuccessful attempt at therapy, his agonizing pain disappeared completely for a period of several months.
- *Catherine's* therapy shows how even a person whose life has been extremely traumatic can experience profound transformation, reach reconciliation with a lifetime of suffering, and approach death with dignity and spiritual vision. Her experience also gave us the opportunity to compare the relative influence that a very difficult life history and a very easy birth can have on the nature of a psychedelic session.
- *Joan's* history is an example of the potential of psychedelic therapy at its best. As a result of her three LSD sessions, she underwent a profound spiritual transformation that totally changed the quality of her remaining days. The new way she handled everyday situations, as well as the practical circumstances of her death, was a constant source of awe and wonder among her relatives and friends. In addition, her husband, who was an educator, was able to have his

own psychedelic sessions within the framework of our LSD training program for professionals. This helped him not only to understand better the process of Joan's dying but also to work through some of his own feelings concerning cancer and death.

Matthew's Case History

Matthew was a forty-two-year-old internist suffering from inoperable cancer of the pancreas. He was well acquainted with our psychedelic therapy program. Several years earlier he had actually referred one of his cancer patients to us, for whom LSD therapy had proven very successful. Since Matthew's wife described his condition on the telephone as critical, we responded to their request for LSD therapy immediately and visited them in their home on the same day.

We found Matthew extremely weak, anxious, and full of despair. He had many unpleasant physical symptoms, such as pain, nausea, feelings of fullness in his belly, belching, flatulence, and progressive loss of appetite and weight. Matthew was fully aware of his condition, not only in terms of diagnosis and general prognosis but also with regard to the stage and progress of his malignancy. He followed his own case closely, reviewed his laboratory findings regularly, and monitored the progressive deterioration of his physiological functions. He was even able to diagnose a minor pulmonary embolism that his attending physician had overlooked.

Matthew seemed completely overwhelmed by his illness. His health had always been perfect and his life rewarding and successful. When the disease struck him, he had a beautiful wife, a good marriage, three children, and a well-established medical practice. He was completely unprepared emotionally, philosophically, and spiritually for this unexpected turn of his destiny. Religion had never meant much to him, and his whole approach to life had been highly rational and pragmatic.

As Matthew's suffering increased, he pondered about the absurdity of his disease and asked why and how this had happened to him. His attitude toward his illness and his predicament had been much better until about two weeks before our first visit, when he was surprised by an episode of severe pain that lasted several days. Although the pain had eventually been controlled by morphine, the severe depression and anxiety that it had precipitated continued. An attempt to tranquilize Matthew with chlorpromazine was highly unsuccessful. If anything, the medication made him feel more depressed, defeated, and hopeless.

The degree of Matthew's physical and emotional distress was such that he experienced every day as an unbearable torture. He begged us to shorten the preparation to the absolute minimum and run the session as soon as possible. We decided to condense the preparatory work into two days. During both days we spent many hours talking with Matthew and his wife, children, and parents. Although this preparation time was relatively short, we had the good fortune to establish a close relationship with all the persons involved, and we obtained all the necessary information about Matthew's past and present situation.

In spite of Matthew's serious condition, the interaction between him and his wife Deborah was very effective, one of the rare examples we had encountered of completely honest and open communication. The only complication the couple was facing at the time was related to Matthew's problem with intimacy. Deborah's impulse was to move toward him and be physically close and loving. Because he had lacked physical and emotional contact in his childhood, Matthew was not comfortable with this approach. He considered physical intimacy a prelude to sexual intercourse. But because of his severe somatic condition, he had developed erectile dysfunction. He experienced Deborah's closeness as a painful reminder of his inadequacy and tended to withdraw. Furthermore, he believed that he should cope with his situation by himself, and saw this kind of support as infantilizing.

Despite our relatively brief contact, we felt so encouraged by our relationship with Matthew and his family situation that we decided to conduct the session without delay. At Matthew's request we obtained special permission to run his session in his home instead of the hospital ward. As we were discussing the range of experiences that could occur in LSD sessions, Matthew was generally very curious about the overall process, but he was incredulous and quite skeptical about the potential spiritual aspect of the treatment. We suggested that he approach the session as a scientific experiment by trying to be as open as possible and then drawing his own conclusions after the experience was over. He was very excited that we would use music in the session, as music was his most important solace in his otherwise dismal situation. Matthew was a musician himself, and in the past he had made attempts at composing. While listening to classical music he could occasionally get so absorbed that he would forget about his serious condition.

Matthew's LSD Session

On the day of his session Matthew received 200 micrograms of LSD. We decided to administer the substance intramuscularly because we were concerned about the ability of his gastrointestinal system to absorb it. The latency period seemed somewhat longer than usual, and for over an hour Matthew appeared to be completely normal. Later his behavior became unusual, but he continued to deny that anything was happening. He was lying on the mattress with the headphones on and listening to classical music. Occasionally he would toss and turn and had episodes of difficult breathing. The visual dimension was almost entirely absent from his session, and this made it more difficult for Matthew to identify clearly the onset of the LSD experience.

Eventually it became quite apparent that Matthew was in a holotropic state of consciousness. He became ecstatic about the quality of the music and deeply immersed in it. He kept asking us to listen carefully and tell him whether we had ever heard anything so fantastic before. The music sounded divine to him, and he was losing his boundaries and merging with its flow. Quite early in the session, Matthew felt an intense need for warmth and reached for Joan Halifax, who was the co-therapist in this session. She responded immediately and held and cradled him for more than four hours. He continued listening to the music in this way with an ecstatic expression in his face. His features showed an unusual mixture of infantile bliss and mystical rapture.

On occasion, he uttered seemingly disconnected sentences, which sounded alternately like excerpts from Buddhist texts and accounts of Jewish and Christian mystics: "One world and one universe...all is one...nothing and everything...everything and nothing...nothing is everything...let it go when it's time...it does not make any difference...disease...injury...it is either the real thing or it is not...lower forms and higher forms...the glittering extremities of his majesty's possession...so I am immortal...it is true! ..."

Deborah, who occasionally came to the door of the living room where the session was taking place, could not believe that these statements were coming from her pragmatic and atheistic husband. In the sixth hour of the session, she came in, took Joan's place, and held and cradled Matthew. He was still wearing eyeshades and headphones and was so deeply immersed in the experience that he barely noticed the shift. They spent a long time in a quiet embrace. Then Matthew took off his eyeshades and enjoyed a glass of orange juice. He kept his eyes on Deborah and felt overwhelmed by feelings of great love and closeness.

While the effects of his session were subsiding, Matthew encountered intense physical discomfort. He felt constipated and made desperate efforts to move his bowels. He felt that this was the only obstacle that he had to overcome to return to a blissful state. He believed that if he could empty his bowels, he would "reach the whole world." However, the constipation was so severe that he had to be relieved by an enema. Later that day, Matthew wanted to take a bath. He sat in the bathtub for almost an hour, listening to music and enjoying himself as he was bathed. He then spent the evening listening again to music and discovering entirely new dimensions in pieces that he knew quite well. Feelings of intestinal pain were the only discomfort in his otherwise pleasant condition.

Interestingly, Matthew did not seem to be able to reconstruct the sequences of his LSD experience and did not remember much of its content. The degree of his memory lapse was quite extraordinary, since most people clearly remember the major events of their sessions. He could only manage to communicate his overall feeling about the day—that the experience was unbelievably beautiful and that he had never experienced anything like that in his entire life. Matthew stated that it had felt like "being in a warm cocoon, surrounded by unending love, feeling helpless, but happy and safe."

He reported that the most powerful experience had been lying on the mattress with Deborah, embracing her, and feeling that he was melting into her. As Matthew recounted this, they were both very moved and cried together. Before we left that evening, Matthew summarized his feelings about the session: "Whether this helps or not, I want you to know that I am very grateful for what happened today. It was truly the most beautiful and fulfilling day of my life. I can't see how this could do any harm…"

Two days after the session, Matthew had to be rehospitalized because of a complete intestinal obstruction. With this harsh reminder of the rapid progress of his disease, Matthew started slipping back into his depression. Since he had a private room in the hospital, we brought him a tape recorder, amplifier, and a set of headphones so that he could benefit from the effect music had on him. We also brought him the recordings of the pieces that we had played during his LSD session. We had previously observed that the music used in psychedelic sessions had a special propensity to bring back some of the feelings that the clients had experienced while listening to it under the influence of the drug.

In a special session, Joan taught Matthew how to combine music with a relaxation technique and meditation. She suggested that he had the option to focus on his disease and physical suffering or to reconnect with the experience from his LSD session. After about twenty minutes, Matthew moved into a peaceful state of mind. With the help of the music and Deborah, who stayed with him for many hours each day, he was able to maintain this new emotional balance for his several remaining days. Matthew's block against intimacy seemed to have been completely removed by his LSD session, and he enjoyed physical closeness enormously. Matthew and Deborah both told us independently that this was the most meaningful period in their marriage.

We were scheduled to travel to Hartford, Connecticut, for two days to conduct a seminar. Before leaving Baltimore, we visited Matthew in the hospital. His physical condition was deteriorating rapidly, and we felt that we might not see him again. He evidently shared our feelings. At the end of our visit he told us: "It makes no sense to fight it any longer, if it is time to leave…Do not worry, it is all right…" While we were in Hartford, Joan was awakened at 3:00 AM by a powerful dream about Matthew. He had appeared to her smiling and repeating his last words: "It is all right." She had a distinct feeling that Matthew had just died. When we called the hospital the next morning, the attending physician told us that Matthew had passed on at 3:00 am that day.

We attended Matthew's funeral and the minyan (prayer) service for him and stayed in touch with the family during their mourning period. The family's recovery was surprisingly easy, considering their close bonds with one another. This suggested that the severity of loss is not necessarily the most important factor influencing the nature of grief. In Matthew's case we had clearly seen that the feeling of meaningful participation in the process of dying can take away much of the despair of the survivors.

Ted's Case History

Ted was a twenty-six-year-old African American suffering from inoperable cancer of the colon. He was married and had three children. We contacted him late in 1971 in the outpatient clinic of Sinai Hospital as a potential candidate for the DPT study. At that time his major complaint was almost constant intolerable pain in the abdomen. In addition, he was severely depressed, irritable, and anxious, and had considerable difficulties in his interpersonal relationships, particularly his marriage. The interaction between him and his wife, Lilly, was very unsatisfactory and complicated, and they both felt deeply alienated from one another. Periods of stubborn silence alternated with angry encounters in which they made various accusations of each other—most frequently lack of interest and affection.

Six years earlier, Ted's disease had first been diagnosed, and he had undergone a colostomy. Lilly had been told by the attending physician that Ted's condition was very serious and that he had only several weeks to live. She had been strongly advised not to disclose his diagnosis and prognosis to him, lest he have a desperate reaction and perhaps even commit suicide. But Ted's will to live and his physical resistance had been enormous, and the duration of his survival had surpassed all expectations. During the months and years when he was defying his disease, Lilly had anxiously avoided any allusions to his diagnosis and prognosis. As a result of this, their interaction had become mechanical, superficial, distorted, and increasingly painful. Lilly had extramarital relationships, became pregnant by another man, and had to have an abortion. Ted, in spite of his severe clinical condition and the handicap imposed on him by his colostomy, had an affair with another woman and made her pregnant.

After a brief interview, Ted was accepted into the Spring Grove program. However, because of the random selection required by the research design, he was assigned to the control group. After the follow-up period was over, the patients previously allocated to the control group had the option of having psychedelic therapy outside of the framework of the study. Ted and Lilly expressed interest in a course of psychotherapy with high doses of LSD. In a private interview, Lilly clearly stated her condition for giving her consent. She insisted that the diagnosis and prognosis not be disclosed to

Ted or discussed with him in the procedure. Our experience had been that sometimes patients with whom the situation could not be openly discussed discovered the truth themselves in the course of psychedelic therapy. In view of Lilly's strong feelings on the subject, we decided to accept Ted with this restriction and started therapeutic work.

In the preparation phase we briefly reviewed Ted's stormy personal history. His entire childhood was characterized by severe emotional deprivation and outright physical abuse. He lost both parents at the age of three and spent several years in various orphanages. Finally he ended up in the house of his uncle and aunt, who became his foster parents. In their home he suffered much rejection and cruel emotional and physical abuse. During his childhood and adolescence, Ted was involved in minor antisocial activities, had frequent fistfights in street-gang skirmishes, and liked rough entertainment. Later when he was drafted into the army, he enjoyed his involvement in the war, where his aggressive tendencies found a socially approved channel. In marriage, he was extremely jealous of Lilly but had strong tendencies toward extramarital affairs himself.

Ted's First LSD Session

On the day of the session, we gave Ted 300 micrograms of LSD. At the very onset of the drug action, he became quite confused. This was his first psychedelic experience, and he was not familiar with the effects of the substance. He felt that he was losing all reference points and did not know what was happening to him; he likened it to "floating on a cloud and not having my feet on the ground." He started thinking about his family and present life and saw the faces of his three children. Then the scene changed, and Ted and Lilly were participating in a television show, something like "This Is Your Life," and their children were in it also.

Later the effect of LSD intensified, and Ted experienced himself as a patient in a large hospital. He was lying on the operating table and was surrounded by a surgical team: doctors, orderlies, and nurses. He observed various surgical instruments—X-ray machines, infusion bottles, syringes, and life-support devices. It was not quite clear to him whether he was reliving one of his past operations or just imagining it all. He felt very close to death and saw many people whose lives were also threatened—soldiers dying in wars, adults and children perishing in epidemics, and various persons killed in accidents. Somehow he could, however, see beyond death. Nobody involved in these situations really died; they experienced merely a transition into a different kind of existence. Astonished, Ted saw eternal cycles of life and death unfolding in front of his eyes. Nothing really ever was destroyed; everything was in eternal flux and transformation.

He then felt transported into his childhood and started reliving various episodes of physical and psychological abuse that he had experienced in his aunt and uncle's house. The feeling was so deep and real that he lost the critical insight of being in an LSD session. He saw me illusively transformed into his uncle and Ilse Richards, my co-therapist, into his aunt. He felt deep mistrust toward both of us and experienced himself as trapped, cornered, and suffocating. In a state of fear and panic, he made several attempts to get up and leave the room, some of them quite assertive and aggressive. It soon became obvious that the memory of his birth was emerging into his consciousness and influencing his behavior.

At the time of the session, Ilse was in the second half of her pregnancy, and her condition seemed to attract Ted like a magnet. He focused much of his aggression on Ilse's full abdomen. On several occasions he tried to send her out of the room: "Lady, you better get out of here, it is too dangerous for you to be here." Ilse, who approximately a year before this session had lost a baby in the sixth month of her pregnancy, was naturally very sensitive to these threats and moved into the corner of the treatment room. Ted's mistrust rapidly increased to a dangerous level. As we later discovered, two more factors were involved in this experience. Ted's memories of his violent behavior and indiscriminate killing during the war were coming to the surface, and he felt we were brainwashing him to confess his war crimes. On the deepest level, he perceived me as the Devil, who was tempting him and trying to steal his soul.

In the most critical moment of the session, when Ted's paranoia was culminating, a painfully loud, shrill, and penetrating siren went off and sounded for full three minutes. In the midst of this havoc, the fire inspector and his helper appeared at the door and demanded that we leave the building immediately because of a very unfortunately timed fire drill. Keeping one eye on Ted, whose mistrust was further nourished by this bizarre scene, and the other one on Ilse, who was terrified and potentially in danger, I tried my best to explain the exceptional nature of the situation to the two men, who were determined to carry out their duty. This was by far the most difficult episode that we had experienced during our psychedelic work, and for a while Ted's session appeared to be a total failure.

Surprisingly, all the problems were resolved by the time the session was over. Ted moved into an ecstatic, relaxed, and painless state. He felt that he had gotten rid of much traumatic material that had been bothering him for years. His enthusiasm about the LSD experience was without end. Before the session had ended, he was already talking about having another one. However, the outcome of his first session was so good that it did not seem necessary or desirable to run another one in the near future. Ted's pain was reduced to the point that he stopped taking analgesics and narcotics. Although he had been previously bedridden, he now took on a voluntary job and was able to keep it for several months. In addition, he began to do all kinds of minor chores around the house.

Ted's clinical situation started to deteriorate rapidly around Thanksgiving Day, five months after his first LSD session. He became depressed and progressively weaker; his pain returned and began to reach an intolerable level. Lilly telephoned us and asked for help. Ilse, who had been the co-therapist in the first session, had discontinued her work in the research center. She had delivered in the meantime and was at home to care for her baby. Joan Halifax agreed to take her place in working with Ted. As a preparation for the second session we had several long meetings with Ted and Lilly. We spent much time exploring recent developments in Ted's situation, his present physical and emotional condition, and the patterns of interaction between him and the other members of the family.

During these talks, Lilly's love and genuine concern for Ted soon became obvious. Yet they were still quite alienated from one another. Their skewed, dishonest, and chaotic interaction seemed to be closely connected with their inability to communicate about Ted's disease, diagnosis, and prognosis. At this time, playing the hide-and-seek game had become an almost unbearable burden for Lilly, and she was gradually accepting the idea that something should be done to correct this situation. In a private talk with Ted, we found out that he had suspected his diagnosis from the very beginning, when he had overheard two interns discussing his case outside the door of his hospital room. Later he had confirmed his suspicion when he read in the *Physician's Desk Reference* that cancer was the only indication for one of the drugs he was taking.

Since Lilly did not discuss the diagnosis with him, he presumed that she had not been told. He decided to conceal the truth from her, as he was convinced that she would leave him if she knew he had cancer. "Who wants to live with a man who has cancer?" he told us when we suggested that the issue of his diagnosis and prognosis should be openly discussed. In a dynamic and stormy session, we catalyzed the exchange of the "secret" between the spouses. After an initial aggressive outburst and mutual accusations of dishonesty, both Lilly and Ted were extremely happy about the new, open situation. Lilly was relieved, because she did not have to lie and pretend any more. Ted was pleasantly surprised and very moved when he discovered that Lilly had stayed with him for several years, even though she had known all along that he had cancer.

Another important topic of our discussion was the problem of intimacy and sexual interaction between the spouses. For the last several months Ted had not been able to have sex, and he felt discouraged and humiliated. At one point he complained bitterly: "What am I good for? I cannot move around, go to work, provide money for the family, or satisfy Lilly sexually." Since the time of his sexual failure, he had been avoiding any physical closeness. We discussed his erectile dysfunction as a natural consequence of the disease process and emphasized that it did not have any bearing on his value as a man or as a human being. We encouraged Ted and Lilly to find nonsexual physical expression of the affection that they felt for each other.

We also spent some time with the children to work through difficulties and blocks in Ted's interaction with them. Ted wanted to be a strong and self-reliant father, able to support his children. But in reality their roles were reversed, and Ted was helpless and dependent on them. Ted found this situation very painful and unacceptable. He did not want to have his children around and frequently chased them out of the room whenever they appeared. We tried to show Ted how his experience was affecting his children's concept of death and their attitude toward it. He finally understood how a dying person might impart an invaluable lesson to the living and realized that he could function as a teacher for his children and communicate a very unique message by the way in which he faced dying. He also was able to accept their help without feeling humiliated and saw this as an important opportunity for them to achieve a sense of mastery.

Ted's Second LSD Session

Shortly before the second LSD session, we reviewed Ted's first psychedelic experience with him, particularly the crisis of trust and the paranoid episode, which had presented serious management problems for us. We emphasized that it was important to keep the experience internalized and trace the unpleasant emotions to their sources in his history.

In Ted's second session, we again used 300 micrograms of LSD, the same dose as in the first session. This time Ted's experience was very powerful, but smooth and without any serious problems. He was able to keep the eyeshades and headphones on all through the session and had very few difficult experiences. Generally he enjoyed this session much more but remembered the sequences less vividly, possibly because he experienced less concrete visual content. The emphasis in the second session was more on emotional states and thought processes.

The first effects of the substance became noticeable about twenty-five minutes after its administration. We spent this time with Lilly, listening to a tape that Ted had recorded the evening before the session. Ted's first experience was an image of crossing a large river. This episode seemed to have some deeper symbolic meaning for him, such as travel to another world, to the Beyond. For a brief period following this opening vision, Ted enjoyed music and experienced himself as playing vibraphone in the orchestra. Then his process became much more dynamic and dramatic. As in his first session, Ted became aware of the repetitive nature of various life cycles and saw again numerous sequences of dying and being killed. Some episodes involved humans in various critical and dangerous situations; others took place in the world of animals. For example, one vision featured the interior of a slaughterhouse, where hundreds of hogs were being butchered.

These scenes of suffering were interspersed with many allusions to Ted's disease. He became aware of his body on a tissue and cellular level and felt that it was decaying. He saw his family as beautiful apples in a basket and himself as the only rotten one among these perfect specimens. Then Ted started envisioning a great variety of scenes from many different nations, races, and creeds throughout centuries. These images were beautiful and interesting, but Ted felt annoyed by them. Mostly he wanted to find God, and this display seemed irrelevant and distracting to him. However, as the session continued, the experiences somehow started to come together, and Ted began to understand the unity underlying all of them.

The session culminated in Ted's experience of his own death, during which God appeared to him as a brilliant source of light. This was a very beautiful and comforting episode, as God told him there was nothing to fear and assured him that everything would be all right. Ted was overwhelmed at the realization that behind the seeming chaos and complexity of creation there was only one God. In the light of these new insights, he now focused on his disease and was trying to find the reason for his suffering and its deeper meaning. He kept asking why God inflicted on him this seemingly senseless and absurd agony. At one point, he felt that he had almost reached an understanding and found the answers to these questions.

Following his encounter with God, the rest of Ted's session was magnificent and ecstatic. He experienced visions of crystals, diamonds, jewels, ornate goblets, and chalices in beautiful colors and supernatural radiance. He sensed an upsurge of loving feelings toward Lilly and his children and also expressed his love and gratitude to Joan and me for having provided the opportunity for his experience. At one point, he envisioned a scene in which the four of us (including Lilly, who actually was not physically present at that time) were sitting near a fireplace in friendly communion, enjoying delicious food and having a good time. There were no more dramatic sequences. Ted had feelings of warmth and wholeness; he was relaxed, and experienced himself as floating on a roseate cloud. His pain seemed to have disappeared, and the mobility and control of his legs increased considerably. His appetite was enhanced, and he enjoyed a substantial dinner in Lilly's company. He spent much of the night reviewing all his experiences and impressions of the day and did not sleep until about four o'clock in the morning.

The changes in Ted after this session were so dramatic that Lilly found it baffling. He was very peaceful, serene, centered, and in good spirits. Lilly's comment on the new situation was: "I can't understand it; he is the one who is dying and I seem to be having all the problems. It is as if he has settled something and accepted the situation…as if he has found the answer, but I did not. For me it is still as difficult and painful as before." Ted himself summarized his feelings after the session: "Something has changed … I feel more peace inside… I feel like I might go to Heaven if I die… I was there…."

Although Ted's mental state was relatively stable, his physical condition deteriorated relentlessly. Because of his problems with urination, an indwelling catheter had to be induced into his bladder and a plastic bag attached to his thigh, adding to the inconvenience that he had with his colostomy and further complicating his everyday life. He now spent most of his time in bed and found the visits to the hospital more and more fatiguing. Although the session considerably alleviated the pain, it did not relieve it completely. Ted found physical movement difficult, because it tended to precipitate episodes of painful sensations.

Ted also faced loneliness and boredom. When Lilly was at work and the children at school, he spent many hours at home alone. At such times he was particularly aware of the lack of meaning in his life. We reminded him that because of his condition and situation there was much he could teach others about a very important dimension of life. We asked him to use a small tape recorder to capture his ideas, feelings, and reflections. Ted very much enjoyed this activity and continued giving us tapes with messages he had recorded for Lilly, his children, and both of us. He found this activity very meaningful and was quite proud of his new role, especially as he was one of few dying people involved in a new experimental program. He realized that this gave special significance to the information he was able to provide.

At this time a BBC television crew contacted us and asked if we would allow them to film the process of psychedelic therapy with a cancer patient. They had heard about our research and wanted to include a segment on it as part of a special program on dying and death. Because of very difficult experiences with the journalists and media in the past, we were reluctant to accept this offer. However, during our negotiations with the BBC team, we came to trust them. With some hesitation we contacted Ted, who seemed to be the logical candidate for this project, and told him about the BBC offer. He immediately became very excited and enthusiastic and saw this as an opportunity to give meaning to his otherwise dismal and hopeless situation. The prospect had such an enlivening effect on him that when the film crew arrived at his house and expected to find him bedridden, he was instead in the backyard, fully dressed and polishing his car.

We tried to arrange Ted's third session in a way that would make the filming as unobtrusive as possible. The session environment was minimally modified—the only change in the treatment room was the presence of the cameraman, along with special lamps and cables necessary for the filming. With the help of closed-circuit TV monitoring, the audio-taping and all the other operations were controlled from outside the room. We had an agreement with the TV crew that Ted's well-being was of primary importance. The filming would be discontinued at any point if it seriously interfered with the course of his session, without regard to the ensuing economic losses.

Ted's Third LSD Session

Under these circumstances Ted received his third dose of 300 micrograms of LSD. The nature of this session combined the elements of his first two psychedelic experiences. At the very beginning, he had a profound religious experience of being in a large cathedral with beautiful stained-glass windows. The presence of God filled this temple, and Ted felt deeply connected with Him. He was again shown that life was an endless sequence of cycles in which becoming, being, and perishing were just chapters in the same great book. However, this was not merely a repetition of what he had understood in his first two sessions; Ted was now able to recognize certain new dimensions and important aspects that had previously remained unexpressed.

Then the element of mistrust began to predominate, similar to an aspect of his first session but in a much less serious form. Ted relived a number of his negative experiences with women and expressed much hostility toward the females in his life—his aunt, a number of his girl friends, and especially Lilly. As the memories of Lilly's extramarital affairs, pregnancy with another man, and her dishonesty about his disease emerged in Ted's consciousness, he felt much bitterness, resentment, and aggression. He took off his eyeshades and, as he was looking at Joan, he saw her illusively transformed into Lilly and later into an epitome and personification of all female deception.

Ted had the opportunity to vent much of his deep-seated anger during these transference projections. After this dramatic episode, when the trust bond between us had been reestablished, he was able to reconnect with the positive feelings that characterized the first part of his session. When Lilly later joined us, Ted actually sensed that after the emotional outbursts directed toward her during his session, his feelings for her were much deeper than ever before. He felt that his mistrust and insecurity in the relationship were fading away and sensed an upsurge of warm, loving feelings. We concluded the day with a family dinner. Ted was coming down from the session in a very good condition and enjoyed the meal enormously. After dinner, we drove Ted and Lilly back home and spent some time by Ted's bed, discussing his LSD experience and the events of the day.

The third session further reinforced Ted's spiritual orientation toward life, toward his disease, and toward death. His tapes were full of statements resembling Buddhist philosophy and Hindu cosmology. He talked about cycles of death and rebirth, causes of suffering, and need for detachment. His fear of death diminished greatly, in spite of his rapidly deteriorating physical condition. Unfortunately, shortly after his third session, Ted developed severe symptoms of uremia. Several years earlier, one of his kidneys had been surgically removed because of a malignant growth. At this point, the ureter of his remaining kidney became obstructed by an infection, and Ted was developing symptoms of intoxication by his own toxic metabolic products. The surgeons, uncertain of the value of an intervention that would at best prolong his life for several additional weeks, kept delaying the operation.

After Ted had spent eight days in progressively worsening uremia, we received an urgent telephone call from Lilly at five o'clock in the morning. That night Ted had seen me in a dream and wanted to discuss an issue that he considered to be of utmost importance. We arrived at the hospital about an hour later; by that time Ted's condition had deteriorated considerably, and he appeared to be in a coma. He was surrounded by several of his relatives, who tried to communicate with him. But Ted did not respond, except for an occasional, quite incomprehensible mumbling. Ted's death seemed imminent. While I was comforting Lilly and the relatives and tried to help them accept the situation, Joan sat down by Ted's side. She talked to him gently, using her own westernized version of the instructions from the *Bardo Thödol*, and suggested that he move toward the light and merge with it, unafraid of its brilliance.

Just when everybody in the room seemed to have accepted Ted's imminent death, a very unexpected event took place. In the last moment, the surgical team decided to operate after all. With no forewarning, two male attendants suddenly entered the room, transferred Ted to a stretcher, and took him to the operating room. All the people in the room were shocked by what appeared to be a brutal intrusion into an intimate and special situation. During the operation, Ted had two cardiac arrests resulting in clinical death and was resuscitated on both occasions.

When we visited Ted in the afternoon in the Intensive Care Unit, he was just recovering from anesthesia. He looked at Joan and surprised her with an unexpected, yet accurate, comment: "You changed your dress!" Unwilling to believe that somebody who was in a coma could have correctly observed the environment and remembered such a subtlety, we started inquiring about the nature of Ted's experiences on the morning of that day. We soon realized that he had correctly perceived the people present in the room, although his eyes had been closed all the time. At one point, he had even noticed that tears rolled down Joan's cheeks. While fully aware of his environment, he also had had a number of unusual experiences that seemed to unfold on at least three levels.

He was able to listen to Joan's voice and responded to her suggestions. The initial darkness was replaced by brilliant light, and he was able to approach it and fuse with it. As he merged with the light, he felt a sense of sacredness and deep inner peace. Yet at the same time, he saw a movie on the ceiling, a vivid reenactment of all his misdeeds. He saw the faces of all the people whom he had killed in the war and all the youngsters he had beaten up as an adolescent hoodlum. He had to suffer the pain and agony of all the people whom he had hurt during his lifetime. While this was happening, he was aware of the presence of God, who was watching and judging this review of Ted's life.

Before we left him that day, Ted emphasized how glad he was that he had had his three LSD sessions. He had found the experience of actual dying extremely similar to his psychedelic experiences and considered the latter excellent training and preparation for death. "Without the LSD sessions, I would have been scared by what was happening, but knowing these states, I was not afraid at all."

Although Ted's critical condition was ameliorated by palliative surgery, his body showed signs of profound deterioration. He was exhausted by the many years of his fight against cancer and further weakened by progressive intoxication from his own metabolic products. He was losing weight at a fast rate and wasting away in front of our eyes. We left Baltimore a month after Ted's last session. Before our departure we visited him, and we all knew that we would not see each other again. Toward the end of our visit, we spent a few minutes in silence, looking at each other. Ted interrupted the silence and said: "My body has had it, my body is all shot with cancer; it is time for me to go. But my mind is all right...I am beyond fear now...I am going to make it...Thank you for all your help..."

We found later that Ted had died several weeks after our last visit. The tube draining his ureter had become clogged, and he had returned to the hospital. Lilly spent much time with him there. On the last day of his life, Ted sent Lilly home to bring him clean pajamas. Lilly left the hospital, and a nurse who entered Ted's room several minutes later found him quietly resting on his pillow. When she came closer, she discovered that he showed no signs of life.

Jesse's Case History

Jesse was referred to our program in a severe physical and emotional condition. At the age of thirty-two he had undergone a partial resection of his upper lip because of a squamous cell carcinoma. Now, thirteen years later, he returned to the hospital with an uncontrollable spread of the same type of cancer throughout his body. Large tumorous masses were visible on the left side of his neck, the right side of his face, and around his forehead. He complained of severe pain, excessive weakness and fatigue, coughing, and difficulties with swallowing. He was also suffering from insomnia, deep depression, and great emotional instability.

Jesse was experiencing frequent crying spells and severe bouts of anxiety with a sense of impending death. He was preoccupied with the aesthetic aspects of his disease—the disfiguration of his face and neck and the intense odor of the bandages soaked with the tissue fluid that was leaking from his skin ulcerations. The malignant process was proceeding rather rapidly, resisting an aggressive regimen of external radiation and chemotherapy. Despite his hopeless physical condition, Jesse was terrified of death and was desperately clinging to life. Since nothing more could be done to arrest his neoplastic process, he was accepted into the DPT program with the goal of alleviating his emotional suffering and physical pain.

During the preparation for his psychedelic session, Jesse shared his complicated life history with me and my co-therapist Ilse Richards. Jesse, one of sixteen siblings, was only five years old when his parents were killed in a car accident. He was raised in an orphanage until the age of fourteen, when he started working and became economically independent. He changed jobs several times and, because of his limited education, he never achieved sufficient skills in any of them. His first job was as a laborer on a farm; later he moved to Baltimore and worked successively as a carpenter, plumber, and roofer.

Jesse had always had great difficulty relating to women. After several superficial relationships, he married a woman with a strict Catholic background, who had just started the process of liberating herself from her restrictive past. The marriage was short-lived and ended after about a year, when his wife became involved with another man. Jesse learned about it and had a fistfight with his rival. His wife walked out on him, and he never saw her again.

During the fifteen years before our meeting with him, Jesse had had a rather steady relationship with Betty, a widowed woman considerably older than himself. The friendship between them had initially been sexual, but their sexual relations had ceased years before Jesse's DPT treatment. Betty and her sister were taking care of Jesse in a most remarkable way—functioning literally as full-time nurses. They shared their small apartment with him and patiently endured the strong odor that Jesse's soaked bandages exuded in Baltimore's hot and humid summer. Jesse, as a convinced Catholic, felt deeply guilty about this relationship. He believed that marriage in church represented an eternal bond that could not be dissolved even by physical death, let alone by separation or divorce. As far as he was concerned, his obligations to his wife remained unchanged by her departure.

During the preparation for his DPT session, Jesse expressed his overwhelming fear of death. When he thought about dying, he saw two alternatives, each one frightening in its own way. According to the first, death was the absolute end of everything, a step into nothingness and darkness. The second possibility was the Christian concept he had been introduced to as part of his strict Catholic upbringing: when one dies, existence and consciousness continue for eternity, and the quality of Afterlife depends on one's conduct on earth. Jesse did not find the idea of posthumous existence sufficiently convincing, and it was not a particularly comforting alternative anyway. If there were the Christian abodes of the Beyond, he saw himself forever condemned, assigned to the tortures of Hell for having lived his life in sin. As a result of this dilemma, Jesse's clinging to life was desperate and fraught with profound anxiety.

Jesse's DPT Session

On the day of his psychedelic session, Jesse manifested an almost childlike fear and was very apprehensive about what might happen. He received 90 milligrams of DPT intramuscularly, and we then had to exert much effort to persuade him to put on the eyeshades and headphones. The beginning of the session was marked by an intense fight against the effect of the drug. Jesse seemed to hold onto reality with the same anxious determination with which he clung to life in his everyday struggle. This fight against the experience was marked by strong physical distress, particularly coughing and nausea, which finally culminated in repeated vomiting. Jesse was overwhelmed by the impact of the material that was pouring out of his own mind. The music sounded rough, loud, and distorted, and he experienced it as an assault. He felt that if he surrendered to the experience he would die. On several occasions, he voiced his deep regret for having taken the drug.

During this heroic struggle, countless images and scenes were passing in front of Jesse's eyes. In all of them he was both the observer and the participant. His nausea was accompanied by visions of gigantic, frightening creatures of various forms that were attacking and trying to destroy him. He envisioned thousands of war scenes, full of aggression and destruction, and other situations in which "people were dying and disposing of themselves." During a long episode Jesse saw numerous scenes of junkyards strewn with corpses, carcasses, skeletons, rotting offal, and trash cans spreading foul odors. He saw his own body in these scenes, wrapped in stinking bandages, eaten by cancer, its skin cracking, leaking, and covered with cancerous ulcerations.

Suddenly a gigantic ball of fire appeared out of nowhere. All the mess and garbage were dumped into its purifying flames and consumed. Jesse's flesh and bones were destroyed in this fire, yet his soul survived. He then experienced a Last Judgment scene where God ("Jehovah") was weighing his good and evil deeds. Numerous memories from his life passed through his mind in what felt like some final reckoning. The positive aspects of his life were found to outweigh his sins and transgressions. Jesse felt as if a prison had opened up and he had been set free. At this point he heard sounds of celestial music and angelic singing, and he began to understand the meaning of his experience. A profound message came to him through some supernatural, nonverbal channels and permeated his whole being: "When you die, your body will be destroyed, but you will be saved; your soul will be with you all the time. You will come back to earth, you will be living again, but you do not know what you will be on the next earth."

As a result of this experience Jesse's pain was alleviated, and his depression and anxiety disappeared. He emerged from the session with a profound belief in reincarnation, even though this concept was alien to his own religious tradition. Jesse struggled deeply with the limitations of his educational background to communicate the nature and scope of his experience. He did not realize that in talking about reincarnation, he was describing a fundamental concept of Eastern religious and philosophical thinking and many other traditions throughout ages. He was very tentative and apologetic in sharing his new conviction with me, afraid that I might consider his new ideas, which conflicted with accepted Christian beliefs, a symptom of mental illness.

After his session Jesse was able to come to terms with his situation and developed a new attitude toward his impending death. The prospect of another incarnation freed him from clinging to his body, which was all but destroyed by cancer. He saw his body as a burden and unfair complication in the lives of Betty and her sister, who had accepted the duty of caring for it. Jesse died peacefully five days after his session, perhaps a little earlier than he would have otherwise surrendered in his struggle against inevitable death. It almost seemed as if he was hurrying to get a new body on the "next earth."

Suzanne's Case History

Suzanne was sent to us by her attending physician from the Department of Gynecology at Sinai Hospital. She was an attractive, sensitive, and intelligent woman, a divorced mother of three children. At the time of our first encounter, she was thirty-two years old and was studying psychology. She had been hospitalized because of advanced gynecological cancer, which had spread all through her pelvis in spite of a radical hysterectomy and subsequent course of intensive radiation. The neoplastic process had invaded the nerve plexuses along her spine, causing excruciating pain that responded only poorly to morphine medication.

Her surgeon had suggested a cordotomy as a last resort—an operation on the spinal cord in which the neural tracts which conduct pain stimuli are selectively severed. Suzanne was facing a serious conflict. She desperately desired alleviation of her pain but was unable to face the risks of this procedure: possible paralysis of her legs and incontinence. She became deeply depressed, to the point of seriously considering suicide. In addition, she felt completely exhausted and lacked initiative and interest in anything. She welcomed the offer of psychedelic therapy, especially when she learned that in many instances it had helped to alleviate intractable pain associated with cancer.

During the preparation period, we became acquainted with Suzanne's difficult and moving life history, particularly her severely deprived childhood. Her mother was an attractive but emotionally unstable person. She was very promiscuous and at times engaged in prostitution; she had had five marriages and many boyfriends. Suzanne spent her childhood mostly alone. Her mother's neglect affected even basic aspects of her daughter's existence. Suzanne remembered many times when, starving, she would sit on the neighbor's doorstep hoping to get something to eat, or she would eat leftovers from trash cans. Her resentment toward her mother was quite obvious; she described her as deceptive, destructive, and domineering. Later in her childhood, Suzanne had been sent to a boarding school. Despite the confining and restrictive regime there, the school seemed a definite improvement over her home situation. Episodes of deep depression with suicidal fantasies, panic, fear of darkness, and terrible nightmares completed the picture of Suzanne's emotional struggles in childhood.

Suzanne's adolescence and adulthood were also fraught with serious problems and conflicts. She had had only a few superficial relationships before meeting her husband. Their relationship was initially quite exciting and fulfilling but deteriorated quickly after they got married. Suzanne was subjected first to emotional and later even physical abuse by her husband. At the time of their divorce, she was so emotionally disturbed that she had to be hospitalized in a psychiatric institution. Because of her emotional problems, her husband was awarded the children. Following the divorce suit, Suzanne saw her children only rarely and missed them very much. Shortly after her divorce, she started living with Michael, an unemployed artist. The couple was financially supported by Suzanne's mother who, according to Suzanne, was attempting to appease her guilt about all the earlier neglect. Her mother used the couple's dependence on her money to manipulate and control them. Suzanne spent much effort trying to free herself from the strong ambivalent bond with her mother and "cut the umbilical cord," but to no avail.

Suzanne's gynecological problems started during a trip to Mexico, where she had fallen ill with dysentery and developed vaginal bleeding. Upon her return, she had a Pap smear and cervical biopsy, both of which came back positive. When she learned of her diagnosis, she responded with fear and depression and cried bitterly for many days. Occasionally she also had episodes of anger and felt that life had played a dirty trick on her. Her suicidal tendencies were very strong, and she would have attempted to kill herself but for her sense that everything happening to her had some deeper reason and meaning.

Suzanne traced the origin of this optimistic feeling to an unusual spiritual experience that had occurred spontaneously shortly after her hysterectomy: she had a convincing sense that she had left her body and was floating above the city of San Francisco. The city was illuminated by thousands of lights, and the view was breathtaking. At that point, all her emotional and physical pain disappeared, and she experienced an ecstatic rapture, deep inner peace, and indescribable bliss. For about a week after this episode she could leave her body at will and have similar experiences, but she was too frightened to explore these states any further.

Suzanne's First DPT Session

Like Jesse, Suzanne was assigned to the DPT psychedelic research project. Her first psychedelic session was very intense and quite difficult. Shortly after the injection of 120 milligrams intramuscularly, she felt that everything began to spin around, as in a giant whirlpool. She became involved in a vicious struggle against an unknown amorphous danger or enemy, a battle of life and death that was overwhelming and totally incomprehensible to her. She felt enormously physically constrained and panted and gasped for breath. Powerful energy streamed through her entire body, and her thighs shook violently. Her prevailing feelings were intense pain and sickness. She tried to stop the experience, but without success. Waves of nausea permeated her whole being and culminated in explosive vomiting, which had a powerful purging quality.

During this difficult period we tried to give Suzanne support, but contact with her was very limited because she was totally absorbed in her experience. Later she told us that she had been desperately fighting her way through a large triangular mass of shiny black material that seemed to be a mountain of anthracite coal with ragged edges. She felt that she was biting and chewing her way and tearing the black mass with her fingers. When she finally made it through the black mountain, she envisioned flowing forms in shining pink and gold colors. She sensed that pink symbolized pain, and gold represented goodness. Then the experience opened into a world of millions of colors and eventually into images of swirling galaxies. Later Suzanne identified the black mountain from which she had been liberated as a symbol of death.

As a result of this session, Suzanne's emotional condition improved considerably. Her depression totally disappeared, her fears were alleviated, and she felt an upsurge of energy and initiative. However, the one improvement that she desperately needed and the one which we all hoped for did not occur—relief from her agonizing physical pain. Since the only remaining alternative was neurosurgery, which Suzanne feared, we scheduled a second DPT session shortly after the first one to give her another chance.

Suzanne's Second DPT Session

In the second session, we used the same dose of DPT, 120 milligrams intramuscularly. Several minutes after the injection, Suzanne started again feeling nauseous.

However, this time the physical sensation of nausea was accompanied by a very clear psychological content. Suzanne experienced herself as a pregnant mother and simultaneously identified with the baby in a toxic womb. She was hypersalivating and experiencing the water in her mouth as amniotic fluid. Suddenly a patch of spattered blood appeared in her visual field and, in the next moment, everything became flooded with bloody splashes.

Suzanne began to go through numerous sequences of dying and being born, in many variations. The most prominent feature in these sequences was a strange mixture of the agony of dying and the ecstasy of birth. She oscillated between feelings of being trapped and desperate attempts to free herself, between agonizing metaphysical loneliness and striving for reunion, between murderous rage and feelings of passionate love. She identified deeply with all the mothers who had ever given birth, and with all the children who had ever been born. Through these episodes of birth and death, she became connected "with all of suffering humanity, with millions and millions of people crying in pain." She was crying with them, and at the same time she identified with them and felt the ecstasy of this union in agony.

Several times she flashed on something that felt like sequences from previous lifetimes or incarnations. In one of them, she became an African native running with her fellow tribespeople on sun-scorched plains in what seemed to be a scene of violent tribal warfare. At the end of this episode, she was struck by a spear, which penetrated deeply through her back into her body. Mortally wounded, she lost consciousness and died. In another sequence, she gave birth to a baby in medieval England. She sensed that this particular death and childbirth in previous lifetimes were somehow meaningfully related to the reliving of her own birth.

Later in the session, as a bird flying through the skies, she was shot by an arrow and fell down to earth with a broken wing. Finally all these sequences of dying and being born seemed to converge into a powerful unifying image. She became the mother of all the men who have ever been killed in all the wars in human history. As she became all these mothers and all these children, she felt that she also became a fetus growing inside of her and trying to give birth to itself. In a final sequence of being born and dying, her adult ego died, and a new self was born. Then she became a tiny speck in space, in an infinite universe filled with beautiful stars.

As the experience was gradually subsiding, Suzanne remembered different periods from her present life. She experienced herself as an infant crying in the crib, relived her childhood nightmares (including how she had needed to sleep with her light on), and saw her mother and father fighting. As she was reliving these episodes she was able to reevaluate them against the background of her new universal insights and cosmic feelings. Then she experienced deep love for her partner Michael and the need for him to join us in the session.

Suzanne's second DPT session was again a disappointment in that it did not alleviate her pain. On the days following the session, her physical suffering was as intense and excruciating as ever. However, in every other respect she benefited enormously from the experience. Her depression had completely disappeared, and she radiated energy and determination. She decided to continue her psychological studies as intensely as her disease would permit. In her new state of mind, she was also able to solve the problem of the cordotomy, which in the past she had feared so much. The risk of paralysis and incontinence now seemed worth taking if it offered a chance to get rid of her pain. She said about it: "I do not care if I am crippled from my neck down and pee all over Baltimore; I want my consciousness clear and not absorbed by this pain." The operation was performed shortly after the session, and its outcome was stunning. Suzanne's pain completely disappeared, and the surgeon managed to sever only the sensitive tracts without the slightest impairment to the motor neurons. None of the feared complications materialized.

The most striking consequence of Suzanne's second DPT session was the change in her concept of death and her attitude toward it. She became open to the possibility that after death part of the energy that constitutes the human being continues to exist in a conscious form. Instead of seeing death as the ultimate disaster, absolute blackness, nothingness, and emptiness, as she had before, she began to think in terms of cosmic cycles and transitions. The concept of reincarnation and a chain of lives had now become quite plausible for her.

Suzanne was able to continue her life without feeling oppressed by her cancer, taking one day at a time, and focusing on the problems of each day as it unfolded. She told us: "That is actually what we all should be doing, whether we are healthy or sick; none of us knows the day and the hour when death will come." For some time it seemed that Suzanne's new attitude would conquer her disease. An exploratory laparotomy conducted a few weeks after her cordotomy actually showed that the tumor was shrinking. That finding confirmed Suzanne's optimism, and for several months she lived as if she had never had cancer: "I don't think about it at all anymore," she said when we asked her how she felt about her disease. During this time, she applied for a fellowship and was determined to complete her psychological studies. The tentative title of her thesis was "The Effect of Psychedelic Therapy on Persons Suffering from Cancer."

Then to her great surprise and disappointment, her pain returned. The initial onset was gradual, but later its intensity rapidly increased until her pain became excruciating again. It originated in the residual tumor and radiated into her pelvis and legs. Another surgical intervention brought only temporary relief. Suzanne continued to lose weight and developed severe side effects of chemotherapy, a treatment which in itself had only minimal effect. The tumor spread into her kidneys and caused irreversible damage. From this point on, Suzanne's disease progressed rapidly. Throughout this painful downhill course she was able to maintain the insight from her DPT sessions that there might be some form of existence beyond physical death, that "there is light on the other side of that anthracite mountain." Despite all her physical suffering, Suzanne's death was very peaceful.

John's Case History

When we first met John during the grand rounds at the Oncology Unit of Sinai Hospital, he was deeply depressed and totally absorbed in his pain. He had been bedridden for several weeks, incapable of getting up even to go to the toilet. He rarely ate his meals, would not listen to the radio, and did not want to read a book or newspaper. He was not even interested in watching the new color TV that his father-in-law had bought especially for him. John was completely preoccupied with the nature and intensity of his pain and physical suffering. He complained that no matter what position he assumed, his pain was intolerable and getting worse every moment. He feared even minor changes of his position, passive or active, and felt literally immobilized by this physical agony that had captured and absorbed all of his attention.

A year earlier the Sinai physicians had discovered that John had malignant hypernephroma, a tumor of his right kidney originating in the adrenal gland. A nephrectomy, radical surgical removal of the afflicted kidney, was performed without delay. However, the tumor had already metastasized. In the following months, John developed progressive symptoms from the secondary growths. By the time we first met him, the tumor had spread to his spinal column and was causing severe neurological problems.

John was thirty-six years old, married, and the father of three children. Both spouses considered their marriage to be better than average. Occasionally they argued about the upbringing of their children, but basically the family manifested a sense of deep loyalty, cooperation, and warmth. John's wife Martha came to the hospital every day around ten o'clock in the morning and stayed until the evening, even though her husband barely communicated with her during these visits and did not show any interest in family affairs. He either complained about his agonizing pain or dozed because he was so heavily medicated. Martha always brought some kind of work with her to the hospital; she would sit quietly in an armchair and was available whenever John needed something.

Martha had learned of her husband's diagnosis shortly after it was made and seemed to be facing the problem with considerable courage. She had kept the diagnosis and prognosis from John for many months, until finally she could no longer do so. Shortly before we met John, she had decided to tell him the truth. John now knew that he had cancer, but he was oscillating between pessimism and optimism about his future. Often he mentioned death and even instructed Martha to arrange a simple funeral to save money for the children. At other times he referred to long-term plans regarding his job and talked about a vacation abroad they would all take after he became well. Shortly after Martha told John the truth, she decided to discuss his situation openly with his mother. However, she decided not to tell John that she had told his mother, because "John would get upset knowing how much this information would disturb her."

John was a rather problematic patient for psychedelic therapy, where psychological preparation and cooperation are considered essential for successful outcome. He was extremely reluctant to establish contact and engage in conversation. He was either so preoccupied with his disease and pain or so mentally altered by narcotics and sleep medication that any focused discussion was essentially impossible. He did not want to talk about his life situation, past history, or the psychological aspects of psychedelic therapy simply because he did not see any direct and immediate link between these topics and his physical pain.

The preparation was thus shortened to a bare minimum, and some of the basic information was obtained from John's wife. Under these circumstances, we were somewhat reluctant to run the session, as we felt that we had not been able to establish sufficient rapport, trust, and understanding—elements that we considered important for safe and productive therapy. Despite our mixed feelings, we finally decided to proceed because of Martha's demands and John's desperate insistence that we give him the promised treatment if it offered the slightest chance of alleviating his pain.

John's DPT Session

In the morning of the session day, John was given 60 milligrams of DPT intramuscularly, a lower dose than usual because of our concern that John was not well prepared and ready for the experience. When the drug started to take effect, we encouraged John to put on the eyeshades and headphones. He reluctantly complied after repeatedly emphasizing that all he could bear was soft, gentle, and unobtrusive music. This was consistent with John's attitude toward sounds and with his behavior in everyday life. He preferred to rest all day in darkness and in absolute silence. Visual, acoustic, and tactile stimuli of any kind seemed to increase his pain and irritate him.

In the early stages of his DPT session, John complained frequently about his physical discomfort, feelings of heat, and intense dislike of the music. He was nauseated and vomited several times. Generally his experiences seemed quite uninteresting and uneventful. He spent much time fighting the effects of the drug and exerting great effort to maintain control. It was extremely difficult for him to let go of his defenses and to face the emerging unconscious material. The content of the session seemed relatively superficial, mostly of recollective-biographical nature. John recalled various periods of his life and relived several traumatic events from his childhood, including a railroad accident that he had witnessed as a young boy and an injury that his three-year-old sister had suffered when her sled hit a tree and she broke her leg.

John also encountered several episodes of violent war scenes, which opened into reliving some memories from his military service. At another point in the session, John had visions of a stormy ocean, sinking ships, and drowning people. After this he reconnected with a memory of a dangerous event on the Chesapeake Bay: John and some of his close relatives had gone cruising on a boat that almost collided with a Japanese freighter. In the second half of the session, John grew progressively more tired and finally insisted on taking off the eyeshades and headphones. He had no sense of any major resolution or breakthrough; the effects of the drug simply subsided, and we all felt disappointed in the session. The only redeeming aspect that John reported from his session was a seemingly trivial pleasant memory of a large bowl or pitcher filled with iced tea. This vision seemed highly relevant to him—connected with some important situation or problem from his childhood. In our discussions during the follow-up sessions, John repeatedly returned to this image. Although he never understood its meaning, the memory filled him with excitement.

When we saw John in the hospital on the day after the session, he was in bed, weak, extremely tired, and almost incommunicative. His condition only confirmed our previous feeling that the session had been unproductive. However, on the second day after the session John's condition suddenly shifted in a dramatic way. His mood improved; he was smiling at people and started communicating with his family and the staff. When he talked with his wife, he showed interest in the children and the family for the first time in months. He asked for a radio and spent time listening to soft music. The new color TV was now on for many hours a day.

To everyone's amazement, John's pain had completely disappeared. This was especially surprising, as one of the metastases located in his spine was encroaching on the radices of his spinal nerves. John was now able to get to the toilet without assistance and even take short walks in the hospital corridor. He stopped talking about his disease and his suffering and enjoyed discussions about political, social, and family issues. According to Martha, John appeared to be totally transformed; he was a "completely different person." Now he often laughed and joked and displayed interest in many different topics.

Interesting additional information about John's session emerged about ten days later, when we were analyzing his answers to the Psychedelic Experience Questionnaire (PEQ). We discovered that he had responded positively to the item "Visions of religious personages (Jesus, Buddha, Muhammad, Sri Ramana Maharishi, etc.)" and had given his experience a rating of 5 on a 0-5 scale. This was surprising, since we had asked him explicitly after his session if there had been any religious elements in his experience, and he had denied it. When asked to clarify this discrepancy, he answered: "At one point I saw large bronze and golden statues of these Oriental...How do they call them...Buddhas. There were some inscriptions under them, but they were all in Latin. I don't read Latin and could not figure them out. That's why I didn't tell you about them."

Shortly after his session John discontinued all medication and was completely free of pain until more than two months later, shortly before his death. The session that was initially considered by everybody involved to be a complete failure thus turned out to be one of the most dramatic therapeutic successes of our study. John's case showed the most significant effect of psychedelic therapy on intractable pain that we had ever witnessed. The incongruence between the content and course of the session, on the one hand, and the therapeutic outcome, on the other, illustrates very well the unpredictable nature of the effect of psychedelic therapy on pain.

Catherine's Case History

Catherine was a sixty-year-old businesswoman suffering from breast cancer and carcinoma of the intestines, with metastases in the liver. Her life history was one of the most difficult we have ever encountered in our patients—a combination of childhood traumas in a severely dysfunctional family, ridicule and abuse she had experienced in her life as a Jew, extremely traumatic sexual history, and difficult marriage. The most important trauma of her life occurred at age thirteen when she was brutally raped and as a result became both pregnant and infected by gonorrhea. Her mother forced her to have an illegal abortion in a very advanced stage of her pregnancy. The aborted fetus was alive, and Catherine watched as the woman who performed the abortion drowned the fetus in a sink and disposed of it. All her adult life Catherine wanted to have children, but the gonorrheal infection had left her sterile.

Knowing Catherine's difficult history, we undertook her treatment with some trepidation. During psychedelic sessions patients are usually confronted by their traumatic past, and a series of sessions is usually required to come to terms with this material. This level of effort is certainly justified, given enough time for systematic therapy and assuming the patients have enough of their life left to enjoy the positive results. But in this case we hesitated to contribute to Catherine's suffering in the short period of life remaining. However, one encouraging circumstance in Catherine's case was that she was the eighth of nine children; her delivery had been easy and had lasted only several hours. In our experience, the nature of her birth was a positive prognostic sign for psychedelic sessions. But it remained to be seen whether the nature of Catherine's session was to be more profoundly influenced by her easy birth or her severely traumatic postnatal life history.

Catherine's LSD Session

On the morning of her session Catherine was given 400 micrograms of LSD. Her first symptom was intense nausea; however, this sensation was not only physical—it had a distinctly spiritual undertone. A brief period of calmness ensued, and then Catherine began to see beautiful emeralds and opals in soft green and bluish colors, spinning and cascading from above. A magnificent beam of brilliant light was illuminating them; the light seemed to be coming from inside her. The precious stones and jewels appeared to have a much deeper meaning beyond their beauty. The green light emanating from them was of a spiritual nature and was relieving her from her sorrow and physical pain.

Then all the beauty disappeared, and Catherine began reviewing various aspects of her life. Tears poured down her cheeks as she relived the frustrations of her childhood, confusions of her heavy sexual history, failures of her marriage, and the humiliation she had experienced as a Jew. During this cleansing and purging life review, much of her caustic self-hatred was transformed into incisive humor. For the first time in her life she even started experiencing genuine feelings of love. Later in the session the music sounded louder and louder to her, like a cyclone spinning at incredible speed, a tornado tearing her gut, very wild and angry. It scooped her up and threatened to throw her out into space, where nothing would be left of her.

She fought the sucking force of this powerful whirlpool, fearful that if she let herself be drawn into the middle of this vortex she would be completely stripped of flesh and bones, and there would be nothing left of her. Then she sensed that a vicious battle was underway, being fought with very primitive weapons such as swords, daggers, halberds, and crossbows. Catherine was directly involved in this bloody warfare—she was fiercely hacking away and being hacked in turn. Simultaneously she felt that she was being carried upward and supported by the music. Two wheels of music were lifting her up and thrusting her forward. The pressure was unbearable, and she was afraid she might burst and explode. Her predicament was so intense that it seemed like a gigantic A-bomb would go off any second, much larger than anything known on earth, one that would destroy the whole universe, not just one area. Her face felt very brittle, like the finest china, and she could hear tiny bones breaking in her cheeks and her head. Then her skull cracked and shattered into a thousand pieces. Blood flooded her face. She felt like a little helpless baby struggling to be born and choking on something in the process of delivery.

The experience had a quality that Catherine later called "shimmering coming togetherness." It culminated in a vision of a gigantic wheel reaching into infinity. All the religions of the world were along the edge of the wheel, on its infinite rim, radiating toward the center and outward. They were represented by images of their divine service, sacred symbols, and obvious or cryptic inscriptions. Catherine was able to recognize some of them and knew them by name—Christianity, Judaism, Islam, Hinduism, and Buddhism. She saw many other creeds that she did not recognize, but she was able to understand their spiritual message and their manner of worship. Catherine was standing in the middle of this wheel, caught right in the center, attracted, lured, and pulled apart by these different faiths. All the religions wanted her and competed for her by putting forward the best they had to offer. Every time Catherine was ready to succumb to one or another, she was able to see their flaws and weaknesses and changed her mind.

Then the wheel rotated, faster and faster until Catherine could not discriminate any more. She was totally immobilized, completely still in the center of time and space. The peripheral segments of the wheel, which represented various creeds, finally fused into one: the Beyond Within, the Divine transcending all forms and boundaries, both formless and the source of all forms. Everything was flooded by warm and soft golden light; she floated and bathed in it, feeling cradled and comforted. This unified divine vision seemed to be what she had been craving and waiting for her whole life. She almost reached the point of total fusion and oneness, but remained just one little step from it. Just before she was about to merge with the divine light, she realized that the Godhead is always male, and she could not surrender and join completely.

After this climax the session subsided, and its termination period was sweet and mellow. Catherine felt immersed in a warm, golden glow and experienced herself as loving and being loved. When we gave her strawberries with fresh whipped cream, she remarked: "This was the most fantastic meal I have ever had in my whole life. It was sensuous, almost to the point of being obscene, and the tastes were unbelievably distinct." At one point, Catherine gazed at my co-therapist Joan for many moments and saw her as a composite feminine figure representing simultaneously her mother, her sister, and her daughter.

Later in the evening she expressed enormous gratitude for her experience and for all the cosmic insights, which she saw as special grace and privilege. She particularly valued two experiences that had the quality of past incarnation memories. In one of them she had identified with a Greek scholar in bondage to a wealthy Roman and a tutor to his children. Although he knew he was being subjugated, he felt above the situation and free in his mind and spirit. In the second, she had experienced herself as an Oriental monk with a shaven head, dressed in saffron robes and radiating joy and inner peace.

Catherine saw the session as a very important event in her life. Beforehand she had been severely depressed and had made serious attempts to procure an effective poison for herself. Her preoccupation with suicide now disappeared completely. She felt as if she had begun a completely new chapter: "I have been *existing* all these years; I started to *live* this past Friday. I honestly feel that I am a new person, with a completely new mind. Even my body feels different; I am pain-free."

Joan's Case History

When Joan volunteered for our LSD program, she was a forty-year-old housewife and mother of four children. Two of these children, a seventeen-year-old daughter and an eight-year-old son, were from her first marriage. She was also caring for an adopted boy of nine and a nine-year-old boy from her husband's first marriage and was involved in many other activities, including encounter groups and a ballet school. Her cancer had been diagnosed in August 1971, after a long period of superficial and transitional gastrointestinal disturbances. The physician whom she had consulted first discovered a gastric ulcer and, when it failed to heal over a period of six weeks, he recommended surgical intervention. The surgeon found a tumor in her stomach and conducted a high subtotal gastrectomy. He noted aggressive regional invasion but no generalized metastases. Microscopic examination of the resected gastric tissue revealed infiltrating, highly anaplastic carcinoma.

Joan was informed of her diagnosis in several stages. First she learned that she had a gastric ulcer and later found out that it was a tumor, but without any details of its nature. Then her doctor told her that the tumor was malignant and finally disclosed to her the most disquieting fact: the malignant tissue reached all the way to the point of resection. She thus had some time to gradually adjust to the diagnosis, with all of its prognostic implications. Initially she reacted with deep depression and anxiety. Later a sense of detachment and withdrawal replaced her feelings of hopelessness and helplessness. At the same time, she decided that she did not want to spend the rest of her life passively awaiting death. She was determined to do something about her disease, to contribute somehow to the healing process, no matter how little her chance for survival. After the physicians had stated that nothing more could be done for her along medical lines, Joan spent some time seeking faith healers and other unorthodox help.

At this point she heard about the Spring Grove Program of psychedelic therapy for persons suffering from cancer. She made an appointment with us to see the facility, meet the research team, and get more specific information about the treatment program. We explained the nature of psychedelic therapy to her and outlined both its therapeutic potential and its limitations. We mentioned that, based on our experience, this therapy could have very beneficial effect on physical pain and on the emotional distress accompanying the disease. We also talked briefly about how successful LSD sessions had affected people's concepts and attitudes regarding death. We made it clear that we had no conclusive data as to what effect psychedelic therapy might have on the cancer process itself. However, we did not explicitly exclude the possibility that a favorable change in the patient's emotional condition could influence the progress of the illness.

Joan came for the first interview accompanied by her husband Dick. As an educator, he was naturally quite concerned about the possible adverse effects of LSD. We carefully explained that with judicious use of LSD the ratio between benefits and risks is drastically different from that of unsupervised self-experimentation. After this issue had been clarified, both Joan and Dick enthusiastically participated in the LSD program. The preparation for Joan's first LSD session consisted of several drug-free interviews with her alone and one meeting with her and Dick. During this time Joan was depressed and anxious. She felt very tired and disinterested in subjects and activities that before her disease had been sources of much joy. In the course of her illness she became very tense and irritable; her frustration tolerance was "at an all-time low."

Throughout our preliminary discussions, her physical suffering was still tolerable. She felt general gastrointestinal discomfort, but her pain had not reached the intensity that, in and of itself, would make her life unbearable or miserable. Her apprehension about the future seemed to be much more significant than her physical suffering at that point. Joan was fully aware of the diagnosis and prognosis of her illness and was able to discuss it quite openly when explicitly asked. Her major concern was to reach a decent and honest closure in her relationship with Dick and all the children. She hoped to leave them resolved and free of guilt, anger, bitterness, or pathological grief, so that they could continue to live their own lives without having to carry the psychological burden of her death.

Joan understood that it was necessary for her to explore her personal history before the LSD session. We explained that the success of her treatment depended on her ability to reach as much clarity and comprehension as she possibly could regarding the patterns and conflicts underlying her life trajectory from birth to the present time. She undertook this task with unusual zeal and wrote a detailed autobiography that we then used as a basis for our further discussions about the most important aspects of her life. Joan's childhood had been very strongly influenced by her emotionally unstable mother, who suffered from severe depressions and was treated by electroshocks during her numerous psychiatric hospitalizations. Joan's relationship with her mother lacked intimacy and was erratic and confusing. Joan felt much closer to her father, who was able to express warm feelings toward her and give her support. However, in later years she became aware of a strong sensual element in their relationship, which became a source of fear and guilt because of her strict Catholic upbringing. The relationship between her parents was disharmonious, with constant fights and quarrels. The marriage finally ended in a divorce.

Joan described herself in her early years as "a moderately withdrawn child with a rich fantasy world." She had only a few friends and interacted very little with her peers outside this close circle. Of her four siblings, she had a close bond and coalition with her younger brother and felt intense rivalry toward her sister. At the time of her LSD treatment, she felt extremely alienated from the rest of her siblings. The puritanical elements in Joan's background were reinforced when she attended a parochial school run exclusively by nuns. Her experience at school contributed further to the difficulties in her sexual development. During adolescence she had problems relating to people in general because of her anxieties, insecurity, and feelings of inadequacy. All these problems were much more intense in regard to potential sexual partners.

Joan's world of rich romantic fantasies contrasted sharply with her actual erotic life. Her several relationships were superficial and short-lived; she did not have any sexual experiences before she got married. Her marriage was plagued by many problems and conflicts, particularly by strong jealousy and possessiveness on the part of both spouses. Her husband, who initially had had strict opinions about premarital sex and monogamy, became interested in other women and had a series of extramarital affairs. His involvement with one of his pupils resulted in pregnancy and expedited separation and divorce. Shortly after she had divorced her first husband, Joan married Dick. The second marriage was much better than the first, but was not free of problems.

In a joint interview with both partners, we tried to identify the sources of difficult interaction and facilitate the communication between them. When asked what she considered the most disturbing aspect of their marriage, Joan pointed to Dick's tendency to impulsive reactions and to his possessiveness. Dick felt that Joan was not sufficiently committed to their relationship and that her emotional investment in their family life was lacking. He found her high degree of independence very disquieting and threatening. As we explored various vicious circles in Joan and Dick's everyday interaction, they both found interesting precedents and possible causes for their fears, insecurities, and specific idiosyncrasies in their childhood experiences. The result of this interview was a joint decision that they would seek new channels of more effective communication on various levels. They agreed that they would try to live each of Joan's remaining days as fully as possible, one at a time, without letting past programs and concerns about the future contaminate their everyday interaction. We all felt that the situation was ready for Joan's first psychedelic session. Joan's description of this session follows.

Joan's First LSD Session

"I began the session with considerable apprehension and found it very comforting to hold onto Stan and Nancy's hands. [Nancy Jewell was the nurse and co-therapist in this session.] About twenty minutes after the administration of 300 micrograms of LSD, I started having floating and vibrating sensations. As I was listening to Brahms' second piano concerto, I experienced myself standing in a gigantic hall of a futuristic, supersonic airport, waiting for my flight. The hall was crowded with passengers dressed in extremely modern fashion; a strange feeling of excitement and expectation seemed to permeate this unusual crowd.

Suddenly I heard a loud voice through the system of airport speakers: "The event that you are going to experience is Yourself. With some of you, as you may notice, it is already happening." As I looked around at my fellow travelers, I saw strange changes in their faces; their bodies were twitching and assuming unusual postures, as they began their journeys into the inner worlds. At that point, I noticed an intense humming sound of a comforting and soothing quality, like a radio signal, guiding me through the experience and reassuring me. It seemed as if my brain was being burned very slowly, revealing its content in one picture after another.

My father's image appeared with great clarity, and the nature of our relationship was analyzed and explored with the precision of a surgical operation. I perceived my father's need for me to be something or someone that I could not be. I realized that I had to be myself even if it disappoints him. I became aware of a whole network of other people's needs—my husband's, my children's, my friends'. I realized that the needs of other people made it more difficult for me to accept the reality of my impending death and to surrender to the process.

Then the inward journey deepened, and I was encountering various terrifying monsters that resembled images from Asian art—vicious demons and lean, hungry, surrealistic creatures, all in strange Day-Glo green color. It was as if a whole panoply of demons from the Tibetan Book of the Dead had been evoked and performed a wild dance in my head. Whenever I moved toward them and into them, the fear would disappear and the picture would change into something else, usually quite pleasant. At one point, when I was looking at some slimy, evil creatures, I realized that they were products of my own mind and extensions of myself. I mumbled: "Uh hum, that's me too all right."

The encounter with demons was accompanied by an intense struggle for breath and feelings of anxiety, but it was of relatively brief duration. When it ended, I felt fantastic amounts of energy streaming through my body. I felt it was so much energy that no single individual could contain it and handle it effectively. It became clear to me that I contained so much energy that in everyday life I had to deny it, misuse it, and project it on other people. I had a flash of myself in various stages of my life, trying on different roles—daughter, lover, young wife, mother, artist—and realized that they could not work since they were inadequate containers for my energy.

The most important aspect of these experiences was their relevance for the understanding of death. I saw the magnificent unfolding of the cosmic design in all its infinite nuances and ramifications. Each individual represented a thread in the beautiful warp of life and was playing a specific role. All these roles were equally necessary for the central energy core of the universe; none of them was more important than others. I saw that after death the life energy underwent a transformation and the roles were recast. I saw my role in this life to be a cancer patient and was able and willing to accept it.

I envisioned and intuitively understood the dynamics of reincarnation. It was represented symbolically as a view of the earth with many paths leading in all directions; they looked like tunnels in a giant ant hill. It became clear to me that there have been many lives before this one and many others will follow. The purpose and task is to experience and explore whatever is assigned to us in the cosmic screenplay. Death is just one episode, one transitional experience within this magnificent perennial drama.

Throughout my session, I had visions of pictures, sculptures, handicraft, and architecture of a number of different countries and cultures—ancient Egypt, Greece, Rome, Persia, as well as pre-Columbian North, South, and Central America. This was accompanied by many insights into the nature of human existence. Through the richness of my experience, I discovered that the dimensions of my being were much greater than I had ever imagined.

Whatever I perceived the world was doing—inventing hostile countries, internecine wars, racial hatred and riots, corrupted political schemes, or polluting technology—I saw myself participating in it and projecting on other people the things I denied in myself. I got in touch with what I felt was "pure being" and realized that it could not be comprehended and did not need any justification. With this came the awareness that my only task was to keep the energy flowing and not to "sit on it," as I used to do. The flow of life was symbolized by many beautiful images of moving water, fish and aquatic plants, and delightful dancing scenes, some majestic and ethereal, others down to earth.

As a result of all these experiences and insights, I developed an affirmative attitude toward the totality of existence and the ability to accept whatever happens in life as being ultimately all right. I made many enthusiastic comments about the incredible cosmic wit and humor built into the fabric of existence. As I allowed the energy of life to flow through me and opened up to it, my entire body was vibrating with excitement and delight. After having enjoyed this new way of being for some time, I curled into a comfortable fetal position.

About five hours into the session I decided to take off my eyeshades, sit up, and connect with the environment. I sat on the couch in deep peace and relaxation, listening to Zen meditation music and watching a single rosebud in a crystal vase on a nearby table. Occasionally I closed my eyes and returned to my inner world. As I saw later on the video taken during the session, my face was radiant and had the expression of quiet bliss found in Buddhist sculptures. For a long period of time, I experienced nothing but a beautiful warm, nourishing golden glow, like a transcendental rain of liquid gold. At one point, I noticed a bowl of grapes in the room and decided to taste a few of them. They tasted like ambrosia, and the grape stems looked so beautiful that I decided to take some of them home as a souvenir.

Later in the afternoon, Dick joined us in the session room. Immediately after his arrival he and I fell into each other's arms and stayed in a close embrace for a very long time. Dick commented that he sensed an enormous amount of energy radiating from me. He was aware of an almost tangible energy field surrounding my body. We were then given about two hours of absolute privacy, which we enjoyed tremendously. This made it possible for me to share my experiences with Dick. One of my best memories from the session was the shower we took together. I felt unusually tuned into Dick's body, as well as my own, and experienced a sense of exquisite sensuality unlike anything I had known before.

Another fantastic experience was a Chinese dinner that we all shared. Although the food was brought from a nearby suburban Chinese restaurant and was probably of average quality, I considered it the best meal I had ever tasted. I could not recall ever enjoying food, or myself, more. The only factor that somewhat inhibited my culinary pleasure was my rational awareness that I should be somewhat conservative with the food because of my subtotal gastrectomy reducing the volume of my stomach. For the rest of the evening, Dick and I shared quiet time together, lying on the couch and listening to stereophonic music. Dick was very impressed by my openness and all my insights. He was convinced that I was tapping some sources of genuine cosmic wisdom that were closed to him. He admired the depth in my reporting and the spontaneous confidence and authority with which I spoke about my experience.

I was elated, in radiant mood, and felt absolute freedom from anxiety. My ability to enjoy music, tastes, colors, and the shower was greatly enhanced. Dick's conclusion was that I was just pure pleasure to be with. This was such a contagious experience that Dick himself felt and expressed his desire to have a psychedelic session. He decided to explore the possibility of participating in the LSD training program for professionals that was also available at the Maryland Psychiatric Research Center. I stayed up for a long time talking to Dick and awoke several times during the night. I had one dream about working in a library and hearing others say: "This Zen stuff does not make any sense." I smiled to myself, knowing it was too simple to make sense to them. The next morning after the session, I felt refreshed, relaxed, and very much in tune with the world. Dick put Bach's Brandenburg Concerto on the record player and it seemed absolutely perfect. The outside world appeared clear, serene, and beautiful. On the road going home, I saw things I had never seen before. The trees, grass, colors, sky—all were a real delight to behold."

For about two months after her first LSD session, Joan felt relaxed, elated, and optimistic. The psychedelic experience also seemed to have opened new realms of mystical and cosmic feelings within her. The spiritual elements that she had experienced in her session transcended the narrow boundaries of the traditional Catholic religion she had been brought up with. She was now embracing universal approaches found in Eastern spiritual philosophies, such as Hinduism and Buddhism. Joan felt so much overflowing energy that it baffled her attending physicians. They found her energetic resources quite incongruent with her serious clinical condition and explicitly expressed their surprise that she was still able to move around on her own and to drive a car. They also voiced their doubt that she would be able to spend the forthcoming summer vacation in California, as the family was planning to do. Joan herself felt very confident and believed that this would be possible.

The future course of events bore out her feelings; the vacation in California proved to be a very meaningful and rewarding time for the whole family. This positive development was drastically interrupted in mid-January, when Joan saw her physician because of continued belching and retching. He discovered a new mass in the area of her spleen, which he identified as metastatic growth. Joan was very disappointed when no concrete medical procedure was suggested and realized that the doctors had given up on her. At this point, both Joan and Dick felt very strongly that Joan should have another psychedelic session. Our staff agreed. Joan was optimistic that the session would improve her emotional condition and deepen her philosophical and spiritual insights. She was also hoping that another psychedelic experience might have a positive influence on the psychosomatic component that she suspected in the etiology of her cancer.

Joan's Second LSD Session

The second LSD session took place in February 1972. Since the dosage of 300 micrograms had had a powerful effect the first time, we decided to use the same quantity again. The following is Joan's summary of the most important events of her session:

> "This session was a grim one for me. It contrasted with my first session in almost every way: black and white rather than color; personal rather than cosmic; sad, not joyous. There was a short time at the beginning when I found myself in a universal place or space where I knew again that the whole cosmos was in each of us and that there was a meaning to our lives and deaths. After that the experience narrowed and became much more personal. Death was the main subject of my session. I experienced several funeral scenes in ornate or traditional church surroundings, sometimes at the cemetery, sometimes inside a church with a choir of many people. I cried often in the course of the several hours. I also asked many questions and answered them; they would lead to ultimately unanswerable ones, and then it would seem funny. Early on, I remember thinking: 'All that ugliness is really beauty.' In the course of the day, other polarities came to my mind—good and evil, victory and defeat, wisdom and ignorance, life and death.

I experienced my childhood, but not any specific scenes, just the general feeling tone—a very sad one. Much of it had to do with very early feelings of frustration and deprivation, hunger, and starvation. It flashed through my mind whether there might be a connection between these experiences and my peptic ulcer that turned into cancer. I remember being once out in the rain with my brothers for what seemed like a very long time. I recall our being turned away from a show or circus by the man in charge. I was feeling very sad as we walked away, not too sure where we were going. The hidden allusion to my present situation is obvious—being denied further participation in the show of life and facing the uncertainty of death.

For what seemed like a fairly long time, I experienced my present family in terms of preparing them for my death. There was a scene in which, after preparing myself for some time, I finally told them. In a sequence of scenes, I was able to say good-bye to my children, my husband, my father, and other relatives, as well as friends and acquaintances. I did it in a very individualized way, with regard to the personality and special sensitivity of each of them. Tears followed but, after a time, there was warmth and cheer. At the end, they all gathered around me to take care of me. I recall their fixing warm and sweet things to eat. After this, I spent some good bit of time saying good-bye to them and to my husband and realizing that there were caring people who were going to look after them. I said good-bye to them, too, and felt that something of me would live on in them.

There was a happy, warm scene toward the end of my session, which I felt I was just observing and was not part of, but I really enjoyed it. It was a scene with adults and children playing outside in the snow. I felt it was in some very northern place. All were bundled up and staying warm in spite of the cold and the snow. The children were being enjoyed and cared for by the grown-ups, and there was laughter and play and general good cheer. Then I remember seeing a whole row of boots, knowing that children's feet were in them and were warm. In the evening after the session I felt good in some ways—quite responsive and pleased to see Dick, but I found myself crying off and on for the rest of the evening. I felt that I saw myself and my situation realistically, that I could handle it better now, but still felt very sad. I wished that the experience could have gone on for a few more hours and that I might have gone on from the grimness to joy."

The second session proved very beneficial for Joan. She became reconciled to her situation and decided to spend her remaining days focusing on her spiritual quest. After a vacation with the family on the West Coast, she decided to say good-bye to her husband and her children. She thought this would save them from the painful process of watching her progressive deterioration and make it easier for them to remember her full of life and energy. In California Joan remained in close contact with her father, who was interested in the spiritual path and introduced her to a Vedanta group which she joined.

Joan's Third LSD Session

In late summer Joan became interested in having another LSD experience. She wrote to inquire about the possibility of arranging the third session in California. We recommended that she approach Sidney Cohen, a Los Angeles psychiatrist and psychoanalyst, who had extensive experience with psychedelic therapy and a license to use LSD. (See Chapter 12 for more information on Cohen's contributions to psychedelic therapy.) The following is Joan's account of her third LSD session, which she had under Sidney Cohen's auspices. This time the dosage was increased to 400 micrograms.

> "My first response after the drug took effect was to get cold, colder, and colder. It seemed that no amount of covers could alleviate the bone-penetrating, angular, and greenish freezing cold. It was hard to believe later that so many warm blankets had been put on top of me because, at the time, nothing seemed to alleviate the cold. I called for hot tea, which I sipped through a glass straw. While holding the hot cup of tea, I went into a very intense experience. The cup became the whole universe, and all was vividly clear and real. The greenish, brownish color of the tea melted into a swirling vortex. No more questions; life, death, meaning—all were there. I had always been there—we all were. All was one. Fear did not exist; death, life—all the same thing. The swirling circularity of it all. The intense desire for everyone to realize the universe is in everything. The tear coming down my cheek, the cup, the tea—everything! What harmony, I felt, is there behind the seeming chaos!
>
> Wanting not to lose sight of this, wanting all to share in this experience; then there could be no discord. I was feeling that Dr. Cohen knew with me. Then my father came in, and I tried to share with him what I could of the intense earlier experience, trying to express the inexpressible: that there is no fear, no question of fear. We have always been where we are going. Just being is sufficient. No need to worry, ask, question, reason. Just be. I told him the importance of us all in keeping things moving in the everyday world. I consumed my hot broth and tea, craving for nourishment

and warmth. After a break, I got back into myself. This time I experienced bleak and sad scenes of my very early life that I was familiar with from my previous sessions. The pictures took the form of small skeletal creatures floating about in emptiness, looking for nourishment, but not finding it. Emptiness, no fulfillment. Scrawny birds looking for food in an empty nest. Some feeling of me and my brothers alone, looking, nowhere to go.

At some point, I got into my sadness, sadness as an overriding theme running from early childhood throughout my life. I became aware of the progressive effort to disguise it—to satisfy what others seemed to want instead: "Smile…look alive…stop daydreaming!" Later in the session, I had the feeling that some are chosen to feel the sadness inherent in the universe. If I am one of them, fine. I thought of all the children looking for mothers who are not there. I thought of the Stations of the Cross and felt the suffering of Jesus Christ or the sadness he had to feel. I realized that other people's karma is to feel the gladness, or the strength, or the beauty, whatever. Why not gladly accept the sadness?

At another time, I was on many cushions with many comforters on top of me, warm, secure. Wanting not to be reborn as a person, but perhaps as a rainbow—orangey, reddish, yellowish, soft, beautiful. At some point in the afternoon, I became aware of the centrality of my stomach. So many pictures of people being comforted with food, my earlier craving for the hot tea, broth, always something coming into my stomach. I realized that I am aware of that in my day-to-day life now, always wanting the tit and substituting spoon, straw, cigarette. Never enough!

I became aware of being a child again, dependent, but now having a mother to take care of me, who wants to and likes taking care of me. I found comfort and pleasure in getting what I never had as a child. There were moments to enjoy the smell and feel of the fruit—a beautiful mango, pear, peach, grapes. While looking at them I saw the cellular movement in them. Much later, I enjoyed the rosebud, velvety, fragrant, and lovely. Toward the end of the day, I became suddenly aware that I had found a way to legitimize my lifelong sadness: to become terminally ill. The irony of this situation was that I then found happiness and felt relief in this discovery. I wanted to get into the sources of my sadness. I saw that from very early my mother had not much to give me, that, in fact, she looked to me to give her. I did indeed have more to give her than she me. I experienced this as a heavy burden.

> I had much discussion with my father about sadness, what is wrong with it and why it is so discouraged by other people. I described to him how much energy I expended pretending to be glad or happy or to smile. I talked about the beauty in sadness—sad sweetness, sweet sadness—allowing yourself and others to be sad when they feel it. Sadness perhaps is not in vogue, as is joy, spontaneity, or fun. These I expended great energy in acting out. Now I am just being; not being this or that, just being. Sometimes it is sad, often peaceful, sometimes angry or irritable, sometimes very warm and happy. I am not sad any longer that I am going to die. I have many more loving feelings than ever before. All the pressures to be something "other" have been taken off me. I feel relieved from sham and pretense. Much spiritual feeling permeates my everyday life."

A member of our team who visited Joan in California a short time before her death gave us a moving description of how Joan spent her remaining days. She maintained her interest in the spiritual quest and spent several hours a day in meditation. In spite of her rapidly deteriorating physical condition, she appeared to be emotionally balanced and in good spirits. Remarkably, she kept her determination not to lose any opportunity to experience the world fully as long as she could. For example, she insisted that she be served all the meals that others were eating, although the passage through her stomach was now totally obstructed, and she could not swallow anything. She chewed the food slowly, savored its taste, and then spat it out into a bucket. She spent the final evening of her life watching the setting sun, totally absorbed by its beauty. Her last words before retiring that night were: "What a magnificent sunset!" That night she died quietly in her sleep.

After Joan's death, her relatives and friends on the East Coast received the invitations for a memorial gathering that she had personally written when she was still alive. After they had all assembled at the appointed time, they were surprised to be addressed by Joan's voice from a cassette tape. It was much more than an unusual and moving farewell. According to the participants, the content and tone of her speech had a deeply comforting effect on those who had come to this meeting with a sense of tragedy and deep grief. Joan succeeded in imparting to them some of the sense of inner peace and reconciliation that she herself had reached in her sessions.

Healing Potential of Psychedelic Therapy

As we have seen, psychedelic therapy has an extraordinary capacity to alleviate, both in dying individuals and their survivors, the emotional and physical agony of what is potentially the most painful crisis in human life. The Spring Grove research projects and clinical studies conducted in many countries in the world have also shown that psychedelics can be used safely and that they are not physiologically addictive. The current political and administrative hindrances that prevent hundreds of thousands of terminal patients from benefiting from this remarkable procedure are unnecessary, indefensible, and even inhumane. Overcautious administrators and legislators have raised many objections against the use of psychedelics in other populations, such as patients with emotional and psychosomatic disorders, mental health professionals, artists, and clergy. Such opposition is absurd, particularly in time-limited, life-threatening situations where the problems involved are so serious that even the taboo against the use of really dangerous and highly addictive narcotics has been lifted.

Swan as an Initiatory Bird. In this shamanic experience of death and rebirth from a session of Holotropic Breathwork, the swan appears as a sacred animal. In the Siberian shamanic lore, the swan is an important power animal associated with love, inspiration, intuition, self-transformation, gracefulness and beauty, and also with traveling to the Otherworld.

Initiatory Dismemberment. The artist's rendering of psychospiritual death and rebirth in a session of Holotropic Breathwork shows a highly typical shamanic initiation sequence–annihilation carried out by initiatory animals (in this case, being torn to pieces by a pack of wolves).

1. Interior View of the Medicine Lodge

Scenes from the Mandan Okipa Festival of the Plains Indians. (Paintings by George Catlin, 1832)

1. The initiates are assembled inside the medicine lodge, and the Keeper of the Ceremonies addresses a prayer to the Great Spirit.

2. During the Buffalo Dance O-kee-hee-dee enters on the left, the Keeper of the Ceremonies leans on the "Big Canoe," and O-kee-hee-dee flees the scene on the right.

3. As part of their ordeal the initiates are suspended on cords attached to skewers piercing their flesh, with weights of buffalo skulls hanging from their bodies; in the center, the Keeper of the Ceremonies smokes a calumet for success of the initiation, and on the right initiates offer their little fingers for sacrifice.

4. The Keeper of the Ceremonies is surrounded by young braves. The initiates run, are dragged, and left in the keeping of the Great Spirit.

2. Buffalo Dance and O-kee-hee-dee

▲ 3. *The Ordeal* ▼4. *The Last Race*

Ehecatl and Mictlantecuhtli. Quetzalcoatl, most frequently represented in Mesoamerican art as the Plumed Serpent and symbolizing the spirit and spiritual rebirth, is shown here in his manifestation as the wind god Ehecatl breathing life into the skeletal figure of the god of death, Mictlantecuhtli. (*Codex Borgia*, Aztec accordion screenfold, probably late A.D. 15th century)

Vision Serpent. The Mayans used the image of a serpent to symbolize their visions. This limestone lintel depicts Lady Choc, wife of Shield Jaguar, encountering the figure of an ancestor emerging from the mouth of the Vision Serpent. (Yaxchilan, Chiapas, Mexico, Mayan Late Classic Period, A.D. 770)

Mayan Bloodletting Ritual. This limestone lintel depicts a tongue perforation. King Shield Jaguar holds a huge torch, which suggests that the bloodletting ceremony occurred in a dark place. His wife, Lady Choc, is pulling a thorn-lined rope through her mutilated tongue. Her blank look implies that she is in a trance induced by massive blood loss. (Yaxchilan, Chiapas, Mexico, Mayan Late Classic Period, A.D. 725)

Mayan Psychedelic Ritual.
Paintings on a Mayan ceramic vase that depict the ritual administration of an enema with psychedelic properties. (Peten, Guatemala, Classic Period, c. A.D. 600)

Tlalocan, Earthly Paradise of the Rain God Tlaloc. In this fresco the deity Tlaloc sits under a magnificent ceiba tree and pours water from both of his hands. He is flanked by two priests, who make offerings and plant seeds. Ethnobotanist Richard Schultes identified the objects lining the streams of these seeds as caps of Psilocybe mushrooms. This suggests that ingesting these mushrooms made it possible for the user to enter Tlalocan. In the lower part of the fresco, the souls of people who have died by water or by storms and lightning enjoy eternal happiness, and are pictured playing games, singing songs, and chasing butterflies. (Teotihuacan, Mexico, 4th–8th century A.D.)

Rapture of Xochipilli. This early 16th century Aztec pre-Columbian statue represents Xochipilli, the Lord of Flowers, seated on a pedestal in ecstatic rapture. Harvard ethnobotanist Richard Schultes identified the floral glyphs decorating the body of the deity, as well as his pedestal, as stylized psychedelic plants: caps of the sacred mushroom *Psilocybe aztecorum,* tendrils and flowers of the morning glory *Turbina corymbosa,* blossoms of the psychedelic tobacco *Nicotiana tabacum,* and buds of *Heimia salicifolia (sinicuichi).* (Unearthed in Tlamanalco, on the slopes of the Popocatepetl volcano)

Sunrise. This scene symbolizes the triumphant emergence of the Sun God in the sky after his nocturnal journey through the Underworld. The goddesses Isis and Nephthys kneel on two sides of the djed, the vertebral column of Osiris, and worship the solar disk emerging under the vault of the sky from the ankh, symbol of eternal life. The six baboons in positions of adoration are the Spirits of Dawn celebrating the sunrise. This symbolism also describes the rebirth of the deceased person and the psychospiritual death and rebirth of the initiate. (Papyrus of Any, Egypt, c. 1420 B.C.)

Sekhet Hetepet, the Fields of Peace. The deceased Anhai worships goddesses, cruises with deities on the Celestial Nile, works in the fields, and adores the Bennu Bird. The boat with oars and steps probably symbolizes the Primeval Mound. (Papyrus of Any, Egypt, c. 1100 B.C.)

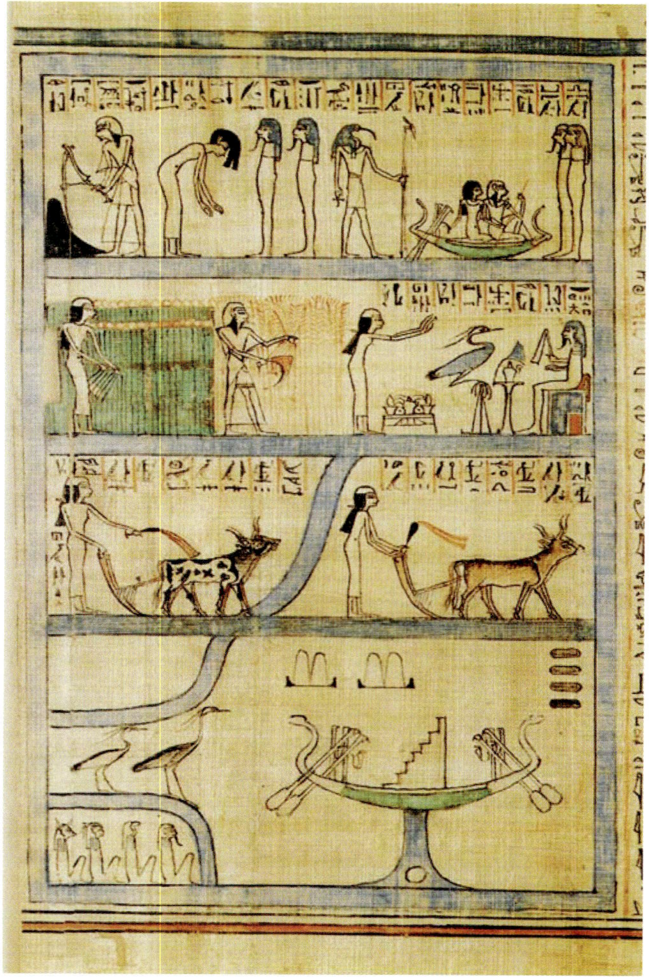

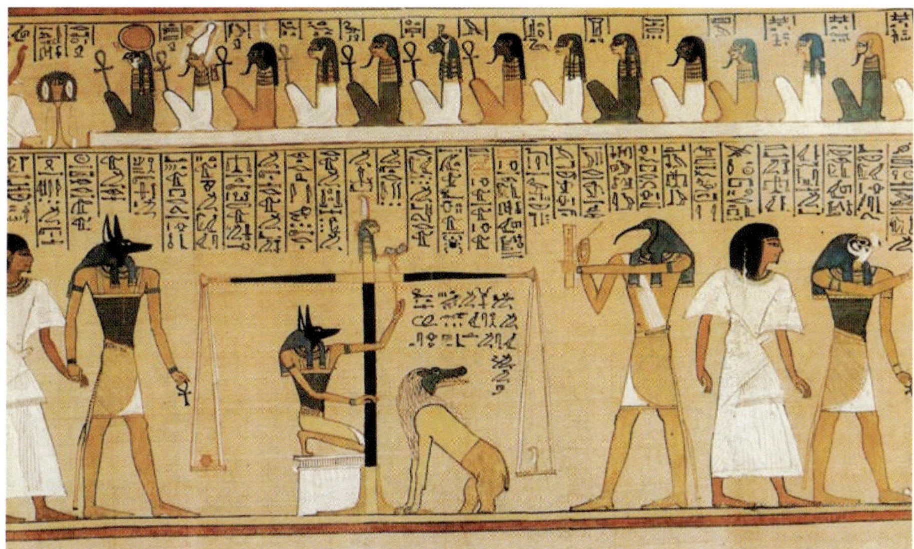

Judgment in the Egyptian Underworld. The deceased Hunefer is brought by the jackal-headed god Anubis to the Hall of Maat, where his heart will be weighed on the Great Balance against the feather of truth belonging to Maat, the goddess of justice. Below the scale waits Amemet, the Devourer of Souls, who eats the hearts of the unjust. On the right, Hunefer has passed the judgment and is taken by the hawk-headed god Horus to be presented to Osiris. (Papyrus of Hunefer, c. 1350 B.C.)

Hunefer's Presentation to Osiris. After the deceased Hunefer has successfully passed the judgment in the Hall of Maat, Horus presents him to Osiris, the ruler of the Underworld, seated on a throne and holding his regalia. In front of him is a lotus supporting the four sons of Horus and behind him are his two sisters, Isis and Nephtys. (Papyrus of Hunefer, c. 1350 B.C.)

Tomb of Sen-nedjem. In this wall painting from an Egyptian tomb, the resurrected Sen-nedjem and his wife are shown in the Happy Fields, where they work and worship the gods. The scene in the tympanum links this situation to the diurnal-nocturnal journey of the sun. Two baboons celebrate the emergence of the solar barque from the Underworld at dawn and worship the falcon-headed Sun God, who holds the ankh as a symbol of rebirth.
(Egypt, Theban necropolis, 19th Dynasty, 1305–1200 B.C.)

The Egyptian Great Mother Goddess. Isis, sister and spouse of Osiris, took the form of a kite to conceive his son Horus. Here she is depicted with her wings outspread as a protectress of the tomb of the pharaoh Tutankhamen. (Egypt, 18th Dynasty, c. 1400 B.C.)

Tomb of Tutmosis III. The tomb is painted with scenes representing the journey of the Sun God during his first hour in the underworld, as described in *Am Tuat* (The Book of What is in the Underworld Tuat), a guide for the deceased during their posthumous journey. (Egypt, 18th Dynasty, 15th century B.C.)

Irinefer's Death and Rebirth. The Bennu bird, Egyptian version of the legendary Arabian phoenix, symbolized the death-rebirth cycle and immortality. It appears here in the solar boat with the deceased Irinefer. The eye of Horus and the solar disc are additional symbols of rebirth. (The Tomb of Irinefer, Thebes, Egypt, 19th–20th Dynasty, c. 1100 B.C.)

Life in the Beyond. The Egyptian Happy Fields were nourished by the waters of the Celestial Nile. Here Uberkhet, a singer of the sun god Ra, drinks from the divine river with the God Geb in the form of crocodile, suggesting transcendence of the distinction between animals, humans, and gods in the Beyond—they are all nourished by the same divine source. (Papyrus of Here-Uberkhet, 21st Dynasty, c. 1000 B.C.)

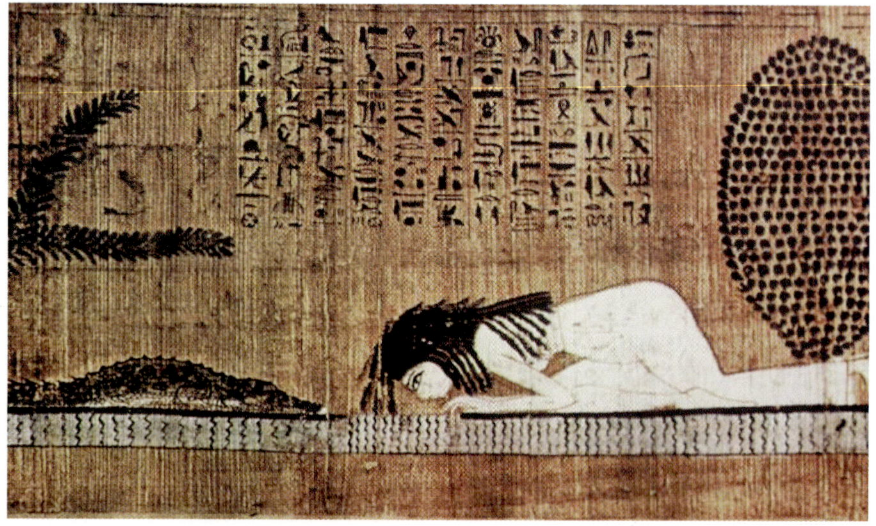

◀ **The Great Guru Padma Sambhava.** One of the most extraordinary representations of Padma Sambhava, who brought Buddhism into Tibet and is considered the author of the Bardo Thödol. Above him is a small figure of Amitabha Buddha in his paradise; arranged around him are various important scenes from his life. (Western Tibet, Guge, 16th–17th centuries)

▶ **Sukhavati,** the Western Paradise of Buddha Amitabha, one of the transcendental Buddhas of the Vajrayana pentad. It is a delightful place, with many beautiful palaces and airy pavilions, resplendent with gold and full of jewels and treasures. The trees are made of precious stones; the lotuses of gems and gold. Amitabha is surrounded by monks, Bodhisattvas, and various celestial beings. (Guge, Western Tibet, 15th century)

Prajnaparamita. A Tibetan wall painting represents *prajnaparamita,* transcendental wisdom that dispels *avidya,* ignorance about our true nature and the nature of reality. (Tholing Monastery, Western Tibet, 15th century)

Wheel of Becoming. This Tibetan *thangka* (contemplative painting) depicts Yama Raja, the Lord of Death, fiercely gripping the Wheel of Becoming. The animals in the center symbolize the three Poisons, or forces that drive the cycles of death and rebirth and are responsible for all suffering: ignorance (pig), desire (rooster), and aggression (snake). The next circle represents the dark descending path and the light ascending path. The segments of the large circle (lokas) signify the six realms into which one can be (re)born. From the top clockwise these are: the realm of gods (devaloka), the realm of jealous, belligerent gods (asuraloka), the realm of the hungry ghosts (pretaloka), hell (narakaloka), the realm of the animals (tiryakaloka), and the realm of humans (manakaloka). (Tibet, 18th–19th century)

Chemchok (Mandala of Fierce and Tranquil Deities). A Tibetan thangka shows the three-headed and winged "knowledge-holding" deity Chemchok Heruka appearing amidst flames in the embrace of his consort. The Peaceful Deities appear in the upper part of the mandala, while all around dance the ferocious human and animal protectors. This thangka belongs stylistically to a special class of esoteric paintings of the 19th century that were used for contemplative preparation for the Afterdeath experience. (Tibetan painting of the Nyingmapa tradition, Eastern Tibet, c. 19th century)

The Bardo Mandala. This germinal mandala represents the development of the deities of the Bardo Thödol from one common cosmic matrix. In this first derivation only the five Tathagatas (as tantric couples) appear as icons identifiable by colors, symbols, mudras, cardinal points, and meaning. Other deities are represented abstractly, by colored dots. (From a painting school of the Nyingmapa sect)

The Three Quick and the Three Dead. A favorite theme of *Ars moriendi* recurs in this story of three young noblemen. During a hunting expedition they discover three coffins with bodies in various stages of decomposition. The noblemen's friends are having a gay party and are immersed in various forms of entertainment, unaware that in the background devils are transporting sinners to Hell. The corpses talk and remind the noblemen that they are witnessing what will happen to them in the future. (Detail from Francesco Traini's *Triumph of Death*, A.D. 14th century)

The Triumph of Death. The inescapable power of death is masterfully captured in this 16th century painting by Pieter Brueghel the Elder, which portrays the medieval concept of equality in death: king, bishop, knights, monks, soldiers, and peasants are attacked and defeated alike. The atmosphere of horrifying catastrophes, such as fires, ship-wrecks, and executions complete the picture.

King and Bishop. ***(Below)*** Detail from *The Triumph of Death* by Pieter Brueghel the Elder shows two figures representing secular and religious authority—the king and the bishop—at the time of death. Their earthly power is of no use at this moment. The skeletons mockingly claim their bodies and collect the gold and silver that these powerful figures of this world have amassed during their lifetime.

Last Judgment. In this magnificent 15th century fresco by Fra Angelico depicting the Last Judgment, Christ appears in a mandorla surrounded by angels and saints to judge humanity. On his right, the just enter the Garden of Paradise to experience eternal bliss. On his left the sinners are summoned into Hell to face damnation and eternal tortures. At the bottom of Hell, Satan, immersed in frozen blood, crushes and devours his victims. Above him, the doomed are experiencing infernal punishments for the seven cardinal sins. (A.D. 1431)

Christian Pantheon. This scene of the Last Judgment sets the Christian pantheon of God the Father, Christ, and the Virgin Mary into a mandorla-shaped opening in the heavens, among saints and angels, with Satan in Hell below. (Bolognese School)

Death and Rebirth. This painting, which shows deep insights into the cycles of death and rebirth in nature and in human life, was inspired by a high-dose psychedelic session with psilocybin. It reflects the concept that life feeds on life and that new life comes out of the old. By choosing the carnation as the flower nourished by the remnants of the past, the artist makes a playful allusion to the process of reincarnation.

The Dún an Óir Series. These paintings and drawings illustrate various aspects of an important past life memory of the battle of Dún an Óir in Ireland, as it was retrieved and relived in sessions of Holotropic Breathwork (the case of Karl, described on pages 186-7).

1. Vision associated with uncanny feelings and anxious expectation shows a mysterious fortress situated on the cliffs overlooking the ocean.

2. In this image of the fortress, blood flows down from the ramparts and colors the beach and the ocean; a scene conveying the sense of a horrifying bloody massacre.

3, 4, and 5. The general layout of the fortress and various aspects of its interior—living quarters, dormitories, corridors, and storage rooms for food and ammunition. (Composites from a number of experiential sequences.)

6. One of the corridors in the fortress.

7. An underground tunnel leading to the beach. This vision was closely associated with perinatal sequences.

8. An impulsive finger painting depicting the experience of being gored by the sword of a British soldier.

9. A representation of death on the beach after the experience of being killed and thrown over the ramparts.

10. Drawing of the priest's seal ring showing initials of his name.

1

2

3

4

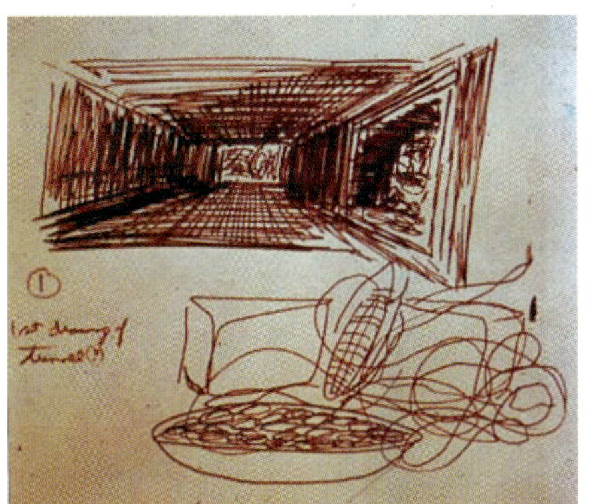

5

6

7

8

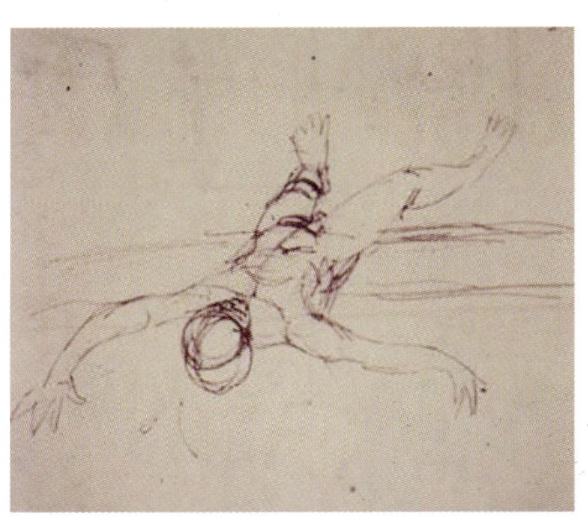
9

10

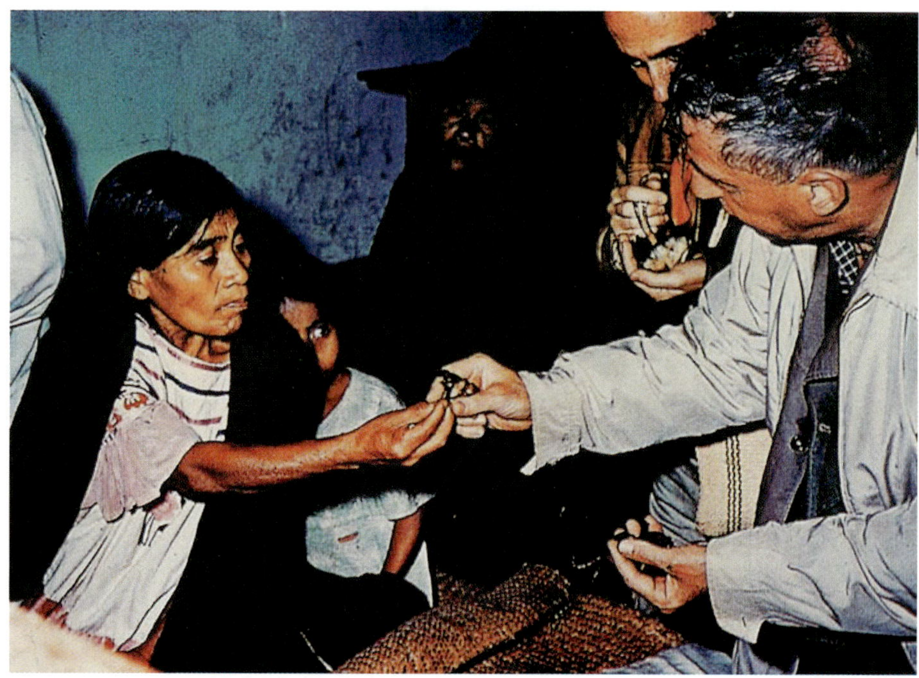

Gordon Wasson receives his portion of magic mushrooms from Maria Sabina at the beginning of the ceremony.

Gordon Wasson and Valentina Pavlovna Wasson in the Mazatec village Huautla de Jimenez, Oaxaca, Mexico, 1955. (Jars contain samples of psychedelic mushrooms.)

15
PSYCHEDELIC METAMORPHOSIS OF DYING

Death is not extinguishing the light; it is putting out the lamp because dawn has come.
– Rabindranath Tagore, Nobel Prize-winning Bengali poet and playwright

DURING OUR RESEARCH, we observed many unique and interesting features of working with dying cancer patients, including the nature of their pre-existing emotional problems and psychological conflicts, the specific content of their sessions, and the factors responsible for the effects of the treatment. In our initial work, we naively expected that the cancer patients would be relatively "normal" persons with a severe physical illness and an understandable and fully commensurate emotional reaction to their situation. This anticipation was quickly dispelled. During psychedelic therapy, many of the cancer patients manifested a variety of serious emotional problems and psychological conflicts that predated the onset and diagnosis of their physical illness. In fact, these emotional problems were so striking and prominent in some cases that they suggested a possible causal connection with the cancer itself.

Emotional Problems and Psychological Conflicts of Cancer Patients

Generally the incidence of depressive states, strong negative attitudes toward life, and even self-destructive and suicidal tendencies seemed to be higher in the cancer patients compared to the general population. While this observation came from clinical impressions and was not studied in a controlled and systematic way, we also saw surprisingly frequent instances of severe guilt, feelings of self-hatred, and self-punishing and self-destructive tendencies that had preceded the clinical manifestation of cancer by years or even decades. During their psychedelic sessions the cancer patients often saw direct links between such tendencies and their malignancies. A less frequent but not uncommon perspective was to view their cancer as punishment for past transgressions. The patients frequently traced these character traits and symptoms back to their early history—to memories of abandonment and deprivation or of physical, emotional, and sexual abuse in infancy and childhood. They saw these intensely painful experiences, which involved loneliness, anxiety, anger, hunger, and other difficult emotions, as possible causes or at least contributing factors of their illness.

We also repeatedly observed that the physical sites of the primary cancer had been the focus of the patients' increased attention for many years before the onset of the illness. These areas often had been the targets of repeated emotional or even physical insults. Some patients reported that the site of the cancer had always been the area of least resistance or the weakest link in the chain of their psychosomatic defenses. The organ or area afflicted with cancer had also often responded in a specific way to various emotional stresses in their lives.

For example, female patients with gynecological cancer often had a previous history of severe sexual abuse and conflicts about sexuality. Similarly several of our patients said that significant psychological problems related to the oral area and ingestion of food had antedated by many years the onset of their stomach cancer. In one instance, peptic ulcer, which is caused by a microorganism but also can be influenced by psychosomatic factors, was an intermediary stage between gastric dysfunction of a neurotic nature and the development of a carcinoma. We also saw cases where a long history of gastrointestinal discomfort preceded the development of pancreatic cancer and where important psychological problems of long duration related to the anal area were followed by malignant changes in the colon. Although this evidence is anecdotal, these connections are sufficiently striking and consistent to merit systematic research in the future.

In an early article, Carl Simonton and Stephanie Matthews Simonton reviewed the medical literature on the relationship between emotional factors and malignancy. In their analysis of more than two hundred relevant articles, the Simontons found a general consensus that emotional factors and malignancy were directly related to one another. The question for them was not the existence or nonexistence of such a connection, but its degree and practical significance, including the therapeutic implications (Simonton and Simonton 1974). The most common personality characteristics of cancer patients and the most plausible predisposing factors mentioned by various authors quoted in the Simontons' review were: significant tendency to hold resentment and a marked inability to forgive; a predilection toward self-pity; difficulty developing and maintaining meaningful long-term relationships; and a poor self-image. The Simontons suggested that history of a persistent pattern of basic rejection might be a possible common denominator behind all these personality characteristics. They observed that this pattern frequently culminates in the loss of a serious love object six to eighteen months before the diagnosis of cancer.

Regarding the psychedelic sessions themselves, many individuals dying of cancer seemed to have strong psychological defenses and were very reluctant to let go and allow the experience to unfold. These patients often resisted taking a deep look into their own unconscious and were able to relinquish their psychological resistances only after very good therapeutic rapport had been established. Once these psychological defenses had been overcome, the nature of the psychedelic sessions with cancer patients did not differ substantially from those of other populations, including various categories of psychiatric patients and mental health professionals.

Content of the Psychedelic Sessions

The general content of the psychedelic sessions was similar for all the populations we worked with, including neurotics, alcoholics, and narcotic addicts, "normal" volunteers in the training program for professionals, and cancer patients. In all cases the session contents consisted of a wide range of experiences, from beautiful colorful fractal-like visions, reliving of traumatic or positive childhood memories, and episodes of death and rebirth to profound archetypal and transcendental states of consciousness.

However, beyond this general similarity, certain characteristics were unique to the sessions of the cancer patients. As might be expected, individuals with cancer generally had a higher incidence of difficult somatic symptoms and were more preoccupied with their bodies. Various psychosomatic manifestations, such as nausea, vomiting, tremors, cardiac complaints, and breathing difficulties, are not uncommon in psychedelic therapy, regardless of the population involved. They are especially frequent during the onset of the pharmacological effect of psychedelic substances. The early LSD researchers referred to this initial activation of the autonomous nervous system as the "vegetative phase." Intense physical manifestations occurring later in the session usually indicate the emergence of emotionally strongly charged unconscious material and are associated with the individual's struggle to break through the usual resistances and defenses. As the patient relives biological birth, intense and often difficult physical feelings, such as suffocation, pain, pressures, muscular tensions, and nausea, reflect the extreme physical discomfort associated with the passage through the birth canal.

Besides these "usual" physical manifestations in psychedelic sessions, our cancer patients occasionally had somatic symptoms that were directly related to their malignancy and reflected specific disturbances in their physiological functioning. These included, for example, nausea and vomiting in patients with gastric cancer or intestinal obstruction and incontinence of urine and feces in patients with pelvic tumors or metastases to the spinal cord. Patients suffering from advanced cancer also seemed to find their psychedelic sessions more debilitating than the other categories of clients with whom we had worked. Especially after the long LSD sessions, many patients felt tired not only in the evening of that same day but also for the entire day after their sessions. Consequently the beneficial effects of the LSD sessions were frequently masked by various degrees of physical and emotional exhaustion and did not become fully apparent until the second day after the psychedelic session.

During the preparation phase of psychedelic therapy, we made every effort to facilitate communication between family members, as explained in Chapter 13. However, some patients had not been informed of their diagnosis and prognosis before their LSD sessions, either because of their strong denial or resistance by close relatives. Often these patients discovered the truth about their disease during the session. Sometimes this discovery was based on insightful review of various clues and observations from the time before the session. Another especially fascinating method of understanding occurred when some patients were actually able to gain experiential access to cellular consciousness of their body tissues and cells. They then witnessed what was happening in their bodies by envisioning the cancerous growth. Images of the cancer site—its anatomical and topographical characteristics, and vascular supply—were common also in the remaining patients who knew their diagnosis. These insights were frequently associated with psychodynamic material that appeared to be involved in the genesis of their cancer.

Occasionally patients in our program made spontaneous attempts at self-healing. They usually followed their intuition as to what the specific therapeutic intervention should be. Some tried to free themselves from emotional or physical blocks in the affected parts of the body. In this approach, reminiscent of the principles of Chinese medicine, patients found that blockages of emotional and physical energy were conducive to disease and that opening the flow of vital energies created the best conditions for healing. Others became consciously aware of destructive energies and emotions underlying the malignancy and tried to discharge them. Sometimes these problems manifested as powerful negative emotions; other times they assumed the forms of vicious archetypal creatures.

Another self-healing strategy that some patients attempted in their psychedelic sessions was to create healing energy fields enveloping the diseased organ or their entire body. They usually associated this field with a specific color that they sensed would have the strongest healing effect, such as green, gold, or blue. Some other alternatives were visualizing the tumor and trying to constrict the surrounding arteries or increasing the immunological defenses of the organism by mobilizing antibodies, leucocytes, and lymphocytes. This type of approach bore striking resemblance to the visualization technique developed in the 1970s by Carl Simonton and Stephanie Matthews Simonton to help individuals with cancer and other tumors actively participate in their own healing. Their method used guided imagery and fantasy exercises to achieve the same goal: boost the psychoimmunological defenses and the intrinsic healing potential of the organism (Simonton, Creighton, and Simonton 1978). Because of the conservative environment we worked in and the lack of knowledge about the nature of cancer, our approach was neither to specifically recommend such therapeutic experimentation nor to discourage it when it occurred spontaneously.

Certain types of experiences that usually occur in psychedelic sessions seemed to happen more frequently in dying individuals or were experienced with more emotional engagement. The emphasis on death as an intrinsic part of life and the search for meaning of human existence was quite understandable in view of the patients' circumstances. Another distinctive theme was an intense focus on family members, close friends, and other important figures in the lives of the cancer patients. Some showed a concerted effort to finish "old business," forget and forgive old grudges, and reach forgiveness for themselves. Others used this opportunity to thank their significant others for all they had done for them and for the role they had played in their lives. These attempts to find emotional closure were extremely moving for everybody involved.

Often during these psychedelic sessions we witnessed episodes similar to those known from the literature on near-death experiences (NDEs). Patients explored their entire present interpersonal and social situation, reviewed and evaluated their past history, and tried to find a meaningful closure in view of their impending death. Also frequent was the sense of a vivid encounter with the spiritual essence of various deceased relatives and a reassuring telepathic exchange with them. As mentioned in Chapter 7, experiences of the "welcoming committee" of deceased relatives and friends have been repeatedly described by thanatologists in the literature on near-death experiences (Osis 1961). Such visions were often vividly and convincingly reported by our cancer patients, who usually found them so real and authentic that they seriously considered the possibility that there might be some form of existence beyond the point of physical demise. In several instances, such encounters with dead relatives and friends introduced an element of joyful expectation and familiarity into a previously terrifying concept of dying and death. A psychedelic session can thus create the kind of situation that existed in many ancient cultures, where a deep belief in the existence of a spiritual realm harboring one's ancestors was a powerful factor in easing the transition from life to death.

Pharmacological Effects and Psychodynamic Mechanisms in Psychedelic Therapy

Many factors are responsible for the often remarkable effects of psychedelic psychotherapy in cancer patients. This modality of treatment involves a complex process that combines pharmacological effects of psychedelic substances with psychodynamic mechanisms. Without a specifically designed controlled study we were unable to determine the relative contribution of these two components to the final therapeutic outcome. We could only speculate as to the impact of the pharmacological effects of the psychedelic substances as such, and the contribution of psychotherapy that preceded, accompanied, and followed the drug session.

The value of either drug-free psychotherapy or LSD chemotherapy alone had been previously demonstrated in terminal cancer patients by studies where each of these modalities had been applied separately. Elisabeth Kübler-Ross, Cicely Saunders, Carl Simonton and Stephanie Matthew Simonton, and others reported noteworthy beneficial effects of psychotherapy in patients with terminal diseases without the aid of psychedelic drugs (Kübler - Ross 1969, Saunders 1967, Saunders 1973, and Simonton and Simonton 1974). Even earlier, priests and hospital chaplains had been able to ease the emotional suffering of patients and their families by providing psychological support.

On the other hand, Eric Kast obtained positive results with a predominantly chemotherapeutic approach and minimal interpersonal interaction. In his experimental treatment Kast routinely used 100 micrograms of LSD without psychologically preparing his patients and without even forewarning them about the unusual effects of the substance. He also terminated the sessions by administering chlorpromazine when his patients reported emotional distress (Kast and Collins 1966). Kast obtained clearly positive results—both in terms of alleviating pain and improving the psychological condition of some of his patients—without any psychotherapeutic effort or intention. These results in this context strongly suggest that the potential therapeutic value of psychedelic substances, in and of themselves, should not be underestimated.

The relative contribution of the pharmacological and psychological factors in psychedelic therapy is more or less an academic question. Psychotherapeutic work and the effects of psychedelic substances are clearly interdependent and form an inextricable amalgam. Combined as they were in the Spring Grove program, both sets of factors—pharmacological and psychological—complement and potentiate each other. The result is a treatment modality that is superior to either of its individual components. The importance of good psychotherapeutic rapport and set and setting has been demonstrated in many studies where psychedelics were used in other categories of patients and in various other experimental subjects, such as mental health professionals, artists, clergy, and scientists. These non-pharmacological factors can clearly maximize the benefits and minimize the risks of LSD administration.

We observed many significant therapeutic results in our cancer patients after their psychedelic treatment. The most important changes occurred in the following five categories:

- Emotional symptoms and problems, such as depression, suicidal tendencies, tension, anxiety, insomnia, and psychological withdrawal.
- Physical pain and distress.
- Fear of death, philosophical concept of death, and attitude toward dying.
- Time orientation, life strategy, and basic hierarchy of values.
- Grief and mourning of the survivors and their ability to accept and integrate the loss.

Alleviation of Emotional Symptoms and Problems

Our previous clinical experiences with various categories of psychiatric patients, as well as data from the existing LSD literature, showed beyond any reasonable doubt that psychedelic therapy can have a positive effect on a wide variety of emotional symptoms and problems. In fact, LSD therapists seemed to agree that depression, anxiety, and general tension—symptoms commonly observed in people dying of cancer—were among those that most readily responded to LSD psychotherapy. Especially striking was the therapeutic effect of LSD therapy on depressed patients who were preoccupied with death and had suicidal tendencies.

Our early work at the Psychiatric Research Institute in Prague yielded extraordinary insights into the psychodynamics of suicide. We learned that suicidal tendencies and fantasies arise when depressed patients confuse the death of the ego with biological death, or egocide with suicide. Such individuals do not understand that their preoccupation with death and their intense wish to die often reflect an underlying craving for psychospiritual death and rebirth and thus ultimately for transcendence, not for destruction of their physical body. In this context suicide results from a tragic error when a person fails to realize that he or she can experience death without physical damage. In practice, the experience of psychospiritual ego death and rebirth in psychedelic sessions proved to be the most powerful remedy against suicidal tendencies (Grof 1985, Grof 2000). Sudden unexpected brush with one's mortality and with impermanence in near-death situations often has the same impact (Ring 1982, 1984).

Given these observations, the positive effects of LSD psychotherapy on the emotional condition of our patients were not particularly surprising in and of themselves. However, the novel and exciting discovery of the Spring Grove Program was that these positive emotional changes occurred in terminal cancer patients, whose depression and anxiety seemed to be a natural and fully understandable response to a very difficult life situation. It seemed plausible that a powerful intervention in the patients' unconscious dynamics might erase a program from infancy and childhood that had outlived its usefulness but continued to have a distorting influence on the patient's emotional and psychosomatic condition. However, a radical transformation of the emotional and philosophical attitude of the patient to currently existing dismal and tragic life circumstances clearly suggested the existence of some powerful psychological mechanisms of an entirely different nature and order—mechanisms previously unknown to mainstream psychiatry.

It is difficult to explain the dramatic alleviation of emotional and psychosomatic symptoms and, particularly, the profound changes in personality structure, world view, and hierarchy of values that can be achieved in psychedelic therapy. Current practices of depth psychology require years of costly and time-consuming systematic psychotherapy to reach much more modest results. In the psychedelic therapy practiced at the Maryland Psychiatric Research Center, preparation for the sessions took ten to fifteen hours. The transformation itself happened within a few hours during the drug sessions, even though full integration of the experience often required days or weeks. The changes occurred in many different areas and on many levels—physical, emotional, psychological, interpersonal, philosophical, and spiritual. Clearly such a powerful process must be very complex and cannot be reduced to a single common denominator. The following discussion summarizes our present understanding of the underlying dynamics.

LSD psychotherapy certainly involves all the mechanisms that are operative in conventional psychotherapeutic approaches, such as recalling and vividly reliving traumatic memories from infancy and childhood, as well as repressed memories from later life; yielding emotional and intellectual insights; providing corrective interpersonal experiences; and facilitating psychological transference. These mechanisms are greatly intensified in psychedelic sessions because of the amplifying effect of LSD. However, the entire spectrum of new and previously unknown therapeutic mechanisms that becomes available in psychedelic therapy can only be understood by thinking in terms of the vastly expanded cartography of the psyche that includes the perinatal and transpersonal domains as well as the biographical-recollective level of conventional psychotherapy (see Chapter 8).

Many of the dramatic emotional and psychosomatic changes facilitated by LSD sessions can be explained in terms of shifts in the interplay of specific memory constellations known as COEX systems, which are discussed briefly in Chapter 8 and more extensively in other publications (Grof 1975, 2000). The governing function of COEX systems can change because of various physiological or biochemical processes occurring inside the organism or as a reaction to a number of external influences of a psychological or physical nature. The LSD sessions seem to represent a deep intervention into the dynamics of COEX systems. Sudden clinical improvements during LSD therapy can often be explained as a shift from a psychological dominance of a negative COEX system to a state where the individual is under the influence of a positive memory constellation. Such a change does not necessarily mean that all the unconscious material underlying the pathological state has been worked through or, for that matter, that any of it has been resolved. It simply indicates an inner shift from one system to another. Such a situation can be referred to as *COEX transmodulation*. A thorough working through of all the layers of a COEX system would result in *resolution of this COEX system*.

A dynamic shift from one COEX system to another does not always mean clinical improvement. A poorly resolved LSD experience could cause a shift from a positive COEX system to a negative one. Such a negative shift is characterized by sudden occurrence of psychopathological symptoms that were not apparent before the session. Another possibility is a shift from one negative COEX system to another negative system with a different main theme. The external manifestation of this intrapsychic event would be a change in psychopathology from one clinical syndrome to another. The most dramatic example of this kind I have observed was a severely depressed and suicidal homosexual patient, who emerged from an LSD session in a state of euphoria and sexually interested in women, but with a classical hysterical paralysis of his right arm. Several additional sessions were required to work through the unconscious material underlying the paralysis before the function of his right arm returned to normal (Grof 1980).

The mechanisms discussed thus far account for many instances of alleviating emotional and psychosomatic symptoms in psychedelic therapy, but they do not adequately explain the most radical and profound healing and transformations that we have observed. These were changes of an entirely different kind and order that occurred after psychedelic sessions marked by strong perinatal and transpersonal elements. For those patients who experienced psychospiritual death and rebirth followed by feelings of mystical union with other people, nature, the universe, and God, the pre-session symptoms often dramatically subsided or even disappeared completely.

Such extraordinary improvement after a single psychedelic session can last for days, weeks, or even months. Many of the positive changes can persist indefinitely. This profound death-rebirth sequence, which the Spring Grove team referred to as the "psychedelic peak experience," clearly constitutes a new and powerful mechanism for eliciting profound therapeutic changes and deep restructuring of the personality. Significant clinical improvement and deep transformation of personality can also result from other therapeutic mechanisms operating on the transpersonal level, such as emergence of an archetype and its full conscious experience and integration, reliving an important past life memory, and experiencing God or the Supracosmic and Metacosmic Void.

The effects of LSD psychotherapy with dying individuals are not limited to the intrapsychic domain. This work can significantly affect the entire network of the patient's interpersonal relations. As the dying individual's emotional condition improves, his or her relationships with family members and significant others are positively affected. This aspect of therapy can also profoundly help the surviving relatives and friends themselves. Clarifying distorted communication, cutting through dysfunctional protective screens, and opening channels of direct and honest interaction are without any doubt important factors of change. Consequently this feature of the treatment process often has a profoundly positive influence on the feelings of hopelessness, alienation, and confusion frequently experienced by persons facing death and by people around them.

Effect of Psychedelic Psychotherapy on Severe Physical Pain

The often dramatic effect of LSD or DPT psychotherapy on severe physical pain is difficult to explain. A single psychedelic session often resulted in considerable alleviation or even disappearance of excruciating pain, pain which sometimes had not even responded to high dosages of powerful narcotics. This theoretically and practically important phenomenon is extremely puzzling. It certainly challenges the simple "telegraph model" of pain, in which the diseased tissue sends a signal through the thalamus to the cerebral cortex and elicits a motor response. Further study of this extraordinary effect could radically revise our understanding of the nature of pain.

The mysterious influence of psychedelic substances on pain also cannot be interpreted simply in terms of their pharmacological action. The relief from pain was not sufficiently predictable and consistent to be considered a pharmacologically-induced analgesia. Moreover, the dose-response relationship characteristic of pharmacological agents could not be established. Dramatic alleviation of pain occurred after some sessions with relatively low dosages, while some of the high-dose sessions had no detectable analgesic effect. For patients who had more than one session, this effect might occur after some sessions but not after others, although the same dosage was used in all of them. In some instances, significant relief from pain was observed for a period of weeks or even months after a single administration of the drug. These observations suggest that psychological factors or perhaps some yet unknown mechanisms in the analgesic effect of psychedelic substances could be operative.

Changes in the experience of pain following psychedelic sessions did not always involve simply a reduction in the intensity of pain; we noticed several distinct patterns. Some individuals reported that following their LSD sessions or shortly thereafter, pain was considerably mitigated or totally disappeared. Others noticed that the pain was still there, but their attitude toward it had changed. Suddenly their pain tolerance was much higher, or the pain no longer relentlessly and irresistibly demanded their attention. Occasionally dying individuals reported quite unusual changes in their perception of pain and attitude toward it. They were able to reevaluate the emotional connotation of their pain and find in it philosophical significance, transcendental experiential qualities, religious meaning, or karmic value.

In the case of Suzanne (see Chapter 14), the psychedelic session significantly eased her persistent depression and fear of death but failed to influence the excruciating pain that made it impossible for her to focus on anything else. However, the session helped her decide on the recommended palliative surgery, which she had previously refused because of her overwhelming fear regarding the potentially adverse side effects. Suzanne's experience clearly shows the potential for contrary effects of a psychedelic session: the overall emotional condition can be dramatically improved even though the level of pain is not.

Often the cancer patients discovered various techniques that allowed them to overcome pain not only during their sessions but afterwards as well. Some of these methods proved so effective that we adopted them and taught them routinely to our patients as part of the preparation for their psychedelic sessions. For example, in many instances it proved quite helpful to direct one's attention away from the pain to the flow of the music, to let oneself be fully involved in the sequences of images and experiences, and to be totally immersed in the here and now. Another useful and opposite approach was to focus and concentrate on the pain, but with an accepting attitude. Initially this caused the unpleasant sensations to be amplified, sometimes to the limits of pain tolerance. The individual was then able to "move through the pain" and transcend it. Thus, paradoxically, accepting pain, yielding to it, "going into it, with it, and through it" can make it possible to move experientially beyond pain altogether. Generally the least useful approach to pain was to let it occupy the center of one's awareness while, at the same time, resisting it and fighting against it.

After their treatment, many of our patients found it unusually helpful to focus in their daily meditations on those images or episodes from their psychedelic sessions that were associated with highly positive emotions and with freedom from pain. Recalling these memories often helped them reconnect with the state of mind and comfortable physical condition that they had experienced at that time. For example, these pleasant memories could be evoked by listening to the same music that had been played in the psychedelic sessions during these episodes. In some instances and with some success, we also used guided imagery in a light hypnotic trance to help the patients move beyond physical and emotional suffering.

While the significance of the psychological component in the relief of pain brought about by LSD is unquestionable, the specific mechanisms involved in this process are yet to be fully understood. We have not been able to find any relationship between the type of the psychedelic session or its content and the degree or pattern of pain relief. Sometimes we observed marked changes in the experience of pain perception after otherwise unsuccessful and poorly resolved sessions that did not have a particularly beneficial effect on other aspects of the patient's clinical condition. Conversely, as in Suzanne's case, we saw sessions that transformed the individual in every other respect except the intensity of their physical pain.

Similarly, the correlation between the level of the unconscious activated in the session and the effect on pain seemed to be minimal. We observed significant pain relief after sessions of any possible type—biographical, perinatal, and transpersonal—yet we worked with a number of individuals where similar sessions did not have any effect on pain. The almost capricious quality of this phenomenon is illustrated by the story of John (see Chapter 14). He was probably the most salient example of the dramatic effect that psychedelic drugs can have on the experience of pain, in spite of the fact that his session appeared to be superficial, uneventful, and unsuccessful.

As emphasized in the articles by Eric Kast and V. J. Collins, pathological pain is a composite phenomenon that has a neurophysiological component, represented by the pain sensation, and a psychological component, namely the pain affect (Kast and Collins 1964). Psychedelic therapy seems to influence the pain experience primarily by modifying the psychological or psychosomatic component—the way the actual neurophysiological stimulation is interpreted and dealt with—rather than by obliterating or reducing the neuronal impulses responsible for the painful sensations. The concept of COEX systems discussed earlier could elucidate some of the mechanisms involved in this process; in certain cases, alleviation of pain could reflect a shift from a COEX system with the central theme of physical suffering to one with a different motif.

Many observations from psychedelic sessions indicate that various physically painful experiences in one's life history are recorded in memory banks closely associated with each other. The resulting memory constellations are then functionally linked with similar experiences on the perinatal and transpersonal level. Episodes of pain and physical suffering from the individual's life related to operations, injuries, diseases, and physical abuse are typically relived in psychedelic sessions in close connection with the birth experience. If an individual is exposed in everyday life to situations that produce actual physical pain—during a disease, accident, or surgical intervention—specific COEX systems become activated that involve physical suffering and threat to body integrity or survival. The nature and content of past painful experiences will then co-determine and color the resulting pain perception and the individual's reaction to it.

Patients suffering from chronic and progressive diseases, especially ones that are considered incurable, also have a strong tendency to experience fearful fantasies of how their pain will continue and increase in the future. This anticipation then seems to increase their present suffering. In his paper entitled "Pain and LSD-25: A Theory of Attenuation of Anticipation," Eric Kast points out that reducing this fearful anticipation could be an important mechanism responsible for at least part of the analgesic action of LSD. He suggests that symbol formation and anticipation, so vital to survival in ordinary life, tend to augment the agony of the individual involved in grave situations (Kast 1964).

The totality of the pain experience thus seems to reflect not only the direct neurophysiological response to the tissue damage, but also the past programming of the individual regarding painful events and anticipation of future suffering. An important effect of LSD and other psychedelic substances is to divest traumatic memories of their emotional charge. This makes it possible for patients to free themselves from the burden of the past and to live more fully in the present moment, a development that is usually accompanied by a comparable decrease of emotional investment in the future. The resulting here-and-now orientation can be an important element in altering the individual's experience of pain.

Another significant aspect of the analgesic action of psychedelics is related to the powerful tyrannizing effect that physical pain usually has on the patient's field of attention. Intense pain quite predictably tends to dominate the individual's awareness at the expense of all the other sensory inputs. Many patients suffering from intense pain find it difficult or impossible to carry on conversations, read books, watch television, or pursue any of their previous activities that could make their difficult situation more tolerable. In extreme cases they even lose interest in keeping up with important events in the lives of close family members.

Due to their powerful mind-expanding effect, psychedelic experiences can break the emotional barriers and sensory impoverishment of cancer patients. During sessions one's field of awareness is flooded with emotionally highly charged material from the individual and collective unconscious and from the sensory organs, particularly the optical system. Fascinating visual displays of colors and forms, sounds, and unusual sensations inundate the consciousness that was previously dominated by the excruciating monotony of pain. Returning from a well-resolved psychedelic session, the patient can once again enjoy the richness of sensory experiences—the beauty of nature, sounds of music, taste of food, or elements of human interaction. This expansion of awareness and emotional interest can persist for days or weeks after a successful session.

Thus some of our patients could shift their attention from pain and physical discomfort and focus on new areas of interest inspired by the experiences in their sessions. Many people discovered new dimensions in music and a new way of listening to it. They purchased recordings of the pieces that had been played in their sessions (or similar selections) and spent much time listening to them. Others developed deep interests in books on mysticism, yoga, reincarnation, Buddhism, shamanism, or nonordinary states of consciousness. A few also used the insights they had in psychedelic sessions to understand how to best spend their remaining days. For example, one patient decided that her dying could become a powerful catalyst in bringing her alienated relatives closer together, and she spent the last weeks of her life working systematically on this task.

The influence of psychedelic therapy on pain associated with cancer cannot be explained in all its complexity within the framework of the traditional neurophysiological theories. Ronald Melzack, professor of psychology at McGill University in Montreal, collected many laboratory and clinical observations that represent equally serious challenges to contemporary concepts of pain. Among them were congenital absence of sensitivity to noxious stimuli and its opposite: spontaneous psychogenic pain occurring without detectable external irritation. Melzack pointed out certain peculiar characteristics of some pain syndromes, such as phantom limb and various neuralgias, and high rate of failure after radical surgical operations aimed at alleviating pain. He also paid special attention to the surprising success of certain unconventional pain-relieving procedures, particularly the analgesic and anesthetic effect of acupuncture. In his book, *The Puzzle of Pain*, Melzack suggested a radical revision of medical thinking about pain (Melzack 1973). His work is very relevant to our findings and is summarized briefly below.

Melzack distinguishes three major components of pain, from the theoretical as well as practical point of view:

- The *sensory-discriminative dimension of pain*, mediated by the specific sensory pathways (the spinothalamic projection system). This dimension uses perceptual information regarding the location, magnitude, and spatiotemporal properties of the noxious stimulus.
- The *emotional and motivational dimension of pain* involving the reticular system of the brainstem and the limbic structures. It contributes the distinctly unpleasant emotional quality and the aversive drive to escape the stimulus and seek relief from pain.

- The *cognitive and evaluative dimension of pain*, which is the neocortical addition to the total experience. This includes cultural learning, the unique history of the individual in relation to pain, the meaning the individual attributes to the pain-producing situation, the effect of suggestion, and the state of mind of the individual at that moment.

These three components of pain, as well as their relative participation in the pain experience, can be selectively influenced by a variety of factors.

Melzack and Wall formulated the so-called gate-control theory of pain, which accounts for many seemingly mysterious aspects of pain. They postulated that a neural mechanism in the dorsal horns of the spinal cord acts like a gate. This gating mechanism can increase or decrease the flow of nerve impulses from peripheral fibers to the central nervous system. The degree to which the gate facilitates or inhibits sensory transmission is determined by the relative activity in large-diameter and small-diameter fibers and by descending influences from the brain. Somatic inputs from all parts of the body, as well as visual and auditory inputs, are able to exert a modulating influence on the transmission of impulses through the gating mechanism. The presence or absence of pain is thus determined by the balance between the sensory and the central inputs to the gate-control system. When the amount of information passing through the gate exceeds a critical level, it activates the neural areas responsible for the pain experience and pain response (Melzack and Wall 1965).

Melzack and Wall's theory provides a plausible theoretical framework for the seemingly capricious effect of psychedelic therapy on the pain experience of cancer patients. The variability of results may reflect a dynamic interaction between the multidimensional nature of the psychedelic experience and the complexity of the neurophysiological structures and mechanisms underlying the pain phenomenon. The clinical observations concerning the effects of LSD and DPT on pain represent an important additional source of supportive evidence for the gate-control theory of pain and are of such theoretical and practical importance that they should be studied in the future.

An unexpected discrepancy in the Spring Grove cancer study was that the relief of pain was not reflected in an equally dramatic drop in the consumption of narcotics. To address this inconsistency, at least four factors must be considered. First, the attending physicians of the patients made no specific attempt to change the pharmacological regime—neither the patients nor the nurses were asked to reduce the narcotic medication if the patients' pain levels diminished. The consumption of narcotics thus reflected the spontaneous interaction between the patients' demands and the response of the medical personnel. In this context the seemingly paradoxical findings could have simply reflected the habitual routine and inertia of the patients, as well as the hospital staff.

Second, most of the patients received a variety of other psychoactive substances in addition to narcotics, such as major or minor tranquilizers, non-narcotic analgesics, and hypnotics. The changes in the consumption of these drugs were not considered or measured systematically in our study. This limitation is especially important in the case of phenothiazine derivatives and minor tranquilizers, which we routinely discontinued a week before the session so that they would not interfere with the effect of LSD or DPT. The reduction of pain achieved by psychedelic therapy thus had to compensate for the previous analgesic effect of the medicines that had been discontinued.

Third, even heavy narcotic medication had failed to control successfully the pain of many of our cancer patients before their psychedelics sessions. Indeed, inadequate response to narcotic medication and persisting severe pain were the main reasons many of the patients agreed to participate in our study. In some cases medication was not reduced after the psychedelic sessions, but the same amount of narcotic became more effective in controlling pain and making life more tolerable. And, finally, the apparent discrepancy between the relief of pain and the demand for narcotics could have reflected not only the element of habituation but actual physiological addiction. This was not unlikely, as many of our patients had been under heavy narcotic medication for many months before their psychedelic sessions.

Fear of Death, Philosophical Concept of Death, and Attitude Toward Dying

An important dimension of the changes in our patients after psychedelic therapy was *profound transformation of their concept of death and attitude toward the situation they were facing*. In LSD therapy of psychiatric patients or "normal" subjects, we frequently heard how radically psychedelic experiences had changed their feelings about death. Individuals who experienced psychospiritual death and rebirth saw this experience as a foretaste of what would happen to them at the time of biological death. They reported that as a result they no longer feared death, and they now viewed dying as a fantastic journey, an awe-inspiring adventure in consciousness. Deep experiences of cosmic unity, convincing past life memories, and certain other transpersonal forms of consciousness seemed to render physical death less important and threatening. These experiences could also profoundly transform the attitudes of patients who were facing physical death in a matter of months, weeks, or days. Our observations suggest that such experiences deserve in-depth research as complex phenomena with the potential to provide fascinating psychological, philosophical, mythological, and spiritual insights. Clearly these phenomena are much more than hallucinations, wishful fantasies, or self-deceptions resulting from altered brain functioning.

Indirect support for the ability of psychedelic therapy to alleviate fear of death came from the research of Charles A. Garfield. In his doctoral dissertation, Garfield explored the relationship between long-term systematic experiences of non-ordinary states of consciousness and the level of death-related fear (Garfield 1974). Garfield used a combination of clinical interviews, psychometric testing, and psychophysiological measurements to study the differences in conscious and unconscious fear of death among 150 male subjects selected from five subcultures: graduate students in psychology, graduate students in religion, psychedelic drug users, Zen meditators, and American-born disciples of Tibetan Buddhism. The groups with extensive experience in holotropic states of consciousness (psychedelic drug users, Zen meditators, and students of Tibetan Buddhism) showed a significantly lower level of death-related fear compared to the student groups.

In an earlier study of psychedelic therapy and fear of death, Eric Kast suggested that some mechanism must protect dying patients from a devastating realization of hopelessness. However, Kast postulated that the "desperate" situation of such individuals is only quantitatively different from that of any other person, since everybody can anticipate death at any time with some probability and ultimately with certainty. Kast therefore assumed that the mechanisms that protect us daily from realizing our own mortality operate with greater force in the dying patient. In both cases, terminal patients and healthy persons, the fright experienced in contemplating death was based on the fear of loss of control over their bodies and their environments. Kast saw the acceptance of the inevitable loss of control during and after LSD administration as an indication that LSD apparently eased the blow which impending death deals to the fantasy of infantile omnipotence (Kast 1964).

Kast also emphasized the diminution of anticipation as an important factor in relieving both the experience of pain and the fear of death. Under normal circumstances, anticipation represents a very important mechanism that is useful not only for orientation but also for defense and procurement of food. However, Kast suggests that anticipation offers nothing to the welfare of the dying persons—it only accentuates their feelings of helplessness. Anticipation requires the ability to use words meaningfully and to form and manipulate symbols. Kast saw the decrease in the power of words and the resulting loss of ability to anticipate, together with the expansion of the immediate sensory life, as the most important factors modifying the attitudes of dying individuals toward death.

The changes of attitude toward death induced by psychedelics cannot be adequately explained in terms of traditional psychodynamic concepts. Such a limited approach reflects deep misunderstanding of the depth and nature of spiritual experiences. Unlike the relief of pain, dramatic changes in the concept of death and attitudes toward it were always associated with specific content of the psychedelic sessions and occurred only when the experiences had a strong perinatal or transpersonal emphasis. Individuals who experienced psychospiritual death and rebirth, feelings of cosmic unity, or deep insights into the cycles of reincarnation typically showed radical and lasting changes in their fundamental understanding of human nature and its relation to the universe. They developed a deep belief in the ultimate unity of all creation and experienced themselves as integral parts of it. This attitude often applied also to their disease and to the painful predicament they were facing. Death, instead of being the ultimate end of everything, suddenly appeared as a transition to a different type of existence. These patients perceived the alternative of consciousness continuing beyond physical death as much more plausible than that of its ceasing at the time of biological demise.

As a result of powerful and convincing perinatal and transpersonal experiences, our patients discovered ordinarily invisible dimensions of existence far beyond their previous world views and belief systems. They also became aware of their own rich ancestral, racial, collective, phylogenetic, and karmic heritage. The sharp demarcation between their everyday identity and the universe-at-large tended to dissolve, and the usual distinction between the inner world of their psyche and external reality became much more arbitrary. The opening of this fantastic cosmic panorama provided a new referential system of such enormous scope that the fact of individual demise lost its terrifying impact.

Clearly these patients benefited from the mystical experiences of their psychedelic sessions. This observation raises a question that is often asked by materialistically oriented scientists: Do mystical experiences of any kind—spontaneous, psychedelic, or induced by some other means—provide ontologically valid information about human nature and about the universe, or are they products of a chemically altered brain or mental illness? Do they reveal authentic dimensions of reality in the sense of what Eastern spiritual philosophies call transcendental wisdom (prajnaparamita)? Are mystics people with a deeper understanding of reality than an average person, or are they mentally deranged individuals suffering from hallucinations and delusions, as contemporary psychiatry portrays them?

In *The Cosmic Game* (Grof 1998), I suggest that the world view emerging from holotropic states, which closely resembles a perspective on reality that Aldous Huxley called perennial philosophy (Huxley 1945), is also surprisingly compatible with many revolutionary discoveries of modern science—from astrophysics, quantum-relativistic physics, and David Bohm's theory of holomovement to new biology and Jungian psychology. Thus the insights from the psychedelic sessions of our clients are corroborated by the most advanced modern science. However, questioning the ontological relevance of mystical experiences is moot in this context. The cancer patients we worked with found the cosmic visions in their psychedelic sessions utterly convincing, and these experiences and insights made their tragic situations much more tolerable.

Changes in Hierarchy of Values and Life Strategy

The striking *changes in the hierarchy of values and life strategy* that we observed in our patients after psychedelic sessions were usually directly related to the spiritual insights associated with perinatal and transpersonal experiences. In the course of psychedelic psychotherapy, many people discover that their life has been inauthentic in terms of certain specific sectors of interpersonal relations. For example, problems with parental authority can lead to specific patterns of difficulties with authority figures, repeated dysfunctional patterns in sexual relationships can be traced to one's parents as models for sexual behavior, intense sibling rivalry can color and distort future peer relationships, and so on. These connections are well known from traditional dynamic psychotherapy. However, the insights from psychedelic sessions are more profound. When the process of experiential self-exploration reaches the perinatal level, we typically discover that our life thus far has been largely inauthentic in its totality, not just in certain partial segments. We find, to our astonishment, that our entire life strategy has been misdirected and therefore incapable of providing genuine satisfaction. Our misdirected life strategy has been primarily motivated by factors that we have not adequately processed and integrated: the fear of death and unconscious forces associated with biological birth. In other words, during our biological delivery we completed the process of birth anatomically, but not emotionally.

When our everyday field of consciousness is strongly influenced by the underlying memory of the struggle in the birth canal, we experience feelings of discomfort and dissatisfaction with our present situation. Our discontent can focus on a large spectrum of issues—unsatisfactory physical appearance, inadequate resources and material possessions, low social position and influence, insufficient amount of power and fame, and many others. Like the child stuck in the birth canal, we feel a strong need to reach a better situation that lies somewhere in the future. Whatever our present circumstances, we find them unsatisfactory. Our fantasy continually creates images of future scenarios that appear more fulfilling than the present. We see our life as preparation for a better future, not yet "the real thing."

This orientation toward existence results in a life pattern that some of our clients have described as a "rat-race" or "treadmill." The image of a hamster hectically running within a wheel and getting nowhere mockingly portrays the strategy and fundamental fallacy of an average human life based on incessant pursuit of goals. It is essentially a loser strategy, incapable of delivering the satisfaction that we desire. Whether our strategy actually brings us fruit in the material world is of little consequence, since we can never get enough of what we do not really need or want. When we succeed in reaching the goal of our aspirations, our basic feelings do not really change. We then assume that our continuing dissatisfaction has something to do with the goal—either it is the wrong goal, or it is not ambitious enough. Consequently we either substitute the old goal with a different one or augment the same type of ambitions. In any case, we have not correctly diagnosed the failure as an inevitable result of a fundamentally wrong life strategy, which is in principle incapable of providing true satisfaction.

Reckless irrational pursuit of various grandiose goals causes much suffering and leads to serious problems on the individual, as well as collective scale. This fallacious strategy is played out endlessly at all levels of importance and affluence, since it never brings true satisfaction. Applied globally, it manifests as plundering non-renewable resources, turning them into pollution, and threatening survival of life on this planet. Mahatma Gandhi put it very succinctly: "Earth provides enough to satisfy every man's needs, but not every man's greed." The experience of psychospiritual death and rebirth, which includes emotional completion of biological birth and confrontation with one's mortality and impermanence, can significantly reduce this irrational drive.

Beyond the trauma of birth and fear of death, psychedelic research and experiential psychotherapy have revealed an even deeper source of our dissatisfaction and striving for perfection. The insatiable craving that drives human life is ultimately transpersonal in nature and is best described by Ken Wilber's concept of the "Atman Project" (Wilber 1980). Our true nature is divine—God, Cosmic Christ, Allah, Buddha, Brahma, the Tao, Great Spirit. Although the process of creation separates and alienates us from our source and our true identity, our awareness of this fact is never completely lost. The psyche's deepest motivating force on all levels of consciousness evolution is the drive to return to the experience of our divinity. However, the constraining conditions of the consecutive stages of development prevent a full experience of our own divinity and force us to search for various surrogates that are ultimately inadequate and unsatisfactory.

Transcendence requires death of the separate self—dying to our exclusive identification with the body/ego. But since we fear annihilation and cling to the ego, we must settle for Atman substitutes, which are specific for each particular developmental stage:

- For the fetus and the newborn, the Atman substitute is the satisfaction experienced in the good womb or on the good breast.
- For an infant, it is satisfaction of age-specific physiological needs and the sense of security.
- For the adult the range of possible Atman projects is large and includes food, sex, money, fame, power, appearance, knowledge, and many others.

Because of our deep sense that our true identity is the totality of cosmic creation and the creative principle itself, substitutes of any degree and scope—the Atman projects—will always remain unsatisfactory. Our deepest needs can only be fulfilled by the experience of our divinity in a holotropic state of consciousness. Thus the ultimate solution for the insatiable greed of humanity is in the inner world, not in secular pursuits of any kind and scope.

It is easy to understand how insights of this kind can ease the psychological suffering of cancer patients. As they accept their impermanence and impending death they realize the ultimate absurdity and futility of exaggerated ambitions, attachment to money, status, fame, and power, or pursuit of other secular values. This realization in turn makes it less painful to face the involuntary termination of one's professional career and the impending loss of all worldly possessions. Psychedelic experiences also deeply affect time orientation; the past and future become less important compared to the present moment. Psychological emphasis tends to shift from plans for large time spans to living "one day at a time," a shift that is accompanied by an increased ability to enjoy life and to derive pleasure from simple things.

The spirituality awakened by psychedelic experiences is usually not based on religious beliefs and dogmas of a specific creed or church affiliation but is typically universal, all-encompassing, and non-denominational. Yet in many instances the psychedelic session has deepened and illumined the dying individual's traditional beliefs and imbued them with new dimensions of meaning.

Psychological Condition of the Survivors and the Nature of the Grieving Process

The significance of psychedelic therapy with the dying transcends the narrow framework of helping the individual patient. This type of treatment can also significantly influence the *psychological condition of the survivors and the nature of the grieving process*. Times of death are times of crisis in any family. While most of the suffering is experienced by the patient, the confrontation with death and the impending separation from the loved ones are matters of profound emotional relevance for all the other persons involved. Close relatives and friends who witness the progressive deterioration and death of a close person are often deeply emotionally affected. In some cases, these persons later suffer long-term adverse emotional reactions. Practicing psychiatrists are well aware that the deaths of parents and other close relatives play a very important role in the future life of the family members. These events can be instrumental in the development of many emotional disorders, either as an original trauma during childhood or as an important trigger of manifest symptoms later in life.

The grieving and bereavement period seems to be fundamentally influenced by the nature and intensity of the conflicts in the survivors' relationships with the dying person. Adjusting to the death of a family member is usually much more difficult if relatives feel ambivalent about their behavior toward the dying person or about the way the entire situation was handled. The inability or lack of opportunity to express one's compassion for the dying, to utter words of gratitude for the past, or to find a way to say good-bye leaves survivors with feelings of dissatisfaction, bitterness, and often intense guilt.

If the therapist can enter the family system as a catalyzing agent and facilitate channels of effective emotional exchange and communication, this difficult time of transition can become an event of profound meaning for everyone involved. Dying and death can take the form of an encounter with the cosmic forces and universal laws that operate in our lives and to which we are all subject. Under the best circumstances, survivors experience very little guilt regarding the suffering and death of their loved one, and the grief period is considerably shorter. Participating in the dying person's process can influence the surviving children and adults' concepts of death and help them approach their own demise in the future. Spending time with dying persons can even precipitate a profound experience of spiritual opening, and is for this reason an important part of the training of Tibetan monks.

Skills and Training Necessary for Successful Psychedelic Therapy

Skillful therapeutic intervention often makes it possible to ease the agony of the dying person and, at the same time, help the survivors absorb and integrate this trauma. Psychedelic therapy is not chemotherapy, nor does it provide therapeutic magic. The quality of the human encounter, sensitive psychotherapeutic guidance of the dying, individual work with the family, and the optimism of the therapist are factors of crucial significance. Fascinating and deeply emotionally moving experiences in psychedelic sessions and subsequent positive changes in feelings, attitudes, and behavior are more than enough to maintain the enthusiasm of the therapists and protect them from burn-out, even in the face of what is frequently a grim reality.

However, enthusiasm and optimism, in and of themselves, are not sufficient qualifications for conducting a successful program of LSD-assisted psychotherapy. Any therapists participating in such a study must receive specialized training. Optimal preparation of therapists requires more than knowing the existing literature, watching selected videotapes of psychedelic sessions, and participating as co-therapist in sessions conducted by experienced therapists. Psychedelic states are largely ineffable—even the best descriptions cannot adequately convey their nature and depth. Consequently it is impossible to obtain any truly relevant understanding of these states by simply reading books and articles in scientific journals. Psychedelic therapy, unlike therapy with ordinary pharmaceutical agents, therefore requires that skilled therapists have personal experience with psychedelic substances to understand their effects and to be able to use them effectively. In our LSD training program for professionals at Spring Grove, psychiatrists and psychologists had the opportunity to experience personally holotropic states of consciousness under the guidance of trained therapists. Such intimate knowledge of the psychedelic experience proved absolutely indispensable for effective and sensitive work with LSD and other psychedelics.

Psychedelic training sessions for future therapists have another important function—they provide the trainees with an opportunity to confront and work through their own fear of death and other important emotional issues that could become activated in working with dying patients and cause problems in the sessions. The equanimity and centeredness of the therapist when he or she is confronted with highly emotionally charged material of the client is one of the most important factors in successful psychedelic therapy. During my work with psychedelic therapy at the Psychiatric Research Institute in Prague and the Maryland Psychiatric Research Center in Baltimore, I repeatedly observed and appreciated the skill and compassion of nurses and other members of the research team who had experienced such sessions themselves as part of their professional training.

With adequate therapeutic training, LSD-assisted psychotherapy can be a safe and promising approach in an area that has thus far been most discouraging. Although members of the helping professions and the public have become aware of the urgent need to help dying individuals, very few effective programs exist. Most dying patients are still faced with a very dim reality, described by Aldous Huxley in his novel *Island* as: "increasing pain, increasing anxiety, increasing morphine, increasing demandingness, with the ultimate disintegration of personality and a loss of the opportunity to die with dignity" (Huxley 1963).

16 PSYCHE AND THANATOS: DEATH IN WESTERN PSYCHOLOGY AND SOCIETY

It seems to me that one of the most basic human experiences, one that is genuinely universal and unites—or, more precisely, could unite—all of humanity, is the experience of transcendence in the broadest sense of the word.
– Václav Havel, President, Czech Republic

DEATH AND IMPERMANENCE, critical aspects of human life, have been largely neglected by mainstream psychiatry and psychology until very recently. Significant early research in this field was conducted primarily by pioneers of depth psychology (including Freud, Jung, Adler), the anthropologist and psychiatric clinician Ernest Becker, and some of the existentialist philosophers, who all believed in their own ways that death played an important role in the human psyche and profoundly influenced human life. They agreed on the importance of coming to terms with death as a prerequisite for a successful strategy of existence. However, they would all be surprised today at the dimensions that subsequent research has revealed regarding the powerful representation of death in the psyche, including the specific form which the presence of death takes on the biographical, perinatal, and transpersonal levels. And none of them anticipated the radical solution of the problems related to death made possible by psychedelic therapy and non-drug experiential methods using holotropic states, work which has led to a new understanding of death and dying, with profound implications for the future of humanity.

Pioneers of Depth Psychology and Existential Philosophy

Sigmund Freud, Viennese neurologist and the founder of psychoanalysis, was foremost among those pioneers of depth psychology who incorporated death into their theory. Given that Freud single-handedly opened this vast new area of psychological study, it is not surprising that his views regarding the relevance of death evolved dramatically over the years. In his earlier writings, Freud saw the human psyche as governed by a dynamic tension between two conflicting forces—the sexual drive (libido) and the self-preservation drive (ego instinct). During these early years Freud also believed that the primary motivating force in the psyche was what he called the "pleasure principle" (*das Lustprinzip*), the tendency to avoid discomfort and seek satisfaction. At this stage of his career, Freud considered the issue of death irrelevant. He viewed the unconscious as a realm beyond time and space, incapable of knowing and acknowledging the fact of death. From this perspective, problems that seemed related to death, such as fear of death, had nothing to do with biological death and masked some other issues. Fear of death could be caused by death wishes toward another person, which the superego found unacceptable and turned against the subject. It could also substitute for fear of an overwhelming sexual orgasm, fear of loss of control, or fear of castration. In Freud's early understanding, fear of death was essentially rooted in the conflicts of the pre-oedipal and oedipal stages of libidinal development (Fenichel 1945).

Freud's thinking about death began to change radically when he discovered the existence of phenomena that clearly were not governed by the pleasure principle: primarily masochism, need for punishment, self-mutilation, and violent suicide. At this point, his previous concept of the psyche became untenable and required a major revision. Freud's struggle with the conceptual challenges associated with this problem made him realize that the phenomena which were "beyond the pleasure principle" could not be understood without bringing in the problem of death. The first indications of this change can be found in his theoretical formulations published between 1913 and 1920, especially in his analysis of Shakespeare's play *The Merchant of Venice* entitled "The Theme of the Three Caskets" (Freud 1925a) and in his essay "Thoughts for the Times on War and Death" (Freud 1925b). In these papers Freud showed that he was revising his earlier thesis that death did not have a representation in the human mind. By 1920, he achieved a synthesis and integration of his divergent views of death and formulated a new comprehensive biopsychological theory of the human personality.

In Freud's new psychology, expounded in his book *Beyond the Pleasure Principle*, the psyche was no longer a battlefield between the sexual drive and the self-preservation instinct. One of the competing forces continued to be the libido (Eros), but he now called the new opposing force the "death instinct" (Thanatos) (Freud 1975). The goal of Eros was to preserve life and that of Thanatos was to counteract life, destroy it, and eventually return it to the inorganic realm from whence it had originally come. Freud saw a deep relationship between these two groups of instinctual forces and the two basic biochemical processes in the human organism, anabolism and catabolism. Anabolic processes contribute to growth, development, and storage of nutrients. Catabolic processes are destructive, breaking down reserves and releasing energy. Freud also linked the activity of these two drives to the destiny of two groups of cells in the human organism—the germinal cells, which are potentially immortal, and the somatic cells constituting the body, which are destined to die.

In his early work, Freud considered almost all manifestations of aggression to be expressions of sexuality and thus basically sadistic in nature; in the new conceptual framework he related aggression to the death instinct. According to this new understanding, the death instinct operated in the human organism from the very beginning, converting it gradually into an inorganic system. This destructive drive could and had to be partially diverted from its primary aim and directed against other organisms. It seemed irrelevant whether the death instinct was oriented toward objects in the external world or against the organism itself, as long as it could achieve its goal, which was to destroy.

Freud's final formulations concerning the role of the death instinct appeared in his last major work, *An Outline of Psychoanalysis* (Freud 1949). There the basic dichotomy between two powerful forces, the love instinct (Eros or Libido) and the death instinct (Thanatos or Destrudo), became the cornerstone of Freud's understanding of mental processes. This concept, which dominated his thinking during the last years of his life and which Freud himself considered to be the most definitive formulation of his ideas, did not generate much enthusiasm among Freud's followers and was never fully incorporated into mainstream psychoanalysis. Rudolf Brun, who conducted an extensive statistical review of papers concerned with Freud's theory of the death instinct, found that 94% of them were clearly unfavorable to Freud's concept (Brun 1953).

While Freud himself saw Eros and Thanatos as biological instincts, they had definite mythological features, not unlike the Jungian archetypes. Many psychoanalysts, including his otherwise ardent followers, considered Freud's interest in death and the incorporation of Thanatos into his theory of instincts to be an alien enclave in the development of his psychological framework. Several critics suggested that Freud's speculations about Thanatos were unfavorably affected by his advanced age and by a variety of traumatizing personal and external factors—his intense thanatophobia, mutilating resection of his jaw for a misdiagnosed tumor, a poorly fitting maxillary prosthetic device, emotional reaction to his cancer of the tongue, death of many family members, and the mass killing in World War I.

Freud's critics contended that the unexpected change in his thinking reflected his pathological preoccupation with death; however, he was actually far ahead of his followers. As discussed later in this chapter, consciousness research over the last five decades has confirmed Freud's general intuition as to the importance of death for psychology. While this subsequent research has not confirmed the existence of a biological death instinct as Freud envisioned it, rich representation of the theme of death has been uncovered in all three levels of the unconscious—biographical, perinatal, and transpersonal. We also now know that the element of death plays an important role in the psychogenesis of many emotional and psychosomatic disorders.

Alfred Adler, psychoanalytic renegade and founder of the school of individual psychology, was another pioneer of depth psychology who considered death very important (Adler 1932). According to his own account, Adler's life and work were influenced by his shattering encounter with death. At the age of five he was stricken with severe pneumonia, and his situation was declared hopeless by his attending physician. After his recovery, he decided to study medicine to gain control over death. As a direct result of his early brush with death, Adler came to see feelings of inadequacy and helplessness and a strong drive to overcome them (the "masculine protest") as the most important driving forces in the psyche. In this context a person's inability to prevent and control death was the deepest core of feelings of inadequacy. Although Adler did not explicitly incorporate the fear of death into his theory, his own lifelong pursuits were certainly deeply influenced by this experience of vital emergency. Adler's therapy emphasized courage and the ability to face the dangerous aspects of life (Bottome 1939).

We have seen in Chapter 9 how profoundly C. G. Jung, another pioneer of depth psychology, was influenced by his near-death experience. Jung also had a keen interest in death, although his understanding differed significantly from Freud's speculations. In his essay "On the Psychology of the Unconscious," he opposed Freud's concept of the two fundamental instincts, Eros and Thanatos, as the forces governing the psyche (Jung 1953). He also disagreed with Freud's thesis that the aim of Eros is to establish ever greater unities and preserve them, and that the purpose of Thanatos is to undo connections and destroy. Jung argued that such a choice of opposites reflected attitudes of the conscious mind and not the dynamics of the unconscious. He saw the logical opposite of love as hate and that of Eros as Phobos (fear). However, the psychological opposite of love is the will to power, a force that dominated the theories of Alfred Adler.

Jung observed that where love reigns, there is no will to power; and where the will to power is paramount, love is absent. Jung contended that Freud was compelled to name Thanatos, the destructive death instinct, as the opposite of Eros because he was making a concession to intellectual logic on the one hand, and to psychological prejudice on the other. According to Jung, Eros is not equivalent with life. But for those who do equate Eros with life, its opposite will naturally appear to be death. We all think that the opposite of our highest principle must be purely destructive and evil. Thus we cannot endow death with any positive qualities, and we tend to fear and avoid it.

Jung's specific contribution to thanatology was his full awareness of how powerfully the motifs related to death are represented in the unconscious. He and his followers brought to the attention of Western psychologists and lay audiences the utmost significance of the theme of psychospiritual death and rebirth, with all its symbolic variations, in the ritual and spiritual history of humanity. They collected and analyzed numerous examples of death/rebirth symbolism from various cultures and historical periods, ranging from the mythology of Australian Aborigines to alchemy. However, they did not recognize and appreciate the relationship of this archetypal symbolism to biological birth and its stages (see the discussion of perinatal matrices in Chapter 8). Jungian psychologists made another major contribution to the understanding of death with their exploration of eschatological mythologies of various cultures and historical periods.

The problems related to death also played a prominent role in Jung's psychology of the individuation process. He emphasized that it was crucial to see death as equally important as birth and to accept it as an integral part of life. If we grant goal and purpose to the ascent of life, why not to its descent? Instead of clinging to the past, one should face death as part of a natural teleological process. A useful perspective is to see death as the end of empirical man and the goal of spiritual man. While sexuality is the dominant force in the first half of human life, the problems of biological decline and approaching death should ideally be the central focus in the second half of it.

Preoccupation with the problem of death emerges under normal circumstances in later decades of life, while its occurrence in earlier years is usually associated with psychopathology. However, avoiding the issues of death and impermanence in later decades is equally problematic. Jung criticized those who were unable to embrace death, and he expressed his opinion quite unequivocally: "To the psychotherapist, an old man who cannot bid farewell to life appears as feeble and sickly as a young man who is unable to embrace it." The process of individuation as Jung saw it resulted in psychological completion of the personality and involved resolving the problem of death. The goal of his therapy was wholeness. A person who only sees life and death as opposing each other certainly is not whole (Jung 1967, 1970a, 1970b).

Another important and influential contribution to the psychological literature on death was Ernest Becker's book *The Denial of Death: A Perspective in Psychiatry and Anthropology* (Becker 1973). Becker was an anthropologist by training but acquired considerable skills as a psychiatric clinician and theoretician as a student of the renowned psychiatrist and critic of this discipline, Thomas Szasz. Becker asserted that the central problem of human existence is that we are mortal and will die. Although this is a self-evident reality of our life, the fear associated with it is so strong and pervasive that we use all possible means to deny it. In Becker's opinion, this denial of death is the cause of virtually all the pathologies to which humans are subject. The particular way in which it manifests is narcissism, an obsessive need to be recognized as important. This constitutes what Becker called "man's tragic destiny"—a desperate effort to: justify one-self as an object of primary value in the universe, be a heroic figure, and make a bigger contribution to the world than anybody else.

Becker saw all cultures as systems that provide their members an opportunity to become the kind of heroes that this "tragic destiny" requires. It makes little difference which form this cultural system has—whether primitive, magical, and religious, or secular, civilized, and scientifically informed. Regardless of its form, the cultural system is still a mythical hero-system, which people are willing to serve in order to achieve a feeling of excellence, meaning in life, and special status. Consequently people build edifices, make scientific discoveries, create pieces of art, perform heroic acts, and found families that span generations. The driving force behind all these activities is the desire to create things in society of lasting value that will outlive or outshine death and decay. Becker believed that, were we to become conscious of our denial of death and of the false cultural structures that we have erected to give ourselves a patina of heroism, the unleashing of this truth would fundamentally change the world. We would realize that the existing cultural systems are artificial, and that whatever we do on this planet has to be done with the awareness of the terror underlying existence.

Death also has an important place in the thinking of the existentialists, particularly in the philosophy of Martin Heidegger. Death plays a central role in his analysis of existence put forth in *Sein und Zeit* (Being and Time) (Heidegger 1927). According to Heidegger, the awareness of impermanence, nothingness, and death permeates imperceptibly every moment of human life before the actual occurrence of biological death or an encounter with it. Existential analysis reveals that life is "existence toward death" (*Sein zum Tode*). All ontological speculations must consider the totality of existence and thus also that part of it which does not yet exist, including the very end. The awareness of death is a constant source of tension and existential anxiety in the organism, but it also provides a background against which existence and time appear to have a deeper meaning.

Heidegger followed the recommendation of his teacher Edmund Husserl that philosophers should turn their attention away from the natural world and toward inner experience. He saw self-exploration as a basic necessity for our apprehension of the world and for our thinking about it. Heidegger claimed to have described fundamental experiences that underlie our everyday perception of the world and yet are beyond and outside the reach of traditional scientific method. His views here are very similar to the insights from holotropic states of consciousness. As explained in Chapter 8, the existentialist world view tends to dominate the thinking of subjects who are under the influence of the second basic perinatal matrix (BPM II), characterized by feelings of "no-exit." In this kind of situation people are unable to find the only solution, namely the experience of transcendence.

Conceptual Revolution of the 1960s

The renaissance of interest in consciousness research and self-experimentation in the stormy 1960s moved the exploration of the human psyche far beyond the boundaries of Freudian psychoanalysis. A major conceptual revolution took place, the full impact and meaning of which have not yet been fully acknowledged and assimilated by academic circles. Albert Hofmann's serendipitous discovery of the psychedelic effects of LSD, and the ensuing laboratory and clinical research of psychedelics and unsupervised self-experimentation with these substances, played a major role in this development. However, important information concerning the nature of consciousness and the dimensions of the human psyche was generated also by work with other therapeutic and laboratory methods capable of inducing holotropic states of consciousness.

Among these methods were the new experiential therapies—encounter groups, marathon and nude marathon sessions, various bioenergetic approaches, primal therapy, Gestalt practice, and hypnosis. Additional sources of revolutionary new data were experiments with laboratory mind-altering techniques, such as sensory deprivation, sensory overload, biofeedback, and various kinesthetic devices. The 1960s also witnessed an unprecedented wave of interest in various mystical traditions, meditation, ancient and aboriginal wisdom, and Oriental philosophies. Many people, including psychiatrists and psychologists, became students of visiting Eastern spiritual teachers or undertook serious study and practice in ashrams and monasteries. Scientific studies were conducted of various meditation techniques and their effects on practitioners.

An important development of this golden era of consciousness research was a quantum leap in the understanding of death and the role it plays in the human unconscious. A major milestone here was Herman Feifel's book, *The Meaning of Death*, a compendium of articles by physicians, psychiatrists, psychologists, philosophers, and theologians that focused on the problems of dying individuals (Feifel 1959). In the years after this book was published, professional circles became more interested in the subject of death, and people grew increasingly aware of the urgent need for change. The Foundation of Thanatology was subsequently created to bring together members of the helping professions, ministers, philosophers, writers, and other individuals interested in the problems related to death and in the management of the dying individuals. This organization was founded in 1968 in New York City by Austin Kutscher, who also became its first president.

This wave of professional interest in the practical and theoretical aspects of dying culminated in the work of Elisabeth Kübler-Ross, M.D., at the psychiatric department of the University of Chicago. In her pioneering book, *On Death and Dying*, she summarized her experiences in psychotherapeutic work with severely ill individuals and in training seminars conducted with physicians, nurses, students, and ministers (Kübler-Ross 1969). Kübler-Ross provided ample evidence that many dying persons were in urgent need of genuine human contact and psychotherapeutic help. She emphasized the importance of open and honest communication, and stressed that it was critical to be willing to discuss any issues of psychological relevance. Approached this way, her dying patients were able to teach the survivors important lessons not only about the final stages of life, but also about uniquely human aspects of existence. Those involved in this process, moreover, emerged from the experience enriched and often with fewer anxieties about their own death.

Working with patients suffering from terminal diseases, Kübler-Ross discovered that their psychological attitudes and reactions to their disease underwent typical progressive changes as their physical condition deteriorated. She described five consecutive stages that all her dying patients seemed to pass through. The first stage, immediately following the diagnosis of terminal illness, was temporary shock response to bad news and *denial*. This was accompanied by withdrawal of friends and relatives leading to a sense of isolation. The predominant reaction in the second stage was *anger*, which could take different forms—anger at God, envy of healthy people, or negativity toward doctors, nurses, and relatives. In the third stage, patients became involved in a process of *bargaining*, offering that in return for a cure they would fulfill one or more promises. *Depression* in the fourth stage was partially a reaction to actual losses, such as the deprivation of job, hobbies, mobility, sexual activity, and other important aspects of life. Another aspect of the depression concerned losses yet to come. The final stage of *acceptance* was the point at which the dying person gave up and realized that death was inevitable.

In Chapter 9 I discussed at some length another major contribution to this revolution in professional attitudes toward death—Raymond Moody's research of near-death experiences and his ground-breaking book *Life After Life* (Moody 1975). The pioneering work of Elisabeth Kübler-Ross focused primarily on the psychological changes in dying people and therapeutic support for them. Moody's book *Life After Life* in turn inspired an entire generation of investigators to explore near-death phenomena, including Kenneth Ring, Michael Sabom, Bruce Greyson, Phyllis Atwater, Barbara Harris Whitfield, and many others.

Psychedelic Research and Experiential Therapies

Psychedelic research and experiential therapies brought fascinating insights into the significance of the theme of death for the human unconscious. The new observations confirmed Freud's general intuition about the importance of death for psychology, but they substantially revised, modified, and expanded his views. Instead of confirming the existence of the death instinct as a biological drive, results from this work enabled researchers to identify and specify the various representations that the theme of death has in the human psyche.

On the biographical level, the element of death is present in the form of memories from postnatal life of events that represented serious threat to survival and body integrity—operations, accidents, injuries, and serious diseases. Especially important are memories of dangerous situations that interfered with breathing, such as diphtheria, severe whooping cough, strangulation, or near drowning. An even deeper representation of death occurs on the perinatal level. Biological birth is a potentially or actually life-threatening event that can last many hours. Some people have actually died in the birth process and been subsequently resuscitated. Beyond the actual vital emergency associated with the difficult passage through the birth canal, delivery also represents the death of the fetus as an aquatic creature and its transformation into a radically different organism, the air-breathing newborn. Reliving of birth in holotropic states, including the concomitant vital emergency, can be so authentic and convincing that the individual involved can believe that he or she is actually dying.

On the transpersonal level, dying and death can take many different forms. We may identify with our ancestors or people from different countries and historical periods who are dying or whose lives are threatened. Such sequences from the collective unconscious can sometimes be associated with a sense of personal remembering, which characterizes them as past incarnation memories. Death can even be experienced in full identification with an animal or a plant. Death is also powerfully represented in the collective unconscious as mythological motifs of death and rebirth and as various eschatological themes, including specific death gods and underworlds of various cultures, the archetype of Death, astral or bardo realms, the posthumous journey of the soul, and the abodes of the Beyond. As we saw in the discussion of perinatal matrices (Chapter 8) and of ritual transformation (Chapter 3), the deities of different cultures representing death and rebirth play an important role in holotropic states. Destruction and death are also intrinsic elements of grand archetypal themes, such as the Christian Apocalypse or the Nordic Ragnarok (the Doom, or Twilight, of the Gods).

All these representations of death in the human psyche are arranged in multilevel COEX systems comprised of biographical, perinatal, and transpersonal elements. Associated with difficult emotions and physical feelings, they underlie many forms of psychopathology—from suicidal depression, phobias, and addiction through sadomasochism to asthma and psychosomatic pains. Conversely, confrontation with death in the course of experiential psychotherapy and conscious processing of the unconscious material related to it has important healing, transformative, and evolutionary potential. Of all the various encounters with death that we can experience on different levels of the psyche, one has a particularly profound healing, transformative, and evolutionary potential: the confrontation with our mortality and impermanence, which occurs on the perinatal level in the context of reliving birth and experiencing psychospiritual death and rebirth.

Episodes of this kind emerge spontaneously in various holotropic states, without any specific programming. They represent one of the most frequent experiences in psychedelic therapy, sessions of Holotropic Breathwork, and in spiritual emergencies. Clearly the human psyche has a strong propensity to exteriorize this deep unconscious material and bring it into consciousness for processing. Incomplete surfacing of unconscious themes related to mortality and impermanence results in emotional and psychosomatic symptoms, whereas full emergence and integration of this material is conducive to healing and transformation. This observation explains the ubiquitous nature of various death-rebirth rituals and the importance attributed to them by all ancient cultures and native societies of the preindustrial era.

Consequences of Psychospiritual Death and Rebirth

The benefits of experiencing psychospiritual death and rebirth are profound. The key element is alleviation or elimination of the fear of death. Western philosophy's usual explanation for fear of death is that it reflects our intellectual knowledge of our own mortality. But research of holotropic states has demonstrated that fear of death has very little to do with our knowledge that we must die. Its sources are instead memories of life-threatening situations from postnatal biography and the memory record of the vital emergency experienced during birth and at the time of various prenatal crises. Additional roots are transpersonal in nature, such as past life memories of events endangering life or body integrity and terrifying archetypal motifs. As this unconscious material begins to reach consciousness, the person experiences emotions of vital threat. But as the death-related themes are allowed to surface fully into consciousness, they lose their power to shape the person's life experience. This explains why fear of death can be significantly alleviated even in terminal cancer patients, for whom the prospect of biological demise is imminent.

Profound spiritual opening is another important consequence of the deep encounter with birth and death on the perinatal level. When the experiential regression reaches the perinatal domain, the experiences typically assume a quality that C. G. Jung referred to as numinous. The sacred and hallowed aspect of the experience is convincing proof of the authentic nature of the spiritual dimension of existence. I have seen many atheists, materialists, skeptics, Marxists, and positivistic scientists reach this point and experience a radical change in their world view. The spirituality that opens up in this context has nothing to do with organized religions—it is mystical, universal, non-denominational, and all-encompassing. This form of spirituality can be discovered whether the encounter with death is symbolic, as in psychedelic sessions, Holotropic Breathwork, spiritual emergency, or meditation; or involves a real brush with death during a heart attack, serious accident, life-threatening operation, dangerous war situation, or internment.

A completed and well-integrated experience of psychospiritual death and rebirth significantly improves the subject's emotional and physical well-being. Those who previously had various forms and degrees of emotional and psychosomatic discomfort typically feel greatly relieved after the experience. Depression dissolves, anxiety and various tensions diminish or disappear, guilt feelings subside, and self-image and self-acceptance strengthen considerably. People report a general sense of physical health, sound physiological functioning and striking increase in zest and joie de vivre. Previous feelings of alienation are replaced by a deep sense of being in tune with nature and the universe. People feel reborn, cleansed, rejuvenated, purified—full of profound serenity and joy.

Many of my clients assert that the death-rebirth process has profoundly changed their sensory perception, as if a subtle film has been removed from their senses. In William Blake's expression, their "doors of perception" have been cleansed. They liken their previous existence to living in a glass cylinder that kept them from experiencing reality fully and being attuned to the world. Following their death and rebirth experience, their sensory input has become extremely rich, fresh, and intense, at times overwhelmingly so. By comparison, they now understand that they had previously never really seen colors, heard music, smelled fragrances and odors, and appreciated the infinite nuances of tastes. Similarly, the ability to enjoy sex and the general capacity to explore the sensual potential of their bodies have been greatly enhanced.

Experiential encounter with death also profoundly influences one's attitude toward other people, animals, and nature, as well as one's hierarchy of values and strategy of existence. Aggressive feelings and impulses are usually markedly reduced; tolerance, empathy, and compassion increase considerably. Differences among people appear to be interesting and enriching rather than threatening or irritating, whether they are related to race, color, gender, culture, political orientation, or religious belief. Everything in the universe seems perfect, exactly as it should be—not necessarily with regard to its status quo, but as a process. Nationalistic and patriotic concerns and feelings of exclusivity are replaced by a sense of planetary belonging and sense of solidarity with all of humanity. This feeling of deep connection and concern extends to other species and nature in general. Refined ecological sensitivity is an important consequence of this transformation, including concern about the quality of water, air, and soil—fundamental and necessary prerequisites for health and survival of all life forms on our planet. Protecting these basic conditions for life is clearly seen as our highest priority, one that should never be overshadowed by economic, nationalistic, political, ideological, and other interests.

When the experience of death and rebirth is followed by feelings of cosmic unity, clients usually see the world and themselves as creations of cosmic energy involved in a divine play. In this context ordinary reality is perceived as essentially sacred. The process of spiritual opening and transformation typically deepens further after such transpersonal episodes as identification with other people, entire human groups, animals, plants, and various processes in nature. Additional sequences provide conscious access to events occurring in other countries, cultures, and historical periods and even to the mythological realms and archetypal beings of the collective unconscious. Experiences of cosmic unity and one's own divinity lead to greater identification with all of creation and bring the sense of wonder, love, compassion, and inner peace.

A marked change of orientation in relation to time is another remarkable consequence of the experience of death and rebirth. This is manifested by a radical shift of emotional focus from being preoccupied with the past and with plans and fantasies concerning the future to fully experiencing the present moment. Closely related is the newly discovered ability to enjoy nature and simple everyday activities—gardening, cooking and eating food, socializing, and lovemaking. Following psychedelic sessions, many people showed a sudden interest in art, particularly music and painting, or their already existing interests in this regard were intensified and deepened. Intellectual interests often shifted in the direction of mysticism, shamanism, ancient cultures, and Oriental philosophies. For some clients these new interests took a purely intellectual form; for others they were associated with a deep commitment to systematic spiritual practice.

Aside from the potential benefits of the death-rebirth process, certain risks are associated with it. Psychedelic sessions engaging the perinatal level can certainly facilitate all the profound positive changes mentioned above, but serious complications can also occur. When, for instance, psychedelic sessions with perinatal elements take place in a problematic set and setting and the experiences are poorly resolved, possible complications can include depression with suicidal tendencies, destructive and self-destructive impulses, paranoid states, or grandiose and messianic delusions. These problems are not in any way unique to psychedelic states. Such dangers are referred to in mystical literature, oral traditions of aboriginal cultures, and various mythological stories. These sources warn of the dangers that threaten a careless and inexperienced seeker or spiritual adventurer, including physical disease, insanity, and even death. Adequate preparation, support, and guidance are critical prerequisites for exploring the deep territories of the human mind.

Research of Holotropic States: Current Status

As we have seen, research of holotropic states has brought many fascinating insights into fundamental problems related to death and dying, such as the phenomenology of near-death experiences, fear of death and its role in human life, survival of consciousness after death, and reincarnation. These insights are of great theoretical importance for psychiatrists, psychologists, anthropologists, and thanatologists. They are also essential for any serious understanding of such phenomena as shamanism, rites of passage, ancient mysteries of death and rebirth, and the great religions of the world. Moreover, this research has expanded significantly our knowledge of the nature and architecture of emotional and psychosomatic disorders, including functional psychoses, and offer new strategies for their treatment.

Since all of us will face death at some point, this new understanding of death and dying represents crucially important information for every single human being. Psychedelic therapy with cancer patients and individuals plagued by other terminal diseases deserves special notice here. Having witnessed the beneficial effects of this treatment in patients with extreme forms of emotional and physical suffering, I feel profoundly sad that this therapy has been denied to countless people who desperately need it. I firmly hope that in the near future, legislators, administrators, and politicians will inform themselves from scientific literature rather than from articles of sensation-hunting journalists, free themselves from the hysteria surrounding psychedelic substances, and return this promising tool into the hands of clinicians and patients.

I am encouraged that longstanding efforts to legitimize psychedelic therapy are now realizing some success. Limited, federally approved research with psychedelics has been resumed in the United States and abroad, thanks to the perseverance of Rick Doblin, President of the Multidisciplinary Association for Psychedelic Studies (MAPS), and other advocates. These new projects include several studies of psychedelic therapy. Dr. Michael Mithoefer is investigating the therapeutic potential of 3,4-methylenedioxy-Nmethylamphetamine (MDMA, also known as "Ecstasy") in a study of MDMA-assisted psychotherapy in subjects with treatment-resistant posttraumatic stress disorder. This is the first ever FDA-approved protocol designed to investigate any therapeutic potential of MDMA.

Other studies of psychedelic therapy are being conducted with cancer patients. Dr. Charles Grob, a psychiatrist at the Harbor-UCLA Medical Center in Los Angeles, is currently conducting a Heffter Research Institute-sponsored study, with approval from the Food and Drug Administration (FDA), to examine how psilocybin can help terminal cancer patients in advanced stages of the disease cope with the emotional and physical pain and spiritual issues associated with dying. Preliminary results show that psilocybin-assisted therapy, administered in a therapeutic setting and in the context of a carefully structured study, may be remarkably beneficial; Grob's patients have experienced observed amelioration of anxiety, improvement of mood, increased rapport with family and friends, as well as reduced pain.

Psychedelic research is also being resumed at Harvard University, more than forty years after the "drug scandal" involving psychologists Timothy Leary and Richard Alpert. The current study, conducted by Dr. John Halpern, Associate Director of Substance Abuse Research at Harvard Medical School's McLean Hospital, received FDA approval in 2004 to administer the psychedelic substance MDMA to advanced-stage cancer patients. More than one year later, the DEA issued its license for this study. Now that the final regulatory approval has been obtained, the Harvard team is moving forward. This project, which received preliminary funding and assistance from MAPS during the initial phases of study design and regulatory approval, is focusing on how MDMA may be used to help alleviate anxiety, reduce pain, and enhance quality of life.

Drs. Grob and Halpern hope that successful results will facilitate the introduction of psychedelic therapy into hospital practice as a way to help many patients facing death. My experience at the Maryland Psychiatric Research Center suggests that this step would substantially contribute to the palliative care strategies that the medical profession can offer people facing death.

Global Implications of the New Understanding of Death

I will close by discussing some of the larger implications that the observations from consciousness research and a new understanding of death might have for the global crisis humanity is currently facing. Contemporary authors, such as Alan Harrington and Ernest Becker, have suggested that massive denial of death leads to social pathologies with dangerous consequences for humanity (Harrington 1969, Becker 1973). During the second half of the twentieth century, psychedelic research, thanatology, and new experiential forms of psychotherapy have not only provided convincing evidence to support this point of view but have also shown quite specifically how our attitude regarding death is related to the fundamental dilemmas confronting us.

In the human psyche death is powerfully represented in the form of biographical memories of life-threatening situations in postnatal life, during birth, and in prenatal existence. Additional themes related to death and impermanence constitute an important aspect of the historical, karmic, and archetypal domain of the collective unconscious. These elements of the personal and collective unconscious play a crucial role in many serious emotional and psychosomatic disorders. They also represent one of the most important sources of two infamous and problematic aspects of human nature: insatiable greed and disposition to what Erich Fromm called "malignant aggression" (Fromm 1973).

Greed and violence are two principal forces that have been driving human history throughout millennia. Until recently their tragic consequences were limited to those who were directly involved in various wars, revolutions, and conquests; they did not threaten the evolution of the human species as a whole and certainly did not pose a danger to the ecosystem and biosphere of the planet. Even after the most violent wars, nature was able to recover completely within a few decades. However, over the last century this situation has radically changed. Rapid technological progress, exponential growth of industrial production, massive population explosion, and especially the discovery of atomic energy have forever changed the balance of the equations involved. It has become imperative for our survival and the survival of the planet as a whole to tame these dangerous tendencies inherent in human nature.

Psychotherapy and self-exploration bring some hope to this dismal situation. Techniques involving holotropic experience make it possible to bring the death-related material from different levels of the psyche to consciousness, experience it fully, and reduce or eliminate the emotional power this material has for the individual. Over the years I have witnessed profound emotional and psychosomatic healing, as well as radical personality transformation, in thousands of people conducting serious and systematic inner quests. Some have been meditators with regular spiritual practice, others have had supervised psychedelic sessions or have participated in various forms of experiential psychotherapy and self-exploration. I have also seen profoundly positive changes in many people who received adequate support during spontaneous episodes of psychospiritual crises.

After experiential confrontation with death, particularly in the context of psychospiritual death and rebirth, the level of aggression diminishes considerably. People become more peaceful, comfortable with themselves and tolerant of others. The experience of psychospiritual death and rebirth and conscious connection with positive postnatal or prenatal memories also reduce irrational drives and exaggerated ambitions. As the emotional focus shifts from the past and future to the present moment, people are more able to enjoy the simple and everyday circumstances of life, such as food, lovemaking, nature, and music. Spirituality also emerges from this process, spirituality of a universal and mystical nature that is very authentic and convincing because it is based on deep personal experience.

This process of spiritual opening and transformation typically deepens further with transpersonal experiences—identification with other people, entire human groups, animals, plants, and even inorganic materials and processes in nature. Related experiences provide conscious access to events occurring in other countries, cultures and historical periods and even in the mythological realms and archetypal beings of the collective unconscious. With the knowledge of cosmic unity and one's own divinity come an increasing identification with all of creation and the sense of wonder, love, compassion, and inner peace. People who connect to the transpersonal domain of their psyches thus tend to develop new appreciation for existence and reverence for all life. One of the most striking consequences of this process is that deep humanitarian and ecological concerns spontaneously emerge, and people often commit to service for some common purpose. This attitude is based on an almost cellular awareness that the boundaries in the universe are arbitrary; each of us is identical with the entire web of existence.

Obviously such a transformation would increase our chances for survival if it were to occur on a sufficiently large scale. This scenario would require official support for "technologies of the sacred" in the form of various spiritual practices, experiential therapies involving holotropic states of consciousness, supervised psychotherapy with psychedelic substances, shamanic rituals, and rites of passage. Even if this condition could be met, it is uncertain whether the radical inner transformation I have repeatedly witnessed in individual cases could be carried out on a large enough scale. An even more important question is whether such transformation could be achieved quickly enough to counterbalance the rapidly escalating global crisis.

The issues of survival of consciousness after death, reincarnation, and karma are also very relevant to the current world crisis. Our behavior is profoundly affected by our beliefs in this regard. More than 2,000 years ago, Plato pointed to the profound moral implications of the belief in immortality. In his *Republic*, Plato's discussion of the immortal soul and ultimate justice concludes with the story of the near-death experience of the renowned warrior Er, who was slain in battle (Plato 1961b). Having returned to life, Er recounted that when his soul left his body, he journeyed to a mysterious region where he witnessed divine judgment and posthumous reward for the just and punishment for the depraved. The concept of postmortem justice appears also in Plato's final work *Laws*, where he quotes Socrates as saying that unconcern for the consequences of one's deeds after death would be "a boon for the wicked" (Plato 1961c).

In previous chapters I have reviewed several observations suggesting the possibility of survival of consciousness after death and reincarnation. While these research data might not be sufficient, in and of themselves, to convert a hardcore materialist, the experiences from which they are drawn are extremely convincing. Such holotropic experiences can affect people so profoundly as to cause fundamental changes in their behavior. The new moral code that results is not based on commandments, injunctions, prohibitions and fear of punishment, but on a cellular awareness of the underlying unity of all creation and the universal laws that govern it.

As a combination of unbridled greed, malignant aggression, and existence of weapons of mass destruction threatens the survival of humanity and possibly life on this planet, we must seriously consider any avenue that offers some hope. However implausible the idea of profound, large-scale psychospiritual transformation might appear, the fact that it can occur regularly on an individual basis is highly significant. In my experience, individuals who are able to confront death and come to terms with it in their inner process tend to develop a sense of planetary citizenship, reverence for life in all its forms, deep ecological sensitivity, spirituality of a universal and all-encompassing type, aversion to violence, and reluctance to view aggression as an acceptable form of conflict resolution. Such radical inner transformation and rise to a new level of consciousness might be humanity's only real chance for survival.

APPENDIX: ALDOUS HUXLEY'S CONSCIOUS APPROACH TO DEATH

Excerpts from Laura Huxley's
This Timeless Moment: A Personal View of Aldous Huxley

AS THE APPENDIX TO THIS BOOK Laura Huxley has graciously contributed some excerpts about Aldous Huxley's conscious approach to death from her book *This Timeless Moment: A Personal View of Aldous Huxley,* along with some introductory comments. The excerpts are from two chapters, titled: "This Timeless Moment" and "O Nobly Born!"

Introductory Comments

> If I were to write something now, the passing of forty-four years might color my expression. Rather than write a new report about the work Aldous and I did on the way of dying, I can do no better than referring to Aldous' own words to Maria when she was dying. The way he spoke to her during the last days and hours of her life is so loving, beautiful and clear—giving the instruction of the Tibetan Book of the Dead in a poetic, loving way as closure to a wonderful thirty-five year marriage. The touching way Aldous encourages Maria to go forward to a greater love is a profound teaching in itself, typically Aldous. Then the chapter "O Nobly Born" is simply the application of what he did and believed in and is 100% authentic and correct in all details. Actually, what I had to do was so clear.
>
> *Laura Huxley*
>
> *August 11, 2005*

Excerpt from the Chapter "This Timeless Moment"

(This excerpt, written by Aldous, describes the death of his first wife, Maria. Aldous explains how he eased Maria's death by using hypnotic suggestions to encourage her surrender to a greater wholeness.)

Laura introduces this account by noting that Aldous:

wrote an account of her death, which he gave to a few friends. It conveys the feeling that death is not the end of consciousness but rather an expansion of it. It is a touching document of human love, which could totally change, in many persons, their tremulous attitude toward death. This is his account.

Maria was in the hospital for two periods of about two weeks each, with an interval of a week between them. During these two periods she underwent a long series of tests and was given twelve X-ray treatments to relieve the pain in the lower spine and to guard against the spread, in that area, of what was suspected to be malignancy. These treatments were tolerated at first fairly well; but the last of them produced distressing symptoms, due, as it turned out, to cancer of the liver. During the last few days in hospital Maria was unable to keep any food or liquid in the stomach and had to be fed intravenously.

She was brought home in an ambulance on Monday, February 7 and installed in her own room. The nurse who had taken care of her after her operation, four years before, was waiting for her when she arrived. Maria had a real affection for this good, deeply compassionate woman, and the affection was warmly reciprocated. Three days later a second nurse was called in for night duty.

On Monday afternoon her old friend, L. the psychotherapist, came in for half an hour, put her into hypnosis and gave her suggestions to the effect that the nausea, which had made her life miserable during the preceding days, would disappear, and that she would be able to keep down whatever food was given to her. Later that evening I repeated these suggestions, and from that time forward there was no more nausea, and it was possible for her to take liquid nourishment and a sufficiency of water for the body's needs. No further intravenous feeding was necessary.

The progress of the disease was extraordinarily rapid. She was still able to find a great and fully conscious happiness in seeing her son, who had flown in from New York on Tuesday morning. But by Wednesday, when her sister S. arrived, her response was only just conscious. She recognized S. and said a few words to her, but after that there was very little communication. Maria could hear still, but it was becoming harder and harder for her to speak, and the words, when they came, were wandering words, whose relevance was to the inner life of illness, not to the external world.

I spent a good many hours of each day sitting with her, sometimes saying nothing, sometimes speaking. When I spoke, it was always, first of all, to give suggestions about her physical well-being. I would go through the ordinary procedure of hypnotic induction, beginning by suggestions of muscular relaxation, then counting to five or ten, with the suggestion that each count would send her deeper into hypnosis. I would generally accompany the counting with passes of the hand, which I drew slowly down from the head toward the feet. After the induction period was over, I would suggest that she was feeling, and would continue to feel, comfortable, free from pain and nausea, desirous of taking water and liquid nourishment whenever they should be offered. These suggestions were, I think, effective; at any rate there was little pain and it was only during the last thirty-six hours that sedation (with Demerol) became necessary.

These suggestions for physical comfort were in every case followed by a much longer series of suggestions addressed to the deeper levels of the mind. Under hypnosis Maria had had, in the past, many remarkable visionary experiences of a kind which theologians would call "pre-mystical." She had also had, especially while we were living in the Mojave Desert during the war, a number of genuinely mystical experiences, and had lived with an abiding sense of divine immanence, of Reality totally present, moment by moment in every object, person and event. This was the reason for her passionate love of the desert. For her, it was not merely a geographic region; it was also a state of mind, a metaphysical reality, an unequivocal manifestation of God.

In the desert and later, under hypnosis, all Maria's visionary and mystical experiences had been associated with light. (In this she was in no way exceptional. Almost all mystics and visionaries have experienced Reality in terms of light—either of light in its naked purity, or of light infusing and radiating out of things and persons seen with the inner eye or in the external world.) Light had been the element in which her spirit had lived, and it was therefore to light that all my words referred. I would begin by reminding her of the desert she had loved so much, of the vast crystalline silence, of the overarching sky, of the snow-covered mountains at whose feet we had lived. I would ask her to open the eyes of memory to the desert sky and to think of it as the blue light of Peace, soft and yet intense, gentle and yet irresistible in its tranquillizing power. And now, I would say, it was evening in the desert, and the sun was setting. Overhead the sky was more deeply blue than ever. But in the West there was a great golden illumination deepening to red; and this was the golden light of Joy, the rosy light of Love. And to the South rose the mountains, covered with snow and glowing with the white light of pure Being—the white light which is the source of the colored lights, the absolute Being of which love, joy and peace are manifestations, and which all dualism of our experience, all the pairs of opposites—positive and negative, good and evil, pleasure and pain, health and sickness, life and death—are reconciled and made one. And I would ask her to look at these lights of her beloved desert and to realize that they were not merely symbols, but actual expression of the divine nature; an expression of Pure Being, and expression of the peace that passeth all understanding; an expression of the divine joy; an expression of the love which is at the heart of things, at the core, along with peace and joy and being, of every human mind. And having reminded her of those truths—truths which we all know in the unconscious depths of our being, which some know consciously but only theoretically and which a few (Maria was one of them) have known directly, albeit briefly and by snatches—I would urge her to advance into those lights, to open herself to joy, peace, love and being, to permit herself to be irradiated by them and to become one with them. I urged her to become what in fact she had always been, what all of us have always been, a part of the divine substance, a manifestation of love, joy and peace, a being identical with the One Reality. And I kept on repeating this, urging her to go deeper and deeper into the light, ever deeper and deeper.

So the days passed, and as her body weakened, her surface mind drifted further and further out of contact, so that she no longer recognized us or paid attention. And yet she must have still heard and understood what was said; for she would respond by appropriate action, when the nurse asked her to open her mouth or swallow. Under anesthesia, the sense of hearing remains awake long after the other senses have been eliminated. And even in deep sleep, suggestions will be accepted, and complicated sentences can be memorized. Addressing the deep mind which never sleeps, I went on suggesting that there should be relaxation on the physical level, and an absence of pain and nausea; and I continued to remind her of who she really was—a manifestation in time of eternal, a part forever unseparated from the whole, of the divine reality; I went on urging her to go forward into the light.

A little before three on Saturday morning the night nurse came and told us that the pulse was failing. I went and sat by Maria's bed and from time to time leaned over and spoke into her ear. I told her that I was with her and would always be with her in that light which was the central reality of our beings. I told her that she was surrounded by human love and that this love was manifestation of a greater love, by which she was enveloped and sustained. I told her to let go, to forget the body, to leave it lying here like a bundle of old clothes and to allow herself to be carried, as a child is carried, into the heart of the rosy light of love. She knew what love was, had been capable of love as few human beings are capable. Now she must go forward into love, must permit herself to be carried into love, deeper and deeper into it, so that at last she would be capable of loving as God loves—of loving everything, infinitely, without judging, without condemning, without either craving or abhorring. And then there was peace. How passionately, from the depth of a fatigue which illness and a frail constitution had often intensified to the point of being hardly bearable, she had longed for peace! And now she would have peace. And where there was peace and love, there too would be joy. And the river of the colored lights was carrying her toward the white light of pure being, which is the source of all things and reconciliation of all opposites in unity. And she was to forget, not only her poor body, but the time in which that body had lived. Let her forget the past, leave her old memories behind. Regrets, nostalgias, remorses, apprehensions—all these were barriers between her and the light. Let her forget them, forget them completely, and stand there, transparent, in the presence of the light—absorbing it, allowing herself to be made one with it in the timeless now of present instant. "Peace now," I kept repeating. "Peace, love, joy, *now*. Being *now*."

For the last hour I sat or stood with my left hand on her head and the right on the solar plexus. Between two right-handed persons this contact seems to create a kind of vital circuit. For a restless child, for a sick or tired adult, there seems to be something soothing and refreshing about being in such a circuit. And so it proved even in this extremity. The breathing became quieter, and I had the impression that there was some kind of release. I went on with my suggestions and reminders, reducing them to their simplest form and repeating them close to the ear. "Let go, let go. Forget the body, leave it lying here; it is of no importance now. Go forward into the light. Let yourself be carried into light. No memories, no regrets, no looking backwards, no apprehensive thoughts about your own or anyone else's future. Only light. Only this pure being, this love, this joy. Above all, this peace. Peace in this timeless moment, peace now, peace now!" When the breathing ceased, at about six, it was without any struggle.

Excerpt from the Chapter "O Nobly Born!"

(This account of Aldous Huxley's death, written by Laura, is taken from the final chapter of *This Timeless Moment: A Personal View of Aldous Huxley*.)

Aldous died as he lived, doing his best to develop fully in himself one of the essentials he recommended to others: Awareness. When he realized that the labor of his body leaving this life might lessen his awareness, Aldous prescribed his own medicine or—expressed in another way—his own sacrament.

"The last rites should make one more conscious rather than less conscious," he had often said, "more human rather than less human." In a letter to Dr. Osmond, who had reminded Aldous that six years had passed since their first mescaline experiment, he answered, "Yes, six years since that first experiment. 'O Death in Life, the years that are no more'—and yet also, 'O Life in Death...'" Also to Osmond: "...My own experience with Maria convinced me that the living can do a great deal to make the passage easier for the dying, to raise the most purely physiological act of human existence to the level of consciousness and perhaps even of spirituality."

All too often, unconscious or dying people are treated as 'things,' as though they were not there. But often they are very much there. Although a dying person has fewer and fewer means of expressing what he feels, he still is open to receiving communication. In this sense the very sick or the dying person is much like a child: he cannot tell us how he feels, but he is absorbing our feeling, our voice, and, most of all, our touch. In the infant the greatest channel of communication is the skin. Similarly, for the individual plunged in the immense solitude of sickness and death, the touch of a hand can dispel that solitude, even warmly illuminate that unknown universe. To the "nobly born" as to the "nobly dying," skin and voice communication may make an immeasurable difference. Modern psychology has discovered how powerful the birth trauma is to the individual's life. What about the "death trauma"? If one believes in the continuity of life, should one not give it equal consideration?

Then, I don't know exactly what time it was, he asked me for his tablet and wrote, "Try LSD 100 micrograms intramuscular." Although, as you see from the reproduction, it is not very clear, I knew that this is what he meant. I read it aloud and he confirmed it. Suddenly, something was very clear to me, after this tortuous talking of the last two months. I knew then, I knew what was to be done. I went quickly to fetch the LSD, which was in the medicine chest in the room across the hall. There is a TV set in that room, which was hardly ever used. But I had been aware, in the last hour or so, that it was on. Now, when I entered the room, Ginny, the doctor, the nurse, and the rest of the household were all looking at television. The thought shot through my mind: "This is madness, these people looking at television when Aldous is dying." A second later, while I was opening the box containing the LSD vial, I heard that President Kennedy had been assassinated. Only then did I understand the strange behavior of the people that morning.

I said, "I am going to give him a shot of LSD—he asked for it."

The doctor had a moment of agitation—you know very well the uneasiness in the medical mind about this drug. But no "authority," not even an army of authorities, could have stopped me then. I went into Aldous's room with the vial of LSD and prepared a syringe. The doctor asked me if I wanted to give him the shot—maybe because he saw that my hands were trembling. His asking me that made me conscious of my hands, and I said, "No, I must do this." I quieted myself, and when I gave him the shot my hands were firm.

Then, somehow, a great relief came to us both. It was 11:45 AM when I gave him his first shot of 100 micrograms. I sat near his bed and I said, "Darling, maybe in a little while I will take it with you. Would you like me to take it also in a little while?" I said "a little while" because I had no idea of when I could take it. And he indicated yes. We must keep in mind that by now he was speaking very, very little.

Then I said, "Would you like Matthew to take it with you also?" And he said, "Yes."

"What about Ellen?" He said, "Yes." Then I mentioned two or three other people who had been working with LSD and he said, "No, no, basta, basta."

Then I said, "What about Ginny?" And he said, "Yes," with emphasis.

Then we were quiet. I just sat there without speaking for a while. Aldous was not so agitated physically. He seemed—somehow I felt he knew—we both knew what we were doing, and this had always been a great relief to Aldous. I have seen him at times during his illness upset until he knew what he was going to do; then, the decision taken, however serious, he would make a total change. This enormous feeling of relief would come to him, and he wouldn't be worried at all about it. He would say, "Let's do it," and we would do it, and he was like a liberated man. And now I had the same feeling: a decision had been made. Suddenly he accepted the fact of death; now, he had taken this moksha-medicine in which he believed. Once again he knew he was doing what he had written in *Island*, and I had the feeling that he was interested and relieved and quiet.

After half an hour, the expression on his face began to change a little, and I asked him if he felt the effect of LSD, and he indicated no. Yet I think that something had taken place already. This was one of Aldous's characteristics. He would always delay acknowledging the effect of any medicine, even when the effect was quite certainly there; unless the effect was very, very strong, he would say no. Now the expression on his face was beginning to look as it did when he had taken the moksha-medicine, when this immense expression of complete bliss and love would come over him. This was not the case now, but there was a change in comparison to what his face had been two hours before. I let another half hour pass, and then I decided to give him another 100 micrograms. I told him I was going to do it, and he acquiesced. I gave him another shot, and then I began to talk to him. He was very quiet now; he was very quiet and his legs were getting colder; higher and higher I could see purple areas of cyanosis. Then I began to talk to him, saying, "Light and free." Some of these suggestions I had given him at night, in these last few weeks, before he would go to sleep, and now I spoke them more convincingly, more intensely.

"Light and free you let go, darling; forward and up. You are going forward and up; you are going toward the light. Willingly and consciously you are going, willingly and consciously, and you are doing this beautifully—you are going toward the light—you are going toward a greater love—you are going forward and up. You are going toward Maria's love with my love. You are going toward a greater love than you have ever known. You are going toward the best, the greatest love, and it is easy, it is so easy, and you are doing it so beautifully."

I believe I started to talk to him—it must have been about 1 or 2 PM. It was very difficult for me to keep track of time. I was very, very near his ear, and I hope I spoke clearly and understandably. Once I asked him, "Do you hear me?" He squeezed my hand; he was hearing me. It was 3:15 PM according to the nurse's records. I was tempted to ask more questions, but in the morning he had begged me not to ask any more questions, and the entire feeling was that things were right. I didn't dare to inquire, to disturb, and that was the only question that I asked: "Do you hear me?"

Later on I asked the same question, but the hand didn't move any more. Now from 2 PM until the time he died, which was 5:20 PM, there was complete peace except for once. That must have been about 3:30 or 4 PM, when I saw the beginning of struggle in his lower lip. His lower lip began to move as if it were going to struggle for air. Then I gave the direction even more forcefully:

"It is easy, and you are doing this beautifully and consciously, in full awareness, in full awareness, darling, you are going toward the light." I repeated these or similar words for the last three or four hours. Once in a while my own emotion would overcome me, but if it did I would immediately leave the bed for two or three minutes, and would come back only when I could control my emotion. The twitching of the lower lip lasted only a little bit, and it seemed to respond completely to what I was saying.

"Easy, easy, and you are doing this willingly and consciously and beautifully—going forward and up, light and free, forward and up toward the light, into the light, into complete love."

The twitching stopped, the breathing became slower and slower, and there was absolutely not the slightest indication of contraction, of struggle. It was just that the breathing became slower—and slower—and slower; this ceasing of life was not a drama at all, but like a piece of music just finishing so gently in a *sempre piu piano, dolcemente...* and at 5:20 PM the breathing stopped.

And now, after I have been alone these few days, and less bombarded by other people's feelings, the meaning of this last day becomes clearer and clearer to me and more and more important. Aldous was appalled, I think (and certainly I am), at the fact that what he wrote in *Island* was not taken seriously. It was treated as a work of science fiction, when it was not fiction, because each one of the ways of living he described in *Island* was not a product of his fantasy, but something that had been tried in one place or another, some of them in our own everyday life. If the way Aldous died were known, it might awaken people to the awareness that not only this, but many other facts described in *Island* are possible here and now. Aldous asking for the moksha-medicine while dying is not only a confirmation of his open-mindedness and courage, but as such a last gesture of continuing importance. Such a gesture might be ignorantly misinterpreted, but it is history that Huxleys stop ignorance before ignorance stops Huxleys.

Now, is his way of dying to remain for us, and only for us, a relief and consolation, or should others also benefit from it? Aren't we all nobly born and entitled to nobly dying?

LITERATURE

Adler, A. 1932. *The Practice and Theory of Individual Psychology.* New York: Harcourt, Brace & Co.

Alexander, F. 1931. "Buddhist Training As Artificial Catatonia." *Psychoanalyt. Review* 18:129.

Allegro, J. M. 1970. *The Sacred Mushroom and the Cross: A Study of the Nature and Origin of Christianity within the Fertility Cults of the Ancient Near East.* New York: Doubleday.

Asch, S. 1967. *The Nazarene.* New York: Carroll and Graf.

Assagioli, R. 1976. *Psychosynthesis.* New York: Penguin Books.

Atwater, P.M.H. 1988. *Coming Back to Life—the After-Effects of the Near Death Experience.* New York: Ballantine Books.

Bache, C. 1985. "A Reappraisal of Teresa of Avila's Supposed Hysteria." *Journal of Religion and Health* 24:21.

Bache, C. 1991a. "Mysticism and Psychedelics: The Case of the Dark Night." *Journal of Religion and Health* 30: 215.

Bache, C. 1991b. *Lifecycles: Reincarnation and the Web of Life.* New York: Paragon Press.

Bache, C. 1996. "Expanding Grof's Conception of the Perinatal: Deepening the Inquiry into Frightening Near-Death Experiences." *Journal of Near-Death Studies* 15:115.

Bache, C. 2000. *Dark Night, Early Dawn: Steps to A Deep Ecology of Mind.* Albany, New York: State University of New York Press.

Barrett, W. 1926. *Death-Bed Visions.* London: Methuen.

Bateson, G. 1972. *Steps to An Ecology of Mind.* San Francisco, California: Chandler Publications.

Becker, E. 1973. *The Denial of Death: A Perspective in Psychiatry and Anthropology.* New York: The Free Press.

Bell, J. 1966. "On the Problem of Hidden Variables in Quantum Physics." *Review of Modern Physics* 38:447.

Benson, H., Lehmann, J. W., Malhotra, M. S., Goldman, R.F., Hopkins, J., Epstein, M.D. 1982. "Body Temperature Changes During the Practice of g Tummo Yoga." *Nature* 295:232.

Bonny, H., and Pahnke, W. N. 1972. "The Use of Music in Psychedelic (LSD) Psychotherapy." *J. Music Therapy* 9: 64.

Bottome, P. 1939. *Alfred Adler: A Biography.* New York: Putnam Press.

Bozzano, E. 1948. *Dei Fenomeni di Telekinesia in Rapporto con Eventi di Morti* (Phenomena of Telekinesis Related to Events Involving the Dead). Verona: Casa Editrice Europa.

Brinkley, D., Perry, P. and Moody, R. 1995. *Saved by Light: The True Story of a Man Who Died Twice and the Profound Revelations He Received.* New York: HarperCollins Publishers.

Brun, A. 1953. "Über Freuds Hypothese vom Todestrieb" (Apropos of Freud's Theory of the Death Instinct). *Psyche* 17:81.

Campbell, J. 1968. *The Hero with a Thousand Faces.* Princeton, New Jersey: Princeton University Press.

Capra, F. 1982. *The Turning Point.* New York: Simon & Schuster.

Cicero, M. T. 1977. *De Legibus Libri Tres.* New York: Georg Olms Publishers.

Clarke, E. H. 1878. *Visions: A Study of False Sight.* Boston, Massachusetts: Houghton, Osgood & Co.

Cobbe, F. P. 1877. "The Peak in Darien: The Riddle of Death." *Littell's Living Age* and *New Quarterly Review* 134:374.

Coe, M. D. 1978. *Lords of the Underworld: Masterpieces of Classic Maya Ceramics.* Princeton, New Jersey: Princeton University Press.

Cohen, M. M., Marinello, M. J. and Back, N. 1967. "Chromosomal Damage in Human Leucocytes Induced by Lysergic Acid Diethylamide." *Science* 155:1417.

Cohen, S. 1965. "LSD and the Anguish of Dying." *Harper's Magazine* 231: 69, 77.

Corbin, H. 2000. "Mundus Imaginalis, Or the Imaginary and the Imaginal." In: *Working With Images* (B. Sells, ed.). Woodstock, Connecticut: Spring Publications 71-89.

Dabrowski, K. 1966. *Positive Disintegration.* Boston: Little, Brown.

Delacour, J. B. 1974. *Glimpses of the Beyond.* New York: Delacorte Press.

Eliade, M. 1958. *Rites and Symbols of Initiation: The Mysteries of Death and Rebirth.* New York: Harper & Row, Publishers.

Eliade, M. 1964. "Shamanism: Archaic Techniques of Ecstasy." *Bollingen Series*, vol. 76. New York: Pantheon Books.

Evans-Wentz, W. E. 1957. *The Tibetan Book of the Dead.* London: Oxford University Press.

Feifel, H. (ed.) 1959. *The Meaning of Death.* New York: McGraw-Hill.

Fenichel, O. 1945. *The Psychoanalytic Theory of Neurosis*. New York: W. W. Norton.

Fenwick, P. and Fenwick, E. 1995. Interview in *The Daily Mail.* London, March 2, p. 47.

Ferenczi, S. 1968. *Thalassa: A Theory of Genitality.* New York: W. W. Norton.

Fisher, G. 1970. "Psychotherapy for the Dying: Principles and Illustrative Cases with Special Reference to the Use of LSD." *Omega* 1:3.

Foerster, H. von. 1965. "Memory Without A Record." In: *The Anatomy of Memory* (D. P. Kimble, ed.). Palo Alto: Science and Behavior Books.

Freud, S. 1925a. "The Theme of the Three Caskets." In: *Collected Papers 4.* London: Hogarth Press.

Freud, S. 1925b. "Thoughts for the Times on War and Death." In: *Collected Papers 4.* London: Hogarth Press.

Freud, S. 1949. *An Outline of Psychoanalysis*. New York: W. W. Norton.

Freud, S. 1975. *Beyond the Pleasure Principle.* (J. Strachey. ed. and transl.). New York: W. W. Norton.

Friend, T. 2003. "Jumpers: The fatal grandeur of the Golden Gate Bridge." *New Yorker*, October 13.

Fromm, E. 1973. *Anatomy of Human Destructiveness.* New York: Holt, Rinehart, Winston.

Garfield, A. 1974. "Psychothanatological Concomitants of Altered State Experiences: An Investigation of the Relationship between Consciousness Alteration and Fear of Death." Ph.D. Dissertation, University of California.

Gennep, A. van. 1960: *The Rites of Passage.* Chicago, Illinois: The University of Chicago Press.

Grey, M. 1985. *Return from Death: An Exploration of the Near-Death Experience.* London: Arkana.

Greyson, B. and Bush, N.E. 1992. "Distressing Near-Death Experiences." *Psychiatry* 55:95.

Grof, C. and Grof S. 1990. *The Stormy Search for the Self.* Los Angeles: J. P. Tarcher.

Grof, S. 1975. *Realms of the Human Unconscious: Observations from LSD Research.* New York: Viking Press.

Grof, S., 1985. *Beyond the Brain: Birth, Death, and Transcendence in Psychotherapy.* Albany, New York: State University of New York (SUNY) Press.

Grof, S. 1988. *The Adventure of Self-Discovery.* Albany, New York: State University of New York (SUNY) Press.

Grof, S. 1992. *The Holotropic Mind.* San Francisco, California: Harper Collins Publishers.

Grof, S. 1994. *Books of the Dead.* London: Thames and Hudson.

Grof, S. 1998. *The Cosmic Game: Explorations of the Frontiers of Human Consciousness.* Albany, New York: State University of New York (SUNY) Press.

Grof, S. 2000. *Psychology of the Future: Lessons from Modern Consciousness Research.* Albany, New York: State University of New York (SUNY) Press.

Grof, S. 2001. *LSD Psychotherapy.* Sarasota, Florida: MAPS Publications.

Grof, S. 2005. "Ervin Laszlo's Akashic Field and the Dilemmas of Modern Consciousness Research." World Futures: *The Journal of General Evolution*, Special issue: "Explorations in the Akashic Field" (Alfonso Montuori, guest editor). London and Budapest: Taylor & Francis.

Grof, S. and Grof, C. 1980. *Beyond Death.* London: Thames and Hudson.

Grof, S. and Grof, C. (eds.) 1989. *Spiritual Emergency: When Personal Transformation Becomes a Crisis.* Los Angeles, California: J. P. Tarcher.

Grof, S., and Halifax, J. 1977. *The Human Encounter with Death.* New York: E. P. Dutton.

Grof, S., Pahnke, W. N. Kurland, A. A., and Goodman, L. E. 1971. "LSD-Assisted Psychotherapy in Patients with Terminal Cancer." A presentation at the Fifth Symposium of the Foundation of Thanatology, New York City, November.

Grosso, M. 1981. "The Status of Survival Research: Evidence, Problems, Paradigms." A paper presented at the Institute of Noetic Sciences Symposium entitled "The Survival of Consciousness After Death," Chicago, Illinois.

Group for the Advancement of Psychiatry, Committee on Psychiatry and Religion. 1976. "Mysticism: Spiritual Quest or Psychic Disorder?" Washington, D.C.

Harrington, A. 1969. *The Immortalist.* Milbrae, California: Celestial Arts.

Hart, H. 1959. *The Enigma of Survival.* Springfield, Illinois: Charles Thomas.

Heidegger, M. 1927. *Sein und Zeit.* Halle: Max Niemage.

Heim, A. 1892. "Notizen über den Tod durch Absturz" (Remarks on Fatal Falls). *Jahrbuch des Schweizer Alpenklub* 27:327.

Hillman, J. 1977. *Re-Visioning Psychology.* New York: Harper & Row, Publishers.

Hunter, R. A. 1967. "On the Experience of Nearly Dying." *Amer. J. Psychiat.* 124: 84.

Huxley, A. 1945. *Perennial Philosophy.* New York and London: Harper and Brothers.

Huxley, A. 1959. *The Doors of Perception and Heaven and Hell.* Harmondsworth, Middlesex, Great Britain: Penguin Books.

Huxley, A. 1963. *Island.* New York: Bantam.

Huxley, A. 1968. *Brave New World.* Bantam Modern Classic. New York: Harper & Row, Publishers.

Huxley, L. A. 1968. *This Timeless Moment.* New York: Farrar, Straus & Giroux.

Hyslop, J. H. 1908. *Psychical Research and the Resurrection.* Boston, Massachusetts: Small, Maynard, & Co.

Irwin, H. J., and Bramwell, B. A. 1988. "The Devil in Heaven: A Near-Death Experience with Both Positive and Negative Facets." *Journal of Near-Death Studies,* 7:38.

James, W. 1929. *The Varieties of Religious Experience.* New York: Longmans, Green and Company.

Journal of the American Medical Association. 2004. Review of Ian Stevenson's "European Cases of the Reincarnation Type." 291: 628-629.

Jung, C. G. 1953. "Two Essays on Analytical Psychology." *Collected Works of C.G. Jung.* Vol. 7, Bollingen Series XX. Princeton, New Jersey: Princeton University Press.

Jung, C. G. 1956. "Symbols of Transformation." *Collected Works of C.G. Jung.* Vol. 5, Bollingen Series XX, Princeton, New Jersey: Princeton University Press.

Jung, C. G. 1959. "The Archetypes and the Collective Unconscious." *Collected Works of C.G. Jung.* Vol. 9, Bollingen Series XX, Princeton, New Jersey: Princeton University Press.

Jung, C. G. 1960. "A Review of the Complex Theory." *Collected Works of C.G. Jung.* Vol. 8, Bollingen Series XX. Princeton, New Jersey: Princeton University Press.

Jung, C. G. 1961. *Memories, Dreams, Reflections.* New York: Pantheon.

Jung, C. G. 1967. "Alchemical Studies." *Collected Works of C.G. Jung.* Vol. 13, Bollingen Series XX, Princeton, New Jersey: Princeton University Press.

Jung, C.G. 1970a. "The Structure and Dynamics of the Psyche." *Collected Works of C.G. Jung.* Vol. 8, Bollingen Series XX, Princeton, New Jersey: Princeton University Press.

Jung, C.G. 1970b. "Civilization in Transition." *Collected Works of C.G. Jung.* Vol. 10, Bollingen Series XX, Princeton, New Jersey: Princeton University Press.

Jung, C.J. 1976. "The Symbolic Life, Tavistock Lectures: On the Theory and Practice of Analytical Psychology." *Collected Works of C. G. Jung*. Vol. 18, Bollingen Series XX, Princeton, New Jersey: Princeton University Press.

Kast, E. C. 1963. "The Analgesic Action of Lysergic Acid Compared with Dihydromorphinone and Meperidine." *Bull. Drug Addiction Narcotics,* App. 27:3517.

Kast, E. C. 1964. "Pain and LSD-25: A Theory of Attenuation of Anticipation." In: *LSD-25: The Consciousness-Expanding Drug.* (D. Solomon, ed.) New York: Putnam Press.

Kast, E. C. and Collins, V. J. 1964. "A Study of Lysergic Acid Diethylamide As An Analgesic Agent." *Anaesth. Analg. Curr. Res.* 43:285.

Kast, E. C. and Collins, V. J. 1966. "LSD and the Dying Patient." *Chicago Med. School Quarterly* 26:80.

Knowlson, J. 2004. *Damned to Fame: The Life of Samuel Beckett.* New York: Grove Press.

Korzybski, A. 1933. *Science and Sanity: An Introduction to Non-Aristotelian Systems and General Semantics.* Lakeville, Connecticut: The International Non-Aristotelian Library Publishing Company.

Kübler-Ross, E. 1969. *On Death and Dying.* London: Collier-Macmillan Ltd.

Kurland, A. A., Pahnke, W. N., Unger, S., Savage, C., and Goodman, L. E. 1968. "Psychedelic Psychotherapy (LSD) in the Treatment of the Patient with A Malignancy." *Excerpta Medica International Congress Series No. 180.* (The Present Status of Psychotropic Drugs 180). Proceedings of the Sixth International Congress of the CINP in Tarragona, Spain, April.

Laszlo, E. 1994. *The Creative Cosmos.* Edinburgh: Floris Books.

Laszlo, E. 2003. *The Connectivity Hypothesis: Foundations of an Integral Science of Quantum, Cosmos, Life, and Consciousness.* Albany, New York: State University of New York (SUNY) Press.

Laszlo, E. 2004. *Science and the Akashic Field: An Integral Theory of Everything.* Rochester, Vermont: Inner Traditions.

Leary, T., Alpert, R. and Metzner, R. 1964. *Psychedelic Experience: A Manual Based on the Tibetan Book of the Dead.* New Hyde Park, New York: University Books.

Leuner, H. 1962. *Experimentelle Psychose: Ihre Psychopharmakologie, Phänomenlogie und Dynamik in Beziehung zur Person.* Berlin: Springer Verlag.

Macy, M. 2005. "The Miraculous Side of Instrumental Transcommunication." A lecture at the Seventh International Conference on Science and Consciousness in La Fonda Hotel, Santa Fe, New Mexico.

Mahdi, L.C., Christopher, N.G., Meade, M. (eds.). 1996. *Crossroads: The Quest for Contemporary Rites of Passage.* Chicago, Illinois: Open Court.

Mahdi, L. C., Foster, S. and Little, M. (eds.) 1987. *Betwixt and Between: Patterns of Masculine and Feminine Initiation.* Chicago, Illinois: Open Court.

Maslow, A. 1964. *Religions, Values, and Peak Experiences.* Columbus, Ohio: Ohio State University Press.

Masters, R.E.L. and Houston, J. 1966. *The Varieties of Psychedelic Experience.* New York: Dell Publishing Company.

Matus, Father Thomas. 1984. *Yoga and the Jesus Prayer Tradition: An Experiment in Faith.* Ramsey: Paulist Press.

Mead, M. 1973. "Ritual and the Conscious Creation of New Rituals." Prefatory statement prepared for the participants of the Fifty-Ninth Burg Wartenstein Symposium on Ritual: Reconciliation in Change, sponsored by the Wenner-Gren Foundation. Gloggnitz, Austria.

Meher Baba, 1966. *God In A Pill?* Walnut Creek, California: Sufism Reoriented, Inc.

Melzack, R. 1973. *The Puzzle of Pain.* New York: Basic Books.

Melzack, R., and Wall, P. D. 1965. "Pain Mechanisms: A New Theory." *Science* 150: 971.

Merkur, D. 2000. *The Mystery of Manna: The Psychedelic Sacrament of the Bible.* Rochester, Vermont: Park Street Press.

Monroe, R. A. 1971. *Journeys Out of the Body.* New York: Doubleday and Co.

Monroe, R. A. 1985. *Far Journeys.* New York: Doubleday and Co.

Monroe, R. A. 1994. *Ultimate Journey.* New York: Doubleday and Co.

Moody, R. A. 1975. *Life After Life: The Investigation of a Phenomenon—Survival of Bodily Death.* Atlanta, Georgia: Mockingbird Books.

Moody, R. A. 1977. *Reflections on Life After Life: More Important Discoveries in the Ongoing Investigation of Survival of Life After Bodily Death.* New York: Bantam Books.

Moody, R. A. 1993. *Reunions: Visionary Encounters with Departed Loved Ones.* New York: Villard Books.

Mookerjee, A. and Khanna, M. 1977. *The Tantric Way.* London: Thames and Hudson.

Morse, M. 1992. *Transformed by the Light.* New York: Piatkus.

Munk, W. 1887. *Euthanasia or Medical Treatment in Aid of an Easy Death.* New York: Longmans, Green & Co.

Nandor, F. 1949. *The Search for the Beloved: A Clinical Investigation of the Trauma of Birth and Prenatal Condition.* New Hyde Park, New York: University Books.

Noyes, R. 1971. "Dying and Mystical Consciousness." *J. Thanatol.* 1: 25.

Noyes, R. 1972. "The Experience of Dying." *Psychiatry* 35:174.

Noyes, R. and Kletti, R. 1972. "The Experience of Dying from Falls." *Omega* 3:45.

Origenes Adamantius (Father Origen) 1973. *De Principiis* (On First Principles). (G. T. Butterworth, transl.). Gloucester, Massachusetts: Peter Smith.

Osis, K. 1961. *Deathbed Observations of Physicians and Nurses.* New York: Parapsychology Foundation.

Osis, K. and McCormick, D. 1980. "Kinetic Effects at the Ostensible Location of an Out-of-Body Projection During Perceptual Testing." *Journal of the American Society for Psychical Research.* 74:319.

Pahnke, W. N. 1963. "Drugs and Mysticism: An Analysis of the Relationship Between Psychedelic Drugs and the Mystical Consciousness." Ph. D. Dissertation, Harvard University.

Pahnke, W. N. 1966. "Report on a Pilot Project Investigating the Pharmacological Effects of Psilocybin in Normal Volunteers." Massachusetts Mental Health Center. Unpublished manuscript.

Pahnke, W. N. 1969. "The Psychedelic Mystical Experience in the Human Encounter with Death." An Ingersoll Lecture. *Harvard Theol. Rev.* 62. I.

Pahnke, W. N., Kurland, A. A., Richards, W. E., and Goodman, L. E. 1969. "LSD-Assisted Psychotherapy with Terminal Cancer Patients." In: *Psychedelic Drugs.* (R. E. Hicks and P. J. Fink, eds). New York: Grune and Stratton.

Pahnke, W. N., Kurland, A. A., Unger, S., Savage, C, and Grof, S. 1970a. "The Experimental Use of Psychedelic (LSD) Psychotherapy." *Journal of the American Medical Association* 212: 1856.

Pahnke, W. N, Kurland, A. A., Unger, S., Savage, C, Wolf, S., and Goodman, L. E. 1970b. "Psychedelic Therapy (Utilizing LSD) with Terminal Cancer Patients." *J. Psychedelic Drugs* 3: 63.

Pahnke, W. N. and Richards, W. E. 1966. "Implications of LSD and Experimental Mysticism." *Journal of Religion and Health.* 5:175.

Peerbolte, L. 1975. "Prenatal Dynamics." In: *Psychic Energy.* Amsterdam, Holland: Servire Publications.

Perry, J. 1974. *The Far Side of Madness.* Englewood Cliffs, New Jersey: Prentice Hall.

Perry, J. 1976. *Roots of Renewal in Myth and Madness.* San Francisco, California: Jossey-Bass Publications.

Pfister, O. 1930. "Schockdenken und Schockphantasien bei höchster Todesgefahr." *Ztschr. für Psychoanalyse* 16:430.

Plato 1961a. "Phaedrus." In: *The Collected Dialogues of Plato.* Bollingen Series LXXI. Princeton, New Jersey: Princeton University Press.

Plato 1961b. "Republic." In: *The Collected Dialogues of Plato.* Bollingen Series LXXI. Princeton, New Jersey: Princeton University Press.

Plato 1961c. "Laws." In: *The Collected Dialogues of Plato.* Bollingen Series LXXI. Princeton, New Jersey: Princeton University Press.

Popov, A. A. 1936. "Tavgijcy: Materialy po etnografii avamskich i vedeevskich tavgijcev." Moscow and Leningrad: *Trudy instituta antropologii i etnografii*, I:5.

Rank, O. 1929. *The Trauma of Birth.* New York: Harcourt Brace.

Raudive, K. 1971. *Breakthrough.* New York: Lancer Books.

Reich, W. 1949. *Character Analysis.* New York: Noonday Press.

Reich, W. 1961. *The Function of the Orgasm: Sex-Economic Problems of Biological Energy.* New York: Farrar, Strauss & Giroux.

Reich, W. 1970. *The Mass Psychology of Fascism.* New York: Simon & Schuster.

Richards, W. A. 1975. "Counseling, Peak Experiences, and the Human Encounter with Death: An Empirical Study of the Efficacy of DPT-Assisted Counseling in Enhancing the Quality of Life of Persons with Terminal Cancer and Their Closest Family Members." Ph.D. Dissertation, School of Education, Catholic University of America, Washington, D.C.

Richards, W. A., Grof, S., Goodman, L. E. and Kurland, A. A. 1972. "LSD-Assisted Psychotherapy and the Human Encounter with Death." *J. Transpersonal Psychol.* 4:121.

Riedlinger, T. 1982. "Sartre's Rite of Passage." *Journal of Transpersonal Psychol.* 14: 105.

Ring, K. 1982. *Life at Death: A Scientific Investigation of the Near-Death Experience.* New York: Quill.

Ring, K. 1984. *Heading Toward Omega: In Search of the Meaning of the Near-Death Experience.* New York: Morrow.

Ring, K. 1994. "Solving the Riddle of Frightening Near-Death Experiences: Some Testable Hypotheses and a Perspective Based on a Course In Miracles." *Journal of Near-Death Studies* 13:1.

Ring, K. and Cooper, S. 1999. *Mindsight: Near-Death and Out-of-Body Experiences in the Blind.* Palo Alto, California: William James Center for Consciousness Studies.

Ring, K. and Valarino, E. E. 1998. *Lessons from the Light: What We Can Learn from the Near-Death Experience.* New York: Plenum Press.

Robicsek, F. 1981. *The Maya Book of the Dead: The Ceramic Codex.* Charlottesville, Virginia: University of Virginia Art Museum.

Roll, W. 1974. "A New Look at the Survival Problem." In: *New Directions in Parapsychology* (J. Beloff, ed.). Lanham, Maryland: The Scarecrow Press.

Rommer, B. 2000. *Blessing in Disguise: Another Side of the Near-Death Experience.* St. Paul, Minnesota: Llewellyn Publishers.

Rosen, D. 1975. "Suicide Survivors; A Follow-Up Study of Persons Who Survived Jumping from the Golden Gate and San Francisco-Oakland Bay Bridges." *West. J. Med.* 122: 289.

Sabom, M. 1982. *Recollections of Death: A Medical Investigation.* New York: Harper & Row, Publishers.

Sabom, M. 1998. *Light and Death: One Doctor's Fascinating Accounts of Near-Death Experiences.* Grand Rapids, Michigan: Zondervan, Church Source.

Saunders, C. 1967. *The Management of Terminal Illness.* London: Hospital Medicine Publications.

Saunders, C. 1973. "The Need for In-Patient Care for the Patient with Terminal Cancer." *Middlesex Hospital Journal* 72:3.

Schultes, R. E. and Hofmann, A. 1979. *Plants of the Gods: Origin of Hallucinogenic Use.* New York: McGraw Hill Book Company.

Senkowski, E. 1994. "Instrumental Transcommunication (ITC)." An Institute for Noetic Sciences lecture at the Corte Madera Inn, Corte Madera, California, July.

Sheldrake, R. 1981. *A New Science of Life: The Hypothesis of Formative Causation.* Los Angeles, California: J. P. Tarcher.

Sheldrake 1990. "Can Our Memories Survive the Death of Our Brains?" In: *What Survives? Contemporary Explorations of Life After Death.* (G. Doore, ed.) Los Angeles, California: J. P. Tarcher.

Sidgewick, H. et al. 1894. "Report on the Census of Hallucinations." *Proceedings of the Society for Psychical Research,* 34:25.

Silverman, J. 1967. "Shamans and Acute Schizophrenia." *Amer. Anthropologist* 69:21.

Silverman, J. 1970. "Acute Schizophrenia: Disease or Dis-Ease?" *Psychology Today 4:62.*

Simonton, C. O. 1974. "The Role of the Mind in Cancer Therapy." Lecture at the symposium entitled The Dimensions of Healing at the UCLA, October.

Simonton, C. O., Creighton, J., and Simonton, S. M. 1978. *Getting Well Again.* Los Angeles, California: J. P. Tarcher.

Simonton, C. O., and Simonton, S. M. 1974. "Belief Systems and Management of the Emotional Aspects of Malignancy." *J. Transpersonal Psychol.* 1: 29.

Stace, W. T. 1960. *Mysticism and Philosophy.* Philadelphia and New York: J. P. Lippincott.

Stevenson, I. 1966. *Twenty Cases Suggestive of Reincarnation.* Charlottesville, Virginia: University of Virginia Press.

Stevenson, I. 1977. "The Explanatory Value of the Idea of Reincarnation." *Journal of Nervous and Mental Diseases.* 164:5.

Stevenson, I. 1984. *Unlearned Languages.* Charlottesville, Virginia: University of Virginia Press.

Stevenson, I. 1987. *Children Who Remember Previous Lives.* Charlottesville, Virginia: University of Virginia Press.

Stevenson, I. 1997. *Reincarnation and Biology: A Contribution to the Etiology of Birthmarks and Birth Defects.* Westport, Connecticut: Praeger.

Sutherland, C. 1992. *Transformed by the Light.* Sydney: Bantam Books.

Talbot, M. 1991. *The Holographic Universe.* New York: HarperCollins Publishers.

Tarnas, R. 2006. *Cosmos and Psyche: Intimations of a New World View.* New York: Viking Press.

Tart, C. 1968. "A Psychophysiological Study of Out-of-Body Phenomena." *Journal of the Society for Psychical Research* 62:3.

Turner, V. W. 1969. *The Ritual Process: Structure and Anti-Structure.* Chicago, Illinois: Aldine Publishing Co.

Turner, V. W. 1974. *Dramas, Fields and Metaphors; Symbolic Action in Human Society.* Ithaca, New York: Cornell University Press.

Ulansey, D. 1989. *Origins of the Mithraic Mysteries: Cosmology and Salvation in the Ancient World.* Oxford: Oxford University Press.

Vondrá□ek, V. and Holub, F. 1993. *Fantastické a magické z hlediska psychiatrie* (The Fantastic and the Magical from the Point of View of Psychiatry). Bratislava: Columbus.

Wambach, H. 1979. *Life Before Life.* New York: Bantam.

Wang, S. 1979. *The Multiple Planes of the Cosmos and Life.* Taipei, Taiwan: Society for Psychic Studies.

Wasson, G., Hofmann, A., and Ruck, C. A. P. 1978. *The Road to Eleusis: Unveiling the Secret of the Mysteries.* New York: Harcourt, Brace Jovanovich.

Wasson, G. and Wasson, V.P. 1957. *Mushrooms, Russia, and History.* New York: Pantheon Books.

Wasson, V. P. 1957. An interview in *This Week*, Baltimore, May 19.

Watts, A. 1961. *Psychotherapy East and West.* New York: Random House.

Weisse, J. E. 1972. *The Vestibule.* Port Washington, New York: Ashley Books.

Whinnery, J. E. 1997. "Psychophysiological Correlates of Unconsciousness and Near-Death Experiences." *Journal of Near-Death Studies* Vol. 15, 4.

Wilber, K. 1980. *The Atman Project: A Transpersonal View of Human Development.* Wheaton, Illinois: The Theosophical Publishing House.

Wilber, K. 1982. *A Sociable God.* New York: McGraw-Hill.

Wunderlich, H. G. 1972. *The Secret of Crete.* New York: Macmillan.

Zaehner, R. C. 1957. *Mysticism Sacred and Profane.* Oxford: The Clarendon Press.

Zaehner, R. C. 1972. *Zen, Drugs, and Mysticism.* New York: Pantheon.

Sources of Illustrations

Black and white plates

i. Source unknown
ii. Both images from *The Road to Eleusis,* by R. G. Wasson, C. A. Ruck, and A. Hofmann, Hermes Press, Los Angeles, 1998 (first edition 1978), courtesy of Robert Forte.
iii. (top) From *Plants of the Gods,* by S. R. Schultes and A. Hofmann, McGraw Hill, New York, p. 216, 1979, © Biblioteca Nationale, Florence. (bottom) Trustees of the British Museum.
iv. Source unknown.
v. Both images from *The Maya Book of the Dead: The Ceramic Codex* by Francis Robicsek, University of Virginia Art Museum, Charlottesville, VA, 1981. (top) Metropolitan Museum of Art, NY. (bottom) Francis Robicsek.
vi. (top) From *The Maya Book of the Dead: The Ceramic Codex* by Francis Robicsek, University of Virginia Art Museum, Charlottesville, VA. 1981, © Museum of Fine Arts, Boston. (bottom) Peter Furst.
vii. Bridgeman-Giraudon/Art Resource, NY.
viii. From *The Tibetan Book of the Dead* by W. Y. Evans-Wentz, Oxford University Press, NY, 1960, p. 167.
ix. From *The Sacred Art of Tibet,* by the Tibetan Nyingmapa Meditation Center and T. Tarthang, Dharma Press, Berkeley, 1970.
x. Snark/Art Resource, NY.
xi. From *Books of the Dead,* by Stanislav Grof, Thames and Hudson, London, 1994.
xii. Both images courtesy of Robert Forte.
xiii. (top) Author's collection. (bottom) Courtesy of Laura Huxley.
xiv. (top) Courtesy of Albert Hofmann. (bottom) Author's collection.
xv. Author's collection.
xvi. Author's collection.

Color plates

I. Author's collection (both images).
II. Smithsonian American Art Museum/Art Resource NY (both images).
III. (top) Denver Art Museum. (bottom) Smithsonian American Art Museum/ Art Resource NY.
IV. From *Akademische Druck- und Verlagsanstalt,* Graz, Austria, 1976, p. 56, © Apostolic Library of the Vatican, Vatican City.
V. Trustees of the British Museum (both images).
VI. (top) Peter Furst. (bottom) Museo Nacional de Antropología, Mexico City.
VII. From *Plants of the Gods,* by S. R. Schultes and A. Hofmann, McGraw Hill, New York, p. 216, 1979, © Museo Nacional de Antropología, Mexico City.

VIII. Trustees of the British Museum (both images).
IX. Trustees of the British Museum (both images).
X. From *Books of the Dead,* by Stanislav Grof, Thames and Hudson, London, 1994, © Hirmers Photoarchiv Munich.
XI. (top) From *Books of the Dead,* by Stanislav Grof, Thames and Hudson, London, 1994, © Kodansha, Ltd., Tokyo. (bottom) Source unknown.
XII. Source unknown (both images).
XIII. (left) From *Art of Tibet* by Pratapaditya Pal, Los Angeles County Museum of Art, Los Angeles, 1983, © Los Angeles County Museum of Art, Los Angeles. (right) From *Wisdom and Compassion* by M. M. Rie and R. A. F. Thurman, Asian Art Museum and Tibet House, New York, H. Abrams, New York, fig. 23, p. 57, © John Bigelow Taylor.
XIV. From *Wisdom and Compassion* by M. M. Rie and R. A. F. Thurman, Asian Art Museum and Tibet House, New York, H. Abrams, New York, fig. 49, p. 176, © Edwin Bernbaum.
XV. From *Books of the Dead,* by Stanislav Grof, Thames and Hudson, London, 1994, © Los Angeles County Museum of Art, Los Angeles.
XVI. Newark Museum/Art Resource, NY.
XVII. From *Tibetan Sacred Art* by Ingo Detlef Laub, Shambhala, Berkeley, CA, 1976, p. 127.
XVIII. Alinari/Art Resource, NY.
XIX. Museo del Prado, Madrid.
XX. Scala/Art Resource, NY.
XXI. Scala/Art Resource, NY.
XXII. Author's collection (all).
XXIII. Author's collection (all).
XIV. Both images courtesy of Robert Forte.

Illustrations within the text

10. Source unknown.
28. Source unknown.
42. Source unknown.
96. From *The Smoking Gods: Tobacco in Maya Art, History, and Religion* by Francis Robicsek, University of Oklahoma Press, Norman, Oklahoma, 1978, fig. 167.
102. From *The Blood of Kings* by Linda Schele and Mary Ellen Miller, George Braziller, New York, 1986.
109, 110, 112, 114, 116 From *Devils, Demons, and Witchcraft: 244 Illustrations for Artists,* by Ernst Lehner and Johanna Lehner, Dover Publications, New York City, 1971. fig. 134–137.
117. Source unknown.

INDEX

E

F

G

H

About the Publisher:
The Multidisciplinary Association for Psychedelic Studies (MAPS)

FOUNDED IN 1986, the Multidisciplinary Association for Psychedelic Studies (MAPS) is a membership-based, IRS-approved 501 (c) (3) nonprofit research and educational organization. Please visit our website: www.maps.org

MAPS' mission is 1) to treat conditions for which conventional medicines provide limited relief—such as posttraumatic stress disorder (PTSD), pain, drug dependence, anxiety and depression associated with end-of-life issues—by developing psychedelics and marijuana into prescription medicines; 2) to cure many thousands of people by building a network of clinics where treatments can be provided; and 3) to educate the public honestly about the risks and benefits of psychedelics and marijuana.

For decades, the government was the biggest obstacle to research. Now that long-awaited research is being approved and conducted, the formidable challenge is funding it. At the time of this publication, there is no funding available from governments, pharmaceutical companies, or major foundations. That means, for the time being, the future of psychedelic and marijuana research rests in the hands of people like you.

Can you imagine a cultural reintegration of the use of psychedelics and the states of mind they engender? Please join MAPS in supporting the expansion of scientific knowledge in this promising area. Progress is only possible with the support of individuals who care enough to take individual and collective action.

Since 1986, MAPS has managed and distributed over 10 million dollars to worthy research and educational projects.

How MAPS Has Made a Difference

- SPONSORED and obtained approval for the first LSD-assisted psychotherapy study since 1972. At the time of this publication, the study is taking place in Switzerland in subjects with anxiety associated with end-of-life issues.
- SPONSORED the first U.S. study evaluating MDMA's therapeutic applications for subjects with chronic posttraumatic stress disorder (PTSD), as well as MDMA/PTSD pilot studies in Switzerland, Israel, Canada, and Spain. The ultimate goal is to develop MDMA into an FDA-approved prescription medicine.
- WAGED a successful lawsuit against the U.S. Drug Enforcement Administration in support of Professor Lyle Craker's proposed MAPS-sponsored medical marijuana production facility at the University of Massachusetts-Amherst; led campaigns to gain support from over 50 members of the U.S. House of Representatives. The Administrative Law Judge, Mary Ellen Bittner, who heard the

case wrote a recommended ruling that Professor Craker be given a license to grow marijuana for research and that the U.S. government should not have a monopoly on the supply of marijuana for research. Despite the judge's recommended ruling, at the time of this publication the lawsuit is being held-up in an appeal process.

- SUPPORTED long-term follow-up studies of pioneering research with LSD and psilocybin from the 1950s and 1960s.
- SPONSORED Dr. Evgeny Krupitsky's pioneering research into the use of ketamine-assisted psychotherapy in the treatment of alcoholism and heroin addiction.
- ASSISTED Dr. Charles Grob to obtain permission for the first human studies in the United States with MDMA after it was criminalized in 1985.
- SPONSORED the first study to analyze the purity and potency of street samples of "Ecstasy" and medical marijuana.
- FUNDED the successful effort of Dr. Donald Abrams to obtain permission for the first human study into the therapeutic use of marijuana in 15 years, and to secure a $1-million grant from the U.S. National Institute on Drug Abuse.
- OBTAINED orphan-drug designation from the FDA for smoked marijuana in the treatment of AIDS Wasting Syndrome.
- FUNDED the synthesis of psilocybin for the first clinical trial under U.S. FDA regulations in a patient population in twenty-five years.
- SPONSORED "Psychedelic Harm Reduction" programs and services at events, concerts, schools, and churches.

Benefits of MAPS Membership

AS A MAPS MEMBER, you'll receive the tri-annual MAPS Bulletin. In addition to reporting on the latest research in both the United States and abroad, the Bulletin includes feature articles, personal accounts, book reviews, and reports on conferences and allied organizations. MAPS members are invited to participate in a vital on-line mailing list and to visit our website, which includes all articles published by MAPS since 1988.

Unless otherwise indicated, your donation will be considered an unrestricted gift to be used to fund high-priority projects. If you wish, however, you may direct contributions to a specific study. Your tax-deductible donations may be made by credit card or check made out to MAPS. Gifts of stock are welcome, as are trust and estate planning options.

The MAPS list is strictly confidential and not available for purchase. The MAPS Bulletin is mailed in a plain envelope. A minimum donation of $20 is needed to receive the MAPS Bulletin. Overseas postage fees are also required.

MAPS
309 Cedar Street #2323, Santa Cruz CA 95060
voice: 831-429-MDMA (6362) • fax: 831-429-6370
e-mail: askmaps@maps.org
Please visit our website: www.maps.org

Other books published by MAPS

LSD Psychotherapy by Stanislav Grof, M.D. (4th Edition, Paperback)
ISBN: 0-9798622-0-5 $19.95

LSD Psychotherapy is a complete study of the use of LSD in clinical therapeutic practice, written by the world's foremost LSD psychotherapist. This text was written as a medical manual and as a historical record portraying a broad therapeutic vision. It is a valuable source of information for anyone wishing to learn more about LSD. The therapeutic model is applicable to other substances, as well; the research team for the MAPS-funded MDMA/PTSD study used *LSD Psychotherapy* as a key reference. Originally published in 1980, this 2008 paperback edition has a new introduction by Albert Hofmann, Ph.D., a foreword by Andrew Weil M.D. and many color illustrations.

The Secret Chief Revealed by Myron Stolaroff
ISBN: 0-9669919-6-6 $12.95

The second edition of the original *The Secret Chief*, this is a collection of interviews with "Jacob," the underground psychedelic therapist who only now, years after his death, is revealed as psychologist Leo Zeff. Leo practiced psychedelic therapy with over 3,000 people before his death in 1988. As "Jacob," Leo relates what sparked his early interest in psychedelics, how he chose his clients, and what he did to prepare them. He discusses the dynamics of the "individual trip" and the "group trip," the characteristics and appropriate dosages of various drugs, and the range of problems that people worked through. Stanislav Grof, Ann and Alexander Shulgin, and Albert Hofmann contribute writings about the importance of Leo's work. In this new edition, Leo's family and former clients also write about their experiences with him. This book is an easy-to-read introduction to the technique and potential of psychedelic therapy.

DRAWING IT OUT BY SHERANA HARRIET FRANCIS

ISBN: 0-9669919-5-8 $19.95

Drawing It Out is artist Sherana Francis' fascinating exploration of her LSD psychotherapy experience, in a series of 61 black-and white illustrations, with accompanying text. The book documents the author's journey through a symbolic death and rebirth, with powerful surrealist self-portraits of her psyche undergoing transformation. Francis' images unearth universal experiences of facing the unconscious as they reflect her personal struggle towards healing. An 8.5 by 11" paperback with an introduction by Stan Grof, this makes an excellent coffee table book.

KETAMINE: DREAMS AND REALITIES BY KARL JANSEN, M.D., PH.D.

ISBN: 0-9660019-7-4 $14.95

London researcher Karl Jansen has studied ketamine at every level, from photographing the receptors to which ketamine binds in the human brain to observing the similarities between ketamine's psychoactive effects and near-death experiences. He writes about ketamine's potential as an adjunct to psychotherapy, as well as its addictive nature and methods of treating addiction. Dr. Karl Jansen is the world's foremost expert on ketamine, and this is a great resource for anyone who wishes to understand ketamine's effects, risks, and potential.

LSD: MY PROBLEM CHILD

BY ALBERT HOFMANN, PH.D. (4th English Edition, Paperback)

ISBN: 978-0-9798622-2-9 $15.95

This is the story of LSD told by a concerned yet hopeful father, organic chemist Albert Hofmann. He traces LSD's path from a promising psychiatric research medicine to a recreational drug sparking hysteria and prohibition.We follow Dr. Hofmann's trek across Mexico to discover sacred plants related to LSD and listen in as he corresponds with other notable figures about his remarkable discovery. Underlying it all is Dr. Hofmann's powerful conclusion that mystical experience may be our planet's best hope for survival. Whether induced by LSD, meditation, or arising spontaneously, such experiences help us to comprehend "the wonder, the mystery of the divine in the microcosm of the atom, in the macrocosm of the spiral nebula, in the seeds of plants, in the body and soul of people." More than sixty years after the birth of Albert Hofmann's problem child, his vision of its true potential is more relevant, and more needed, than ever. The fourth edition's foreword is the eulogy that Dr. Hofmann wrote himself and which was read by his children at his funeral.

Ayahuasca Religions: A Comprehensive Bibliography & Critical Essays
by Beatriz Caiuby Labate, Isabel Santana de Rose, and Rafael Guimarães dos Santos (translated by Matthew Meyer)
ISBN: 978-0-9798622-1-2 $11.95

The recent decades have seen a broad expansion of the ayahuasca religions, and it has also witnessed, especially since the millennium, an explosion of studies into the spiritual uses of ayahuasca. *Ayahuasca Religions* grew out of the need for an ordering of the profusion of titles related to this subject that are now appearing. This publication offers a map of the global production of literature on this theme. Three researchers located in different cities (Beatriz Caiuby Labate in São Paulo, Rafael Guimarães dos Santos in Barcelona, and Isabel Santana de Rose in Florianópolis, Brazil) worked in a virtual research group for a year to compile a list of bibliographical references on Santo Daime, Barquinha, UDV and urban ayahuasqueiros, including the specialized academic literature as well as esoteric and experiential writings produced by participants of these churches. Ayahuasca Religions presents the results of that collaboration.

Shipping and handling for any title:

Shipping varies by weight of books. Approximate costs for shipping one book are as follows:

Domestic priority mail (allow 4–7 days)...$5.00
Domestic media mail (allow 2–4 weeks)...$3.00
First-class international mail (allow 1–2 weeks)...$20.00

Bulk orders welcome, contact MAPS for details.

Order books published by MAPS via:

- Secure credit card transaction or PayPal at www.maps.org
- Call 831-429-MDMA (6362)
- Your favorite local bookstore
- Send orders to: MAPS, 309 Cedar Street #2323, Santa Cruz, CA, 95062

ABOUT THE AUTHOR

Stanislav Grof, M.D., is a psychiatrist with over fifty years of research experience in non-ordinary states of consciousness and one of the founders and chief theoreticians of transpersonal psychology. He was born in Prague, Czechoslovakia, where he also received his scientific training: an M.D. degree from the Charles University School of Medicine and a Ph.D. from the Czechoslovakian Academy of Sciences.

Dr. Grof's early research in the clinical uses of psychedelic substances was conducted at the Psychiatric Research Institute in Prague, where he was principal investigator of a program that systematically explored the heuristic and therapeutic potential of LSD and other psychedelic substances. In 1967 he was invited as Clinical and Research Fellow to the Johns Hopkins University in Baltimore, Maryland. After completing this two-year fellowship, he stayed in the United States and continued his research as Chief of Psychiatric Research at the Maryland Psychiatric Research Center and as Assistant Professor of Psychiatry at the Henry Phipps Clinic of Johns Hopkins University.

In 1973 Dr. Grof was invited to the Esalen Institute in Big Sur, California, where he lived until 1987 as Scholar-in-Residence. During this time he wrote several books and articles, gave seminars and lectures, and developed, with his wife Christina Grof, Holotropic Breathwork, an innovative form of experiential psychotherapy. He also served on the Board of Trustees of Esalen Institute.

Stanislav Grof is the founder of the International Transpersonal Association (ITA) and is its past and current president. In this role, along with Christina Grof, he has organized large international conferences in the United States, the former Czechoslovakia, India, Australia, and Brazil. He lives in Mill Valley, California, writes books, conducts training seminars for professional in Holotropic Breathwork and transpersonal psychology (Grof Transpersonal Training), and gives lectures and seminars worldwide. He is also Professor of Psychology at the California Institute of Integral Studies (CIIS) in San Francisco and at the Pacifica Graduate School in Santa Barbara.

In 1993 he received an Honorary Award from the Association for Transpersonal Psychology (ATP) for major contributions to and development of the field of transpersonal psychology, given at the occasion of the 25th Anniversary Convocation held in Asilomar, California. In 2000 he also received an Honorary Doctorate in Humane Letters from Burlington College, Burlington, Vermont.

He has published over 140 articles in professional journals, as well as numerous books, which have been translated into sixteen languages.

Other books by Stanislav Grof:

Realms of the Human Unconscious: Observations from LSD Research. New York: Viking Press, 1975.

The Human Encounter with Death. New York: E. P. Dutton, 1977 (with Joan Halifax).

LSD Psychotherapy. Sarasota, Florida: MAPS Publications, 1980.

Beyond Death: Gates of Consciousness. London: Thames and Hudson, 1980 (with Christina Grof).

Ancient Wisdom and Modern Science. Albany, New York: State University of New York (SUNY) Press, 1984 (ed.).

Beyond the Brain: Birth, Death, and Transcendence in Psychotherapy. Albany, New York: State University of New York (SUNY) Press, 1985.

The Adventure of Self-Discovery. Albany, New York: State University of New York (SUNY) Press, 1988.

Human Survival and Consciousness Evolution. Albany, New York: State University of New York (SUNY) Press, 1988 (ed.).

Spiritual Emergency: When Personal Transformation Becomes a Crisis. Los Angeles, California: J. P. Tarcher, 1989 (ed. with Christina Grof).

The Stormy Search for the Self: A Guide to Personal Growth Through Transformational Crises. Los Angeles: J. P. Tarcher, 1990 (with Christina Grof).

The Holotropic Mind: The Three Levels of Consciousness and How They Shape Our Lives. San Francisco, California: HarperCollins Publishers, 1992.

Books of the Dead: Manuals for Living and Dying. London: Thames and Hudson, 1994.

The Cosmic Game: Explorations of the Frontiers of Human Consciousness. Albany, New York: State University of New York (SUNY) Press, 1998.

The Transpersonal Vision: The Healing Potential of Nonordinary States of Consciousness. Boulder, Colorado: Sounds True, Inc., 1998.

The Consciousness Revolution: A Transatlantic Dialogue. Rockport, Massachusetts: Element Books, 1999 (with E. Laszlo and P. Russell).

Psychology of the Future: Lessons from Modern Consciousness Research. Albany, New York: State University of New York (SUNY) Press, 2000.

When the Impossible Happens: Adventures in Non-Ordinary Realities. Boulder, Colorado: Sounds True, Inc., 2006.

Holotropic Breathwork

Information for readers interested in experiencing

Holotropic Breathwork

or to enroll in the

training for Holotropic Breathwork:

Grof Transpersonal Training (GTT) Website

www.holotropic.com

Mailing address: 38 Miller Ave, PMB 516,

Mill Valley, CA 94941

Tel: (415) 383-8779

fax: (415) 383-0965

E-mail: gtt@holotropic.com